T0384306

Fierce Desires

Fierce Desires

A New History of Sex and Sexuality in America

REBECCA L. DAVIS

W. W. NORTON & COMPANY
Independent Publishers Since 1923

Printed in the United States of America
First Edition

For information about permission to reproduce selections from this book, write to
Permissions, W. W. Norton & Company, Inc., 500 Fifth Avenue, New York, NY 10110

For information about special discounts for bulk purchases, please contact
W. W. Norton Special Sales at specialsales@wwnorton.com or 800-233-4830

Manufacturing by Lakeside Book Company
Book design by Chris Welch
Production manager: Lauren Abbate

ISBN 978-1-63149-657-8

W. W. Norton & Company, Inc., 500 Fifth Avenue, New York, N.Y. 10110
www.wwnorton.com

W. W. Norton & Company Ltd., 15 Carlisle Street, London W1D 3BS

1 0 9 8 7 6 5 4 3 2 1

For my students,
past, present, and future.

You ask all the right questions.

Contents

PART THREE
SOLVING SEXUAL PROBLEMS
1938–2024

Introduction

Americans love to talk—and fight—about sex. We argue over sexual identities, consent, and gender. We variously endorse and oppose limits on sexual freedoms and on sexuality's influence in our culture. Questions of what we can or should *do* about any of this are among the most hotly contested issues in American life. These observations are important, but they're also familiar. What is less often remarked upon is that many Americans seem to agree that sexuality doesn't have a history.

To hear conservatives tell it, little related to sexuality changed until leftist radicals and feminists forced their ideas about liberation and bodily autonomy onto an American public perfectly content to keep things the way they were (and always had been). A counterargument, common in progressive circles, insists that today's sexual identities are authentic because they are eternal. In this way, the left, too, is prone to anchoring its claims outside of history.

The first of these assertions is demonstrably false. The stories that fill this book reveal four centuries' worth of transformation to Americans' sexual ideals and behaviors. Claims that abortion was always criminal or that gender-fluid people did not exist until recently fail the most rudimentary tests of historical evidence. The second argument overlooks how novel the concept of sexual identity is, an omission that ironically diminishes how crucial history is to sexuality as we understand it today. Individuals in the past fiercely contested the meaning and consequences of their desires, long before the concept of sexual identity existed. Their struggles—and pleasures—only magnify the stakes in more recent debates over sexual rights. Those challenging draconian anti-abortion or anti-trans laws have real antecedents to call upon.

Fierce Desires presents a new account of sex and sexuality in America. It documents the persistent presence of gender nonconformity, of people who preferred non-heterosexual sex, of efforts to control the frequency of pregnancies, and of conflicts over the boundaries of permissible sexual behavior. It demonstrates that sexual desires mattered greatly to people living hundreds of years ago. But it is also a history of dramatic and often surprising changes. Over the last four centuries, Americans have shifted from interpreting sexual behaviors as reflections of personal preferences or values—such as those rooted in faith or community norms—to defining sexuality as an essential part of what makes a person who they are. Legislators, police, activists, and bureaucrats transformed the role of government in the regulation of sexual behaviors. And, more than once, Americans upended their ideas about the sexual natures of men, women, and individuals whose gender defies that binary.

This is far from the first book to examine sex and sexuality in America, but it is the first in more than thirty years to try to encompass the sweep of this complex, varied, and important history. It stands on the shoulders of John D'Emilio and Estelle Freedman's *Intimate Matters: A History of Sexuality in America*, which first appeared in 1988. *Intimate Matters* explained that a sexual system organized around marriage and reproduction in the seventeenth through nineteenth centuries made way in the twentieth century for a culture that prioritized individual pleasure, a phenomenon the authors identify as a transition to "sexual liberalism." D'Emilio and Freedman synthesized a staggering amount of evidence about "the dominant language of sexuality" in each of the eras they covered.[1]

In the years since the publication of *Intimate Matters*, an outpouring of scholarship on the history of sexuality has had an effect that is less akin to renovating a kitchen than to tearing an entire house down to the studs and building it anew. Sexual histories of nonwhite Americans have exposed the extent to which ideas about racial difference developed in tandem with theories of gender and sexuality. Scholars have critically examined the connections between sexuality, religion, and politics; investigated the role of federal and state bureaucracies in formulating the very meanings of sexual identity; and creatively illuminated lives that left scarce historical traces.[2]

We have learned, for instance, even more about the importance of gender to the history of sexuality. For much of the period this book covers, a person's gender, more than the object of their desires, determined their social acceptability. In the mid-nineteenth century, a woman who shared the same bed with another woman exclusively for decades usually avoided her neighbors' disapproval as long as she did not assert the privileges of manhood. A person assigned female at birth with a self-understood masculine gender could likewise attain work in a typically male occupation and even find a wife without much fear at all of community backlash or legal jeopardy, if their behavior was otherwise unremarkable. That gender-based system made way, in the early twentieth century, for a new concept of sexuality that focused, instead, on sexual object choice. It was only in the mid-twentieth century that Americans and Europeans distilled the formerly generic category of "sex" into the distinct concepts of biological sex, gender, and sexuality. Even so, defining what it is we talk about when we talk about sex remains a strikingly complex task. Well into the twentieth century, some Black and Latinx communities used the term "gay" for any combination of embodiment, attire, and sexual object choice other than cisgendered heterosexuality. (The word "cis" indicates a gender identity that matches the bodily sex assigned at birth.)[3]

More recently, the concept of "queerness" has come to signify any configuration of genders, bodies, and desires that defy a particular culture's expectations for "normal" sexuality. Once a pejorative term for same-sex-desiring people, "queer" has been reclaimed as a usefully descriptive word for non-normative sexualities and gender roles. The concept of queerness draws our attention to the interplay of gender, sexual desire, and identity. Put more precisely, queerness refers to what one scholar calls "sexual personhood," comprising not only an individual's erotic interests but their relationship to maleness, femaleness, or nonbinary gender.[4]

Informed by this scholarship, this book focuses on how and why Americans came to believe that sexuality was a singularly significant aspect of their identities. Over the four hundred years that the book covers, sexuality shifted from a reflection of social and religious status to a source of self-recognized personhood. By the twentieth century, new movements demanded erotic and reproductive autonomy as fundamental rights.

This book is also, necessarily, a history of pleasure. The enjoyment of erotic experience will strike many readers as the obvious aim of sex, but finding telltale historical sources can be difficult. Some individuals documented gratifying sex, even notating their journal entries with coded symbols to indicate orgasm or a particular act. Stashes of love letters, poetry, and diary entries recount longing and delight. But many more surviving documents depict moments when something went terribly wrong. We have trial testimony from fornication and rape prosecutions, first-person testimonies about abuse, and police records of arrests for "vice," among other evidence of sexual pain and discrimination.

A search for first-person accounts of sexual desire and identity reminds us that people in the past did not always have the means or opportunity to write down and preserve their thoughts. Candid sexual self-expression has proved especially complicated—and often dangerous—for nonwhite people and immigrants in the United States, who contend with assumptions that their race determines their sexuality. Pernicious stereotypes about Black men as hypersexual and of Black women as lascivious, of Mexican women as hyper-fertile, and of Asian and Middle Eastern people as sexually "exotic"—among other false generalizations—have imposed sexualities on individuals that they would typically not claim for themselves. One of the most profound transformations of the second half of the twentieth century was the formation of social justice movements that centered the sexual freedoms of previously marginalized people.

Even though most of the voices of sexual pleasure prior to the 1850s are those of white men, we can read "against the grain" to locate traces of other people's erotic encounters. Medical records diagnosing "perversion" are in many ways pathologizing, but they often show what kinds of sex their subjects preferred. The same holds true of police records. Learning that men in Portland, Oregon, were arrested for performing oral sex in the 1910s tells us, at the very least, that they were doing it. That said, several chapters in this book address sexual violence not because those were the only records I could locate but because actual and feared abuse has harmed far too many people. There are some constants in this history; that is one of them.

Fierce Desires unspools these arguments largely by telling stories. Some of these stories are well known and some are hardly known at all. Some present individuals at odds with their communities while others discuss larger social movements for or against sexual freedom. There are stories here about culture, politics, religion, and race. Many individuals appear in a single chapter, but a few are featured across numerous ones. Narrative writing suits the larger points this book makes: that individual and collective experiences have given sexuality its meaning, that the intimacies of sex bear upon our politics and culture, and that the stories we tell about this history alter our ability to grapple with its complexities today.

I have organized these stories into three parts, each addressing a particular era. When Part One begins, in the seventeenth century, Americans viewed desire as a reflection of other forces in their lives, such as their religious faith or their community's standards. Their identities—as "gentlemen" or servants, freemen or enslaved, Indigenous or English, and so on—were not intrinsically sexual. Rather, their sexual behaviors indicated their success or failure in cultivating civility, faith, and other valued qualities. They took offense at efforts by authorities to tell them how to behave because relative degrees of sexual freedom indicated a person's place in the world. Indigenous North Americans, for their part, seem to have understood sexual acts as expressions of both desire and the division of female and male energies reflected in nature.

Stereotypes of priggish Puritans have warped our perceptions of the sexual cultures in early America. Euro-Americans esteemed marriage as the singular site for moral sex, but they rarely pried open bedroom doors to identify exceptions to the rule and bristled when magistrates prosecuted engaged couples for fornication. Well into the nineteenth century, Americans were far less troubled by same-sex and gender-nonconforming desires than we might imagine, largely ignoring intimacies that did not disrupt communities, lead to out-of-wedlock pregnancies, or challenge the privileges of the male head of household. Although sodomy remained religiously forbidden and illegal, relatively few were arrested for it, let alone convicted, until the early twentieth century. The history of sex in America is not a narrative of fixed, timeless desires, but neither is it one of simple, linear "progress." Earlier generations were far more open about sex than we might think.

Instead, Americans fixated on the marketplace for erotic enticement, which grew dramatically after 1750. Erotica became ubiquitous. Improvements to printing technology accelerated the circulation of pornographic texts and images, and nifty devices such as the stereoscope permitted viewers to see scenes of Paris—or naked women—in three dimensions. Americans also grappled with the horrific commerce in enslaved people, whether to denounce or justify the valuation and sale of human beings for overtly sexual purposes.

Ideas about women's sexuality, the purposes of marriage, and the boundaries of permissible sexual violence also transformed across these decades. A small but influential group of reformers insisted that accessible information, especially for women about their bodies, could bring about a host of improvements, including better health and more loving marriages. These efforts to empower women were impeded by a countervailing development: the democratization of white, male sexual privilege. Anglo-Americans had long recognized men's sexual entitlements within their own households, rarely punishing men who abused their wives, children, servants, or slaves. But traditionally, only higher-status men had the privilege of sexual access to women and other subordinates beyond their households. After 1800, that prerogative extended to nearly all white men.

Part Two opens in the mid-1800s, when small numbers of rebels and seekers argued that sexuality itself had meaning and value. They recognized desire as a fundamental element in their lives and rejected laws that hindered sexual expression. Nearly all these reformers focused on the appropriate parameters of male-female sex, imagining monogamous marriages in which women were men's equals. The radicals among them advocated for nonmonogamous reconfigurations of the family and even communal experiments. Religious iconoclasts envisioned worlds beyond this one in which unorthodox sexual relations would create the conditions necessary for the arrival of a new millennium. Women's rights activists and advocates for Black equality critiqued a political culture that discouraged them from speaking about sexual matters, bringing to light the prevalence of sexual violence as a matter of public concern.

Ironically, the most far-reaching attempt to rein in sexual desires, the Comstock Act of 1873, ended up making sex more visible and more relevant to U.S. governance than it had ever been before. Named for its author, the obsessively anti-sex Anthony Comstock, the law prohibited the use of the U.S. mail to send anything Comstock considered obscene. In addition to banning erotic photographs and texts, it also criminalized the distribution of printed materials explaining how contraception and abortion worked. On the heels of Comstock's national campaign, police departments began to identify certain sexual behaviors as threats to civil society. Many gender nonconforming, queer, and feminist people rejected these attempts at repression; condom sales and sex work did not decline in the late nineteenth century but moved, instead, to a black market.

A new science of sex—"sexology"—sought explanations for the nonmarital sex acts that Comstock and police surveilled. Sexologists variously classified sexual perversions as things a person might inherit from a parent or as a kind of social contagion that put vulnerable populations at risk of infection. By the early twentieth century, new definitions of "normal" sexuality emphasized heterosexuality (a word not yet widely known) and conventional gender roles. Such theories cast queer desires as evidence of deviance, but they also contributed to emerging communities of people whose gender expressions and sexuality defied the norm.

Part Three begins in 1938, when sex researcher Alfred C. Kinsey taught his first class on marriage to undergraduates at Indiana University. The revelations of his 1948 and 1953 "Kinsey Reports" on human sexual behavior shined a national spotlight on the kinds of sex acts that Americans performed, and with whom. Arguments over the acceptability of premarital sex, queer sexuality, and masturbation, however common they might be, crowded into the public square. Two major contentions—that sexuality is a fundamental aspect of human freedom, and that everyone possesses a sexual identity—began to strike many Americans as axioms close to common sense. Harsh federal and state policies, however, limited the civil rights of lesbians and gay men and constrained women's reproductive health, in turn inspiring activists to organize to defend their sexual autonomy. Feminists weighed the importance of sex to women's liberation, pushed for protections from sexual harassment, and otherwise challenged the presumption of male sexual privilege that often seemed as entrenched in the 1980s as it had been centuries earlier. Campaigns for LGBTQ+ rights and the response to HIV/AIDS provided more evidence of the power of social movements to change how Americans think about, express, and respond to matters of sexual equality and safety.

But a counter-proposition endured: that sexual desires and behaviors are reflections of individual self-control and belief systems, not inherent in the self. The anti-abortion movement that took shape in the 1970s, in other words, was less of a "backlash" against feminism than a reassertion of a long-standing view: that sex is secondary to morality. As the thinking went (and still goes, for many Americans), behaviors contrary to the heterosexual norm undermine principles of right and wrong and threaten the authority of those who decide which is which. Conservatives in the late twentieth and early twenty-first centuries relied on the apparatus of government to enforce their beliefs about sexuality, much as Comstock had when he launched his anti-obscenity crusade in 1873. But contrary to earlier eras, since 1970, such efforts have confronted movements for sexual liberation much larger and more popular than anything that came before. Plenty of Comstock's contemporaries sneered at his censorship, and a few free-speech radicals defied him (often at great personal cost), but those individual actions lacked the muscle of the campaigns for sexual equality that emerged out of the twentieth century's feminist, reproductive justice, and LGBTQ+ equality movements.

Debates over sexual self-expression have taken center stage in American life not because sex is suddenly important to people, or because the sexual revolution threw a wrench in some supposed national consensus about sexual ethics, but because the very nature of desire remains a subject of passionate disagreement. Today, struggles over abortion rights, the ability of transgender people to access medical care, and the inclusion of books with LGBTQ+ themes in public libraries, among many other issues, demonstrate yet again how fiercely Americans value their desires and what they are willing to do to defend them.

A Note on Language

The words people use to define themselves, their behaviors, and their desires have changed over time. Few topics have witnessed as much linguistic innovation as sex, sexuality, and gender. The word "transgender," coined in the 1960s, did not circulate in U.S. vernacular speech until the 1990s, but we can find people who expressed a third gender with their community's endorsement—or who did so in defiance of contemporary social expectations—just about everywhere, in all historical epochs. The words used to name that experience have shifted dramatically, and often very quickly. Terms such as "transgendered" and "transsexual" were widely used by LGBTQ-identified people and their allies in the 1990s and early 2000s, but as I write in 2024, both already sound archaic, displaced by "trans" or "transgender." I employ "same-sex-desiring" and "queer" as imperfect but more precise ways to indicate nonnormative sex acts and the people engaging in them in eras before "homosexual," "heterosexual," "gay," "lesbian," and myriad other contemporary terms were coined. Anachronism can obscure the historical events that breathed specific meanings into these words. Readers may also notice that I mention "gay men and lesbians" in chapters about the post–World War II United States; "LGBT" (lesbian, gay, bisexual, and transgender) people by the 1970s; and "LGBTQ+" (with the addition of queer and acknowledgment of other nonnormative genders and sexualities) in sections on the early twenty-first century. More recent variations of the acronym, such as "LGBTQIA+," incorporate other letters to represent asexual, intersex, aromantic, and other identities.

Pronouns present a challenge for historical writing about sex and sexuality. Several of the people who figure centrally in the book would possibly place themselves under the umbrella of transgender identity had today's language and concepts been available to them. Where it is clear that a person saw themselves as either *both* male and female or *neither* male nor female, I use they/them pronouns. If the person appears to have identified as a sex different from the one assigned to them at birth, I use the pronoun of the sex they chose. When in doubt, I use they/them. Throughout, I call attention to the complex and fascinating variation in how people have understood gender and sex differences, including the experiences of people who believed that they could change their gender or their sex during their lifetimes. When discussing gender-expansive Indigenous people, I use "two-spirit," a term created by Indigenous scholars and activists in the late twentieth and early twenty-first centuries for Indigenous people believed to contain the essence of both male and female. I have tried to be transparent about my decisions, all of which the reader is welcome to dispute. I do not advocate a single, "correct" way to describe gender fluidity in the past. Instead, we may choose among several possibilities, aiming in each instance to learn from the people we write about.

Given the geographic scope of this book—the lands that became the United States—I have attempted throughout it to acknowledge the Indigenous nations of North America and to name the regions I discuss without assuming that imperial assertions of territorial control superseded Indigenous presence. For the original inhabitants of North America, I use the terms American Indians and Native Americans interchangeably and also refer to the Indigenous inhabitants of the continent. Whenever possible, I indicate a specific tribe or nation, employing the name preferred by members of that community (such as Diné for the people who have also been known as Navajo). My discussions of slavery attempt to recognize that it was a condition of labor and legal subjugation imposed on certain people, not a status of personhood. For that reason, I use the language of "enslaved people" rather than "slaves" and refer to "enslavers" rather than "owners" or "masters." These distinctions recognize that slave labor did not emerge organically from ready-made social divisions but was instead a practice that some people chose to enforce.[1]

PART ONE

ESTABLISHING ORDER

1600–1870

Chapter 1

To Confound the Course of Nature

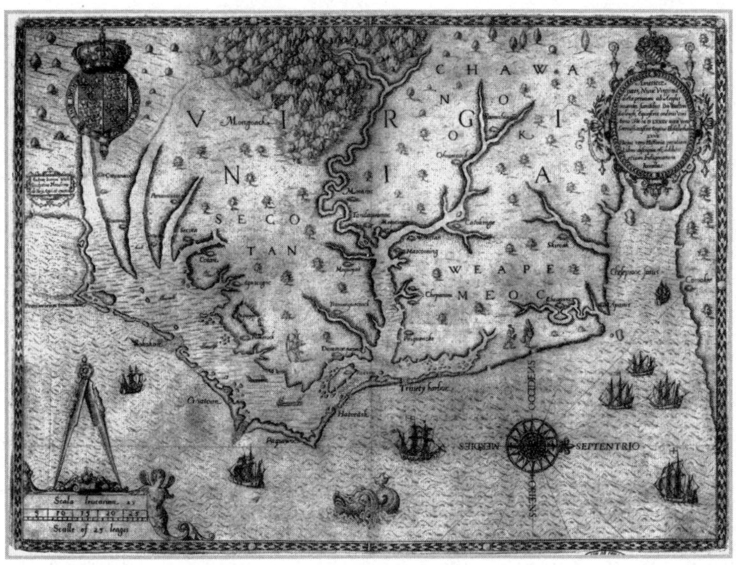

Two people in colonial Virginia shared a bed, which was common enough in the early modern Atlantic world. In this instance, rumors spread that two servants in Warraskoyack, a small settlement across the James River from Jamestown, might have engaged in illicit sex of some kind. Two people slumbering side by side was hardly

Early depictions of Virginia and the Chesapeake Bay proved influential for explorers, investors, and early colonists eager to establish themselves in the "new" world. Visual materials, like this illustrated map created by John White and reproduced by Theodor de Bry in 1590, shaped European understandings of the mid-Atlantic and its Native inhabitants.

shocking in a community where the combination of scant furniture and cold winters made bed-sharing both necessary and desirable. This was different. The commotion centered on whether a domestic servant named Thomasine Hall, discovered in bed with a female servant named Besse, was in fact a man named Thomas.

The question of Hall's bodily sex so concerned residents of the nascent settlement that several of them, unencumbered by ideas of personal privacy, forcibly examined Hall's body for physical indications of male or female sex traits on four separate occasions. Hall is absolutely male, several people concluded. Hall is unquestionably female, others pronounced. I am both, Hall objected, refusing to identify as either a man or a woman. Pressed by local authorities to pick one sex or the other, Hall refused. So confounding was the case that it ended up before the General Court in Jamestown on March 25, 1629, after these examinations and inquiries failed to determine Hall's sex conclusively.[1] (I use they/them pronouns for Hall except when quoting primary sources, which provide key evidence about how Hall's contemporaries interpreted Hall's social and sexual roles.)

Hall's experience is extraordinary, not least because the few pages of depositions and testimony within the minutes of the Virginia General Court and Council that describe these events are unlike anything else in our records of early America. This episode is also, in many ways, as much about gender—cultural expectations for a person understood as a man versus cultural expectations for a woman—as about sexuality. English Virginians held contradictory ideas about the relationship between a person's genitals and their role as either man or woman, permitting a surprising degree of fluidity in some circumstances and demanding narrow conformity in others.

For the leaders of Warraskoyack and Jamestown, Hall's ambiguity mattered when it became a source of discontent among other English servants, distracting them from cultivating the tobacco crops that would ensure their agricultural venture's survival. These leaders also wanted to demonstrate the advantages of Englishness to their Indigenous neighbors and to the Spanish, French, and other European nations with colonizing projects in North America. Sexual behavior and living arrangements were among the most important indications, in their minds, of whether they were replicating the "civility" they considered indicative of English people's superior refinement.

Their efforts to impose this order met with intense resistance from non-elite English people who had their own ideas about permissible sexual activity. The limitations that the colony's leaders placed on servants' bodies—in terms of the labor they had to perform and the kinds of pleasures they could seek—may have motivated some of these servants to reveal Hall's body for what they believed it was. The disparity between law and lived experience—on topics such as gender roles, fornication (sexual intercourse with an unmarried woman), and sodomy, among others—helps us understand why Hall's refusal to claim a single gender was urgent enough to require a court order.

The remarkable story of Thomas/Thomasine Hall introduces the themes that animate Part One of this book. Hall and the people they met in England and Virginia organized their societies as hierarchies in which class, gender, status, and, increasingly, race were supposed to determine a person's sexual liberties. Across the lands and subjects Part One covers, those liberties expanded for white men of all classes while they constricted for most others. Yet we might see Hall's insistent self-definition as a reminder that individuals and communities defended their distinct beliefs about the value of their own desires.

The English people who settled New England and Virginia in the seventeenth century held ideas about gender that might surprise today's reader. Although they usually attributed one's status as man or woman to bodily traits, there were exceptions. Under certain circumstances, a person might adopt a man's *or* a woman's role. English people in New England in the 1600s believed that a woman might become a "deputy husband" if her husband was absent for long periods of time, assuming the privileges of patriarchy in his absence. From a religious perspective, they condemned any sexual behavior outside of marriage, but they thought about sexual morality less in terms of whether the object of desire was male- or female-bodied than whether the desire originated in "unclean" lusts or contravened their ideas about social hierarchy.[2]

English Puritans were dissenters from the Protestant Church of England who demanded simpler styles of worship and stricter adherence to biblical law. Puritans believed that experiences of Jesus Christ's divinity required the believer to assume a receptive role akin to how a wife was expected to behave toward her husband. When a Puritan man submitted himself to Christ, he did so as a bride. In 1651, Boston minister John Cotton asked the members of his congregation if they fantasized about spiritual sexual intercourse with Christ: "Have you a strong and hearty desire to meet him in the bed of loves, when ever you come to the Congregation, and desire you have the seeds of his grace shed abroad in your hearts, and bring forth the fruits of grace to him?" Such descriptions of spiritual ecstasy might appear profoundly homoerotic; for some of these men, it may have been. But erotic language describing Puritan men's "penetration" by Christ's love made sense to Puritans not because they embraced same-sex desires but because they considered the soul to be an essentially feminine entity, well suited for submission.[3]

These allowances for moments when a person's gender role bore no relation to their bodily sex coexisted, however, with other fairly rigid ideas about the distinct privileges of men. "Deputy husbands" notwithstanding, English people of the early seventeenth century believed that nature had made men the superiors of women, divinely designed to provide the moral and intellectual guidance that a woman required in order to become a virtuous "good wife" who avoided dissolution and sin. Christian women bore the curse of Eve; far from the guardians of chastity that white women would later become in the popular imagination, prior to the American Revolution, they were more often considered temptresses. The minister of a church in Andover, Massachusetts, warned in the late 1720s about the "lewd and designing Woman" who led men toward "forbidden Pleasures."[4]

Nor did a gentleman and a male-bodied servant share the privileges of patriarchy equally. Indentured servitude was the primary labor system in 1620s English settlements in Virginia. These servants, who made up more than half of the white immigrants to English settlements in North America before 1750, exchanged between four and seven years of unpaid labor for the cost of passage across the Atlantic Ocean and room and board upon arrival. Elites tried to control their servants' private lives. Many indentured servants signed contracts that prohibited them from marrying (or required that they first obtain a master or mistress's permission), which left them no legal means of having sex. But one of the challenges for elites in seventeenth-century Virginia was that the distinctions of social rank were far more dynamic there than in England. A male servant in a North American colony who completed his term of indenture had what, for the time, was an unprecedented opportunity to purchase a farm and even, in a few instances, acquire wealth befitting a gentleman. If male, then Hall might one day become a patriarch of his own household, the governor of a miniature state who was expected to keep his dependents in line and maintain the family's reputation. But if female, Hall would always suffer from the irrational passions people at the time (including women) thought all women possessed, traits that made the governance of a wiser man—whether father, husband, or master—both necessary and good.[5]

A preoccupation with demonstrating English and Christian superiority over all other cultures informed these ideas about gender and sexual behavior. English travelers to West Africa alternately marveled at the extraordinary beauty of the people they encountered and described those people as less than human, their "heathen" bodies better suited to brutal labor conditions than "Christian" people's were. Europeans depicted African women's breasts as startlingly distended, like an animal's, a savage counterpart to the supposedly high-breasted figure of European women. Englishman William Towerson's account of his travels to Guinea in West Africa in 1555 conferred beast-like qualities on the women's breasts, "which in the most part be very foule and long, hanging downe low like the udder of a goate." However physiologically impossible, Towerson's vivid account helped make theories about supposed distinctions of race appear real, rooted in observations of the "natural" world.[6]

Servants such as Hall and Besse labored alongside some captive Native people and a small but growing population of free and enslaved Africans in Virginia. Spanish and Portuguese traders had been purchasing and selling enslaved people from major ports along the West African coast since the 1400s. As early as 1513, enslaved people from Africa likely accompanied Spanish explorers who traveled north from Mexico to the Pacific coast; in 1526, Spanish soldiers forced one hundred enslaved people to help them create a colony in present-day South Carolina. Europeans also enslaved Indigenous people they encountered in the Americas. Some white men proudly described how they captured Indigenous women as rewards for their journeys, conflating the Indigenous women's relative nakedness with an invitation for sex. More than 700,000 Africans were enslaved and sold on the far side of the Atlantic Ocean, primarily in the Caribbean and South America, between 1580 and 1640. Dutch and English slave ships soon outnumbered those bearing Spanish or Portuguese flags. In 1625, only 23 Africans lived among 1,200 English people in Virginia. (By 1640, those numbers had increased to 300 Africans and 15,000 English Virginians. The number of enslaved Africans in the English colonies rose precipitously after 1660.)[7]

Perhaps more immediately, the English residents of Warraskoyack contended with Native people whose land and resources they had claimed for themselves. That reality contrasted with widely circulated sexual fantasies about America's submission to the wills of English men. English travelers waxed eloquent about the sexual possibilities of travel to the New World; poet John Donne described America as a woman he undressed, as he "discovered" her in a conquest of her "virgin" land. Those erotic metaphors gave many English people a false sense of entitlement to Native people's lands, ones that they would possess as a man possessed a woman.[8]

At the same time, many English settlers described Native North Americans as "savages" who did not deserve the lands they occupied.

For proof, they depicted Native men as simultaneously promiscuous leches and impotent failures. Correct sexual behavior became an essential means of distinguishing Christian from heathen, civilized from savage, and white from "red" or "black." The English feared that sexual intimacy with Indigenous or African people would lead them into the savagery they associated with all non-English people. For English elites who wanted to reestablish civil society in the New World, proper sexual relations would be a measure of their success.[9]

It is no wonder, then, that Thomas/Thomasine Hall's refusal to define themself as either man or woman confounded their neighbors and local authorities. At stake were some of the most fundamental assumptions that English people of the early seventeenth century held about what distinguished one person from another and determined their place in society.

In or about 1603, a person who would be christened Thomasine Hall was born in England. Early on, Hall assumed male or female gender according to their circumstances. At age twelve, Hall went to live with an aunt in London and learned skilled women's work. Hall first dressed as a man about ten years later, when they enlisted in the English Army. Hall's brother had recently served in England's 1625 expedition in Cadiz (one of the deadliest battles in what became a five-year English–Spanish war), and Hall seems to have wanted to follow in their brother's footsteps. To do so, Hall "cut of his heire and Changed his apparell into the fashion of man," presenting for duty as a twenty-two-year-old soldier named Thomas Hall. After a year's service in France, Hall sailed back to Plymouth, England. Once again attired in women's clothing, Hall made a living sewing lace, a woman's occupation. In 1627, Hall again wore men's clothing aboard the ship that carried them to Virginia.

The small settlement of Warraskoyack was named for the Algonkian village whose residents the English had forced out, after a series of attacks by the Powhatan people killed as much as one-third of the English population in Virginia. The celebrated marriage between the

Powhatan chief's daughter, whom the English called Pocahontas, and English captain John Rolfe had forged a temporary truce in 1615; the couple traveled to London with their infant son and met members of the royal family. Their story ended tragically in Pocahontas's death aboard a ship for the return voyage in 1617. As warfare surrounded Jamestown, English migration to Virginia stalled.[10]

Thomasine Hall would have been one of a small number of English women in the labor-intensive tobacco plantations of Virginia. Warraskoyack, established in 1622, included two major tobacco-farming plantations. Women often worked in tobacco fields and factories, and they also typically knew more than men did about gardening, weaving, and other productive tasks that English people considered women's work.[11]

The shortage of English women in the Chesapeake was sufficiently dire that the Virginia Company rounded up and shipped over women who could provide male colonizers with sexual pleasure, domestic labor, and, through their reproductive labors, English children. The company's treasurer, Sir Edwin Sandys, pledged to find a "fit hundredth" of "maids young and uncorrupt to make wifes to the inhabitants and by that meanes to make the men there more settled." All told, between 1620 and 1624, the Virginia Company sent more than two hundred English women to Jamestown, each valued at £150 that their prospective husbands would repay to cover the cost of their transport to the colony. Even so, in 1624, adult women totaled just 230 of the 1,250 Europeans living in Virginia.[12]

Soon after disembarking in Virginia, Hall became a maidservant in the home of John and Jane Tyos. The well-ordered household, the English believed, was emblematic of their civility and thus essential to their demonstration of superiority over both their Indigenous neighbors and other Europeans venturing to the New World. A skilled seamstress, Hall likely engaged in a variety of arduous tasks, including food production and preparation, hauling water for cooking and cleaning, laundering, and the making of candles, soaps, clothing, and other material goods that aided the settlement's continuance. Presenting as a woman,

Hall was a useful domestic servant in the Tyos household. Tyos, as patriarch, benefitted from the labors of an indentured servant such as Hall but was also expected to keep his dependents out of trouble.[13]

The commotion in Warraskoyack about whether Hall was a female servant began sometime in late 1628 or early 1629. A man known as Mr. Stacy, about whom little else is recorded, seems to have raised the alarm over the ambiguity surrounding Hall's sex, but women in the community were the first to investigate the matter. After Mr. Stacy told other English residents of Warraskoyack that Hall was "as hee thought a man and woeman," rather than a clearly female servant, women in the community exercised their authority over women's bodies to force an examination of Hall's genitals. When English communities or courts needed intimate knowledge about a person's body, community members of the same sex obtained it. Women more broadly had a degree of power in matters related to female sexuality; nearly all midwives at the time were women, recognized as experts on matters related to reproductive sex. Because Tyos believed his servant to be a woman, three women, Alice Longe, Dorothye Rodes, and Barbara Hall, conducted the first of several inspections of Hall's body.[14]

The surviving record gives no indication that Hall resisted, but as a servant, they had limited power to refuse. These were surely, at the very least, uncomfortable if not deeply upsetting events for them. The women reached an unambiguous conclusion: they "found (as they then said) that hee was a man." John Tyos, meanwhile, "swore the said Hall was a woeman." Was Hall male or female? What norms or laws would govern the labor or the sexual behavior of a person who was *both* man and woman?

All of this commotion about Hall's ambiguity brought the issue to the attention of Captain Nathaniel Basse. He was Warraskoyack's unofficial leader and the proprietor of the newest tobacco plantation, determined to earn a profit from tobacco despite the colony's recent losses. Basse had served in Virginia's House of Burgesses and would soon be a member of the Governor's Council of Virginia. His high military rank and roles in colonial government endowed him with civil stature and authority over servants such as Hall.[15]

As the nominal leader of the settlement, Basse asked Hall directly what sex they were. Hall "replyed that hee was both." Elaborating, Hall explained that they had both male and female genitalia. The surviving minutes of the General Court were partially destroyed, but the extant text includes Hall's explanation that while unable to get an erection ("hee had not the use of the mans parte"), Hall's body included "a peece of fleshe growing at the [missing section] belly as bigg as the top of his little finger, [an] inch longe" and "a peece of an hole." Perhaps Hall had a larger-than-average clitoris and a small or truncated vagina. Hall's description of male impotence suggested an awareness of the English common-law requirement of sexual consummation for a valid marriage. If that was the case, Hall would have been exempted from the expectation to become a husband.[16]

Early twenty-first century Americans use words like "transgender" to describe people who have a fluid relationship to gender or whose gender expression is different from the norms associated with the sex assigned to them at birth. Another useful term is "intersex," employed to account for a wide variety of anatomical, hormonal, and chromosomal differences that affect 1 of every 200 people whose bodies do not conform to a simple male/female binary. Although neither Hall nor Hall's contemporaries knew these words, early modern people in England and in North America grappled with the possibility that sex was a fluid or changeable trait. "Hermaphrodites" and "androgynes" had populated European legal texts and poetry since 200 CE. Early modern people recognized that some people were born with ambiguous genitalia, but they typically insisted that a person choose one gender—and stick to it. In their refusal to align with a single gender, Hall was unusual.[17]

An elongated clitoris is often related to an intersex condition known today as congenital adrenal hyperplasia, which occurs when a person with XX chromosomes produces an atypically large amount of androgen, the hormone that generates male sex characteristics. Hall's contemporaries of course lacked knowledge of either chromosomes or endocrinology, relying instead on their visual observations of Hall's body and their preexisting assumptions about which traits made someone a man or a woman. Basse overruled the assertions of the women who examined Hall's body and ordered that Hall wear "woemens apparell." Respectful enough of authority to think Basse might know more than they did, Longe, Rodes, and Barbara Hall second-guessed their initial determination. They "stood in doubte of what they had formerly affirmed."[18]

The community's ambivalence about Hall's bodily sex persisted, despite Basse's public pronouncement of Hall's femaleness. Longe, Rodes, and Barbara Hall decided they must take a second look to see if their earlier conclusion was an error. John Atkins had recently purchased Hall's term of indenture from Tyos, acquiring a maidservant called Thomasine. The three curious women entered the Atkins home and examined Hall while Hall slept. Their search reaffirmed their initial observation: "and then allsoe [they] found the said Hall to bee a man." The women urged Atkins to see for himself, but he refused to inspect his servant's body, explaining that Hall was "seeming to starre as if shee had beene awake." Was Hall lying inert but fully conscious during this second examination? Did Hall stare at Atkins as a challenge or as an appeal for help? (Or did Hall sleep with their eyes open?)

A week later, Longe, Rodes, and Barbara Hall returned to the Atkins home, now with two more women, to conduct a *third* inspection of Hall's body. Atkins did not stay away this time and agreed with the five women that his servant was male. He ordered Hall to wear men's clothing, using his authority as head of household temporarily to invalidate Basse's earlier ruling.

A determination of whether Hall was a man or a woman became more urgent after a rumor circulated in early 1629 that Hall "did ly wth a maid of Mr Richard Bennets called greate Besse." Longe, who had already searched Hall's body on three occasions, may have spread this rumor. She said the source of the gossip was one of Tyos's servants. Greate Besse was likely an indentured servant just as Hall was. Had T. Hall and Greate Besse committed the crime of fornication?

Fornication was prosecuted throughout the English colonies in North America. The devout Christians who settled in Virginia and New England created legal systems that combined English common law, which stressed the value of patriarchal household government, and biblical injunctions against sexual relations outside of marriage. In the first century of English settlement, courts from New England to the Chesapeake not only charged unmarried people with fornication but even brought fornication charges against married couples retroactively if the bride gave birth to a full-term child in eight months or less after the wedding date. Ministers often led such couples before their assembled congregation to beg forgiveness for committing both a sin and a crime.

White women faced prosecution for illicit sex more often than white men did. Female fornicators also endured far greater social ostracism, even in cases involving sex with a minor or "ravishment." In 1677, a servant named Mary Manning tried to avoid this stigma when she asked the court of New Castle, Delaware, to mercifully "Cleare hur from the threats and future scandall" of her association with Jeremy Farrington, who had "deluded her from [her employer]" and falsely promised to marry her. The court ruled in her favor. More often, even when female servants alleged coercion, they rarely succeeded in convincing local justices to absolve them of the charge of fornication.[19]

This aggressive pursuit of fornication charges, handed down by high-ranking men, infuriated non-elite Anglo-Americans. They believed that a betrothal rather than formal marriage was the point at which sex became permissible. Non-elites not only made allowances for premarital sex, they recognized couples as married irrespective of a minister's blessing or legal contract. This culture of informal marriage survived in many regions of the American South well into the 1700s, eliciting a steady stream of consternation from Protestant ministers who bemoaned generations of children they believed had been born into sin. Servants in Warraskoyack knew the penalties for disobeying their masters but also sustained their own ideas about legitimate sexual behavior.[20]

Greate Besse, whose opinion of her involvement with Hall was apparently not pursued by the officials who recorded testimony for the case, was both the legal dependent of her employer and a member of his household. Her employer (whom the surviving records do not identify) would have been expected to maintain control of his dependents—wives, children, indentured servants, and enslaved laborers—lest he appear insufficiently patriarchal. Because colonial governments in New England as well as in the Chesapeake were limited and weak, they relied on male heads of household to govern judiciously. Property-owning families proved to be especially adept at protecting their own relatives from negative legal outcomes; single, indentured, and enslaved women were more exposed. (Domestic leadership was especially important because the English insisted that everyone live within households; given the paucity of English women in the Chesapeake until much later in the seventeenth century, this expectation resulted in numerous homes comprised solely of men.)[21]

English residents of Warraskoyack would not have assumed that a man named Thomas coerced Besse into bed. They viewed women as the "lustier" sex and denigrated servant women as "wenches" with untamed erotic impulses. Given their understandings of how the reproductive system worked, men of the time would have not only acknowledged women's capacity for erotic pleasure but, presumably, often actively pursued it. Both men and women emitted a seed during orgasm, the thinking went, the combination of which created the potential for human life. A still-trusted scientific authority had written in 1583, "unwilling copulation for the most part is vain and barren: for love causeth conception." That theory nevertheless worked against women who became pregnant because of an assault. When sixteen-year-old Priscilla Willson was charged with fornication in 1683 in Essex County, Massachusetts, members of the community testified that Samuel Appleton, a wealthy merchant, had forced himself on her. Their attempts to defend Willson failed because she became pregnant, which the local authorities interpreted as evidence that she had enjoyed the sexual encounter.[22]

A child born out of wedlock to an indentured servant such as Greate Besse would have created additional complications. Colonial authorities in Virginia appeared less worried about sexual sin than the financial costs of a child born to an unwed mother. Any potential child would impair the mother's ability to work while she recovered from childbirth and burden her employer with additional expenses. One of the ways English colonial settlements tried to recoup those losses was to require the father to pay damages to the woman's employer. Local governments attempted to identify the father (often by interrogating the woman during the most intense stages of childbirth). Men of lower status were more likely to be found guilty of bastardy and ordered to pay child support. Servant women who bore a "bastard" faced the forced indenture of their child and had one or two years added to their own terms of indenture. The more fortunate among them might marry their employers, or another landowner might pay the balance of a pregnant servant's indenture and marry her. Southern English colonies prosecuted bastardy more often than fornication or any other sex-related crime. By the 1670s, a woman convicted of bastardy had even more years of service added to her indenture, and her sexual partner owed steeper monetary damages to her employer.[23]

The situation in Warraskoyack in 1628 and 1629 was perhaps less about profit than privilege: Was Hall, male-bodied but female-attired, getting away with sexual play otherwise forbidden to indentured servants toiling in Virginia? Two young men in particular insisted on knowing whether Hall was male or female. Roger Rodes and Francis England worked on the same plantations as Hall did. (Perhaps Roger was the husband of Dorothy.) Rodes and England "laid hands upon the said Hall" and "threw the said Hall on his backe" to determine the nature of Hall's genitals for themselves. England thrust his hands into Hall's clothing and "pulled out [Hall's] members whereby it appeared that hee was a perfect man." England demanded that Hall explain why they wore women's clothing if their body indicated male sex.

Hall answered that they wore women's clothing "to gett a bitt for my Catt." The precise meaning of that phrase has vexed historians. Perhaps it meant to "earn a living." Or perhaps, given that "bit" was an early modern English slang for a morsel of food, women's attire improved Hall's chances while begging for something to eat. The time Hall had spent in France suggests a more subtle, humorous, and defiant assertion: a too-literal translation of the French slang, *pour avoir une bite pour mon chat,* or "to get a penis for my cunt." After enduring this fourth bodily search, Hall apparently asserted an erotic playfulness in response to England and Rodes's physical and verbal intrusions.[24]

The issue now had clear legal repercussions and went before the General Court in Jamestown, the colony's highest judicial authority.

The commotion over Hall's bodily sex—and possible sexual misbehavior—occurred as English people in North America were beginning to argue that a person's status depended not only on their social position as master or servant but on whether they traced their ancestry to England, America, or Africa. Enslaved Africans, captive Indians, and indentured servants lived under varying forms of unfreedom in the North American colonies. On farms and in towns, enslaved Africans worked alongside indentured servants, and some even lived with one another. In Hall's time, an African-born woman known as Mary and her African husband, Antonio, earned their freedom and became property owners; Mary's children were free. In the earliest years of English settlement in the Chesapeake and New England, it was not yet clear that slavery was lifelong or that it was a status that an enslaved woman's children inherited. Mixed-race unions thus did not initially raise questions about whether their child would be enslaved.[25]

Instead, colonial English courts at first handled fornication cases involving combinations of English, Native, and African people according to the same laws against fornication that ensnared indentured servants who had sex with one another or with a free English person. Whether enslaved or a servant, the man convicted of fornication was typically whipped and fined. But very soon, the calcifying rules of Atlantic slavery meant that an African-descended man found guilty of fornication might be sold to compensate his sexual partner's master. The children of these unions suffered: colonial courts often demanded that "mulatto" children born to convicted fornicators serve an exceptionally onerous thirty-year indenture to compensate for the cost of their upbringing. In Virginia, these revised fornication laws also reflected English colonists' fears about sex between baptized Christians (mostly members of the Church of England) and "heathen" Africans or Indians. Religion, like race, became yet another marker of inherited difference.[26]

More than thirty years after Hall's interrogation, as England's participation in the Atlantic slave trade expanded, a 1662 law in Virginia, for the first time, defined slavery as a perpetual inheritance, passed down from mother to child. That law also made any sexual contact between an African and English person illegal; prior to 1662, a free Black man and a free English woman could legally marry in Virginia. Leaders of the English colonies in North America wanted to prevent English indentured servants, who would attain the status of "free" people once they served their terms, from creating households or producing children with enslaved Africans. A 1664 law in Maryland scolded "diverse freeborn Englishwomen," most likely indentured servants, who "to the disgrace of our Nation doe intermarry with negro slaves." The law stipulated that any white woman who married an enslaved man would become enslaved to her husband's master. In 1692, Maryland's legislature spelled out additional punishments for interracial fornication, indenturing for seven years any woman who gave birth to a mixed-race child of an enslaved man; if the child's father was a free Black man, then the father, too, would serve seven years' indenture.[27]

Eventually, English laws and the French Code Noir, issued by the French government in 1685 for their colonies in the Caribbean and adapted for Louisiana in 1724, quoted the Latin principle of *partus sequitur ventrem*—"status follows womb." In societies otherwise organized around patriarchal inheritance, this principle assigned a child's status—free or enslaved—based on the condition of their mother, her identity reduced to the "womb" that birthed them. Slavery thus marked African women as a distinct kind of maternal being, a difference that was intended to ensure the enslavers' control of their offspring.[28]

An official determination that Hall was a man might have subjected Hall or Besse to fornication charges, but criminal allegations were far less likely if the court concluded that Hall was female. Sex between two female-bodied people or two male-bodied people was both a sin and a capital crime according to English faith and law, but it was rarely prosecuted. For resource-strapped English settlers, it did not present the immediate financial peril of a fatherless child or a disobedient servant.

Surviving records document only two cases of women punished for sex with women in the seventeenth or eighteenth centuries in the English colonies of North America. In 1642, the Essex County quarterly court in Massachusetts sentenced Elizabeth Johnson to be whipped and fined for "unseemly practices betwixt her and another maid." In 1649, Mary Hammon and Sara Norman, from Yarmouth in Plymouth Colony, were convicted of "leude behavior each with [the] other upon a bed." Norman was also charged with "divers Lasivious speeches," suggesting that she had not only acted but spoken immodestly. While Norman was sentenced to publicly acknowledge "her unchast behavior," Hammon was not punished. New Haven Colony, which was strictly governed according to biblical law, was the only colonial jurisdiction to outlaw sex between women. When the Connecticut Colony absorbed New Haven in 1664, Connecticut's laws took precedence, and sex between women was nowhere illegal—or, for that matter, legally defined—in the English colonies of North America.[29]

"Sodomy," generally defined in English and Dutch colonial law as penetrative sex between men, was a capital crime understood to be a serious violation of God's commandments, but it, too, was seldom prosecuted. (New Haven Colony, yet again the exception, identified sodomy as anal penetration of a man *or* a woman.) Men convicted of sodomy rarely received the death penalty. Plymouth Colony's first sodomy trial, in 1636, found two men guilty but sentenced them to whippings and branding rather than death. The only executions for sodomy in New England occurred in New Haven Colony. The few colonial sodomy cases that resulted in the death penalty involved not simply the crime of sodomy but the outrage of forced sex—of penetration without consent or otherwise in violation of acceptable norms of adult sexual interactions.[30]

Yet in Windsor, Connecticut, half a dozen young men complained over the course of thirty years about unwanted sexual advances from Nicholas Sension, a wealthy resident, before authorities finally charged that he "most wickedly committed, or at least attempted, that horrible sin of sodomy" in 1677. The criminal case might never have commenced at all if Sension hadn't sued one of his former servants, Daniel Saxton, for defamation. Saxton claimed that Sension had tried to force himself on him. The court determined that Sension's accusation against Saxton was meritless and that Sension in fact deserved to stand trial. Witnesses recounted decades of Sension's sexual abuse. "I was in the mill house and Nicholas Sension was with me, and he took me and threw me on the chest, and took hold of my privy parts"; "Sension came to me with his yard or member erected in his hands, and desired me to lie on my belly, and strove with me." A jury comprised of Sension's peers—white "freemen" who could vote and hold office—convicted him of attempted sodomy. They sentenced him to stand under the town's gallows with a rope around his neck, be whipped, and pay fines to cover court costs and ensure future good behavior. He also forfeited his rights as a freeman.[31]

Still, the fact that there was a conviction at all seems due to Sension's apparent assault of his sexual partners. Indeed, the complaints against Sension remind us both that violence—sexual and otherwise—suffused the life experiences of these colonial settlers and that these individuals were outraged by certain kinds of assault.

Laws governing interracial sex in the English colonies, meanwhile, grew stricter as the enslaved population increased in the second half of the seventeenth century. In Virginia, a 1691 statute that outlawed interracial marriage not only introduced the word "white" into Virginia's legal code for the first time but legislated the unequal treatment of women. "English or other white women" were now prohibited from marrying or fornicating with "negroes, mulattoes, and Indians," in order to prevent what legislators derisively called the "abominable mixture and spurious issue" of those unions. The number of women and men arriving in Virginia as indentured servants had declined by the 1680s and 1690s; lawmakers perhaps hoped to keep the white women of the colony for themselves. At the same time, the law made no mention of sex between white men and Black or Indian women; the sexual privileges of white men were becoming clearer, even as they went unspoken.[32]

In 1629, when the inability of Basse and other residents of Warraskoyack to settle the question of Hall's sex brought the case to the General Court in Jamestown, the only matter the court addressed was whether Hall was a man or a woman. Perhaps some members of the court additionally pondered whether Hall, a man, committed the crime of fornication with Besse, or if Hall, a woman, engaged with Besse in other "lewd" acts. If so, they did not leave a record of those concerns. What emerged clearly was a community mobilized to resolve the perceived social chaos that followed from sexual ambiguity.

The General Court's ruling was astonishing, and, as far as we know, unique. The governor and his council concluded that Hall was *both* male and female. The court effectively created a new gender category for Hall, but in doing so it mocked Hall's identity. Likely hoping to prevent Hall's ambiguity from leading to illicit sexual behaviors, the court punished Hall by requiring them to dress as two sexes at once: "it shall bee published in the plantation where the said Hall lyveth that hee is a man and a woeman, that all the Inhabitants there may take notice thereof and that hee shall goe Clothed in mans apparel, only his head to bee attired in a Coyfe and Crosecloth [female headcovering] wth an Apron before him."[33]

In the end, Hall's sentence was a kind of sartorial humiliation, a decree to wear men's clothing with women's accessories. Cross-dressing itself would not become a crime in any of the English colonies until the end of the seventeenth century. Rather, in a society where attire signaled a person's place in the social order, Hall's punishment emphasized dislocation. As both man and woman, Hall was legally unsexed: they could not marry and thus could not have licit sexual relations at all.

Any attempt to determine the "real" sex or gender identity of an individual such as Hall risks imposing a twenty-first-century frame on people who lived in a society far different from our own. Hall defined themself as both male and female centuries before such words as "nonbinary," "intersex," or "transgender" might have matched their self-understanding. Yet until the General Court sentenced Hall to wear both male and female attire, Hall consistently self-presented as one sex, perhaps reflecting an awareness that while they considered themself "both," they moved within a social world that permitted only one or the other.

The inventiveness and defiance in Hall's expression of their gender hints at how people at the time thought about the naturalness of sex. The women who inspected Hall's body made the case that genitals determined gender: a person with a penis was a man. At various moments, Hall's employers offered more ambivalent appraisals of their servant's sexual identity. They may have cared less about what was "natural" than what was useful to their risky experiments in tobacco farming. Hall chose to live outside these expectations and define gender on their own terms.

Two pages of a court proceeding comprise the entirety of the historical record about T. Hall. Did they spend their remaining years wearing both male and female clothing as ordered by the court? Did Hall leave Warraskoyack—sail north to Plymouth or New Haven, south to Barbados, or even east on a return trip to England—to regain control over their gender? Perhaps Hall grew acquainted with one of the Algonquian-speaking peoples of the Chesapeake or survived an overland journey south to the Carolinas, yet unknown to English people but home to dozens of Indigenous nations. That may be a fantastical notion. Yet there—or farther west, among the Pueblo of New Mexico, where our story continues—Hall would have encountered Native communities that valued and accepted a two-spirit person.

Chapter 2

Sacred Possessions

Juana Hurtado was still a child the day in 1680 that Diné (Navajo) warriors on horseback stormed her father's ranch in what is today New Mexico. Documents and archaeological evidence contain a host of details about these events, but how they unfolded from the perspective of a child is a question about which we can only speculate.

Zía Pueblo people believed in a recurring, repeating life cycle that began when the gods gave them fire and taught them to build their houses. Perhaps it was inside a two- or three-story adobe home like those pictured here that Juana Hurtado learned about the origins of her people from her mother, a Zía Pueblo woman.

Perhaps the drumbeat of hooves against packed dirt sent Juana racing to the house from a garden patch she tended. A bucket of water from the Jemez River thrown aside to free her small legs to run faster, an armload of firewood discarded along the path: our imaginations crave details from the ungenerous historical record of the 1680 attack.

Maybe seven-year-old Juana cried for her mother, a Pueblo woman whose brother, Juan Checaye, was the governor of Zía Pueblo (a Pueblo village). Juana's mother would have reached adulthood having absorbed stories about the origins of her people, stories in which sexual desires, reproduction, nature, and the spirit world wove a web of connection with the ancestors. Franciscan friars, who established missions throughout New Mexico in the sixteenth and seventeenth centuries, would have tried to teach Juana's mother that anything other than marital fidelity according to Roman Catholic teaching would condemn her soul to hell. In 1673, this woman came to reside in the home of Capt. Andres Hurtado, likely as a servant, and bore Juana, one of the hundreds of *coyotas*—people of mixed Native-Spanish parentage—in seventeenth-century New Mexico.

Or Juana might have called out to her father, Captain Hurtado. He was an *encomendero*, a Spanish man who had been granted land in the viceroyalty of New Spain from colonial authorities in Mexico as a reward for his contributions to their recent military conquests. The Crown's gift permitted him, as far as the Spanish were concerned, to force Native people to work that land. He would likely also have seen Juana's mother as another sort of reward to which his birth entitled him. He had been raised in a culture of machismo that understood the control of women's sexuality as a demonstration of a man's status. Those ideas taught Spanish men to associate their personal honor with their ability to exert power over other people. In New Mexico, a Spanish man might consider both his military victories over Indigenous people and his control over women in his household as proof of his masculine strength.[1]

Everything about young Juana's life to that moment had taught her to understand the threat of angry men on horseback. But a child, even a clever one, cannot outrun horses or defend herself against a man with a gun. Grabbed from the yard or seized inside her home, Juana became a captive among the Diné, ancestral enemies of her mother's people. Her life followed a common, if violence-ridden pattern, shaped by the ongoing skirmishes among the Pueblo, Diné, and Spanish. Yet she would one day become a wealthy, sexually defiant landowner. She would be known as Juana la Coyota, an appellation that recognized not only her mixed birth but also her authority.[2]

Sacred stories of Pueblo sexuality were an inheritance that a Pueblo mother could pass down to her daughter. Juana's Pueblo kin traced their origins to a time when gods gave them fire and taught them to build their houses. They told the story of the Corn Mother, an ancestor born under the earth whose own children became their foremothers and whose protection enabled them to grow the harvests that sustained them. Seeds from the Corn Mother symbolized the female power of generation; the Hopi Pueblo word *posumi* translated both as corn seed and as nubile woman.[3]

Rituals surrounding birth emphasized the connections between human sexuality and natural abundance. Women of the Zuni tribe, a subset of the Pueblo people, celebrated the birth of a daughter by placing a gourd filled with seeds over her vulva and praying that she would grow to have large and fruitful sex organs. They greeted the birth of a boy by sprinkling his penis with water and praying that it would remain small. Pueblo men who loathed that tradition's emphasis on women's dominant role in procreation engaged in rituals of their own. They wore immense artificial penises carved out of wood while singing, one Hopi man explained, "about the penis being the thing that made the women happy."[4]

Pueblo communities taught that pleasure pervaded the natural world and flowed through their benevolent spirits. Neither the body nor sexual conversation were shameful. In warmer weather, both women and men typically wore small coverings over their genitals but did not cover their chests. They observed evidence of sexuality in nature—seeds and rain, earth and sky—and believed that human sexuality reflected it. Sexual intercourse forged cosmic harmony, uniting and balancing the masculine sky and the feminine earth. Some Pueblo people performed a ceremony at the solstice that concluded with intercourse.[5]

Mutual exchange and kinship, not hierarchy, shaped Pueblo ideas about gender and sexuality. Their beliefs emphasized contrasts between male and female sexual energies, differences that structured everything from the division of labor within and beyond the pueblo to rituals for healing and warfare. As the complement to men's role as warriors and hunters, women could, through their sexual energies, pacify the spirits of a slain foe by symbolically enacting sexual intercourse on the scalps of vanquished enemies, as they did with the hides of deer that men of the community had hunted. Intercourse between a foreign man and a Pueblo woman was also often understood as a means for women's erotic power to mollify antagonistic spirits or to forge new trade or diplomatic bonds. In the Pueblo worldview, women's sexual desires were not shameful. They were considered essential for community cohesion and relationships with outsiders.[6]

Indigenous marriage practices throughout the continent reflected values of kinship and reciprocity. Marriage among the Pueblo, as among many Indigenous North Americans, required only mutual commitment rather than a priest's or an elder's blessing. Young Pueblos freely engaged in premarital sex, with girls and women using herbal contraceptives and practicing abortion. Most Indigenous families were "matrifocal": a new bride brought her husband home to live among her people rather than his. Kinship bonds stretched vertically through multiple generations and horizontally to include female kin and their households. In 1601, an observer noted that Pueblo people "make agreements among themselves and live together as long as they want to, and when the woman takes a notion, she looks for another husband and the man for another wife." A Zuni wife needed only to leave her husband's belongings outside her dwelling to indicate that she no longer considered him her spouse.[7]

Pueblo women prized their sexuality as the source of future generations of their people and of their own pleasure. If married, sex was a wife's gift to her husband to acknowledge his contributions to her mother's household. If not married, then the woman expected a man she had sex with to give her something in return, perhaps a blanket or salt or hides. Throughout North America, Europeans repeatedly misinterpreted these and similar practices as evidence of Indigenous prostitution.[8]

Pueblo men's power came from their expansive connections to the world beyond their homes and villages: agriculture, hunting, and warfare. (Women supervised agriculture in many other Indigenous cultures.) Pueblo women were kept out of men's domains, just as men were excluded from the management of food storage or family life. Men abstained from sex for four days before and after warfare or hunting to renew the vitality of their masculine powers. A medicine man similarly avoided sex (as well as salt and meat) for four days before attempting to cure a disease.[9]

The clear lines between men's and women's roles nevertheless coexisted with an acceptance of individuals who contained both male and female essence. At least 155 American Indian and Alaska Native nations had members of their communities who had a "two-spirit" identity, such as the Diné *nádleehí*, the Lakota *winkte*, and the Sauk and Fox *aya'kwa*. The Northern Algonquin word *niizh manitoag* connotes a person who possesses a combination of masculine and feminine qualities. A Jesuit missionary living among Illinois and Nadouessi people near Lake Superior observed boys who "while still young, assume the garb of women, and retain it throughout their lives." Some two-spirit people worked alongside women at tasks associated with women's work, such as caring for the sick and injured, weaving, food production, and agriculture. The Chumash, a tribe in California, celebrated individuals they called *joyas* as the consummate combination of male and female natures, imbued with spiritual gifts and worthy, in some cases, of marriage to a chief as a second wife. The prevalence of these two-spirit people fascinated and often confused white colonists, who complained that Native American people were inveterate "sodomites."[10]

Gender transition among children assigned female at birth occurred less often, but parents in some cases raised these children to perform masculine roles such as hunting and warfare. Some of the earliest records from Spanish travelers in what are today Florida and New Mexico noted the power of female chiefs and warriors. These individuals seem to have married other women.[11]

Juana's mother was claimed by Captain Hurtado as Spanish soldiers asserted control over New Mexican towns, but sexual intimacies between Indigenous women and European men across North America often occurred on terms that Native women set. Throughout the 1600s and 1700s, many Native nations retained their culture's sexual values, despite European desires to change them. This was partly due to their sheer numbers: one historian describes seventeenth-century North America as "a vast Indigenous ocean speckled with tiny European islands." Indigenous people's control of the trade routes upon which Europeans depended also allowed them to maintain considerable autonomy long after Europeans arrived in North America.[12]

Some Native women welcomed French and English traders into their homes. It was a familiar economic and political strategy among the Indigenous people of North America, even before the arrival of white colonists. These sexual relationships expanded Indigenous kinship networks. The Caddoan people of Louisiana and eastern Texas had long approached intermarriage as a political and economic strategy, using it to consolidate three American Indian confederacies in the sixteenth and seventeenth centuries. The French men who began to arrive in the early eighteenth century struck Caddoans as another people who might become allies in war and partners in their established commerce in horses, furs, and human captives. By helping traders survive in a strange land, these relationships sustained European financial ventures.[13]

In the Northeast and Great Lakes region, cross-cultural sex became essential to the success of the monumentally lucrative fur trade through which hundreds of thousands of pounds of beaver pelts became moccasins, leather belts, and other luxuries for European and American consumers. French and English men who married Indian women typically formed households according to Indigenous practices, sealing their bonds by smoking a calumet. Colonial administrators and missionaries initially tolerated these marriages for their usefulness but soon sought (white) "Christian" wives whose reproductive and domestic labors could help them build permanent settlements of their own.[14]

By the time of Juana's capture, devastating changes over which Indigenous people had no control threatened their survival. From the moment Spanish forces first landed in Mexico in 1519 and declared war on the Native inhabitants, they and their livestock transmitted pathogens that were more lethal than the bullets from their guns. In a pattern repeated across the Americas, epidemic diseases ravaged the Indigenous population of New Mexico. About 86,000 Pueblos farmed and hunted in the area in 1598, when Spanish leaders backed by a few hundred soldiers declared that New Mexico was a Spanish colony. In 1680, the Indigenous population in the area had plummeted to just 17,000. Demographic catastrophe affected sexual behaviors. Many of the hundreds of Indigenous nations in North America already permitted a man of high status to marry more than one wife; amid the challenges posed by colonialism, this practice expanded as a strategy to extend kinship bonds.[15]

Juana's mother had come of age as Franciscans' efforts to enforce Catholic sexual morality became especially violent. Franciscans arrived in New Mexico at the vanguard of Spanish conquest, eager to convert the inhabitants of Pueblo villages. They believed that God's laws commanded chastity before marriage, fidelity within marriage, lifelong and indissoluble monogamy, and modesty. They even critiqued the sexual position that Pueblos apparently preferred, calling it "bestial": "like animals, the female plac[ed] herself publicly on all fours." Such a dishonorable means of copulation, the friars warned, lowered people to the level of animals. They advised that the only Christian position for sexual intercourse had the man and woman lie face to face, with the man on top—thus the "missionary position." The friars preferred it because it favored what the Catholic Church officially considered the primary end of marital sexual intercourse, the conception of children.[16]

Franciscans believed they could educate Pueblos to avoid the wages of sin. Men and women who violated Christian laws might be put in the stocks and publicly whipped. Priests cut off disobedient men's hair, leaving them with what the Pueblo considered shamefully short locks. Franciscans' own behavior undermined their efforts to set a virtuous example. Taos Pueblos complained to the Spanish governor in 1637 and 1638 that the friar there had punished insolent children by castration and acts of sodomy. That friar was eventually relieved of his duties, but resentment built against the friar who replaced him, frustration that culminated in an attack in 1639 that killed the friar and two soldier-settlers.[17]

Seven-year-old Juana, meanwhile, traveled with her captors to a Diné village. She could already speak both Keres (the Zía language) and Spanish; now she learned the Diné language. Linguistic fluency was a valuable commodity in a region rife with intercultural alliances and conflicts. Juana entered the Diné community as a captive, but at some point she was likely adopted into a Diné family or married to a Diné man. She would leave their custody as something closer to kin.[18]

While Juana walked or rode into Diné territory in 1680, her Pueblo kin were secretly organizing a massive rebellion against the Spanish-Catholic presence. Fury over Franciscan attempts to suppress polygamy and other Pueblo sexual practices fueled the rebels' determination. They also observed the weakness of the colonizer's power. Spanish reinforcements arrived only once every three years from Mexico City, the nearest colonial center. Spanish power in the region was never firmly established, and it declined year after year. What became known as the Pueblo Revolt of 1680 left 400 Hispanics dead, including 21 priests. Soldiers from multiple Pueblo communities seized control of New Mexico and drove out 1,500 Spanish soldiers, friars, *mestizos* (people with a mix of Spanish, Indigenous, and often also African ancestry), and Indigenous servants. Those exiles retreated to El Paso, a community that came into existence as a refugee settlement. Perhaps Juana's Spanish father and half-brother were among that beleaguered party.[19]

Juana "la Coyota" Hurtado lived twelve years among the Diné. The captivity that she experienced typified a form of slavery that had existed across North America and around the globe since ancient times. As early as 700 CE, captive labor enriched the powerful and possibly tyrannical leaders of the pueblos of the Southwest and within the vast agricultural power centers that emerged along the Mississippi River and its tributaries. Warring tribes seized people from their enemies' villages to trade among themselves. At annual trade fairs, captives could be "ransomed" while bison meat was traded for vegetables such as squash, beans, and corn. That hierarchical Indigenous power structure had crumbled by the time Juana's Pueblo grandmother was born, brought down by prolonged droughts and famine that undermined the authority of oppressive chiefs. Captivity did not end when those cultures collapsed, but it did morph into something less severe. (Servant captives, for instance, were no longer ritually killed and buried alongside a recently deceased master.) Indigenous slavery in the seventeenth century was nonetheless violent and disruptive. In warfare and diplomacy, tribes traded women and children. Only someone who was a foreigner, an outsider, could be a captive.[20]

In 1692, Juana's Spanish half-brother Martín Hurtado "ransomed" her during Spain's bloody reconquest of New Mexico. Spanish forces in El Paso had spent years plotting, and they recaptured all major Pueblo villages by 1693. Now a young woman, Juana requested and received a land grant near Zía Pueblo. There she established a prosperous *rancho* where Diné, Pueblo, and Spanish people traded for a half century. Juana eventually possessed three houses on two ranches, husbanded hundreds of livestock, kept more than thirty horses, and filled her homes with material possessions.[21]

She shared much of her post-captivity life with a man named Galván from Zía Pueblo. They had four children together by 1727, all of whom the Franciscans considered illegitimate because Galván was married to another woman. Juana disagreed. She went by the name Juana Hurtado Galván, adding her lover's last name to her own. In doing so she honored a Pueblo (and more broadly American Indian) emphasis on kinship rather than wedlock as the foundation for intergenerational and community bonds.

Juana Hurtado Galván operated her businesses and conducted her personal life according to her own fusion of Zía Pueblo and Catholic values. She acted as an interpreter between the Diné people who frequented her ranches and the Franciscan priests who wanted to evangelize them. "They [the Diné] had kept her for so long," Fray Miguel de Menchero wrote, "[that] the Indians of the said Nation made friendly visits to her, and in this way the father of the said mission has been able to instruct some of them." She was esteemed among Pueblo, Diné, and Spanish alike, "favored by certain people," one of her contemporaries noted, so that she could defy laws that attempted to punish her sexual behaviors. Spanish ideals of honor and chastity dictated social ostracism for such a woman as Juana, but she died secure in her wealth, power, and family bonds in 1753, at the age of eighty.[22]

Juana's notable refusal to conform to Catholic sexual morality could not, of course, dampen the zeal of the Franciscans determined to convert what they considered the heathen people of North America. By the mid-eighteenth century, with Spanish outposts in New Mexico more secure, colonial authorities in Mexico turned to establishing settlements along the coast of "Alta California," a vast Mexican province that stretched north from the Baja Peninsula along the Pacific coastline. Founding Catholic missions in Alta California was the great passion of Fr. Junípero Serra, a Franciscan priest who created Mission San Diego, the first in Alta California, in 1769. By 1773, Franciscan priests had established five missions, but they were small and largely unsuccessful.

Spanish priests and administrators in California confronted sexual dilemmas similar to those facing English and French colonists: how to

Franciscan priests established Catholic missions in Mexico and California throughout the mid- to late-eighteenth century with varying levels of success. Father Junípero Serra (1713–1784), who founded Mission San Diego in 1769, hoped not only to convert Indigenous people to Catholicism but to eliminate what he viewed as depraved sexual practices between Native men and women.

build a permanent settlement while prohibiting their men from cohabiting with local women. Serra recognized that celibate priests could not model the Christian marital sexuality that he wanted Native people to emulate. In 1773, he petitioned the Spanish government in Mexico to send him Spanish families so "that the Indians, who until now have been very surprised to see all the men without any women, see that there are also marriages among Christians." Fourteen Spanish families settled San José in 1777, but fewer than 500 Hispanics lived in San José by 1810.[23]

A new Hispanic identity emerged among residents of this region who claimed Spanish ancestry, a heritage that they believed entitled them to lands that Spanish colonists had seized from Indigenous people. Most of the first Hispanic settlers of California were not, in fact, "pure" Spanish but mestizo. Those family histories shaped an emerging Hispanic sexual subculture. Among Hispanic men and women who lived throughout New Spain in the mid- to late eighteenth century, honor depended not as much on private behavior as on public reputation. Like their Anglo-

American contemporaries, they tolerated premarital sex as long as it resulted in marriage.[24]

Fr. Luis Jayme, a priest at Mission San Diego, shared Serra's understanding of sexual behavior as both a tool of conversion and a measure of the convert's obedience. Jayme believed he could transform heathen polygamists into married Christian monogamists. He boasted that Native converts displayed their new faith by abandoning their tribes' sexual norms: "They do not marry relatives [once they convert]," he explained, "and they have but one wife. The married men sleep with their wives only." The "bachelors" at the mission slept in a separate dormitory rather than in the family groupings that Native people more often preferred. Jayme proudly disciplined Indigenous people who failed to comply with Christian sexual morals: "If a man plays with any woman who is not his wife, he is scolded and punished by his captains." Punishments included public whippings.[25]

Spanish soldiers, who built presidios, or forts, near the missions, threatened the priests' aims. Already by 1772, the residents of Indigenous towns near Mission San Diego prepared to attack the mission because, Jayme explained, Spanish soldiers terrorized locals, who fled their homes each morning "so that the soldiers will not rape their women." This violence was not a distinctive horror of Spanish rule. In 1752, leaders of the Lower Creek nation complained to an agent of the South Carolina government that "the white people in general [were] debauching their wives and mentioned several in particular that were found guilty, and said if his Excellency would not punish them for it, the injured persons would certainly put their own laws in execution." Women healed themselves using purification rituals, but the abuses continued.[26]

Fury over these sexual assaults fueled a wave of violent rebellions. In 1771, soon after Mission San Gabriel was established in California, a large group of Indigenous people avenged the rape of a woman from their tribe by ambushing two Spanish soldiers on horseback. The Spanish counterattacked, bringing the head of the local chief back to their presidio. Indigenous nations that had previously been enemies formed a council to mount a unified front against the Spanish. Only the arrival of Spanish reinforcements at the mission foiled their plans. A Spanish soldier's rape of a woman married to another chief similarly instigated an insurrection at San Luis Obispo. Spanish soldiers intercepted the attack, but not before Native people demonstrated their outrage at Spanish behavior.[27]

Time and again, Native people refused to abandon their longstanding sexual practices even as they accommodated some of the friars' religious requirements. Many compromised, complying with Catholic marriage within the mission's walls while holding to their Indigenous sexual values beyond them. Serra complained to the governor of California that the Indigenous men he oversaw "have, each, a gentile woman with them, and have left their Christian wives here at the mission." Priests grilled converted Indians about their sexual desires and behaviors at annual confessions and during prenuptial investigations, inquiring whether they had "carnal" dreams about men, women, or animals; whether they became aroused at the sight of animals having sex; whether a man had raped or had sex with a *joya* (a two-spirit person); and whether they had ever tried to prevent a pregnancy, among other questions. The answers they recorded reveal not the scrupulous avoidance of sin but the lengths to which many Indigenous Catholics went to embrace both Catholic and Indigenous teachings about sex.[28]

Antonio Pablo was a *neófito,* an American Indian who had converted to Catholicism and who resided just outside the walls of the mission at San Juan Capistrano in California in the early 1800s. A widower, he decided after his wife's death that he wanted to share his bed with a woman named Felicitas. While the priests who kept records at the mission did not make note of Pablo's tribal identity, the Native people of California included dozens of distinct language groups and polities.[29]

The Franciscan friars at San Juan Capistrano, though, berated Pablo for living "obscenely" with Felicitas and committing adultery: Felicitas was married to another man. Religious education in Mission San Juan Capistrano had instructed Antonio Pablo in the Catholic Church's teaching against fornication and adultery, but much as Juana Hurtado had in early eighteenth-century New Mexico, he rejected the notion that he had committed a religious offense.[30]

Europeans brought disease and warfare, but their arrival did not extinguish Indigenous people or their cultures. Juana's story reveals how individuals who experienced captivity and possible sexual assault might continue to choose which sexual norms they wanted to follow, despite considerable pressure to adopt a colonizer's moral code.

Chapter 3

Under the Husband's Government

When Abigail Abbot Bailey realized her husband, Asa, had deceived her, carrying her into New York State in 1792 and then abandoning her there, she called upon God to guide her back to her children, relatives, and religious congregation in New

To an eighteenth-century viewer, the many offspring of this husband and wife represented the ideal outcome of marriage. Historians believe that the younger, seated woman holding an infant is the adult child of the older woman, also seated with an infant, suggesting that mother and daughter had both recently given birth. The toddler-sized child, painted in a somewhat translucent hue, might represent a child who died very young.

Hampshire. For years she had waited for God's will to reveal itself, until she finally pursued an informal separation from Asa. She hoped "to suffer him to flee . . . and . . . go to some distant place, where we should be afflicted with him no more," if only he would fairly divide their property between them and then leave her alone. Asa initially refused to do that, even after Abigail confronted him with evidence of his sexual abuse of their teenage daughter Phebe. Like many women of her era, Abigail hesitated to seek a divorce, "the dreadful scene of prosecuting my husband." The laws of New England permitted divorce on limited grounds, including adultery and cruelty, but her Protestant faith in the marriage covenant had led her to seek an alternative.[1]

Abigail's experience of marriage in the eighteenth-century United States was a terrifying one, but it needn't have been. When Abigail Abbot reached the age of twenty-two in the 1760s, she could have reasonably expected that marriage would bring her joy and fulfillment. Her religion taught her to put her trust in God, and it also promised her companionship with her husband. Law defined a wife as her husband's inferior, but Abigail also hoped that love might blossom in her home and pleasure reach her bed. Poetry and essays in popular Anglo-American magazines in the mid-eighteenth century celebrated romance; by century's end, letters exchanged by courting couples—and rationales given in court for a divorce—often referenced the presence or absence of affection and the suffering of the brokenhearted. Husbands were the family patriarchs, but patriarchs were expected to be kind. As Boston preacher and Harvard College president Benjamin Wadsworth explained in 1712, within the family hierarchy, "the Husband is call'd the Head of the Woman," and governs the wife accordingly. Yet a husband should not treat his wife "as a Servant, but as his own flesh; he must love her as himself."[2]

Neither the religious ideals nor the legal options of the time accounted for a husband like Asa. His violent domination subverted the terms of his marriage covenant and endangered the lives of his dependents. Abigail prayed for Asa's redemption and wrote in her journal about her desire to understand how God's plan for her included the endurance of domestic terror.

Ideals of marriage, love, and sexual pleasure had deep roots among New England Protestants. Contrary to modern assumptions of their prudery, seventeenth-century Puritans described marriage as an ideal friendship, and they emphasized that both husband and wife should find erotic satisfaction within it. "If ever two were one, then surely we," the seventeenth-century Puritan poet Anne Bradstreet wrote to her husband. A popular understanding that women were, if anything, more driven by sexual desire than men prompted the authors of domestic advice manuals to emphasize that conjugal love should be not only romantic but mutually satisfying. One midwifery text urged husbands to "entertain" their wives "with all kind of dalliance, wanton behavior, and allurements to venery" to ensure her "content and satisfaction." New England courts upheld divorce petitions from wives whose husbands were impotent, ruling that a man who could not sexually perform for his wife had failed to meet one of the most basic requirements of marriage.[3]

This Protestant celebration of conjugal desire contrasted to the increasingly vociferous disparagement of sodomy. Few sodomy cases made it to court, but ministers preached against it regularly. By the 1730s, American newspapers carried articles about gathering spots in London for men seeking sex with one another called Molly houses, with similar enterprises known by other names in the Dutch Republic, Lisbon, and Paris. Coverage of these "sodomitical clubs" hinted at a nascent concept of sexual identity among these "vile Wretches" and the sexually defined communities they formed, but we have no record of any comparable groups taking shape in Anglo America.[4]

The idea that sexual behavior reflected the state of a person's soul, rather than an internal sexual identity, nevertheless allowed for leniency toward men who had sex with men. In 1756, when the General Meeting of Baptist Churches suspended Stephen Gorton, a minister of a church in New London, Connecticut, for "unchaste behaviour with his fellow men when in bed with them," Gorton's contemporaries bemoaned that his tendency toward sin manifested in forbidden sexual behaviors. The General Meeting determined that Gorton's "offensive" conduct, "frequently repeated for a long space of time," was evidence of "an inward disposition . . . towards the actual commission of a sin of so black and dark a dye." Yet because Gorton's contemporaries believed that his behavior reflected his chronic disposition rather than his desires, they also had faith that repentance could absolve him. He confessed his sins before his church, and the members voted by a two-thirds majority to reinstate him.[5]

The key for prosperous white men was to maintain a reputation for self-mastery. William Byrd II, an eighteenth-century Virginia enslaver and politician, kept a diary in which he recorded his sexual interests and acts. Byrd viewed his sex life as an expression of his privileged social status. He used a combination of genteel and military language to describe his marital and nonmarital encounters, such as when he wrote in the 1710s that he "gave [his] wife a flourish" or characterized intercourse as "mount the guard." He noted the various times he "rogered" his wife, including her displeasure when he did this while she was ill, and recorded his assaults against various other women. ("Roger" was slang for penis.) He referred to sex workers as "ladies of universal gallantry"—surely a joke, but one that allowed him to see his patronage of sex workers as further evidence of his civility.[6]

The Protestant revivals that swept from the Carolinas to New England during Abigail's childhood called believers to a purer ideal of sexual virtue. From the pulpits of Congregationalist churches to the tent revivals of Methodist itinerants, mid-eighteenth-century Protestants emphasized the emotional vulnerability and passion of the converted sinner's experience. Women and men wept at Baptist and Methodist gatherings as they confronted their sins and begged for God's forgiveness. Churches required confession and penitence for sinners, but these practices showed differing understandings of men's and women's weaknesses. Women, far more often than men, were disciplined for sexual misconduct, while secular and church law punished men more often for the sins of avarice and inebriation. Indeed, popular wisdom assigned men a greater capacity for self-government, an ability to regulate their "passions" that women, left to their own devices, generally lacked.[7]

When Asa courted Abigail in the 1760s, he may have visited her father's home to bring her gifts, stay for conversation, and possibly take the first steps toward sexual intimacy. By the mid-eighteenth century, rather than family patriarchs arranging marital partners for their children, young men and women chose for themselves. Asa would have asked Abigail's father for his approval, but Mr. Abbot most likely did not select Abigail's husband.[8]

Their courtship coincided with the heyday in New England of a practice called "bundling," imported from northern Europe, in which parents permitted their daughter's suitor to spend the night in her bed. Bed-sharing remained as common in the mid-1700s as it had been in the 1620s when T. Hall lay beside Greate Besse. Travelers often crawled into bed with one of their hosts, even a young woman of the house. But bundling was different. An English visitor to Massachusetts 1759–1760 observed that after the "old couple" of the house went to bed, "the young ones . . . get into bed together also, but without pulling off their undergarments, in order to prevent scandal." It was common in the small New Hampshire towns where the Abbot and Bailey families lived too. A young farmer in Keane named Abner Sanger wrote in his journal that he and other young men he knew enjoyed what they called "girling of it," casual overnights in the beds of young women their age. Bundling seems to have been especially common among rural and non-elite people. Clergy warned against it. In 1753, minister Samuel Hopkins condemned behaviors that "have a tendency and lead to the gratification of lusts," including "unseasonable company-keeping" and "lying on the bed of any man with young women." Hopkins seems to have held a minority opinion. For most New Englanders, bundling was neither outrageous nor clandestine, and a household's senior residents allowed it for couples who were not even engaged.[9]

Bundling's popularity grew as the American legal system's concern with sex crimes declined. Throughout the seventeenth and into the mid-eighteenth centuries, New England authorities vigorously prosecuted fornication and heard white women's allegations of forced sex. But after about 1750, courts in British North America rarely took on cases involving sexual assault, bastardy, or fornication. Commercial disputes filled their dockets instead. Families and communities assumed responsibility for sexual matters and negotiated informal resolutions. Those changes deprived many women of the ability to have their voices heard in court. Now when accusations of illegitimacy or forcible sex came before the bar, they did so more often as lawsuits for reputational damage brought by one man against another.[10]

The acceptance of bundling suggests not only that playful premarital intimacy filled the lives of many young people of the time but that it gave young women—and their families—significant leverage at a time when they could no longer reliably litigate fornication, illegitimacy, or sexual assault. A young woman likely had some control over whether she and her bedmate remained fully or partially clothed. In the small homes of the time, other members of the household would have easily heard if she called out for help. And a parent whose daughter "bundled" with a suitor would have known whom to hold responsible (and pressure into marriage) if she became pregnant.[11]

Bundling may have contributed to high rates of premarital sex: by the 1770s, between 30 and 40 percent of the brides in New Haven were already pregnant when they spoke their marriage vows. Abigail was not pregnant on her wedding day. Given the intensity of her faith, she likely would have strongly preferred to save her first sexual experiences for her marriage bed. She might also have wanted to make sure that Asa followed through on his promises.[12]

Marriage was hardly a bedrock of "tradition" or Christian morality among white Americans. In the South, where ministers were in much shorter supply than in New England, marriage was a frequently informal arrangement. In 1711, Reverend John Urmstone, an Anglican, bemoaned the "troublesome and unsettled country" of colonial North Carolina, a "barbarous and disorderly place." Nothing captured that disorder, he complained, more than the sexual indiscretions of married women. More than fifty years after Urmstone's tirade, in 1766, Anglican minister Charles Woodmason complained that the white inhabitants of the South Carolina backcountry lived in a "stage of debauchery," with polygamy "very common," "concubinage general," and "bastardy no disrepute."[13]

Americans extolled marriage as a partnership of loving companionship, but they still privileged the power of household patriarchs and the needs of the larger community. Marriage in the United States adhered to the common-law principle of *coverture*, according to which the husband's legal identity "covered" the wife's. Under coverture, a married woman—a *feme covert*—could not establish a separate residence or enter into any contracts without her husband's permission.

Despite those restrictions, the laws of marriage in New England were more liberal than those in Britain or even in the mid-Atlantic and southern regions. In most colonies and states, it was easier to obtain a legal separation (usually separation "of bed and board," with no legal right to remarry) than a civil divorce, but divorces became more common after the Revolution. The most frequent means of separation remained "self-divorce," when husband and wife simply parted ways without legal formalities. (Self-divorce on occasion led desperate husbands to pay for newspaper notices warning others not to enter into contracts with their estranged wives, whose debts, under coverture, they would be legally obligated to honor.) Throughout the new United States, women made up most plaintiffs in divorce cases.[14]

Abigail's hopes for marriage reflected the era's celebration of romantic love as well as her religious worldview: through prayer and subordination to Asa within the marriage covenant, she would serve God. Protestant theology granted spiritual equality to men and women, but a wife could exercise authority only indirectly. A woman married to a deeply disturbed, violent man, who was otherwise a pillar of his community, had to tread carefully.[15]

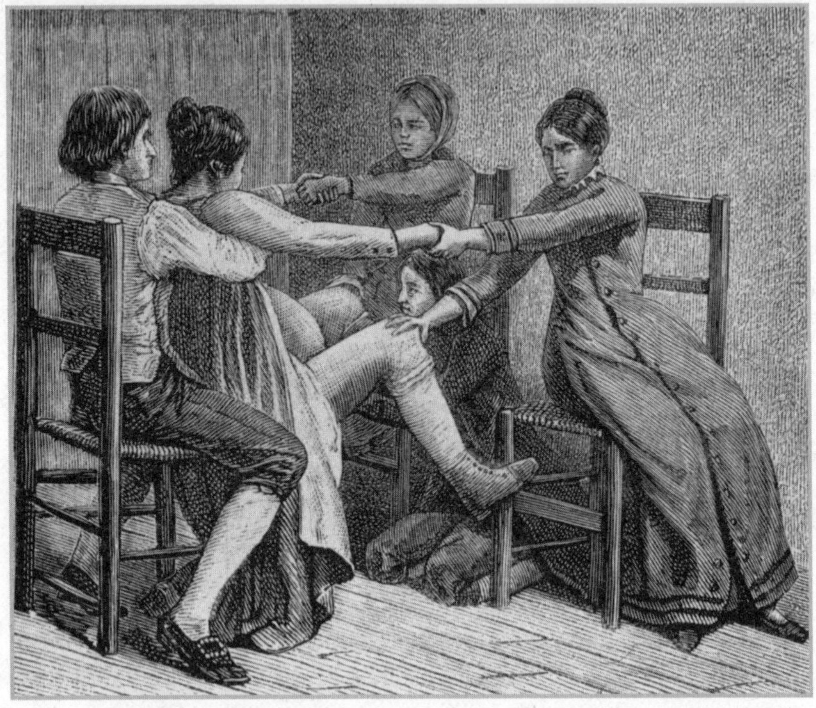

Depicted by a French historian, this portrayal of childbirth in early America illustrates both its intensity and normalcy. Dressed in everyday clothing and sitting on household chairs, a small group of men and women brace the mother and help deliver the child. Indeed, these scenes were not uncommon in eighteenth- and early-nineteenth century America; in 1800, the average white woman experienced seven live births in her lifetime.

Initially, at least, Asa Bailey's sexual energies burnished his reputation for being a capable patriarch. Abigail married Asa in 1767 when she was twenty-two and gave birth to their first child ten months later. For the twenty-five years that Abigail lived with Asa, helping him manage a farm in Bath, New Hampshire, she had sixteen pregnancies, including two sets of twins. Only one of these pregnancies ended in a miscarriage, and two of Abigail's children died in infancy. The babies usually arrived at eighteen-month intervals, but her son Samuel was barely two months old when Asa came to her bed and they conceived a daughter, Phebe, who was born in April 1772.[16]

Abigail's prolific fertility was exceptional and fast-paced even for the New England colonies, which had an astonishingly high birth rate compared both to England and to the English colonies of the Chesapeake. A white woman in British North America typically bore children every two years until she entered menopause, averaging perhaps five to ten pregnancies, with three to eight surviving children. Birth rates for enslaved women varied; they were lower on a large South Carolina plantation than at Thomas Jefferson's labor camp at Monticello, likely the result of harsher living conditions in the Carolinas. Between this reproductive success and ongoing immigration (including the forced migration of enslaved people from Africa), the population of the British colonies in North America exploded from 251,000 in 1700 to 2,464,000 in 1773.[17]

Abigail was fortunate to have survived those many times she was "brought to bed," as women of her generation were in constant danger of death in childbirth. As it was, all of those pregnancies, childbirths, and lactations took a toll on her health. She was often exhausted and felt physically weak. Yet she seemed to understand that bearing children reflected God's plan for her life. No evidence suggests that Asa and Abigail attempted to have fewer children.

Women of Abigail's generation who wanted to limit the frequency of their pregnancies employed a variety of methods. Withdrawal prior to ejaculation was a common form of fertility limitation, although contemporaries may have overestimated its efficacy. A white man in colonial Massachusetts defended himself against charges of illegitimacy by telling the court he could not be the child's father because he "minded [his] pullbacks." Folk-medicine traditions taught lactating women that breastfeeding might suppress their fertility, and they also discouraged sexual intercourse with a lactating woman; many women extended the number of months they kept a baby at the breast to space their pregnancies further apart. Other women also used pessaries, a substance or device placed in the vagina to block or neutralize sperm, varieties of which had existed since ancient times.[18]

Women made decisions about whether to prevent or end a pregnancy based on a widely shared understanding that the fetus's life began with "quickening," the moment at which a pregnant person perceived fetal movement. To restore "blocked menses," women consumed herbs like pennyroyal, sage, snakeweed, calamint, and tansy; brewed teas; laid on poultices; and tried other popular remedies. "Blocked menses" was an ambiguous phrase that connoted the cessation of menstruation due either to ill health or to pregnancy. In 1760, a druggist named Nathaniel Tweedy advertised that his store carried "small ivory syringes," as well as Hooper's Female Pills and Fraunce's Female Elixir, both known as remedies for menstrual irregularity. Syringes might be used for douches, to dilate the cervix, or to intrude into the uterus to induce abortion.[19]

However often early Americans discreetly intervened to prevent or end a pregnancy, they publicly celebrated their fecundity. They showered respect and admiration on the fathers of large families. Women's fertile bodies symbolized abundance; almanacs and newspapers used adjectives like "teeming," "lusty," and "breeding" to describe the expanding bodies of pregnant women. Wealthy American women paid portraitists to depict them seated with fruits in their laps, like wombs ripening with new life. Abigail's descriptions of her fatigue and ill health attest to the physical burdens of frequent pregnancy and childbirth, but her fertility would have burnished Asa's reputation.[20]

The window in Abigail Bailey's bedroom framed a bucolic scene. For as far as her eye could see, cultivated fields and flocks of sheep and cattle adorned the fertile valley west of the White Mountains. She spent many weeks of her adult life in that room, resting during difficult pregnancies, laboring during childbirth, and nursing the infants who arrived in steady succession. She prayed there, too, begging God's forgiveness for what her husband was doing with the young women living under their roof.[21]

Abigail had been Asa's wife for only three years when he had a sexual relationship with a live-in domestic servant. Abigail believed the relationship was consensual, although she did not consider (as no one at the time would have) that an employer's power over a servant's livelihood limited the very concept of consent. To Abigail, what mattered was that this young woman was "rude, and full of vanity" and that "her ways . . . were pleasing to Mr. B." A man of high status like Asa Bailey could get away with a lot. Like many white men of his era, Asa presumed that Black, enslaved, and white working-class women would agree to sex and that force was an appropriate response if they refused.[22]

In the mid-1770s, another woman hired to perform domestic chores for the Bailey household alleged that Asa "made violent attempts on her." (English common law defined rape as "unlawful carnal knowledge of a female over ten years of age by a man not her husband through force or against her will." After American Independence, states adopted versions of that definition.) Asa had approached this servant with his standard opening gambit. First, he flattered her, trying to get her to laugh. When she refused what Abigail described as his "unseemly" conduct, he used force. She fought back and got away from him. Abigail had more sympathy for this woman than for the woman who had sex with her husband earlier in her marriage. She confronted Asa after she heard about the attempted assault, maintaining a calm demeanor that, she believed, was evidence of the depth of her faith (and also, likely, a practical attempt to avoid a reprisal).

Still, Asa became so enraged that Abigail feared for her life. "He fell into a passion with me," Abigail wrote. "He was so overcome with anger" that he collapsed and spent the rest of the day in bed. Asa could not tolerate Abigail's refusal to express anger or agitation. "I never saw such a woman as you," he spat. He transformed her stalwart commitment to "peace" into a justification for his own rage.

Evening fell as Asa remained prostrate, nursing his supposed wounds. The cows needed milking, and Abigail knew that tending to them would leave her vulnerable—out of doors, alone, bent over, and ill prepared to run. She was five months pregnant and had four small children, none older than five, waiting for her back in the house. It seemed only too possible that her "poor husband . . . might not be suffered to add to his other crimes that of murder." She went to the barn anyway; God, she believed, would protect her. For good measure, she whispered a prayer for her husband while she filled her pails and returned to the house.

Abigail had been right to think that Asa might kill her. He admitted as much. Calmer now, he told her that he had "thought that he would put an end to [her] life" but had decided not to. Cultivating Abigail's pity, he declared a newfound interest in discovering Christ's love. Asa had never been as devout as Abigail was (she had converted when she was eighteen, but Asa was unconverted), and although in the past she greeted his pledges to dedicate himself to Christian morals with optimism, she at last doubted his sincerity. Even so, she hoped that he might yet convert. Any means of household comity was welcome.

The young woman they had employed was not satisfied with Asa's professions of faith and went to a grand jury in 1774, attesting that Asa tried to coerce her to have sex with him. "All but the violence used, Mr. B. acknowledged," Abigail noted. The Baileys would now be the subject of neighborhood gossip about their unruly household. It was yet another burden that Abigail would have to bear. Yet within just a few years, Asa was given a major's commission at the head of an army regiment. "He was indeed a man of abilities," Abigail conceded. The family's reputation, for now, was intact.

Malicious gossip, far more than prosecution for sex crimes, threatened abusive white men. Sexual reputation affected their ability to amass wealth. Because the era's financial networks relied on personal ties as much as business interests, it was other men's opinions that mattered to a merchant's ability to get credit. In taverns, coffeehouses, and print culture, men mocked other men who had failed at business as harpies or described them as feminine victims of rape, "ruined," much as a seduced woman was, by a scoundrel. As long as a man's sexual adventures enhanced rather than diminished his reputation for virile patriarchy, he could still brag of his conquests without fearing a loss of social standing.[23]

The legal system gave wide latitude to white, landowning men accused of rape such as Asa but meted out harsh punishments for similarly accused men of African descent. Black men accounted for the overwhelming majority (80 percent) of men executed for rape in British North America and the United States between 1700 and 1820. White men accused of rape were far more often charged with lesser forms of sexual assault. Several colonies specified brutal punishments for Black men; Delaware sentenced an enslaved man convicted of rape to four hours with his ears nailed to the pillory and then "cut off [his ears] close to his Head." White men who exploited free or enslaved Black women faced no legal punishment. The sexual abuse endemic to the transatlantic slave trade was so pronounced, and its effects so enduring, that it was part of the very fabric of American life.[24]

Ideas about white women's virtue emerged in tandem with stereotypes about Black men. During the American Revolutionary period, Americans started to think about white women as uniquely sexually fragile. This ideal applied far more to middle-class women like Abigail than to the servants who worked in her home. It marked a dramatic change. In Philadelphia, a city known for having an especially relaxed attitude toward nonmarital sex, popular ditties and poems in almanacs of the 1750s through 1770s teased about lusty maidens and sexually frustrated widows, portraying men, by contrast, as torn between their erotic impulses and their pursuit of mastery over their desires. Revolutionary politics abetted a notable shift: patriotic literature urged white women to recognize that they served their country by modeling virtue for their husbands and sons, as the wives and mothers of the new republic's male citizens. Presumptions that women were submissive, chaste, and even "passionless" supplanted earlier stereotypes of lusty temptresses descended from Eve. These ideas rendered middle-class and elite white women nearly immune from suspicions of sexual immorality.[25]

Stereotypes about lusty maidens were instead transferred onto working-class and non-white women. An anonymous diarist in the 1790s cataloged his sexual engagements, claiming he had "topped" thirty-six "wenches" the year before, maintained two mistresses, and paid five women for sex. The word "wench" was a derogatory term that conflated a woman's poverty with her sexual availability. This diarist created pretexts for his wife to leave the house so that he could harass a household employee, Nancy Jones, with demands for sex. When she complained to his wife, he fired her. By the late eighteenth century, white people used "wench" to describe Black women of all classes.[26]

Asa and Abigail Bailey's eldest child, a daughter named Abigail, was only six years old when, in 1774, a jury acquitted her father of attempting to forcibly rape their household servant. As she and her siblings grew to adolescence, they learned to fear their father's "severe chastisement upon his children." Ruth, the second eldest child, married a man named Ebenezer Bacon when she was sixteen, leaving her father's home to tend to her husband's household at a significantly younger age than most women of her generation. We might ask what motivated her. Another daughter, Phebe, was thirteen when Ruth married and moved out. Abigail Bailey later described the "hard and cruel treatment" she experienced as Asa's wife, but it paled in comparison to what Asa inflicted on Phebe.[27]

Asa Bailey was financially secure by the 1780s, with hundreds of acres of farmland in his name. For more than two decades, he violated his marriage vows and committed numerous acts of sexual violence before he faced any threats to his reputation, let alone to his freedoms. In this, he was not unusual for a white, landowning man in early America.

But Asa had grown increasingly erratic. He speculated about moving the family westward. Abigail had recurrent dreams that he sold the farm and took three of their children with him. In one dream, he murdered the children. For years, Abigail had practiced "prudent management with him" to navigate his "unhappy temper," but Asa's standing in their community was faltering. The respected citizen who had been awarded a major's commission in the mid-1770s was by the early 1780s embroiled in land disputes, part of a "rabble" that tried to knock a local official off his horse when he delivered unwelcome news about their land titles.[28]

To Phebe's horror, her father's eye turned toward her. Much as he had with the young women they employed, Asa first tried to obtain Phebe's agreement to sex. "A great part of the time he now spent in the room where [Phebe] was spinning," Abigail recalled, "and [he] seemed shy of me and of the rest of the family." Asa joked with Phebe, told her stories, and sought her attentions. When he informed Abigail that he wished to take Phebe with him to Ohio to care for him, she grew alarmed.

Abigail described the abuse as a corruption of her marriage. "My room was deserted," she explained, as Asa lavished attention on their daughter instead. Asa continued to expect sex from his wife, as she may have expected it from him as well; their twins Judith and Simon were conceived the same month that the abuse began.

Phebe was terrified of her father and kept younger siblings around her to avoid his predations. But she could not stop him. Asa raped Phebe when Abigail traveled to see friends or family or was otherwise out of the house. When Phebe resisted her father's "vile conduct," he beat her with a beech stick "large enough for the driving of a team."

The assaults continued for over a year, from December 1788 to April 1790. Phebe's younger siblings witnessed much of it, eventually telling all to an older sister who lived elsewhere. In her memoirs, Abigail relayed the grim story in her own terms. She defended her decision not to leave Asa as soon as she learned of the incest by explaining that she was sick at the time she discovered it; she was pregnant with the twins, born in September 1789, one of whom lived only seventeen days. As she recovered, Asa "proceeded in his wickedness."[29]

When Phebe turned eighteen and was no longer her father's legal dependent, "she immediately left us, and returned no more." Within a few months of Phebe's departure, Abigail was once again pregnant. (Legally, Abigail herself had no basis for refusing sex with an abusive husband. His marriage rights included the right to sex with his wife.) Another daughter, Patience, was born on May 27 or 29, 1791.

Abigail began to seek an informal agreement with Asa that he would leave their home, allow her to raise the children, and give her half the value of their property. Abigail also knew that if she left home without some kind of settlement from Asa, she would be penniless and might lose any legal entitlement to her children.

Rumors seemingly carried by "birds of the air" spread word of the incest and of Abigail's demand for an informal separation. Abigail warned her children "that they must no longer expect to derive the least advantage from being known as the children of Major Bailey." In political print culture and coffeehouse conversations of the Revolutionary era, rape symbolized the excesses of a louche aristocracy, while virtuous citizens of a republic displayed self-control. A piece in the *Boston Journal* in 1780 reminded patriotic men that British soldiers had harmed the property of patriots, "their farms laid desolate;—their property plundered;—their virgins *ravished*." Abigail likely worried about her family's reputation, including how it would shape Phebe's marriage prospects. But that reputation was already shattered.[30]

Proving adultery—the legal fault that would permit divorce—required Phebe's testimony, something that the shy and possibly terrified girl was unwilling to give. Abigail shared Phebe's fear of shame and exposure, which would be "inexpressibly painful." They had reason to avoid provoking a man who had threatened to kill them. Yet Abigail also resented Phebe's recalcitrance.

This seeming lack of sympathy for Phebe is difficult to comprehend. Perhaps Abigail was too exhausted from frequent pregnancies to defend her daughter from Asa's attacks. Her reticence may also reflect her understanding that, under coverture, Asa possessed all of the parental rights. As a *feme covert,* Abigail could not establish a separate residence without his permission. She could not even claim her children as her own in a custody dispute.

Abigail may also have believed that she was successfully fulfilling her maternal obligations. She had reached adulthood understanding that it was her role to be a faithful wife and a fruitful mother; she loved her children by bringing them into the world and teaching them to love God. She might even have learned from her ministers' sermons to interpret Phebe's suffering as a test of her own religious practice of patience and submission. If Abigail did not outwardly express sympathy for her daughter until she learned the full extent of Asa's abuse, she behaved in ways that her contemporaries would have found familiar; reports of child abuse and incest in divorce cases from the eighteenth century rarely expressed outrage on the children's behalf. Even as ideas about natural rights and liberty reshaped American public life, how those rights extended to children remained unsettled. Ideas about motherhood as the center of family nurturing—of intensive, emotionally astute care for a smaller number of children—would emerge in the lifetimes of Abigail's grandchildren, but not in hers.[31]

Amid Abigail's attempts to negotiate a mutually agreeable separation, Asa took Abigail out of New Hampshire on the pretext that he had undergone a change of heart and would seek a buyer for their farm. The proceeds would allow an amicable division of their property—or so Abigail believed. No sooner had they crossed into New York State than Asa revealed his true intentions. He would keep the money from the sale on "terms, that would better suit himself" and abandon her, unless she agreed to be "a kind and obedient wife." Likely predicting that Abigail might decide under these circumstances to seek a divorce after all, he waited to reveal these aims until they had entered a state with some of the strictest divorce laws in the country, where even an abused and neglected wife would have little recourse. Abigail faced this crisis hundreds of miles from her children, brothers, and church friends; informal networks of support often aided married women navigating a legal system that tilted toward the husband's desires. (New York did not grant a single divorce between 1675 and 1787. That year, a new law allowed divorce only on grounds of adultery.)[32]

Smallpox had devastated several of the towns the couple passed through in New York, during weeks of what Abigail described as "captivity." When Abigail and Asa arrived in Whitestown, where their eldest son, then about twenty-one, was living, Abigail was inoculated against the smallpox at the son's urging, but she became ill from the disease nonetheless. Asa did little to attend to Abigail's basic needs, instead forcing her to rely on the goodwill of strangers. In a small settlement where homes made from roughhewn timber lacked roofs and windows, the charity she received was barely enough to keep her alive. She survived as she had for so many years, praying and writing in her diary, and seeking any means she had to barter or labor for cash. Faith and fortitude had sustained her through years of Asa's infidelity and violence—not to mention the births of seventeen children.[33]

After four months in Whitestown and other small settlements, Asa decided to walk back to their New Hampshire farm, still scheming about land deals and westward migration. He abandoned Abigail in a "hut" with no roof (although, inexplicably, he left without his horse). Abigail was certain that once he arrived at their farm he would take their young children—those who had not moved elsewhere—away from her forever. The law would certainly permit him to. But God, she believed, had other plans.

Abigail concluded that this was her chance to flee. She took out a piece of paper and recorded two sets of instructions for herself: directions to New Hampshire and the lyrics to hymns, including the words "Faith is our guide, and faith our light." She closed her eyes and pictured the congregation in Haverhill, New Hampshire, where she worshiped among people "who kept holy day."

She set out alone, on Asa's horse, for the 270-mile journey home in late May of 1792, with less than a dollar in her possession. Her saddlebags contained clothes she might exchange for a night's rest in a tavern, and she also resolved to sell her beads, shoe buckles, and stone sleeve buttons if necessary. She was desperate to see her children, the youngest of whom was just over a year old. She trusted in God to bring her back to them alive, not knowing if they had survived her absence. If in the past she had prayed for Asa's redemption, she now recognized that she could not save him.

Abigail rode alone across rivers and up mountainsides, often finding shelter from charitable innkeepers who accepted silver clasps and articles of clothing in exchange for room and board. After months of additional travail, she reached the town where her youngest children had

After the American Revolution, a new ideal of motherhood encouraged women to have a smaller number of children, whom they could educate and nurture intensively as future citizens of the young nation.

been staying. Even then, Asa had a co-conspirator attempt to kidnap them. With help from friends at her church and from her brothers, Abigail reunited with her children. They had suffered in her absence.

Only the very real possibility of standing trial for a capital crime (incest) persuaded Asa to sign a formal separation agreement, which gave Abigail a portion of the value of their farm and custody of all their minor children except one son, who went to live with Asa and two adult brothers. Those sons eventually left Asa and returned to their mother. Nearly another year passed before the divorce she petitioned for was final. Despite the divorce settlement, Abigail's financial situation was precarious. She lived in a rented room and "put out" several of her children into apprenticeships. When Abigail died in 1815, she was living with her son Asa Jr. His father Asa Bailey lived to be eighty-two, an advanced age in that era, dying in 1826 in West Newbury.[34]

The sexual violence of the Bailey home seems to have influenced the choices of Abigail and Asa's children. Their daughters at the very least made different decisions than their mother had about childbearing. Phebe and Patience never married, but seven of their sisters did. Abigail (b. 1768), Anna (b. 1777), Sarah (b. 1779), and Chloe (b. 1782) each had seven children, a dramatic reduction from their mother's seventeen births. The sisters bore fewer children in part by marrying later; both Sarah and Chloe married when they were about twenty-eight years old. Olive (b. 1786) had her first and only child after she married in 1826 at the age of forty. Judith (b. 1789) had four children.[35]

In doing so, they followed many of their late-eighteenth-century contemporaries, a growing number of whom began to limit their fertility intentionally by combining familiar methods with new, more determined intent. Their efforts transformed pregnancy, childbirth, and nursing from the perpetual condition of adult female existence into a significant but briefer stage of adulthood. White American women in 1800 averaged seven live births; by 1850, it was five.[36]

Asa Bailey was a deeply troubled man, and the horrors of his household are not representative of the broader experience of marriage in the early national period. Sexual coercion—or the fear of it—was nevertheless a common experience for individuals living in all kinds of communities in the eighteenth century. Female indentured servants who married their masters, often because they were already pregnant, may not have entered those marriages happily. Individuals who experienced violence might protest against it, as the servant who brought charges against Asa did in the 1770s, but no organization or movement against domestic violence, rape, or corporal punishment advocated on behalf of victims. Violence was a specter that lurked as a possibility in everyone's lives. As Abigail and her daughter Phebe learned, families and communities stepped in to defend women when courts failed to intervene, but not always soon enough.[37]

Chapter 4

Slavery's Intimate Bonds

" The Sabbath among Slaves."

The roots of the cotton plant are voracious. Tendrils that sprout from seeds planted in early spring soon extend further into the soil, consuming nutrients and water. As summer sunshine warms the ground above, their stems sprout bolls, fluffy blossoms that will burst open by harvest season. If wrenched from the dirt and chewed

---

The Sabbath offered much more than rest to enslaved men, women, and children. Saturday evenings and Sunday mornings also provided the opportunity to dance and make music, as represented in this engraving, or to visit loved ones at nearby labor camps.

into a pulp, cotton roots produce intense abdominal contractions in the person who consumes them. A woman who has reason to suspect—and fear—that she is pregnant might use cotton roots to expel from her body the beginnings of a life.

When a group of American rebels declared independence from Britain in 1776, slavery existed throughout the new United States. Tobacco and rice plantations had proliferated in Virginia and the Carolinas in the eighteenth century. Many smaller farms and urban households, in all regions of the British colonies, also depended on enslaved laborers. Newly steady birthrates, combined with arrivals from Africa and the Caribbean, added to the enslaved population. By the time the United States conducted its first population census in 1790, nearly 700,000 of the nation's approximately 4 million inhabitants were enslaved.[1]

The cotton economy that spread across the South starting in the 1790s augured a more violent epoch in the already terrible history of American slavery, and it opened an equally troubling chapter in the history of American sexuality. Demand for cotton drove slavery's expansion in the new nation. Southern planters in need of laborers relied on coffles of chained men, women, and children, who were dragged south from Virginia, first to Georgia in the 1780s; by the 1820s to plantations in Alabama, Mississippi, and Louisiana; and, after 1848, to Texas. The domestic slave trade thrived after the closing of the international slave trade in 1808, tearing apart families as dealers bought and stole people to sell to men eager to force them into cotton fields. The number of enslaved people living in Mississippi, for example, rose from 17,088 in 1810 to 436,631 by 1860.[2]

Harvesting those cotton bolls were children and adults, some with babies strapped to their backs, others aching for newborns left in the shade or in cabins a mile or more away. They were lovers and siblings, spouses and kin, neighbors of many generations and people so recently arrived that few others knew their names. Illness and pregnancy rarely merited a reprieve from labor. When the price of cotton fell, their enslavers demanded that they pick faster and work harder.

The domestic trade alone did not provide enough laborers to plant the seeds or harvest the bolls from cotton plants. Women who were forced to labor in those fields or the homes of their enslavers knew the worth of their wombs. Slavery's supporters concocted a toxic mix of profit-seeking, misogyny, and racism to defend their treatment of Black women's sexuality as a commodity they could freely exploit. In 1861, on the eve of the Civil War, there were nearly 4 million enslaved people in the United States, a population increase explained by higher birth rates. But in a system that made any child an enslaved woman bore the property of the same person who owned her, resistance grew from those roots.[3]

January Colbert picked cotton in Alabama in the decade before the Civil War began. Tall and proud, he was the sort of older brother who inspired both awe and affection from younger siblings. He reached adulthood walking rows of cotton six days of the week, knowing that Saturday nights and Sundays brought the week's only reprieve. The residents of the slave quarters gathered outside to sing and dance on Saturday nights, to share food and drink, to laugh and carouse, if they could.

At one of these get-togethers or on a Sunday morning at church, perhaps, January met a woman about his age. She worked on a different plantation—a labor camp, really. They spoke enough to make plans to see each other again at her camp. During the week, his back bent over cotton plants and weighed down by a sack growing fuller by the row, January may have fantasized about her and imagined their reunion.

This young woman, her name unrecorded, likely had her own ideas about their anticipated visit. Young women who grew up enslaved were taught an ideal of premarital chastity, as were white and free Black women, but with the tacit understanding among enslaved people that they often did not control their sexual experiences. All could face sexual attack from a white man or woman; enslaved Black women, as the property of white families, were most acutely threatened. Minne Folkes, who was enslaved, learned from her mother and other women to "let nobody bother yo' principle; 'cause dat wuz all yo'had."[4]

Folkes's lessons in sexual respectability meant nothing to men such as the pro-slavery ideologue William Harper. He regarded Black women as a "class of women who set little value on chastity," but he was describing his fantasies rather than social reality. Enslaved people wanted to marry by choice; like anyone else, they typically sought love, fidelity, and mutuality.[5]

Men such as January initiated courtship under slavery. Young men in Georgia, for instance, often brought a small food item, like roasted peanuts, to the cabin door of the woman whose affections they sought. Young people teased and flirted. January seems to have made the walk to his sweetheart's labor camp alone, but sometimes young men traveled together. Mariah Callaway lived and labored on a farm in the Georgia upcountry and recalled that "often in the evenings, boys from the other plantations would come over to see the girls . . . they would stand in large groups around the trees, laughing and talking." They flirted, wooed, and "took up" with partners they desired. Adeline Willis had fond memories of Lewis, the man who became her husband, as a sweet if empty-handed suitor. He "never brought me any presents," she explained, "'cus he didn't have no money to buy them with, but he was good to me and that was what counted."[6]

January and the young woman he courted might have called each other "sweethearts." It was a term of art for short-term relationships among people who did not always have the option of remaining monogamous. The phrase "taking up" likewise described intimate bonds that resembled marriage but might involve partners who did not live together. If two enslaved people decided to marry, they had the option of seeking their enslavers' permission to form an "abroad marriage" across two labor camps. Enslaved men may also have appreciated having abroad marriages because it kept them from having to bear witness to white men's predations on their wives, assaults they had no power to prevent. Some enslaved men had more than one family, informally marrying and having children with women on several different farms or plantations. Some enslavers attended the weddings, and a few hired ministers for the occasion.[7]

These were marriages of the heart if not the law. In slave states, marriages involving enslaved people had no legal standing. Lunsford Lane understood how enslavement affected his marriage vows: "I was bound as fast in wedlock as a slave can be. God may at any time sunder that band in a freeman; either master may do the same at pleasure in a slave." Enslaved people pledged fidelity and lifelong union but accepted the reality of serial monogamy. Many adults forged new sexual and romantic relationships after surviving the horrors of being sold away from their loved ones.[8]

Freedom for either January or his sweetheart prior to the 1863 Emancipation Proclamation would not have immediately solved their problems. Colonial-era prohibitions against marriage between enslaved men and women remained in effect in the early nineteenth century. Several states began using these same laws to criminalize sex and marriage between enslaved and free Black people. Local white authorities throughout the South even leveled fornication charges against free Black people whose spouses were enslaved. In 1846, North Carolina's Supreme Court upheld a lower court's conviction of a free Black man, Zadock Roland, for marrying an enslaved woman, Peggy, rejecting Roland's efforts to convince the court that Peggy's enslaver had approved the marriage.[9]

Those who had permission from their enslavers to formalize an "abroad marriage" might travel peaceably between camps from Saturday night to Sunday to spend time with their spouse. Doing so required a "pass" from the enslaver. Unmarried people could also ask for a pass allowing them to travel elsewhere for the evening. They walked from one labor camp to another to visit relatives, sweethearts, and spouses, temporarily creating something akin to a Black neighborhood. January, young and impetuous, left his cabin one Saturday to see his sweetheart, but he stayed out an hour longer than what was permitted by his pass.[10]

Late that night or in the still of the predawn hours, he made the return journey. When he reached the clearing in front of the cabin he shared with his parents and siblings, Jim Hodison, his enslaver, caught him. Hodison tore off January's shirt and tied him to a pine tree, whipping him again and again with a "long mule skinner." Hodison may have had a different woman in mind for January, a woman he owned and whose children would increase his labor force. Or maybe he wanted to shame January for defying his authority. Whatever the reason, he created a public spectacle of January's humiliation. It was a lesson that January's younger brother, who watched alongside his parents, recalled many decades later. Lash after lash, January refused to beg for mercy. Only as blood poured from the open wounds on his back did he relent; his brother bore witness and wept. Enslaved people learned from such acts of torture that American slavery prized their sexuality solely when it conformed to the desires of the people who considered them human property.[11]

Sexual stereotypes were foundational to American slavery. Fantasies about African people's bodies filled the travelogues of Dutch and English travelers to the African continent in the fifteenth and sixteenth centuries, whether in descriptions of African men's allegedly large genitals or of African women's supposedly painless childbirths. By the time of the Revolution, defenders of slavery insisted that Black women were sexually loose, there for the taking, in stark contrast to the alleged chastity and faithfulness of respectable white women. They explained that the sexual exploitation of enslaved women also prevented white men from debauching "pure" white women. Instead, Black women provided "easy gratification" for white men's "hot passions" and kept them from violating the Southern code of honor. That said, a white man who appeared to enjoy sex with Black women he did not enslave might be called a "whore" in the eighteenth-century Carolinas, even though "whore" was usually reserved for women who had sex outside of marriage.[12]

Indeed, Southerners still viewed non-elite white women, and especially white servant women, as "lusty" and thus more likely to be the agents than the victims of illicit sexual behavior. A poorer white woman who had sex with a Black man—even if she accused an enslaved Black man of rape—could not count on other white people in the community to believe her. Enslaved men were of great financial value to their owners, who on occasion preferred to defend the innocence of their human property than credit the allegations of a lower-status white woman. Elite white women were at the top of the Southern caste system, their virtue presumed and protected. White men of various ranks might socialize together in taverns, but elite white women kept themselves apart from lower-status white women.[13]

Lower-status white women's sexual reputations remained precarious, but they slowly and fitfully acquired more of the privileges of white Southern womanhood. Especially after the Civil War, as African Americans asserted their rights as emancipated citizens, poorer white women found it easier to benefit from the ideal of Southern white womanhood. Those changes appeared to make lower-status white women's rape accusations against Black men more credible to other white people, shifting stereotypes of lusty sexual aggression more fully onto Black people. Elite white men in the South advanced their own political and economic agendas by convincing less-prosperous white men that, as patriarchs, they shared a common concern with governing their household dependents, particularly women. In state legislatures and in the marketplace, yeoman farmers heard from wealthy white men that the racial privileges of slavery formed a common culture that ennobled white manhood and womanhood regardless of class or wealth.[14]

The violence enacted upon January reflected a system of sexual abuse, one that January's sweetheart would have well understood. In enslavers' houses and in the fields, during forced marches to cotton labor camps and in the brothels of New Orleans, Black boys and girls grew to adolescence knowing that the fear or experience of exploitation had shaped the lives of their parents, that it may have resulted in their own lives, and that they would confront it too. This particular form of cruelty against Black people was an ever-present and pervasive fact of American slavery.[15]

This young woman likely faced a series of fraught decisions if her enslaver desired her as a sexual partner. Enslavers and overseers sometimes bargained with enslaved women, offering better food and clothing, education for the woman's children, or even a degree of freedom as rewards for sexual companionship.

Thomas Jefferson was in France on a diplomatic mission for the new United States in the 1780s when he propositioned Sally Hemings, an enslaved teenaged girl he had brought with him to help care for his young daughter. Hemings embodied the intergenerational consequences of white men's sexual access to Black women. She was the half-sister of Jefferson's late wife Martha. Her parents were Jefferson's father-in-law and an enslaved woman, who was herself the child of a white man and an enslaved woman of African descent. Jefferson promised Hemings that if she agreed to leave France, where she might be able to seek emancipation, and return to the United States as his sexual companion, he would emancipate her future children when they turned twenty-one. Hemings was pregnant when they arrived back in Virginia in 1790. Regardless of whether Hemings developed genuine affection for Jefferson over the years of their relationship, she understood the decision to share his bed as one that would ensure her children's freedom.[16]

Others had little choice at all. Young, lighter-skinned Black girls were especially vulnerable: there was a market for enslaved girls whose hair, skin tone, and facial features resembled those more commonly associated with Euro-Americans. Louisa Piquet was fourteen when she was forced into concubinage in New Orleans in the early 1840s. Just as Sally Hemings descended from a woman forced into a sexual relationship with a white man, Piquet was the product of generations of nonconsensual interracial sex. Piquet, however, wrote a narrative of her experiences that helped fuel the abolitionist cause. When she was still an infant, she and her mother were sold by their enslaver, who was also her father, to David R. Cook, a Georgia cotton planter. Cook made Piquet's mother his concubine, and she had three children by him. The cotton economy's cycles of easy credit and collapsing prices upended their lives again when Cook went bankrupt and demanded that they flee with him to Mobile, Alabama.[17]

Cook insisted that Louisa take her mother's place as his concubine; he brutally whipped her when she refused. Creditors from Georgia caught up with Cook, who covered his debts by selling Louisa's mother and one of her brothers to a man in Texas. He sold Louisa to John Williams, a divorced man from New Orleans, for $1,500, an astonishingly high price. On the boat ride down the Mississippi River to New Orleans, she recalled, "Mr. Williams told me what he bought me for. He said he was getting old, and when he saw me he thought he'd buy me, and end his days with me. He said if I behave myself he'd treat me well: but, if not, he'd whip me almost to death." She bore four children with him. One white woman tried to protect Piquet from Cook's predations, but for the most part, she was on her own, seeking ways to survive and escape.[18]

White Southern women often knew that their husbands, sons, and brothers were forcing sex on Black women, but they rarely rose to Black women's defense. These white women were as invested in American slavery as many white men were. As representatives of their race, they held a significant stake in protecting their families' reputations and sustaining white supremacy. Female enslavers further exploited the reproductive sexuality of enslaved women by demanding that they serve as wet nurses to their own infants or by renting out lactating Black women, for a profit, to other white families.[19]

White women themselves sometimes became sexual predators. The white abolitionist Richard J. Hinton testified to the American Freedmen's Inquiry Commission in 1863, "I have never yet found a bright looking colored man . . . who has not told me of instances where he has been compelled, either by his mistress, or by white women of the same class, to have connection with them." Female enslavers could promise freedom—or threaten sale—in exchange for sex. (Accounts of male enslavers' intimacies with their enslaved Black valets are scarce but similarly suggestive of sexual coercion.)[20]

Fighting back came with a price, above all for enslaved women. In Jacksonville, Florida, Jacob Bryan enslaved Celia Bryan and her mother.

In 1847, Jacob "retired" Celia's mother as his concubine and decided to take Celia next. She bludgeoned him to death with a hoe. Another enslaved woman named Celia, in Calloway County, Missouri, killed Robert Newsome after five years of sexual abuse that started when she was fourteen and resulted in the births of two children. In love with an enslaved man, pregnant for a third time, and desperate to end Newsome's assaults, this Celia fought off Newsome's next attempted rape, beating his head with a stick until she crushed his skull. Both Celias were convicted of murder and hanged.[21]

January's enslaver wanted to make an example of him by punishing him publicly. He and many other enslavers used these demonstrations of sexual control to "teach a lesson." Black children were forced to witness, and even participate in, the physical punishment of women who rejected white men's sexual demands. Henry Gerald, who was blond, blue-eyed, and enslaved by his father, was born in 1853 in South Carolina. Henry recalled that his father "beat my mama. He beat her until the blood ran down her back. . . . He beat her because she refused to have relations with him." Henry's father-enslaver forced the child to "wash her back off with salt water." His mother bore four children by her enslaver before emancipation.[22]

Abolitionists in the North took note, accusing enslavers of transforming Southern states into brothels in which white men openly exploited Black women's bodies for their own pleasure. Anti-slavery activist Lydia Maria Child argued that the sexual abuse of enslaved women was evidence of slavery's evil. Her 1833 pamphlet, *Appeal in favor of that class of Americans called Africans,* was received by much of the nation as inflammatory. It inspired other abolitionists to discuss rape. Eager to discredit Child, slavery's defenders alleged that she and other antislavery activists desired interracial sex, or "amalgamation."[23]

By midcentury, fugitives of slavery authored autobiographical narratives that portrayed sexual abuse as a constant, torturous aspect of enslavement. In *Incidents in the Life of a Slave Girl* (1861), a lightly fictionalized account of her life, Harriet Jacobs described how her enslaver attempted to have sex with her from the time she was fourteen or fifteen years old. She chose to partner with another white man, also much older than she was, in order to protect herself from her legal owner. In writing about her experiences following her dramatic escape from the South, Jacobs was one of many Black writers who emphasized sexual violence.[24]

Incidents sold thousands of copies, but Northern white people were often as outraged as white Southerners were by the idea of Black equality, especially if it led to sex between a white woman and a Black man. When Child and fellow radical abolitionist William Lloyd Garrison pushed to overturn the Massachusetts ban on interracial marriage in 1832, anti-Black animus increased throughout the North. Black abolitionists in New York City, fearful of racist attacks, issued reassurances that their pursuit of political equality would not lead to sex across the color line. These activists knew how incendiary allegations of interracial sex could be in New York, which had the largest enslaved population of any city outside of the South until it ended slavery within its borders in 1827. In 1840, after New York City newspapers reported that "a very pretty white girl" had flirted with a Black man, mobs attacked a group of abolitionists. Gatherings of anti-slavery activists not only elicited accusations of interracial sex but of gender chaos. An editor sympathetic to the 1840 mob described the abolitionists as being "of all colors and sexes, and some of no sex at all." Antislavery activists fought back in the press. They accused their assailants of "false delicacy," contriving a defense of white womanhood not out of chivalry but to mask a system of white male sexual license. That system put the virtue of all African Americans at risk.[25]

After 1808, with the end of the international slave trade, enslavers who needed more laborers in their fields and factories looked to new births to replenish and expand their labor forces. It was a project that many Southern planters undertook with enthusiasm. They discussed the best methods for "raising negroes," as one man wrote in 1838, much as they raised livestock, and noted the benefits of enslaving a "good breeding woman." Pro-slavery publishers printed advice for enslavers about how to pair people to "render them prolific." Some enslavers demanded that

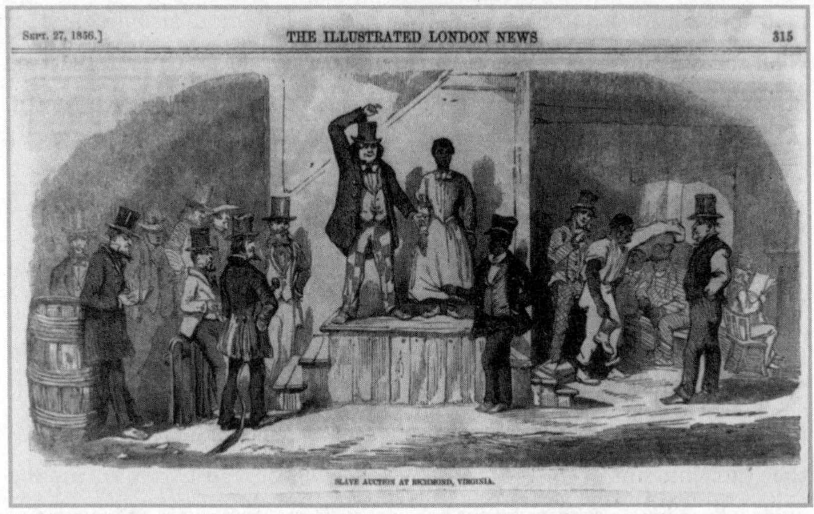

Black girls and young women who grew up enslaved endured traumatic episodes of objectification, especially when being displayed for sale, as depicted in this engraving of an 1856 Richmond, Virginia, auction. These horrors shaped enslaved Black women's understandings of chastity and demanded constant vigilance against the threat of physical and sexual violence.

physically strong men "breed" with several different women or rented out presumptively fertile men to other enslavers. According to one formerly enslaved man, "If a man a big, stout man, good breed, dey gives him four, five women." When fourteen-year-old Rose Williams went on the auction block in the early 1860s, she heard the auctioneer entice bids by saying, "She's never been abused and will make a good breeder."[26]

Not all enslavers viewed enslaved women's pregnancies as a benefit; some considered it evidence of fornication and a drain on their budgets. In New England, where enslaved people typically labored in households or shops rather than fields, some enslavers punished pregnant enslaved women in ways similar to what pregnant indentured servants endured. Enslavers might sell a woman they considered overly fecund.[27]

More often, in the South, an enslaver who traded away someone's spouse might select the replacement, forcing men and women who were strangers to each other into intimate arrangements. After an enslaver sold one man's wife, the enslaver pointed out a different woman and told him, "That is your wife." As the man recollected years later, "I was scared half to death, for I had one wife whom I liked, and didn't want another . . . there was no ceremony about it." Moses Jeffries used his enslaver's desire for pregnancies to his own advantage: "If I went on a plantation and saw a girl I wanted to marry, I would ask my master to buy her for me. It wouldn't matter if she were somebody else's wife; she would become mine." Most enslaved people, however, refused to call such forced pairings marriage.[28]

Some women learned to love the men they were compelled to marry, but others experienced these intimacies as rapes. "Master Hawkins," who enslaved Rose Williams and her parents, forced her to share a cabin with an enslaved man named Rufus when she was likely about seventeen years old. After Williams violently repelled Rufus's advances with a poker, Hawkins threatened to whip her if she did not consent to get pregnant by Rufus. Fearful that Hawkins might separate her from her parents, Williams concluded that she must "yield." It is possible to imagine that Rufus also felt sexually exploited when Hawkins demanded that he have sex with Williams.[29]

A young woman living under slavery learned that the intimate details of her reproductive health interested the white people who hoped to profit from it. Some white men and women made note of how often the women they enslaved menstruated or counted months and years from a male-female couple's "taking up" to the onset of the woman's first pregnancy. Young men and women who had already demonstrated their fertility fetched higher prices in the domestic slave market; the infertility of an otherwise healthy enslaved person offered some enslavers reason enough to sell them. Enslavers and slave traders lobbed lawsuits at one another when a woman advertised as fertile developed menstrual irregularities or had a diseased uterus.[30]

Black midwives cared for pregnant and laboring Black women whenever they could, albeit with the knowledge that enslavers benefitted whenever a midwife successfully delivered a child to a healthy mother. When "granny midwives" assisted enslaved women across the South, they accepted fees for their services or bartered. Their effectiveness in not only delivering babies but in helping induce abortions led the Virginia legislature in 1843 to make it a misdemeanor for any free Black person "to prepare or administer . . . any medication of any kind" and a felony for a Black person to provide a "chemical" abortion.[31]

Despite the intrusions of enslavers and physicians, Black women nurtured distinct bodies of knowledge and methods of care for their bodies. They noted lunar phases to track their menstrual cycles and ingested emmenagogues like sage tea if their periods ceased. Resistance to and subversion of enslavement's brutality occurred not only in slave rebellions but in these intimate acts.[32]

A growing number of white physicians meanwhile sought out partnerships with enslavers. Their interests overlapped: enslavers wanted to improve the fertility of the people they held in bondage, while physicians wanted to refine their surgical expertise. James Marion Sims, later recognized as the "father" of modern gynecology, ran a hospital in Mount Meigs, Alabama, where he developed his method for repairing fistulas—holes that can develop between a person's bladder and upper vaginal tissue during childbirth. Between 1844 and 1849, enslaved women served as his research subjects and as skilled nurses. Sims planned to offer the surgical service, once perfected, to white women, whom he described as "the loveliest, of all God's creation." His brutal medical experiments were typical of how contemporaneous white physicians tested dangerous surgical techniques; all the cesarean sections performed in Louisiana before the Civil War were done on enslaved women.[33]

Sometimes an enslaved woman who was pregnant received more nutritious food, but pregnancy brought no guarantees of better treatment. Some enslavers feared that women pretended to be pregnant to wrangle benefits. A physician's intrusive vaginal examination, to which the enslaved woman's consent was irrelevant, might help determine if she was being truthful.[34]

After giving birth, an enslaved woman might get a month or merely a few days of rest before being forced to resume fourteen-hour stretches in the fields, stooped over rows of cotton plants or performing physically demanding domestic tasks in the enslaver's home. Using advice she learned from mothers, aunts, midwives, and other enslaved women, she wrapped her abdomen with cloths to ease her cramps and to soak up the blood her body expelled. These conditions placed infants at risk; postpartum women had few opportunities to feed their newborns during the day. Throughout the South, Black women's babies died at twice the rate of white women's babies. In American slavery's last decade, fewer than two-thirds of Black children survived past the age of ten.[35]

Some enslaved women chose to abort pregnancies rather than suffer beatings while pregnant or subject a child to slavery's violence. Chewing cotton root was so prevalent among enslaved women in Louisiana and Texas during the final decade of American slavery that it may have accounted for a declining birth rate. Other women miscarried after ingesting calomel, turpentine, or indigo. Mary Gaffney later explained that she "cheated Master" by chewing cotton root "all the time," never bearing any children while enslaved. After emancipation came, she carried several pregnancies to term.[36]

January Colbert likely ceased his courtship after his brutal beating. Perhaps he sought out sexual partners among the women who labored alongside him. (Logic suggests that at least some enslaved men had male partners, and suggestive evidence alludes to such intimacies.) His enslavers may have chosen a sexual partner for him.

When the Civil War came, January would not have waited for a white person to tell him he was free. As sectional conflict became civil war, Black men fled their enslavers en masse, crossing Union lines in pursuit of food, safety, and manumission. Union Army chaplains officiated marriage ceremonies for Black men and women previously denied that legal status. "Marriage under the flag" helped legitimate relationships between spouses and with their children. When the war ended and the Republican-led government established the Freedmen's Bureau to administer Reconstruction in the South, the bureau issued marriage licenses to thousands of formerly enslaved people.[37]

What became of the young woman January had pursued years before? Did January or she take to the roads with thousands of others who searched for lost lovers, children, and kin? Amid tearful reunions there were countless people like Mary Ferguson, who "ain't never seed nor heared tell" any of her family members after their sale when she was thirteen. Men and women who found each other after involuntary separations often dealt with the reality of prior marriages, whether desired or forced. Wives asked husbands' forgiveness for the children they had borne to other men. With emancipation, one of the first steps that many formerly enslaved people took was to seek out the person they considered their "true" spouse, leaving behind the person an enslaver had chosen for them.[38]

The cotton gin that Eli Whitney patented in 1794 separated seed from fiber as fast as the hands of laborers could pick it. Histories of technology and slavery credit the cotton gin with the acceleration of cotton farming—and cotton-derived wealth—across the American South and into the Southwest. But it was people, not plants, who transformed seeds into profit. Those people and their descendants inherited a legacy of sexual pain, abuse, and loss, but also of parenting, pleasure, and love. That legacy would resonate into the twenty-first century among Black people who insisted on setting their own terms for sexual freedom.

Chapter 5

A Woman of Pleasure

As an orphan of fifteen, Fanny Hill made her way to London and sought employment in "any place that such a country girl as I might be fit for." She found it in what she thought was a genteel home, so "magnificently furnished" that it seemed to belong to "a

By the turn of the eighteenth century, technological changes in the production of paper and in printing made the distribution of printed works cheaper and easier, enabling more Americans to get their hands on salacious stories, bawdy illustrations, or outright erotica. This cartoon, published in 1842, depicts a chambermaid resisting an advance from her employer, warning him to "Take care of the Warming pan, Sir."

very reputable family." Presuming that she had been hired as a domestic servant, Fanny obliged when her mistress's female "cousin" climbed into her bed. "Her hands became extremely free," Fanny said, "and wandered over my whole body . . . every part of me was open and exposed to the licentious course of her hands which, like a lambent fire, ran over all my body, and thawed all coldness as they went." Her libidinal awakening continued on two occasions when she watched women of the house entertain male guests.

Fanny Hill: Memoirs of a Woman of Pleasure (1748–49), by Englishman John Cleland, was a work of fiction, the outlines of its story likely familiar to many Anglo Americans. Its plot followed a familiar narrative arc. "The Harlot's Progress" (1721), a series of six prints by the English artist William Hogarth, depicted a country girl's descent into sex work, poverty, disease, and death. Fanny's lesbian initiation into sexual adventure likewise echoed scenes in *Onania*, a book of unknown authorship published around 1716. *Onania* railed against the deleterious effects of the "solitary vice" among men and women, marking the beginning of a new era of Anglo-American anxieties about masturbation. Like Hogarth's widely replicated prints, *Onania* was a consumer item, its vivid descriptions of women's masturbatory pleasures, including voyeuristic scenes of lesbian sex, a key selling point. Cleland broke with convention by giving his heroine a happier ending. Writing from debtors' prison in the British East India Company's settlement in Bombay, he was eager for a commercial hit and perhaps also determined to test the limits of English anti-obscenity laws.[1]

He created Fanny as a personification of male heterosexual fantasies. When one man disrobed and revealed "naked, stiff and erect, that wonderful machine," Fanny recalled that "every vein of my body circulate[d] liquid fires." Fanny brought herself to "at last the critical extacey [*sic*]; the melting flow into which nature, spent with excess of pleasure dissolves and dies away." Only when an older man tried to force himself on her did guileless Fanny concede that she was employed in a brothel. Embracing sexual joy, she gave her "maidenhead" to a handsome young man named Charles. Over the next few years he and other men variously kept her as their mistress; she worked at brothels when the men departed or turned her out. Her years of happy whoring ended when Charles returned from years at sea and wed her, a love match achieved despite her past as a woman of pleasure. As a book ostensibly recounting erotic episodes from a woman's perspective, *Fanny Hill* instead popularized a male imagining of female sexuality as perpetually eager to submit to a man's desires.[2]

Fanny Hill became an international sensation. The original English edition was translated into French and Italian, and copies crossed the Atlantic for sale in Philadelphia. In the early 1800s, printers in Boston, Vermont, Philadelphia, and New York reset the type without concern for errors or embellishments (or the weak and mostly unenforced 1790 Copyright Act), producing the first American editions of one of the most sexually explicit publications of the age.[3]

Prior to Cleland's book, depictions of explicit sex in European drawings or essays were usually intended to portray religious or political leaders as in some way indecent. These sexual critiques might titillate, but arousal was not their main purpose. *Fanny Hill* marked the arrival of a new genre of erotica stripped of any overt message about clerical hypocrisy or political corruption. Instead, Cleland and others invited presumptively male readers to imagine a world in which women craved physical domination.

It was also a far cry from the medical texts that had previously doubled as erotic stimuli. In 1744, the esteemed Northampton, Massachusetts, minister Jonathan Edwards investigated rumors of "lascivious and obscene discourse among the young people." Adolescent boys and young men in his congregation had apparently read two popular medical texts, from which they learned about female sexual anatomy, orgasm, and the danger of "greensickness," an illness one book described as the consequence of abstinence. The youths then teased girls in the community about "what nasty creatures they was." When Edwards attempted to rid his congregation of "bad books," many members of his community sided with the boys: what they did in private, it was argued, was of no concern to the minister.[4]

Cleland's novel, first published just four years after the Northampton episode, contained scenes of explicit sex that surpassed everything else available to English readers. By the early nineteenth century *Fanny Hill* was no longer quite as exceptional as it had been. Brothels, newspapers, and erotica became regular features of young men's lives in cities from Boston and New York to Baltimore and New Orleans. *Fanny Hill* still stood out for its louche explicitness, its mimicry (and mockery) of the conventional novel's form, and the fact that its fictional narrator was a woman. Seemingly fantastical and accessible at the same time, Fanny offered boys and young men a way to imagine themselves as the admired customers of an adventurous sex worker, a fantasy that had real-world consequences in the early decades of the United States.

Fanny Hill left her rural home to find employment in London, a fictional example of the countryside-to-city path that innumerable young people followed as imperial trade, industrial revolution, and consumer markets transformed life on both sides of the Atlantic. The result was a volatile global economy in which women like Fanny—and the men who purchased her services—increasingly relied on wage work. Wildly fluctuating agricultural yields and currency valuations fostered a capitalist economy dependent on credit and anxious for cash. Sex was one of the commodities on offer.

Enterprising Americans discovered, as Cleland had, that they could profit from portrayals of sexual desire and its satisfaction. Peddlers who trekked along New England's dirt roads carried copies of *Fanny Hill* in their satchels and carts, its salacious narrative for sale alongside sewing needles, leather goods, and metal tools. In Concord, New Hampshire, alone, four bookstores kept it in stock.[5]

The book cost $2, but there were more affordable alternatives for the American reader in search of erotic stimulation. In the 1760s, almanacs printed bawdy poems, rumors of sexual indiscretions, and lewd humor about nonmarital sex. These compendiums of agricultural forecasts and local gossip portrayed both women and men as lusty pleasure-seekers, although they hardly promoted gender equality. Stories of cuckolded husbands mocked men who could not control their wives, and writers warned women to satisfy their husbands lest the men stray. Considering that bastardy rates in Philadelphia during the 1790s were three and a half times higher than they had been from 1767 to 1776, *Fanny Hill* found an American audience seeking pleasures—and grappling with nonmarital sex's consequences.[6]

This sexual conversation included tales of same-sex and otherwise queer pleasures. American booksellers sold homoerotic literature as early as the 1750s, when they began to import a new genre of fiction that simultaneously denigrated same-sex sex and provided readers with voyeuristic descriptions of it. In Philadelphia, Tench Francis operated a bookstore on Front Street, where his July 1754 inventory included what historian Clare Lyons describes as "classical Greek and Roman texts with homoerotic content, Restoration satire employing homoerotic sex and politics, French erotica depicting pairs of women making love and the *chroniques scandaleuses* of the French aristocracy, English novels with homoerotic and prostitute adventure narratives, and trial reports of criminal prosecutions for sodomy." One of the books most often checked out of Thomas Bradford's circulating library in mid-eighteenth-century Philadelphia was *Roderick Random,* a novel that featured a homoerotic relationship and an effeminate character.[7]

By the 1820s and 1830s, news of sex workers featured prominently in shoddy newspapers known as the "penny press," upstart enterprises that relied on daily sales rather than the subscriptions that funded established newspapers. Erotic content also appeared in provocatively named weekly newspapers, such as the *Flash* and the *Rake,* which glorified a male youth culture of drinking, gambling, prizefighting, and prostitution—the "sporting life." Articles about brothels and erotic entertainment gave the names and addresses of notorious sex workers and peep shows, doubling as guidebooks for the adventuresome.

In 1841, a New York City paper, *Dixon's Polyanthos*, provided a room-by-room overview of the sex workers at a well-known brothel on Leonard Street. "Feminine tastefulness," the author promised, "and exquisite delicacy . . . are here impersonated in the most attractive form." Catering to an audience of young economic strivers, the papers' articles and cartoons mocked wealthy gentlemen as effete buffoons who failed to seduce buxom women. These papers also discussed voyeurism, masturbation, sadomasochism, and female same-sex sex.[8]

Competition did nothing to dampen demand for *Fanny Hill*—and no wonder. Cleland's description of Fanny's initiation into sex with a man emphasized her desirability as well as the pleasure she took in the act. Narrating her story as a grown woman looking back on her youthful exploits, Fanny recalled how her sexual innocence rendered her white, nubile body irresistible to Charles: "My bosom was now bare and rising in the warmest throbs, presented to his sight and feeling the firm hard swell of a young pair of breasts, such as may be imagined of a girl not sixteen, fresh out of the country, and never before handled." Yet not even so stupendous a set of breasts could distract Charles from the rest of Fanny's fair body: "even their pride, whiteness, fashion, pleasing resistance to the touch, could not bribe his restless hands from roving; but giving them the loose, my petticoats and shift were soon taken up, and their stronger centre of attraction laid open to their tender invasion." The narrative highlighted Charles's excitement, his thrill in seeing Fanny naked, and his eagerness for sex. It also fixated on both Fanny's and Charles's pale complexions; she admired the whiteness of his body—of his forehead, "which was high, perfectly white and smooth," and of his chest, "whiter than a drift of snow." These racially specific descriptions made the couple's eventual union in matrimony both legally possible and socially desirable for readers who read to the book's abrupt conclusion.[9]

A "tender invasion" suggests a confusion of care with violation; similar elisions of violence and pleasure recur throughout the novel. By the late eighteenth century, white men in the Atlantic world tended to presume that sex with a woman necessarily involved her resistance and his force.

Fanny's narrative was rooted in this convention: "My fears . . . made me mechanically close my thighs; but the very touch of his hand insinuated between them, and opened a way for the main attack." Men at the time unselfconsciously bragged of their assaults. A Philadelphian gloated in his diary about "a Ruination at a Soiree," when he danced with a young woman who "aroused all my passion." In a scene reminiscent of Fanny's deflowering, he wrote that this woman "resisted much holding her limbs together, but my flame being up I thrust her vigorously and she opened with a scream—a real joyful fuddle—she screaming much at [Incursion?]." *Fanny Hill* offered a fantasy of domination, one that validated existing practices and may have enticed other men to see their use of force as a necessary complement to female reluctance. It was a model of male-female intercourse that prevailed in American law by the early 1800s, depicted in *Fanny Hill* in scenes of delight.[10]

Fanny's pale breasts aroused Charles, but forbidden mixed-race sex fired many Americans' erotic imaginations. American slavery created a marketplace for the description and pursuit of illicit sexual acts. A newspaper story chiding white men who pursued sex with Black women might also titillate readers with descriptions of interracial intimacy. The *Daily Orleanian* in New Orleans ran stories about notorious "quadroon balls" at which wealthy white men paid for the company of free Black women. Newspapers' discussions of sexuality could also serve to shame white Southern women who defied white men's control. The *Daily Orleanian* published short stories and news articles that denigrated white women who formed "liaisons" with Black men, particularly white women who were arrested for violating the law against interracial sex.[11]

White enslavers produced an erotic literature premised on Black women's sexual victimization. Sex was front of mind for many of the men who owned, sold, transported, priced, and negotiated the sales of women. Slave traders calling themselves robbers, as if they were outlaws, chatted in their letters to one another about "fancy girls"—younger and lighter-skinned Black women whom they expected to satisfy their sexual desires. Isaac Franklin, an enslaver in New Orleans, sent a letter in 1834 to Rice Ballard, a well-connected trader: "The fancy Girl from

Charlottesville, will you send her out or shall I charge you $1100 for her? Say Quick, I wanted to see her . . . I thought that an old Robber might be satisfyed with two or three maids." The language of sexual predation became part of a vocabulary for financial jousting. Traders accused business partners of "raping" them out of their profits, and a few referred to themselves as a "one-eyed man," the enslaver and the penis conflated into a single agent of both sexual and financial domination.[12]

The first American women's groups dedicated to eliminating the kind of male sexual license that *Fanny Hill* endorsed were formed amid a wave of social reform movements in the 1830s. Journals such as the *Friend of Virtue* and the *Advocate of Moral Reform* portrayed the libertine rake as a threat to the innocent farm girl whom he seduced, abandoned, and in the parlance of the time, "ruined." Short stories in the penny press and inexpensive novels featured titles like *The Mysteries of Boston, or, a Woman's Temptation* that parlayed the seduction narrative into potboiler fiction. But reformers insisted that the dangers were all too real. The New England Female Moral Reform Society, composed of middle-class white women, argued that male sexual aggression was an imminent threat to women's virtue. Focused on the eradication of both prostitution and the sexual double standard, they persuaded the Massachusetts legislature to pass a law requiring the licensing of cabdrivers (lest unlicensed drivers abscond with unsuspecting young women) and pushed for a criminal anti-seduction statute. Parents and guardians initiated most seduction cases as civil suits against men who reneged on promises of marriage after having sexual intercourse with their daughters or wards; the members of the Female Moral Reform Society wanted seducers to face prison time. The legislature did not pass the criminal statute these women proposed, but reformers' efforts added an important counterpoint to the era's celebration of sex work and sexual coercion.[13]

An influential group of health educators challenged these male-centric portrayals of sexual pleasure. From the 1820s through the

Frances Wright (1795–1852) was a freethinker who wanted to circulate scientific information about all aspects of the human experience, including anatomy and reproduction. She opened the Hall of Science in New York City with her colleague and was one of the most outspoken women of her time. Henry Inman, Frances Wright, 1824, oil on canvas, 16 5/8 × 12 3/4 in., 1955.263, New-York Historical Society.

1850s, they organized lectures and published books about the pleasures of sex for women as well as for men. Frances Wright was an heiress, radical intellectual, advocate for workers' rights, abolitionist, and lightning rod for controversy. She belonged to a small but vocal group of secular reformers who preferred the scientific rigor of Enlightenment thought to the pieties of evangelical Christianity. In the 1820s she lectured to large, mostly male audiences as newspaper editors warned that Wright "unsexed herself" by doing so. She wrote in favor of interracial sex and sexual passion ("the best joys of our existence") and against marriage, but she insisted that women maintain control over their bodies. Knowledge, not legal or religious doctrine, she argued, should regulate passion. "Fanny Wrightism" soon became a vernacular pejorative, a way to mock and discredit a woman who spoke frankly about sex or women's emancipation.[14]

Using her inherited fortune, Wright purchased a building in lower Manhattan that she renamed the Hall of Science. She dedicated it to scientific knowledge, including the findings presented in the book *Moral Physiology* (1831) by her friend and fellow religious skeptic Robert

Dale Owen. In the book, Owen made a bold case for women's absolute authority to determine the frequency of pregnancy, a power that he argued was essential if married women were to enjoy sex with their husbands.[15]

Health reformers risked fines and imprisonment to share information about "physiology" that they believed was essential for adult health. They did so with limited scientific understanding of ovulation or conception. Owen recommended the withdrawal method to control fertility. A Massachusetts physician named Charles Knowlton took a different approach. In his book, *Fruits of Philosophy; or the Private Companion of Married People,* first published in 1832, Knowlton suggested that women use a postcoital douche to prevent conception. Both men argued that sex was natural and that its enjoyment was healthy. Prosecuted for obscenity under state law, Knowlton was fined and sentenced to three months of hard labor. He defiantly published increasingly explicit editions of his book, with sections that attempted to explain the mechanics of erections and discussed women's capacity for erotic pleasure separate from reproduction. There was an audience for these books: *Fruits of Philosophy* was in its tenth edition by 1877.[16]

Most health reformers of the time focused not on women's sexual freedom but on *Fanny Hill*'s intended audience—erotica's self-pleasuring subject. An anti-masturbation movement preached the dangers of the solitary vice. At first, physicians and moral reformers directed most of their concern toward young men on the make in the nation's growing cities, where the exercise of self-control might determine not only the progress of their souls but the success of their careers in a competitive market economy. Reformers warned that erotica and prostitutes led young men to abuse their bodies and diminish their chances of becoming financially secure citizens or worthy husbands. Likening sex workers to alcohol, reformers lamented how easily young men became completely preoccupied with the pursuit of sex once exposed to it. They portrayed masturbation and patronage of sex workers as self-indulgent behaviors that spread like contagions among young men and their peers—gateway drugs to complete sexual debasement. In the 1830s, women committed to the cause of moral reform teamed up with male physicians to raise the alarm about the dangers of undisciplined desires that led to "self-pollution." After the 1850s, reformers advocated what one scholar memorably called a "spermatic economy," advising young men to moderate their ejaculations lest they deplete their bodies' "vital energies," their sperm wasted like dollar bills thrown into the sea.[17]

The white Christian reformer Sylvester Graham was the most influential anti-masturbation activist in the country. An evangelical Protestant, he believed that individuals must learn to control their inclination to sin. The problem was the overly excited body, for which Graham recommended cold baths, bland diets, and his eponymous crackers, all with the goal of preventing self-pollution. So long as Graham presented these theories to audiences of men, he encountered little opposition.[18]

Graham risked life and limb to share his presentations about sexual anatomy and masturbation with all-female audiences. It was "reprehensible," a newspaper editor in Portland, Maine, wrote in 1833, for a man to discuss such subjects with women in the absence of their husbands. More to the point, these men seem to have objected to Graham's depictions of sexual passion as just as strong in women as it was in men. (Graham's point, of course, was that women needed to exercise as much restraint as men did.) Rowdy crowds of men and boys gathered outside lecture halls threatening to tar and feather Graham. In 1837, at a Boston lecture rescheduled after threats of violence on its original date, Graham hid "locked up in a nice little room" as female supporters held off an angry mob. He later fled the city after some of these men chased him from his hotel, "maltreating" him along the way. Female reformers who endorsed Graham's message depicted his adversaries as "libertines, whoremongers, drunkards, and theatre-frequenters." They concluded that the mob's supposed outrage over the indelicacy of the subject matter masked the men's own licentious interests in keeping women ignorant about their bodies and maintaining the idea that sex was a man's prerogative.[19]

Proper sexual comportment was a matter of special concern for Black people, given the pernicious sexual stereotypes that suffused American racism. African American educator Sarah Mapps Douglass, a contemporary of Graham's, approached sexual knowledge as a tool for realizing Black equality. Self-control, she instructed her students, was as available to Black women as to white women. Before she became a sex educator, Douglass was a leader of the Philadelphia Female Anti-Slavery Society, an interracial women's organization that called for the abolition of slavery and improvements to the living conditions for Black women in their city. For several decades, she ran the Institute for Colored Youth, a school that provided tuition-free education in science as well as literacy; students read anatomy texts and handled specimens from a cabinet of minerals. Douglass herself enrolled in classes in the 1850s at the Female Medical College of Pennsylvania to deepen her knowledge of anatomy and physiology.[20]

Equipped with the latest theories about the virtues of moderation, Douglass joined a growing chorus of health reformers who argued that the act of masturbation might cause insanity. Her point was not that sexual pleasure was in any way something to avoid. Instead, she taught her students about the naturalness of heterosexual intercourse and of sexual pleasure for both men and women, at least when it was experienced within marriage. She shared this outlook with many leading health reformers of her day, who taught that women, like men, needed sexual release *within marriage,* to remain physically and mentally healthy. For these reformers, masturbation was a dangerous diversion of sexual energy.[21]

Fanny Hill: Memoirs of a Woman of Pleasure portrays male-female sex as ecstatic—and very, very wet. The night of her first, painful sexual encounter with Charles, Fanny's awareness of physical injury subsided as "the warm gush darts through all the ravished inwards; what floods of bliss, what melting transports, what agonies of delight, too fierce, too mighty for nature to sustain." She experienced "the relief of a delicious momentary dissolution, the approaches of which are intimate by a dear delirium, a sweet thrill, on the point of emitting those liquid sweets,

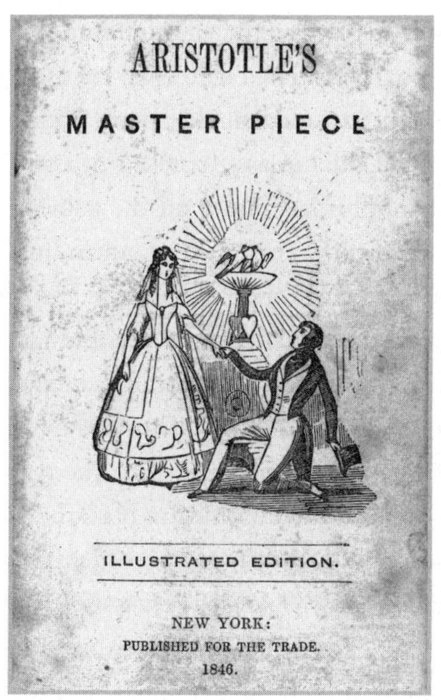

A quasi-medical guide written by an unknown English author or several authors, Aristotle's Masterpiece *piqued the erotic imaginations of people on both sides of the Atlantic from its publication in 1684 until the nineteenth century. For average readers during this period, the text provided some of the only printed advice about human sexuality, pregnancy, and childbirth available in English.*

in which enjoyment itself is drowned, when one gives the languishing stretch out, and dies at the discharge." Gushes, floods, melting, liquid sweets, drowning, and discharge appear in many other depictions of orgasm in the novel too.[22]

These passages in Cleland's narrative revealed the influence of *Aristotle's Masterpiece*, a widely copied and reprinted book whose title originated not with the Greek philosopher but with anonymous writers and editors in seventeenth-century England, possibly working with translations of older Latin treatises about sexual health. With sections devoted to pregnancy, childbirth, and venereal diseases, it was the sort of book that a town physician or midwife might reasonably possess but that was explicit enough to appear improper or lewd in nonexpert hands, to be hidden in chimneys or under mattresses. It contained the most commonly printed advice about human sexuality, pregnancy, and childbirth available from the late seventeenth through the nineteenth centuries in English for the average reader. A compendium of ancient and early modern folklore, it was also a book that piqued some people's erotic imaginations, much to Jonathan Edwards's chagrin when it fell into the hands of young men in his congregation. By the late eighteenth century, the version printed in the United States included ribald poetry about marital compromises and wedding-night dilemmas. *Aristotle's Masterpiece* went through more editions than all other books on the subject combined, with more than one hundred different printings, including publications in Philadelphia, Boston, and New York.[23]

Aristotle's Masterpiece presented an understanding of the human body as composed of four main fluids, or humors. Humoral medicine dated back to the real Aristotle. He taught what some historians have since named a "one-sex model" of human difference, in which the relative quantities of the body's four humors—blood, phlegm, black bile, and yellow bile—determined whether an individual was male or female. That humoral model led the Greek physician Galen of Pergamon (CE 130–200) to describe men and women as anatomically similar but differentiated by body heat. Men had more hot and dry humors, and for that reason they were usually rational. Women, by contrast, had more cold and moist humors, which made them emotional and weak. The cooler female was an inferior subset of the male; women had men's genitals, but they were turned inward.[24]

Physicians and anatomists dismantled this theory in the 1600s, but the idea that fluids regulated human sexuality—and accounted for the conception of new life—persisted well into the nineteenth century. Even as physicians and midwives turned to newer sources of information, chapters in *Aristotle's Masterpiece* about overcoming sterility and about the health benefits of frequent, mutually pleasurable heterosexual sex kept these ideas in circulation. The book even contained folklore about heredity, explaining that a child resembled whatever its mother happened to look at during intercourse. Even if she were to have sex with someone other than her husband, conjuring her husband's image in her mind at that crucial moment would imprint his features on the newly conceived child.[25]

The "floods of bliss" and "liquid sweets" in *Fanny Hill* reflect a theory dating to ancient times, and restated in *Aristotle's Masterpiece,* that both men and women emit a "seed" during orgasm, the union of which pro-

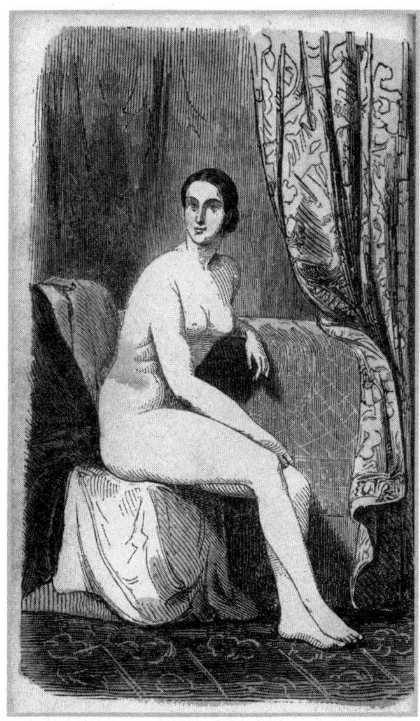

Aristotle's Masterpiece *served as both a medical guide and a source of erotic amusement for its readers. Earlier versions had cruder woodcuts of naked figures, demons, and "monstrous" births. The illustrations in this nineteenth-century edition maintain the excitement of female nudity while adding the refinement of a sofa and luxurious curtains.*

duces a new human life. The authors of *Aristotle's Masterpiece* argued that conception required female as well as male orgasm, although they wondered if the "seed" might in fact be an egg, somewhat like a chicken's. (Scientists did not begin to understand the relationship between ovulation and conception until the early nineteenth century.) Part of the fantasy in Cleland's book was that his heroine managed to have virtuoso orgasms while miraculously avoiding pregnancy throughout her adventures.[26]

One young American man who almost certainly knew about Cleland's novel was Richard P. Robinson. For if Fanny's story had taught men like him anything—aside from the fact of women's immense enjoyment of sexual intercourse with men of all endowments and predilections—it was that all women, even the ones that he might have thought of deri-

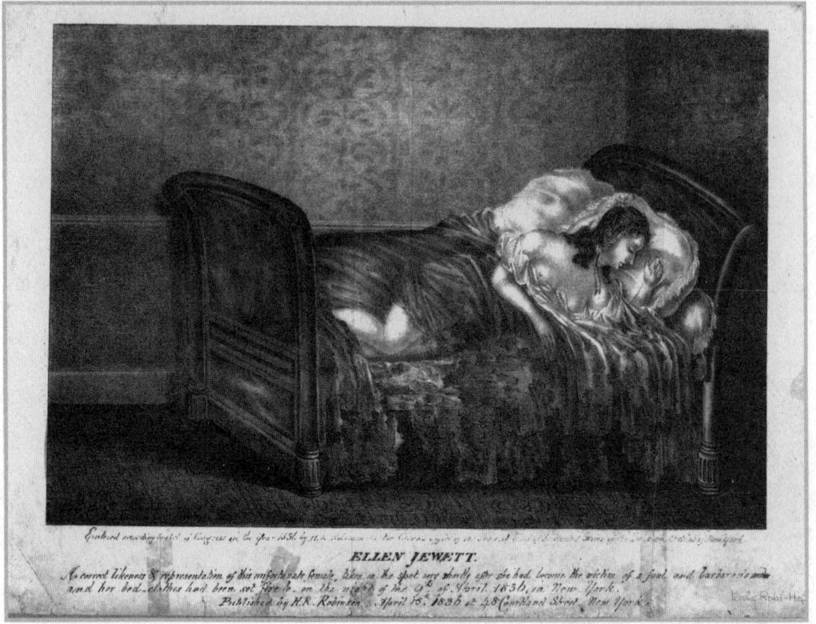

The murder of Helen Jewett, a sex worker in New York City, became a sensationalized news event. Newspapers often misspelled her first name as Ellen, as here in what is described as a "correct likeness & representation" of Jewett immediately following her death on April 9, 1836.

sively as "whores," longed for romance and owed fidelity to the men who claimed them. Like the fictional Fanny, he left the countryside for the city—in his case, a small town in Connecticut for New York. By 1835, he was an office clerk and lived in a boardinghouse with other young, unmarried men. He spent his evenings attending theaters, where he could afford upper-balcony seats, and drinking in saloons. Robinson's immersion in what his peers called "the sporting life" acquired a new focus that summer: he saved every penny for trysts with Helen Jewett, one of the city's most desired sex workers, whom he thought of as his sweetheart. She resided in a notorious yet elegant house on Thomas Street; he was not her only lover. Educated and fanciful, Helen had made her own journey from countryside to city a few years earlier. From their first months of acquaintance, Helen and Richard exchanged pas-

The prime suspect in the murder of Helen Jewett, Richard Robinson was a young clerk in New York City who hoped to become her exclusive love interest. Like many young white men living in America's cities in the early nineteenth century, Robinson enjoyed the "sporting life" of male-centric and commercially available leisure. He was found not guilty.

sionate love letters. Sex with Helen was not enough for Richard; he wanted her to pledge herself to him alone. Surely, he thought, she owed him that.

Helen could hardly promise Richard constancy, and she may have begun to tire of his jealousy. One bitterly cold Saturday night in April of 1836, the acrid smell of smoke roused the other women of the house on Thomas Street. They found Helen murdered by an ax blow and partly burned from a fire that her assailant had set in her bed. Speaking to police officers who rushed to the scene, women who worked with Helen identified Robinson as the man they had admitted to her room that night. Police arrested him the next morning at his boardinghouse, charged him, and locked him in Bridewell Prison. It was one of the first sensationalized murder trials in U.S. history. The case against Robinson filled newspaper pages for months, inspired erotic images, pamphlets, and novellas, and demonstrated how dramatically the erotic commerce within America's cities had expanded since the Revolutionary era. By 1837, Richard was himself a character in a quasi-pornographic fictional retelling of Jewett's murder.[27]

Helen's tragic story reminds us that sex work was part of the makeshift economy that many women took part in, and increasingly so by the 1820s and 1830s. Proprietors of brothels and "bawdy houses" rented or owned space in densely populated areas, while some sex workers plied their trade on the street. These businesses blended in with the commercial life and leisure of the city. The Corner House in Baltimore, for example, hosted ladies' meetings and fundraisers on its upper floors; the basement-level restaurant, meanwhile, functioned as a bawdy house, a place where sex workers from nearby brothels would come for meals and to solicit customers. In Richmond, Virginia, sex workers picked up customers in grocery stores. Theaters permitted sex workers to roam the third tier during performances. Sex work was, in a word, ubiquitous. "The prostitutes in Philadelphia are so many," a visitor remarked in 1798, "that they flood the streets at night, in such a way that even looking at them in the streets without men you can recognize them." In New Orleans, white women owned many of the brothels, where they sold the services of enslaved women they kept there.[28]

Many women who engaged in sex work did so infrequently, to survive personal financial challenges, for instance, but others forged careers. A father's death, or his violence, led many younger women to leave home and to discover that sex work, while risky, was one of the few occupations available to them. It tended to pay much better than domestic service (which was not without its own hazards, sexual and otherwise). Survival in an emerging wage economy necessitated improvisation. Sex workers in Baltimore occasionally turned to the almshouse for aid, while others sold scraps or bartered sex for materials like yarn and cable that they could transform into items they could sell. Occasionally, women took pride in sex work as a form of entrepreneurial independence. In an echo of the main character in *Fanny Hill*, a thirty-eight-year-old white woman named Mary Bower told census takers that she was "a lady of pleasure." Sex work became an integral part of urban economies in the United States.[29]

Women who provided or enabled interracial sex work faced terrible risks. After a Black woman named Betsey Hawlings was arrested in 1813 at a disorderly house, she was "committed & sold," suggesting that her arrest may have led to her enslavement. In 1853, Richmond authorities fined a white woman named Jane Wright "for keeping a disorderly and ill-governed house . . . where people of every sex and color congregate and associate by day and night." When Wright continued to operate her business despite police orders, locals attacked and tore down the building. All that was left was the chimney.[30]

Cleland opened Fanny Hill's narrative with her declaration of honesty: "Truth! stark naked truth, is the word; and I will . . . paint situations such as they actually rose to me in nature, careless of violating those laws of decency, that were never made for such unreserved intimacies as ours." Fanny confesses that she depends on the reader's sophistication, which would allow them to appreciate her candor: "you have too much sense, too much knowledge of the *originals*, to snuff prudishly and out of character, at the *pictures* of them."[31]

Far from presenting heterosexuality as unspeakable, however, *Fanny Hill* and other pornographic productions contributed to a vast conversation about male-female sex. The pretext of scandalous content may have amplified the reader's excitement about encountering the forbidden. The era's profusion of written and visual depictions of penis-vagina sex (and of lesbian sex as a form of voyeuristic foreplay) ultimately reassured consumers of erotica that heterosexual desire was a natural part of the human condition. Same-sex sexualities, between men or between women for their own sake, became the unspeakable desires.

Cleland later bemoaned his book's popularity, not least while facing prosecution in England for obscene libel, but his reputation remained linked to the imagined delights of his titular and indefatigable sex worker. Nor were his subsequent books, including *Memoirs of a Coxcomb*, which rewrote *Fanny Hill* from a man's perspective (though one could argue *Fanny Hill* itself was already written from a male perspective), any less explicit.[32]

Fanny Hill remained infamous—and in print—for generations. Affordable prints and texts traversed the nation's canals and nascent railroad lines, packed into the bags of men heading to Texas and California in the hope of claiming land, fighting Indians, or discovering gold. So, too, did contraceptive cures, condoms, and advertisements for abortion pills and potions. Peddlers, mail-order catalogs, and corner stores sold images and texts that stoked the erotic imagination alongside the more practical implements that reckoned with heterosexual sex's potential consequences. In 1852, when a man named Richard Hickman came upon piles of personal possessions abandoned by men who had traveled the Platte River before him, he found "books of every sort and size from Fanny Hill to the Bible."[33]

The book occasioned the first obscenity trial in the United States, an 1819 case against a Massachusetts printer, Peter Holmes, who was found guilty of selling it and fined. Similar cases followed in New York. One hundred and fifty years later, in the 1960s, *Fanny Hill* was pivotal to a U.S. Supreme Court case that finally lifted obscenity restrictions on literature. Cleland's portrayal of Fanny Hill's fantastical erotic enthusiasm was censored, but its endorsement of rowdy masculine sexual assertiveness endured. Giving voice to women's sexuality from a female perspective, and apart from the gratification of men's desires, would require nothing short of a revolution.[34]

Chapter 6

Perfect Confidence and Love

When Alonzo Choate wrote a letter to his friend Hubbel Pierce in the late summer of 1865, Alonzo's sister Hannah added a postscript. She called Hubbel "my brother's old woman," and urged him to write back soon. "When you send your Wife your picture," Hannah added, "you can send his sister one if you please."

Rebecca Primus and her family were active members of the Talcott Street Congregational Church, the first Black Congregational church in Connecticut. The congregation, pictured here circa 1922, was known for its fierce commitment to abolitionism and public education for Black children. Rebecca Primus stands in the second row, seventh from left.

Alonzo and Hubbel had met in the late spring of 1864 as soldiers in Battery B of the First Michigan Light Artillery; Hubbel was then sixteen, Alonzo a year or two older. Battery B spent weeks marching to Atlanta, enduring what Alonzo called "the perils and dangers of a soldiers life." Their company reached the city shortly before Gen. William Sherman captured it. After a year of war, Hubbel and Alonzo were back in Michigan. They said their farewells when Battery B mustered out. Hubbel gave Alonzo a ring.[1]

Their letters traversed the twenty-odd miles that separated their families' farms. Alonzo called Hubbel "My Dear beloved Husband" in one letter and "my good Old Woman" in another. They teased each other about their marriage-like bond even as they pursued marriages to women. News in the fall of 1865 that Hubbel was engaged to a cousin named Mary prompted Alonzo to congratulate his friend in a jesting letter: "Well Hub you haven't got married yet have you. I think you had better wait until you get a divorce from your Old Man, if you don't I tell your wife what times we used to have sleeping together." They joked about their sexual familiarity even as family members read and commented on their missives.[2]

Alonzo and Hubbel never formally named their relationship or their lust. They did not know the words "homosexual" or "bisexual," nor did anyone else at the time. In fact, their use of conventional marital terminology to describe intimacy, combined with their normatively manly appearance (as soldiers and, later, homesteaders), helped their bond appear ordinary. Gender variance was part of the world they knew; Confederate and Union soldiers alike wrote home about the wild cross-dressing performances that soldiers staged for one another, some of which inspired liaisons between officers and appealing "boy-girls." But neither Hubbel nor Alonzo understood himself as a separate kind of person based on his gender identity, nor did they or their relatives assume that any sexual intimacies they shared marked them as categorically different sorts of people. Marital conventions helped them naturalize their love for each other as men.[3]

Alonzo and Hubbel expressed their affections during one of the last moments of the nineteenth century when two men could do so without attracting scorn or risking arrest. Until then, talk of love and marriage did not raise suspicions of immorality or criminality. In the late eighteenth and early nineteenth centuries, most states replaced colonial-era laws that defined sodomy and buggery as capital crimes with new laws that punished "crimes against nature" with lengthy prison sentences. (North Carolina and South Carolina were exceptions, not jettisoning the death penalty for sodomy or buggery until 1869 and 1873, respectively.) According to the criminal statutes of the day, sodomy meant penetration of the anus; oral-genital contact between two people assigned male at birth was often treated with disgust but not (yet) criminally prosecuted. (Pennsylvania passed the first criminal statute for oral-genital sex in 1879.)[4]

As in the seventeenth and eighteenth centuries, early nineteenth-century law and popular press associated these crimes with aggression, not with effeminacy or an innate condition. The "sodomite" was a man who engaged in a "crime against nature," not a man who loved another man, and definitely not a woman who had sex with another woman. (There was no criminal category for women's erotic acts with other women in the nineteenth-century United States because lawmakers believed that, in order to be sexual, an act must involve penetration by a penis.) None of these laws specifically dealt with gender variance nor presumed that gender nonconformity was proof of a sexual identity. Americans of the time condemned specific sexual acts, and sodomy especially. But although the law continued to prohibit sex of any kind outside of marriage, same-sex and otherwise queer expressions of desire were common and mostly unpunished.[5]

Health reformers of the 1830s worried about excessive sexual interest, including girls' desires that "polluted" their female friends, but a moderate amount of passion aroused little concern. One advice manual warned young women that "kissing and caressing of your female friends should be kept for your hours of privacy, and never indulged in before gentlemen." Others recognized that young women might have passionate feelings for each other but that those desires must "be buried and come to life again" as love for their husbands. Women who did not seem to need or desire to have men in their lives, at any point, incited far more consternation than girls or women who kissed each other. Frederick Hollick, one of the most outspoken health reformers to name women's desires in the 1850s, characterized masculine women as of "doubtful or double sex," sexual "monstrosities" with pathological drives. Women who loved women otherwise experienced relative freedom. (Chapter 8 considers cisgendered women's relationships with gender-nonconforming individuals at length.)[6]

Within a few decades, a new science of sex (sexology) would introduce categories of "perversion" and illness to describe desires between people of the same sex or with gender-variant people. Sexology, as it came into focus in the 1880s and thereafter, viewed gender variance as evidence of "homosexual" or "lesbian" identity. Law enforcement followed close behind, with police forces newly insistent on arresting "sex deviants" (usually men and gender-variant people) on mere suspicion of illegal activity.

Until then, ambiguity nurtured possibility. Outside of courtship and marriage, people loved and lusted after one another without a distinct vocabulary to name their desires. Unencumbered by categories of sexual identity, same-sex and genderqueer friendships could be *loving* without the presumption of being *sexual*. Prior to marriage, many young people engaged in same-sex or queer erotic play without facing accusations of immorality. Novels, books of poetry, stories published in high-circulation magazines, and biographies discussed same-sex couples unabashedly, with a candor that would seem inconceivable by the early twentieth century. Some individuals were tormented by the possibility that they were committing sinful acts by engaging in nonmarital sex, but they rarely thought of themselves or their lovers as sexual deviants.[7]

Marriage was the framework for sexual love that Alonzo and Hubbel best understood. For Rebecca Primus and Addie Brown, two Black women who found love with one another around the same time, friendship and sisterhood also provided metaphors of intimate belonging. For both pairs of lovers, an ideal of conjugal affection simultaneously enticed and eluded them. Lacking a pathway to public recognition of their relationships, such individuals tried to stake out a compromise. Some formed marriage-like households. Others expressed their affection by penning love letters to the people they could only dream of living with as future female husbands or male wives, identities that recognized the interplay of gender and sexual desires in ways that the law did not. It is not surprising that same-sex desires and queer relationships existed in the nineteenth century. What may surprise is just how common same-sex and otherwise queer desire was, before it was named, categorized, and distinguished from the norm.

Hubbel and Alonso found warmth and companionship in Union Army tents, but it did not take a war to bond men to one another. A twenty-two-year-old Thomas Jefferson ("Jeff") Withers queried his former bedmate, nineteen-year-old James ("Jim") H. Hammond, in 1826, to "learn whether you yet sleep in your Shirt-tail, and whether you yet have the extravagant delight of poking and punching a writhing Bedfellow with your long fleshen pole—the exquisite touches of which I have often had the honor of feeling?" Withers teased Hammond for jabbing his bedmates with "the crushing force of a Battering Ram," in language that mingled jokes about penis size with metaphors of aggressive penetration. Withers again asked Hammond about his "fleshen pole" a few months later, wondering if his friend was "charging over the pine barrens of your locality, braying, like an ass, at every she-male you can discover." After making this disparaging comment about a genderqueer or transfeminine person, Withers then shifted abruptly in his letter to a consideration of early marriage and relationships with women. Even as Withers mocked Hammond about the latter's desire for a gender-nonconforming lover, he displayed an uncomplicated awareness of their concurrent plans to marry women. They viewed their sexual play with each other as an acceptable part of the transition from innocent boyhood to the adult obligations of marriage.[8]

Lust and arousal figured in many men's friendships. Men who had every intention of marrying and having sex with women mutually masturbated with their boyhood friends, exchanged passionate kisses with male companions, and cozied up in bed. Abraham Lincoln formed his closest emotional bond with his friend Joshua Speed. The two men became bedmates in 1837. Speed, then twenty-four, was the proprietor of a general store. Within minutes of their acquaintance, he invited the twenty-eight-year-old Illinois legislator to share his wide bed. They slept side by side for years. Based on stories that Speed told late in life, the two men may have visited the same sex worker, a practice that was fairly common among working- and middle-class male friends at the time. Once separated, they wrote to each other about their engagements and marriages to women, but their friendship held special meaning. Perhaps Speed and Lincoln needed morally pure women for marriage, sex workers for sex, and men for love. What's clear is that their intimacy fit easily within their era's norms.[9]

Sailors at sea often engaged in mutual masturbation (going "chaw for chaw," in sailors' slang) and, less often, in anal sex. According to the mid-nineteenth-century diary of a United States Marine, sex acts involving an adult sailor with a boy or youth were especially common. Marines called these pairings "chickenship," when an older, higher-ranking adult gave a boy clothes, money, and protection in exchange for sex. The U.S. Navy did not formally outlaw sodomy; when John Adams wrote the first rules for the new organization in the 1770s, he copied much of the Royal Navy's regulations but, for unknown reasons, omitted a prohibition against sodomy, which the Royal Navy had defined as a capital crime since the 1660s. The U.S. Navy charged a marine with sodomy for the first time in 1805. The brief proceeding concluded without a conviction. The next naval sodomy trial was thirty years later, and it resulted in a not-guilty verdict. In the latter case, a boy said he had "frigged" (masturbated) a lieutenant. A contemporaneous account of British sailors described men on prison ships in Bermuda paired up with partners that they referred to as their spouses. Most of these men never faced criminal charges, but during the Civil War, the U.S. Navy prosecuted several sailors for "improper indecent intercourse." While officially prohibited, queer sex among sailors was pervasive and, occasionally, romantic.[10]

The predominantly male mining camps of the California Gold Rush also nurtured queer intimacies. After the United States claimed California in 1848, thousands of Americans traveled west to land they felt entitled to dominate. Heroic tales of western conquest portrayed a barren landscape where white men fought Indians and seduced white women, but the region was remarkably diverse, if disproportionately male. Foreign-born people (mostly Mexican, Chilean, and Chinese men) joined the local population of Miwok Indians. Some men had sex with other men; Jason Chamberlain and John Chaffee, both white, sailed from Boston to San Francisco (via Cape Horn) in 1849, and lived together in a mining town for more than fifty years. In the domestic spaces of the mining camps, many white men performed conventionally female tasks, cooking and caring for each other. Some Mexican, French, and Miwok women married white miners, but others supported themselves by selling sex in the mining camps' brothels, saloons, and dance halls. The rough-and-tumble American West was distinctly queer. Men at a camp along the Tuolumne River in California gave the name "Sister Stilwell" to a young person (assigned male at birth) who had a "fresh complexion, lack of beard, and effeminate appearance." As fiddlers played at the miners' raucous balls, anyone wearing what one diarist memorably described as "a patch on a certain part of his inexpressibles" danced the ladies' parts.[11]

Bedsharing did not always lead to sex, not all sex was romantic, and, of course, not all nineteenth-century friendships were erotic. James Blake and Wyck Vanderhoef, both engineers, met in 1848 while they were in their twenties. In his diary, Blake wrote of the emotional and physical intimacy he found with Vanderhoef: "Long have I desired a friend, one whom I could trust myself with upon this journey of life . . . [It is] a beautiful thing . . . [to] retire from the cold selfish arms of the world, and receive the pure embrace of friendship." They shared a bed, and this "pure embrace" was not mere metaphor. Blake described a night they spent together: "We retired early, but long was the time before our eyes were closed in slumber, for this was the last night we shall be together for the present, and our hearts were full of that true friendship which could not find utterance by words, we laid our heads upon each other's bosom and wept, it may be unmanly to weep, but I care not, the spirit was touched." The ambiguity of their relationship was a consequence, in part, of the flowery prose of these nineteenth-century romantics. What is clear is how ardently many nineteenth-century men felt about their male and gender-nonconforming friends, and how eager they were to express that love.[12]

This acceptance of queer desire between friends, sailors, and schoolmates coexisted with animosity toward men who appeared to enjoy sex with men to the exclusion of all other sexual practices. In her *Incidents in the Life of a Slave Girl,* Harriet Jacobs included the story of Luke, an enslaved man mistreated and, she implied, sexually assaulted by his master. She described the master as "a mere degraded wreck of manhood," a "cruel and disgusting wretch" who demanded that Luke "submit" to acts "too filthy to be repeated." Abolitionists depicted male enslavers who pursued sex with enslaved men as "loathsome," an adjective that emphasized their larger argument about the inherent depravity of slavery. In 1885, writer F. S. Ryman noted in his diary that his friend "Fuller" was "a 'C—sucker' & that he loves & enjoys that d—d custom so revolting to every right minded person . . ." The absence of the word "sodomy" in Ryman's private journal reflects the pervasive use of euphemisms to describe allegedly disreputable sex acts. It is also possible that Ryman's disgust was a response to his friend's preference for oral-genital sex, a practice associated with sex work.[13]

Lawyers and judges tended to portray men accused of sodomy as "assaultive, ungodly, and monstrous." When William S. Davis was charged with assault and "attempting to commit *Sodomy*" in 1810 in Baltimore County, Maryland, prosecutors described his intended sex act as the "most horrid and detestable crime, (among Christians not to be named,) called *Sodomy.*" Even as the details of penis-vagina sexual intercourse proliferated in *Fanny Hill* and midwifery texts, sodomy remained largely unutterable. *The Whip,* one of New York City's gossip papers, inaugurated a series of articles in January 1842 ridiculing those "who follow that unhallowed practice of Sodomy." Warning that a sodomite's breath was "death to inhale," the paper depicted same-sex desire as a contagion "foreign to our shores," an un-American deviation. Newspapers portrayed sodomites as middle-aged or older men who sought out young men or gender-variant people for sex, occasionally by paying them for it. One was not necessarily born a sodomite, however; sodomy was viewed, instead, as a communicable disease that any man might catch.[14]

A considerable portion of the American population nevertheless appears to have tolerated queer sex, depending on the circumstances. Men known for their exclusive pursuit of sex with other men might get a reputation for moral depravity or "loathsome" behavior. But people at the time would not have recognized any commonality between those "sodomites" and other men who engaged in queer sex play in their youth or while living far from the company of women. And no one at the time identified an overarching category akin to "homosexuality" that would encompass both men and women who enjoyed queer sex.[15]

Addie Brown stayed up late writing to Rebecca Primus, telling her that their nights together set her body aflame. "If you was a man what would things come to they would after come to something very quick," Addie wrote at the end of a long day's labors. Self-educated and orphaned, she spent her days scrubbing floors, washing dishes, and caring for white people's children in Waterbury, Connecticut, a short distance from Rebecca's family home in Hartford. They lived a world apart in terms of class and opportunity. Rebecca was a high school graduate, the child of Holdridge, a small businessman, and Mehitable, a seamstress. The Primuses were active members of the Talcott Street Congregational Church, known for its fierce commitment to abolitionism and to public education for Black children. The family rented rooms to Black workers like Addie and ran an informal employment service for white families seeking domestics. Perhaps Addie and Rebecca met at church or when Addie came to the Primus home to seek work. However they first encountered each other, by late summer 1859 their bond was such that Addie insinuated that a comparable degree of physical affection with a man might get her pregnant.[16]

Theirs was a love story. Addie treasured her visits with Rebecca. In Hartford, Mehitable welcomed Addie as a member of the family, and the young women shared Rebecca's bed. In the first of Addie's surviving letters to Rebecca, dated August 2, 1859, she thanked Rebecca for sending her a long-awaited letter, and added a postscript: "one sweet kiss." She wrote again a few weeks later, having returned to her employer in Waterbury after a visit to Rebecca's home: "Dearest Dearest Rebecca my heart is almost broke I don't know that I ever spent such hours as I have my loving friend . . . it seem to me this very moments if I only had the wings of a dove I would not remain long in Waterbury although we cant allway be together O it tis hard." Addie's letters to Rebecca conveyed an intense desire for intimacy.[17]

Addie's trysts in Rebecca's bed were not her only experiences of sex. She wrote occasionally of difficulties in her employer's home: "Rebecca don't you think I am very foolish I don't want anyone to kiss me now I turn Mr Games away this morning no kisses is like yours." Did Mr. Games often make sexual advances on her? While Addie reassured Rebecca that Mrs. Games was kind to her, offering her some sewing work for additional income, she also alluded to wanting a new place of employment. Mainly, she wanted to live closer to her beloved Rebecca. Her punctuation and unconventional spacing of words conveyed urgency: "Rebecca my Dearest love could any one love a person as Love you   I cannot I cannot stay here any longer with out you I must I must be near you."[18]

Addie wrote these words in defiance of a culture that presumed that women's sexual desire lay hidden, like a bulb planted in the fall, awaiting the warmth of a man's interest to sprout and bloom. Few people would have imagined that Rebecca and Addie shared anything other than friendship. If it was men's insistent demands that provoked women into sexual activity, what erotic act could possibly occur when two women shared a bed?[19]

It is somewhat ironic, then, that Addie's letters to Rebecca, far more than Alonzo's letters to Hubbel, provide details. Addie's grammar reveals a breathless longing to be with Rebecca. "I dreampt of you last night," she wrote in October 1861. "I thought I was seting on your lap with my head on your bosom other things connected with it. I will not tell you at present. When I wake up in the night and found it was all a dream I was so disappointed." By 1861, Addie lived with and worked for a Black family in New York City that operated a restaurant and bar. She wrote Rebecca: "your most Affec letter to me was like pieces of meat to hungre wolfe I will not tell how often I pursue the contents of it this eve for the first time since I left that I gave vent to tears O Dear Dear Rebecca no one knows the heart of your Dear Friend . . . Dear Rebecca if I had the energy of the dove how swiftly I would fly to the arms of my love." The voracious wolf and the peaceful dove: Addie may not have had any formal education, but she was a poet.[20]

Interspersed among mundane descriptions of her daily labors, Addie professed her love with words of kinship: "Think my Dearest Sister," she wrote in March 1862, "I am near the breathing the same air with your arm gently drawn around me my head reclining on your noble breast in perfect confidence and love." They were too often apart, and their separations pained her: "But alas the dream is over the charm is broken I alook to the stern realities of my position but to find myself alone of what would I not give at this moment to be with or near you my longs for it ask for it . . ." Familial terms seem to have given Addie and Rebecca ways to express their devotion. They called each other "beloved sisters."[21]

Addie's daydreams often returned to the possibility of a home with Rebecca. In a letter from September 1861 she asked, "do you ever think that we will live together anymore or live within two or three miles of each other is it possible that we are not able to clasp each other in our arm but once a year . . ." She thought very little of most men: "what they say goes in one ear and comes out the other sometimes when I get to thinking about different things in particular the fact I almost hate the site of a man." Addie viewed marriage principally as a way out of domestic service. Twenty years old in 1861, she was courted by a Mr. Lee she met in New York. "I like him as a Friend and nothing more then that but Dear Rebecca if I should ever see a good chance I will take it for I'm tired roving around the unfriendly world."[22]

Forming a household with another woman was an unlikely but not impossible goal. In 1807, Sylvia Drake and Charity Bryant began living together in a rented house. Two years later they built a one-room home in Vermont and opened a tailoring business. For more than forty-four years, Bryant and Drake spent every night in the same bed, toiled side by side as skilled seamstresses, worshiped together in their Congregationalist church, cared for their nieces and nephews, and nursed each other through injury, illness, and loss. Bryant assumed the masculine privileges of the husband (privileges widely acknowledged within their community), with Drake performing the wife's domestic chores. No formal bonds of matrimony united them, of course, but their neighbors considered them husband and wife. Bryant's gender nonconformity—her manly gait, habit of pipe smoking, and assertive business acumen, even as she continued to identify as a woman—was more controversial than her public union with Drake. Because they lived according to contemporary expectations for marital respectability and operated a successful business, they earned some local toleration and privacy.[23]

Some couples cohabited and wed when one partner, assigned female at birth, lived as a husband. Gender-variant people formed queer households often enough that stories of their "discovery" became their own genre. The figure of the "female husband" recurred in British and U.S. newspapers, court cases, and popular narratives. British author Harry Fielding had popularized the phrase with his 1746 pamphlet, *The Female Husband*, a "true" story of George/Mary Hamilton, who married multiple women and crossed the Atlantic in an unsuccessful attempt to evade punishment. This and other reports of female husbands, which became especially popular by the early nineteenth century, offered tales of disguise, cunning, and sexual escapades. Newspaper reporters expressed disbelief upon the revelation of a female husband's "true sex," but the sheer number of exposés suggests that many more people assigned female at birth lived long and unremarkable lives as men who pursued and often married women. Female husbands and their wives thought of themselves as conventional marriage partners.[24]

Other couples lived openly as two people of the same sex, as Bryant and Drake did. By the late nineteenth century, some elite white women formed "Boston marriages," a phrase that drew upon the relationship between two female characters in *The Bostonians* (1886) by Henry James. James likely based the characters on his sister Alice James and her romantic partner, Katharine Peabody Loring. Often the partners in these unions had professional occupations or found success as writers, actors, or artists. Others inherited wealth. Economic self-sufficiency was nearly impossible for nineteenth-century women to achieve through wage-earning, but it was essential to the formation of women's same-sex households.[25]

Americans remained ambivalent about intimacies between women, but unconventional gender, more than sexual acts, could mark a person as perverse. In Louisa May Alcott's 1870 novel, *An Old-Fashioned Girl,* the characters Rebecca Jeffrey and Lizzie Small "live together, and take care of one another in true Damon and Pythias style." But Alcott, who never married or expressed any romantic interest in a man, and whom family members called "Lou," had another character call these lovers a "different race of creatures" who were, thankfully, not "mannish and rough." Decades before sexologists named the lesbian and the invert as pathological sexualities, Americans attuned to the experience of queer desire recognized it both as a source of comfort and a potential danger.[26]

By the fall of 1865, Rebecca had moved to Royal Oak, Maryland. An emissary of the Hartford Freedmen's Aid Society, she raised funds to build a schoolhouse and stayed until 1869, enduring threats and harassment from local whites. Addie imagined that if they were legally married, she would have been able to accompany Rebecca on her mission to educate formerly enslaved people: "What a pleasure it would be to me to address you My Husband and if so do you think for one moment you would be where you are with out me? . . . you say absence strengthens friendship and our love will not grow cold mine never will I will always love you and you only if you were to remain there how pleasant it would be for me to come there too . . ." When her descriptions of male suitors provoked Rebecca's jealousy, Addie was quick to reassure her: "Dear Rebecca no ones know the love I have for you I have tried to tell you but have not any more than I do and you are the only that I love or ever try to love nobody will come between us in love . . ." Truly, she wrote with unmistakable passion.[27]

Even so, Addie teased Rebecca that other girls were in hot pursuit. In 1867 she was employed at Miss Porter's, an all-girls (and overwhelmingly white) boarding school in Connecticut. Apparently, several students wanted to share Addie's bed with her. Like many girls' schools and women's colleges, this one afforded plenty of opportunities. As Addie wrote to Rebecca, "The girls are very friendly towards me. I am either in they room or they in mine every night often and sometime just one of them wants to sleep with me. I am not very fond of White I can assure you." Rebecca responded with a teasing suggestion: Perhaps Addie's breasts attracted these new bedmates. Addie replied, "If you think that is my bosom that captivated the girl that made her want to sleep with me she got sorely disappointed enjoying it for I had my back towards her all night and my night dress was button up so she could not get to my bosom. I shall try to keep you favorite one always for you." Had Rebecca designated one of Addie's breasts as her favorite? They appear to have shared a tender, teasing, and mutually gratifying intimacy.[28]

Addie Brown does not appear in census records, city directories, or any other surviving sources that document her life beyond what she wrote in her letters to Rebecca. In the late 1860s she left Miss Porter's and moved to Philadelphia, where she married a man named Joseph Tines. And then she was gone, her death at age twenty-eight revealed only by Rebecca's handwritten note on an envelope: "Addie died at home, January 11, 1870." Sometime between 1872 and 1874, when Rebecca was at least thirty-six years old, she married Charles Thomas, a man she knew from Maryland. He became the doorman for the Connecticut State Senate, a highly regarded occupation for a Black man in an era of explicit workplace segregation. They did not have any children. Rebecca died in 1932, at age ninety-five, her accomplishments celebrated in an obituary in the *Hartford Courant*.[29]

In her later years, Rebecca arranged for the disposition of her belongings. Her remarkable family and her acclaimed career as an educator drew the interest of a local historical society. Sorting through decades of correspondence, she decided which items should be preserved for posterity. Social attitudes toward unmarried women's passionate friendships had shifted drastically by the 1920s and 1930s, as law enforcement and mental health professionals began to describe a woman's sexual interest in another woman as proof of deviant desires and mental illness. Other women burned diaries or letters that implicated them in same-sex relationships. Rebecca refused to be ashamed. She stacked Addie's letters neatly and included them among the records she sent to the historical society, a final act of love.

Alonzo and Hubbel called one another husband and wife, even if they did not imagine the possibility of marriage to one another. In a letter Alonzo wrote in the fall of 1866, reflecting on Hubbel's upcoming wedding, Alonzo winked at the bond he enjoyed with his wartime friend: "I am fully aware of the affections of a good and true woman, having enjoyed them for over a year." A year later, at last newly married himself, Alonzo lamented that he had lost Hubbel's ring: "I was real sorry for it always reminds me of you and of the times we used to have together in the army." And then he promised to send Hubbel a photograph of him and his wife just as soon as they could have one taken.[30]

By then, he would have known that Hubbel didn't end up marrying Cousin Mary. After the engagement ended, Hubbel had taken up with Viola Keyes, an ambitious young woman who had attended boarding school in New York. She had exchanged letters with a few men, Hubbel among them, throughout the war years. Viola saved Hubbel's letters, including the twenty he received from Alonzo between 1865 and 1868. It was she who preserved a record of the affection he shared with his wartime companion, if not with her.[31]

Hubbel and Viola's marriage was long, childless, and unhappy. In 1879, Viola prepared to follow Hubbel to the homestead he was establishing in the Dakota Territory. Hubbel sent her letters with detailed information about what to pack, his need for cooking and farming implements, and the weather. The only words of affection in these otherwise mundane dispatches concerned another man, Frank. The two men lived together when they first arrived in the Dakota Territory, before their wives joined them. "I like him ever so much he is as good as he is big. He says he will tell you how I perform when you come. We have pretty pleasant times planning whether our wives will like it here." The letter is at once tantalizing and frustrating: What did he mean, "how I perform"? Hubbel and Viola were burdened with debts and troubled by Hubbel's precarious physical and mental health. He complained of his stomach; Viola worried about his "nerves." Viola and Hubbel both died in the flu pandemic of 1918–1919 when they were in their early seventies, after more than fifty years of marriage.[32]

Same-sex and queer companionship met within narrow beds and in pledges sealed by rings and kisses. Suspicions about what "really" went on in those beds might occasion gossip, but same-sex and queer relationships of the eighteenth and nineteenth century were generally tolerated so long as they were not "flaunted" or disruptive to neighbors. Many people in same-sex or queer relationships did not classify their desires, let alone themselves. Neither law nor language yet set these relationships apart, nor fully included them. Instead, marriage, kinship, and friendship all provided metaphors of intimate partnership for such couples. Hubbel and Alonzo called each other husband and wife; Addie wrote to her "beloved sister." Yet we should not allow this familial language to fool us into questioning the erotic intensity of these romantic friendships.

PART TWO

REDEFINING SEX

1840–1938

Chapter 7

Then Shall They Be Gods

THE CRISIS OF A LIFE—ENTERING INTO POLYGAMY

The summer air in Nauvoo, Illinois, was thick with gossip about sex.

It was 1842, and the followers of Joseph Smith, the prophet of the Church of Jesus Christ of Latter-day Saints, had lived in Nauvoo only since 1839. The Latter-day Saints, or Mormons, had followed Smith from

Fanny Stenhouse's memoir about her twenty years' experience as a polygamous wife to a Latter-day Saint was one of many sensational depictions of Mormon marriage as a form of slavery for women, a portrayal that members of the LDS Church vehemently disputed.

upstate New York to Kirtland, Ohio, and then to Independence, Missouri, where local authorities grew increasingly wary of Smith's plans to build an autonomous society. When mobs threatened Smith, he and his followers once more went in search of an enclave of their own. They believed they found it in Nauvoo (formerly called Commerce), which occupied land that the U.S. government had seized from the Sauk people in the 1810s and sold to white speculators. Smith was optimistic. Here, he declared, the Mormon church would build its Zion according to the divine revelations he had received and which had become the *Book of Mormon*, their sacred text. Wilfred Woodruff, one of Smith's closest associates (and future church president), envisioned the nascent settler community as "the kingdom of God." At first, only Smith's closest confidants knew that the Zion they were building included unorthodox sexual arrangements.[1]

The beginnings and eventual demise of Mormon polygamy prompted a transformation in how the federal government responded to sexual nonconformity, one step in the dramatic investment of local, state, and national government agents in the regulation of sexuality from the mid-1800s to the mid-1900s. Sex and sexuality during these hundred years became increasingly integral to American governance, with the Comstock Act to ban "obscenity," police vice squads arresting suspected sex workers or "deviants," and progressive reformers looking for ways to reform "delinquent" youth. Individuals began to see their desires as sources of their personal identities—and challenged regulations that got in the way of expressing them. Young people socialized more often in mixed-sex groups, away from their families, and enjoyed the recreational pleasures that money could buy. Sexual modernity celebrated the individual pursuit of pleasures and considered a person's desires to be a reflection of their fundamental nature. Fantasies of racial difference, whether in the response to the LDS church or through the emergence of queer subcultures in American cities, shaped the creation of that modern sexuality, too.

Mormon polygamy was one of several dramatic attempts to widen the parameters of sexual morality in the nineteenth-century United States. The iconoclasts considered in this chapter—not only within the LDS church but also among free lovers and the Oneida Perfectionists—led the first collective efforts in the United States to build the world anew by rewriting the rules about sex. Their challenges to convention far surpassed the provocative booklets that Fanny Wright distributed about contraception or Sylvester Graham's lectures about the solitary vice. Mormons, free lovers, and Oneida Perfectionists defied laws that privileged monogamous marriage, and each claimed to liberate women from traditional marriage's oppression. Ironically, their efforts prompted the U.S. government to assert its authority over intimate relationships in ways that amplified white men's marital authority, just as the government was also demanding marital monogamy among Indigenous people.

When Smith and his followers arrived in Nauvoo, the U.S. government was a whisper of the size it would attain by 1896, the year that Woodruff received a new revelation calling for an end to the church's unconventional marriage practices. State legislatures, not Congress, set and enforced laws related to marriage, divorce, and sex (as they still do). But as the government in Washington expanded its enforcement powers across the nineteenth century, adding agencies to administer the Civil War and care for widows and the wounded after it ended, it also asserted a new role as an arbiter of the nation's sexual morality. The federal government's investment in marital monogamy was unprecedented.

In places governed by federal authorities, such as the Utah Territory, where Smith's followers later settled, and on Indian reservations, Washington legislators and bureaucrats attempted to do in the second half of the nineteenth century what missionaries had pursued in the seventeenth and eighteenth: eliminate polygamy through incentives or, if necessary, force. The government demanded that Mormons, Indigenous people, and other nonconformists adhere to a monogamous marital norm. In reality, fidelity and monogamy were hardly the rule in the mid-nineteenth-century United States. Westward migration promised both land and personal reinvention, as tens of thousands of people rode or walked in search of opportunity. Untold numbers of Americans committed de facto bigamy when they deserted spouses and moved across the ever-growing expanse of U.S. territory to marry again. Men enjoyed greater freedom to travel and were far more common sights along the rough roads and unmarked trails west, but women picked up and left their homes too. (Gender-variant people made these journeys as well, often arriving at their destination as the woman or man they understood themselves to be, a subject that Chapter 8 discusses.) When agents of the U.S. government forced Indigenous people to live on single-family farms rather than reservations or arrested Mormon men for adultery, they insisted they were doing it for the people's own good.[2]

The alarming reports emanating from Nauvoo inspired a series of federal actions—military deployments, legislation, and judicial decisions—that asserted the responsibility of national leaders over intimate living arrangements. Critics of polygamy portrayed it as a kind of slavery that subjected women to powerful men's obscene desires. A great deal of erotic fantasy circulated in these ostensible arguments against polygamy. But monogamy did not win the day on the strength of these arguments alone. The Latter-day Saints held out for decades and relented only after the federal government stripped them of nearly all their assets. These intense conflicts over sexual behavior contributed to an idea of sexuality that was just beginning to take shape. Like many Americans, the Mormons understood desire as a reflection of a person's soul. But over time, the national preoccupation with polygamy helped magnify sex's importance to American governance and, eventually, to individual identity.

In a clandestine temple ceremony in 1841, a member of the all-male LDS priesthood "sealed" Smith and Louise Beman in "celestial marriage" that would endure, they believed, for eternity. The following year, Eliza Snow, one of Smith's most faithful followers and a leading figure within Mormon women's organizations, was also sealed in celestial marriage with Smith. Sisters Zina Jacobs and Presendia Buell each already had a husband when they received the priest's blessing for their sealing with Smith. Mormons soon learned that a woman married "for time" to a Gentile (as they described the unconverted) or to a fellow Latter-day Saint could yet marry "for eternity" a man whom Smith had anointed a priest in a special temple ceremony. To Smith and his followers, temporal laws mattered little compared to God's blessings (mediated through his prophet, Joseph Smith). By 1844, Smith had wed more than thirty women, and about 100 of his 12,000 followers (perhaps 3,000 of whom were women of childbearing age) practiced celestial marriage.[3]

In this life, Smith was already married to Emma Smith, who initially knew nothing about these covert rituals. When Emma got wise to her husband's behavior, she was furious, possibly even threatening to have extramarital affairs. According to one of Joseph's friends, "She thought that if he would indulge himself she would too."[4]

Critics within the growing Mormon community sounded the alarm. They amplified the rumors of extramarital sex and bigamous marriage, and they portrayed Smith as a louche seducer. Newspaper exposés written by Gentiles and former Latter-day Saints alleged coercion and abuse, including the story of a woman trapped in a room for two days until she assented to a plural marriage.[5]

Formerly faithful disciples rejected polygamy and urged a return to Smith's prophecy "as originally taught." Smith refused. He led both his church and the Nauvoo government, had a militia that reported to him, and foresaw the creation of a Mormon theocracy. When the *Nauvoo Expositor*, a dissident press, voiced critiques, Smith had the Nauvoo city council, which he controlled, declare the newspaper a public nuisance, and its presses were destroyed.[6]

On June 27, 1844, Smith, his brother Hyrum, and other members of his inner circle were arrested and taken to Carthage, the county seat, on charges of destruction of public property. Outraged over Smith's combined affronts to monogamous marriage and the rights of Gentiles, a mob stormed the jail and shot into the second-story cell that held Joseph, Hyrum, and their companions. Injured, Joseph leapt from a window to his death below.[7]

Brigham Young, a close disciple of Smith, claimed the mantle of prophecy from his mentor and led the Saints out of Nauvoo. Beginning in

1847, thousands of Latter-day Saints made the "trek" to the Great Salt Lake Basin, hoping to elude agents of both state and federal law enforcement. When the area that Young and his followers settled became part of the Utah Territory in 1850, the church once again had to contend with federal authority.[8]

Latter-day Saints in the Utah legislature created a novel legal system that exempted the spouses within polygamous marriages from common-law prohibitions on bigamy. They also established wider grounds for divorce. Laws governing marriage in the rest of the United States still limited married women's legal personhood; coverture restricted married women's rights to property and wages. Mississippi's legislature in 1839 and New York's in 1848 passed Married Women's Property Acts that allowed wives to own property in their own names, but these laws were exceptions. New York did not allow wives to retain their wages until 1860. These impediments to women's equality had dire consequences for women in abusive marriages. The temperance movement that formed in the 1840s drew attention to the predicament of wives whose husbands suffered from "habitual drunkenness." These women, activists argued, needed options foreclosed by the legal principle of marital unity, which presumed that a husband owned his wife's body. Some mid-nineteenth-century judges even continued to define rape as "tolerable cruelty" that did not abrogate a husband's marital rights.[9]

Missionaries for the LDS church pointed to the limitations of American marriage law. They advertised polygamy as one of the benefits of conversion—a virtuous union that, they argued, gave women more rights than traditional marriage did. New converts poured in from Canada and Europe, and for many of them, men and women alike, polygamy was part of the draw. The prospect of entering a marriage in which one man had licit sexual relations with more than one woman appealed to them. Polygamy, they argued, was a purer expression of human sexuality than monogamy because it prevented naturally lustful men from seeking out sex workers or carrying on clandestine affairs. Others viewed polygamy as a religious duty, a sacred obligation that proved their devotion to divine truths. Some women left the church because of polygamy, but most stayed.[10]

Women who converted to the Mormon church before Joseph Smith introduced celestial marriage often had the most difficult adjustments. Vilate Kimball was forty-three years old in January 1850 when she gave birth to her tenth child. This was Vilate's final pregnancy, but that year and the next, her husband, Heber, fathered nine more children by eight other wives. When Vilate complained, Heber urged her to appreciate the larger purpose of celestial marriage: "What I have done is according to the mind and will of God for his glory and mine so it will be for thine," he explained. As one of Joseph Smith's original apostles, Heber reminded Vilate that celestial marriage was from God: it sanctified the temporal patriarchy that oversaw all aspects of both Mormon religious practice and government.[11]

White Americans had long associated polygamy with the "heathens" of Indigenous nations and "infidels" in Arabia. The boundary between moral monogamy and licentious polygamy was marked by racial as well as religious differences. Anti-Mormon diatribes portrayed Smith, Young, and their followers as heathens and harlots who pretended to promote a well-ordered patriarchy when they in fact cultivated an immoral "harem" beset by sexual anarchy. "This Bluebeard of Salt Lake City," one paper warned, had been "lecturing his own harem" to accept polygamy. Young, the article continued, "bawls to his sultanas . . . to depart, if they are not contented . . . But where are these Hagars to go?" The message was clear: Christian self-control, combined with the superior intellect allegedly possessed by those of European descent, should enable Christian men to control their lust.[12]

Latter-day Saints argued that it was monogamy that caused sexual immorality. Polygamy in this life, they explained, enabled patriarchs and the women who devoted themselves to bearing and raising their children to achieve exaltation in the hereafter. Their philosophy of marital sex combined a celebration of bountiful reproduction with criticism of what they considered sexual excess. Polygamy's defenders argued that plurality prevented prostitution, even as they denied that they practiced polygamy out of lust. Man's desires originated with God, they said, in the call to be fruitful and multiply, so it was duty, not desire, that called them to plural marriage. To critics who condemned Latter-day Saints for making virtuous women into prostitutes and trapping them within harems, the church's defenders countered that polygamy honored women by making marriage and motherhood available to nearly all.[13]

One of the most damning criticisms of Mormon polygamy compared it to "free love," a phrase first employed by northeastern and mid-Atlantic newspaper editors in the 1820s to describe adulterers, bigamists, and polygamists—anyone having sex with a person of another sex to whom they were not married. Marriage reformers themselves disagreed about free love's meaning. A few free lovers were "varietists," embracing a romantic philosophy that did away with commitment, while others advocated for the ability to exit an unhappy marriage and remarry according to one's affections. Any of these options would have necessitated massive changes to American divorce law, which varied dramatically from state to state in the mid-nineteenth century just as it had in the 1790s when Abigail Abbot Bailey's husband deserted her in New York, where divorce was difficult to obtain. By the 1850s, Connecticut and Indiana were both considered "havens" for dissatisfied spouses due to their relatively liberal divorce laws. South Carolina, by contrast, provided no means of legal divorce.[14]

Like the health reformers who warned about the hazards of the solitary vice, free lovers preached restraint. Sex radicals throughout the United States asserted that because marriage without love was the real adultery, lack of affection should be grounds for legal divorce. Some went further in their critique of marriage by warning, as temperance reformers did implicitly, that women in abusive marriages experienced rape.[15]

Two of the most notorious free-love radicals were Mary Gove Nichols and Thomas Low Nichols, whose book *Marriage* (1854) argued against marital monogamy. Having endured an awful first marriage to a man whose sexual demands she found loathsome, Mary Nichols was inspired by the lectures of Sylvester Graham to take to the lecture circuit herself. She wrote and spoke about the necessity that wives be able to refuse sex with their husbands. Here the similarity to Graham ended. When Mary and Thomas married in 1848, their wedding vows pledged fidelity of love but not sex. Thomas took an even more remarkable position about the naturalness of sexual self-expression, writing in support of consensual sex between men. However commonly men had sex with men in the mid-nineteenth century, Nichols's position was exceptional. In 1853, Mary and Thomas resided at Modern Times, a utopian community on Long Island of about one hundred people drawn to its founders' ethos of "individual sovereignty."[16]

These free lovers prioritized women's right to sexual consent and mutual pleasure but deplored "sensualism," by which they meant loveless lust. Love, not marriage, they argued, sanctified sex. Free lovers additionally sought an end to the sexual double standard by legitimating women's sexual desires, endorsing coitus interruptus or postcoital douching to unburden women of the fear of continual pregnancies. Their inclusion of women's pleasure in the campaign for women's equality was radical. Not until the twentieth century would movements for women's equality in the United States return to these ideas about the importance of women's sexual gratification.[17]

These nuances aside, "free love" was more often invoked to tarnish another person's reputation than to affirm a new kind of sexual liberty. Dozens of antipolygamy novels characterized free love and the Mormon church as catalysts for sexual chaos. To be sure, when Brigham Young argued that marriage required affection, and that a marriage without it offered grounds for divorce, he sounded much like free lovers on the East Coast. Augusta Cobb, who left a husband in Boston to marry Young, similarly explained "that the doctrine taught by Brigham Young was a glorious doctrine for if she did not love her husband it gave her a man she did love," a sentiment that echoed free lovers' principles. (Back in Boston, her husband divorced her on grounds of adultery.)[18]

"Free love" and polygamy became epithets during the sectional crisis of the 1850s and 1860s. For decades, northern critics of slavery had decried the "harems" that white Southern elites formed with enslaved women. In 1856, the Republican Party platform condemned the "twin relics of barbarism," slavery and polygamy, blaming each for elevating the powers of corrupt patriarchs. This ideology esteemed male-female marriage, by contrast, as the antithesis of the sadism and suffering they associated with Mormon households. Apologists for the South, meanwhile, cast Northerners as dissolute free lovers. *The New York Herald*, which favored the pro-slavery Democratic Party, in 1857 insinuated that white men in the antislavery movement had "free love" in mind when they supported Black women's abolitionist societies.[19]

One of the founders of Modern Times, Stephen Pearl Andrews, took what we would today consider a libertarian approach to sex, arguing for removing the state from intimate decisions. Ready to take on any of free love's opponents, Andrews found a new voice for his theories in the early 1870s when he met Victoria Woodhull. Much like Mary Gove Nichols, Woodhull had survived a miserable first marriage and remarried, setting up an unconventional household in New York City that included her first husband, Calvin Woodhull (who was an ailing alcoholic), and her second husband, Col. James Harvey Blood, as well as her mother, children, and sister Tennessee Claflin. Woodhull and Claflin worked their way into the good graces of millionaire Cornelius Vanderbilt, who gave them enough money to open a brokerage (the first in the United States owned by women) and launch a newspaper. Andrews began to provide Woodhull with content for the paper, often published under Woodhull's name, to circulate his free love ideas. Woodhull was a believer; "Yes, I am a free lover," she announced in 1871, an unscripted moment during a lecture otherwise authored by Andrews. Like Andrews, she was a varietist who believed that for sex to be pure it must be a spiritual meeting of two souls.[20]

Yet even radical free lovers held fairly conventional views on the importance of sexual purity. They typically had little to say about race or slavery, aside from invoking it as an analogy for women's status within marriage. Instead, they addressed their philosophy to a presumptively white audience. Nor did free lovers challenge ideas about the fundamental differences between men and women. They assumed that men had much stronger desires for sex than white women did.

Despite accusations of debauchery, free lovers were, to the contrary, usually opposed to masturbation and libertinism. Male sexual excess resulted, they believed, when husbands ignored their wives' desires. Mutual love, by contrast, would nurture a healthy sexual restraint and reinforce sexual purity.[21]

A communal experiment led by John Humphrey Noyes in Oneida, New York, lay much further outside the mainstream. Calling themselves Bible Perfectionists, the Oneidans never numbered more than a few hundred people, although the abundant newspaper coverage they received brought them considerable attention. Noyes trained at Yale Divinity School but was expelled when he declared to his classmates that he had discovered the way for men and women who had been reborn in Christ to become morally "perfect," incapable of sin. From the late 1840s through the late 1870s, the Oneida Community practiced "Bible Communism" in their housing, wages, child rearing, and male-female sexual encounters. Much as free lovers had, Noyes compared marriage to slavery, an exclusive arrangement that subjected individual affection to the whims of state control. Unlike free lovers, Noyes abolished monogamy in his community. He taught his followers that spiritual perfection rendered secular marriage laws irrelevant.[22]

Noyes created a radical sexual system he called Complex Marriage. Every adult male in the Oneida community was a potential sexual partner of every adult or adolescent female there. Noyes and other adult males sexually initiated girls once they reached puberty, and he argued that the Bible did not prohibit sex between nieces and their uncles. Complicating matters, Noyes dictated every male-female pairing. Fanatical about his rule that all adolescent girls and women remain available to all adolescent boys and men, Noyes broke apart couples when the partners grew too attached or exclusive—"sticky," in the community's terminology. Sexual frequency and variety were intrinsic to his theology; intercourse should not occur only for the purposes of procreation, he explained, but instead was essential for moral communal life. Noyes

John Humphrey Noyes (1811–1886), pictured here in the 1850s, was the leader of the Bible Perfectionists in Oneida, New York. In Noyes's view, intercourse should not occur for the purpose of procreation only but also for personal enjoyment and the pursuit of spiritual perfection. In fact, most sex had at Oneida was not reproductive; Noyes demanded his male followers practice coitus reservatus by not ejaculating during intercourse and thus avoiding unwanted pregnancies.

preached that sex elevated lovers to heights of spiritual perfection. Such a system, of course, would require men to have sexual intercourse frequently and with as many adolescent girls and adult women as possible while avoiding perpetual pregnancies, which put women's lives at risk. (Noyes's own wife, Harriet, had five difficult pregnancies that resulted in only one live birth.)[23]

It was not simply that Noyes controlled *who* would have sex with whom; he also wanted to regulate *how* men and women had sex. Ejaculation, he warned, was "a momentary affair, terminating in exhaustion and disgust." He urged his male followers to practice coitus reservatus, controlling their desire by not ejaculating during intercourse. Men who mastered this technique, he explained, could enjoy "social" or "amative" sex, in which the male partner stopped before the "going over the falls" of the "ejaculatory crisis" and orgasm. Like a sort of tantric sex coach, Noyes taught men to "choose in sexual intercourse whether they will stop at any point in the voluntary stages of it, and so make it simply an act of communion, or go through to the involuntary stage, and make it an act of propagation." Noyes believed that this practice would enhance rather than dim the enjoyment of sex. He argued that it was the "action of the seminal fluid on the internal nerves of the male organ," not orgasm, that produced male pleasure. Noyes said nothing about how women experienced penetrative "presence" or about any connection between the man's "muscular exercise" and a female partner's pleasure.[24]

Noyes apparently found ejaculation a revolting and demoralizing experience. Nor did he advocate for masturbation as a healthy way for men to release their sexual energies, calling it a "useless expenditure of seed." Contemporary anti-masturbation reformers such as Graham and Sarah Mapps Douglass would have agreed with that much, but they held few other beliefs in common. While Graham and Douglass recommended marital "continence," or restraint, Noyes had other ideas.[25]

The sexual system at Oneida was pedantic and intrusive, but for enthusiastic members of the community, it was a source of tremendous sexual satisfaction. Tirzah Miller was Noyes's niece—and one of his favorite sexual partners. After one encounter, when Miller would have been about twenty-five and Noyes about fifty-seven, he praised her for being a sexual partner with "an immense . . . power to please sexually": "I always expect something sublime when I sleep with you." She returned the compliment. When her uncle declined to have sex with her or her friend Mary one evening in order to sleep with two younger women, Tirzah wrote that she was "glad we were out of the way, so that those other girls could get the same benefit from association with him that we had." The following evening, when he asked Tirzah to once again share his bed, she was euphoric: "I never realized so much as I have to-day what a life-giving thing it is to have fellowship with him. I had an unusually nice time." Miller was known among the members of the community for her sensuality, and she appreciated the myriad opportunities that her uncle's philosophy afforded her for sexual experiences with a variety of men.[26]

Scandalized observers of the Bible Communists and of the Latter-day Saints characterized them both as harems and the women who lived in these communities as prisoners, and readers of these pages might agree. Such an interpretation renders Tirzah Miller's enthusiasm for the Oneida system and Augusta Cobb's eagerness to become one of Brigham Young's plural wives as delusional responses to a charismatic but predatory leader. Those two things may have been true, to varying extents. But it would be wrong to deny the agency of at least some of the women who gravitated toward and stayed in these religious groups for any period. Among the sexual options available to them at the time, they chose polygamy and Complex Marriage.

Among the most controversial innovations at Oneida was "stirpiculture," a proto-eugenic experiment Noyes began in the 1860s. He permitted certain men and women to have procreative sex if he believed they would conceive a spiritually elevated child. Generations of selective breeding would bring his community closer to perfection, the pinnacle of which, he taught, was immortality. Noyes suggested that his system gave women a measure of control to "bear children only when they choose," but he alone decided which male-female pairs should take part. Quite often, he chose himself: he was the father of ten of the sixty-two children born of this plan between 1869 and 1879.[27]

Complex marriage and stirpiculture strained Oneida's cohesion. Some community members preferred the option of sexual exclusivity, while others simply wanted Noyes to stop determining their partners. After Noyes died in 1886, his nephew took control of the community, moving quickly to conceal evidence of stirpiculture from public view. A new generation of leaders remade Oneida as a profitable manufacturing center, its eponymous silverware cleansed of associations with sexual experimentation. Yet while Bible Communism fell apart, the Mormon church endured, albeit by making dramatic concessions to mainstream sexual norms.[28]

Polygamy locked Utah's territorial government out of statehood. In 1862 Congress passed the Morrill Act for the Suppression of Polygamy, which criminalized bigamy in the territories and dis-incorporated the Mormon church. The law was unenforceable, and it was never challenged in court. Pressure on Mormon leaders intensified as Congress debated laws that would punish polygamists by confiscating their property, compel polygamous wives to testify against their husbands, and imprison polygamous husbands. The U.S. government grew more determined than ever to eradicate polygamy within its borders, marking it as a sign of "barbarism" unsuited to American democracy.[29]

Whether polygamy degraded women animated the national debate over women's suffrage and Utah statehood. Women suffragists highlighted the stories of ex-Mormon women. They described the tyranny of patriarchal governance and the need for women to have an equal political voice. These activists characterized white women like themselves as innately more chaste than men and thus in need of the protective shield of the franchise. The Utah Territory granted suffrage to adult women in 1870, largely as a rebuke to critics who likened polygamy to female enslavement. To the shock and consternation of women's suffrage advocates and anti-polygamists, Mormon women did not use the franchise to end polygamy but instead continued to defend it as a system that protected them from the misery of celibacy, enabled them to fulfill their obligation to procreate, and guarded Mormon men and women from the "degradation" of prostitution. Even better, LDS women argued, polygamy made men more virile and healthier while enriching their prospects for the afterlife.[30]

Difficult years followed for the Latter-day Saints. A series of congressional acts and court decisions threatened their property, disenfranchised most of the faith's male adults, and dissolved the territorial militia. Perhaps even more damaging to Mormon morale, federal courts unleashed a torrent of sex-crime charges against them. Among the approximately 2,500 cases brought against members of the church between 1871 and 1896, more than 95 percent involved charges of fornication or bigamy. While many church leaders (who were all men) went "underground" to evade prosecution, from 1887 to 1890 more than two hundred Mormon women were indicted on fornication charges for pregnancies that resulted from relationships not sanctioned by legal marriage. In 1887, Congress passed the Edmunds–Tucker Act, which made adultery, incest, and fornication into federal crimes. By

1905, about 140 people in the New Mexico territory had been arrested for adultery. Those imprisoned, however, were overwhelmingly Hispanos who were not members of the Mormon church.[31]

The federal government extended its marital authority over Indigenous North Americans too. Many Indigenous people shared with the Latter-day Saints a tradition of polygamous marriage. Both groups populated the imaginations of white Christian Americans as bloodthirsty and uncivilized. Congress passed the Dawes Severalty Act the same year that it passed the Edmunds–Tucker Act. The Dawes Act was intended to end the reservation system and destroy Indigenous cultures by splintering communal lands into individual "allotments." The law also sought to change families from within. It trained Indigenous men in various forms of wage work and sent home economics specialists to instruct Indigenous women in Euro-American domestic arts. At a time when other white Americans called for the extermination of Native Americans, "assimilationists" touted the salutary effects of the patriarchal household. As white "friends of the Indian" asked a reservation agent in 1890, peppering him with questions about life on the reservation, "Do they not sometimes grow manly, under the influence of having a family to work for?" The Dawes Act, much like the treatment of polygamous Mormons, inscribed sexual monogamy into federal law.[32]

The Kiowa people who lived on the Kiowa, Comanche, and Apache (KCA) reservation in Indian Territory (today, principally Oklahoma) confronted those pressures. For white reformers and federal agents, Kiowa toleration of women's premarital sexual autonomy, polygamy, and serial monogamy indicated cultural inferiority. For centuries, the Kiowa had organized their community according to *topadoga* (kindreds), in which the eldest brother was the leader. A *topadoga* might encompass twelve or fifty tipis, and their composition fluctuated when disputes, social visits, or marriages sent some people from one *topadoga* to another. Sororal polygyny (marriage to two or more sisters) strengthened the family unit and provided men with additional female laborers for the strenuous but essential work of preparing buffalo hides for trade.[33]

Much as white Europeans had two and three centuries earlier, assimilationists concluded both that Indigenous women were mistreated and that they were promiscuous. They disparaged Indigenous men as debauched. Yet while Juana Hurtado had managed, in the first half of the eighteenth century, to ignore Franciscan efforts to control her sexual choices, by the late nineteenth century the force of American military power and the desperate poverty of many Native people made such resistance nearly impossible. To be "assimilated" into the general U.S. population, the Kiowa needed to change their sex lives.[34]

The Dawes Severalty Act broke apart *topadoga* and created male-headed, single-family households. Only single men or men who led a marital, single-family household received a land allotment. The Code and Court of Indian Offenses, which was enacted on the Kiowa reservation in 1888, explicitly outlawed polygamy.[35]

But sexual practices and family forms long valued by Kiowa people did not simply vanish, replaced by parceled lots or federal requirements. During the 1880s, a Kiowa artist drew scenes of their people in a plain ledger book, an item given as a gift by a soldier or missionary, or perhaps stolen, a small response to the theft of land. With colored ink, the Kiowa artist depicted reservation life across the ledger's pages. In one striking domestic scene, two figures, one male and one female, stand outside a painted tipi. The female figure, positioned near the tipi's entrance, wears a multicolored blanket, adorned with a chevron of blue, pink, white, and yellow above rows of vibrant patterns. She faces the viewer, while the male figure, more distant from the tipi, looks at her. He is wearing a striking blue blanket or robe above a bright yellow-and-red patterned skirt. Matrifocal households appear to have endured; perhaps the man has arrived to live in the woman's tipi. The household also appears to be monogamous, as no other women are present to suggest more than one wife. Colored stripes adorn the tipi's flap, and while three crosses also decorate the tipi, there is little else to suggest Christian ideas dominated the imminent consummation of this conjugal household.[36]

A Kiowa artist living on the Kiowa-Comanche-Apache (KCA) reservation created this domestic scene, likely between 1880 and 1890, on the pages of a ledger book. It appears to depict a wife welcoming her husband to her home. The U.S. government forced the Kiowa to abandon their long-standing practice of sororal polygamy in order to receive meager but life-sustaining government rations.

Officially, the Latter-day Saints became monogamists in 1896, when church president Wilfred Woodruff banned the practice of polygamy in exchange for an end to what he and his flock saw as federal harassment. Only then did Congress admit Utah as a state. Marital monogamy, as defined by the Protestant men who dominated all aspects of the U.S. government, was the price of citizenship. (The Fundamentalist Latter-day Saints were Mormons who refused to renounce polygamy. They broke away from the main church body and operated in secrecy.)

Yet even as Mormons and Indigenous peoples were being accused of sexual deviance, the values of white Protestant America were changing. Divorce rates climbed steadily upward in the second half of the nineteenth century. Ideas about women's bodily autonomy animated the pages of sex radical journals—whose readership stretched from New York to Kansas to the Oregon territory—and the socially conservative temperance movement, where women obliquely emphasized the hazards that a drunken husband presented to his wife. Newspaper editors disparaged "free love" and described the scandal of polygamy, but in doing so they circulated images and ideas far beyond the tight-knit communities of Modern Times, Oneida, or Salt Lake City. Theories about the proper aims of sex stirred up heated debates, but all might agree that sex had become a subject of urgent public concern.

Chapter 8

A Typical Invert

Alice Mitchell, age nineteen, thought about murder while she sat at a desk in her parents' home in Memphis in August 1891. Then Alice dipped a pen in ink, set its tip on a sheaf of paper, and proposed marriage to Freda Ward for the third time. Alice first met Freda at Miss Higbee's School for Young Ladies, an elite, white girls'

Annie Hindle, a Memphis native, had a successful career on the stage, often playing male parts, and had several female lovers, even marrying one of them. She was in the news just months before Alice Mitchell brutally murdered Freda Ward, whom Mitchell had once hoped to marry.

academy, from which they had since graduated. Freda, who was seventeen, had accepted Alice's proposal twice already, but Alice sought confirmation. Alice had given Freda a ring. Originally from Memphis, Freda now lived fifty miles away with her older, married sister in a Tennessee town called Gold Dust. Alice and Freda visited each other when they could and exchanged passionate letters when they couldn't. "Sweet love," Freda wrote just weeks earlier, "you know that I love you better than anyone in the wide world."[1]

The arrival of August put the lie to July's promises. Alice pressed the pen into the paper. It had been an awful month. Freda had started to wear a ring given to her by Ashley Roselle, a young man who secured her family's approval. When Alice responded furiously, Freda begged forgiveness. "I will be true to you this time," Freda pleaded. Their love reaffirmed, Alice and Freda rehearsed their plans: Alice would put on a man's suit and get a short haircut to become Alvin J. Ward. (Alice later told Dr. B. F. Turner, a psychiatrist, that shaving would enable a mustache to grow.) Rev. Dr. Patterson, a Memphis minister, would unite Alvin and Freda in marriage. They would catch the next steamboat to St. Louis and live there as man and wife.[2]

This detail brings us to the question of which pronouns we should use to describe Alice. Alice wanted to be known as Alvin and to be a husband (not a wife) to Freda. The world described Alice as a tomboyish girl who grew up to be a deranged young woman. Today, we might recognize Alice as a butch lesbian or as a transman. Those identifying terms were not available to Alice. Did Alice view a new identity as Alvin simply as a vehicle for being able to marry and form a household with Freda? Or did Alice want to *live* as a man? I interpret the evidence as pointing toward the latter conclusion, but because Alice did not clarify their plans, I refer throughout the remainder of the chapter to Alice using they/them pronouns.

Weeks earlier, Freda had promised Alice that Ashley meant nothing to her. She marked the riverboat timetables and packed her small bag for Memphis. "I will be perfectly happy when I become Mrs. Alvin J. Ward," she pledged. (They planned to share Freda's last name.)[3]

But now Alice feared betrayal. "Do you remember what I said I would do if you would deceive me?" they wrote. "I love you, Fred," Alice added, using Freda's nickname (one used by everyone in her family; it was not intended, at least by most, to have a masculine ring to it), "and would kill Ashley before I would see him take you from me." Alice contemplated violent retribution: "I had the nerve to price the pistols."[4]

A letter intended for a lover instead fell into hostile hands. Freda's older sister, Ada Volkmar, and her husband, William Volkmar, took their supervisory responsibilities seriously. William suspected that Freda was planning to run away, and he spent one night guarding his yard, Winchester rifle in hand. At the sound of a steamboat whistle, he caught Freda out of bed and fully dressed, her bag packed. She would not take a steamship journey to Memphis after all, nor marry Alice Mitchell. Alice learned about this turn of events in another letter. "I return your 'engagement ring,'" Ada Volkmar informed Alice, fury dripping from the page. "Don't try in any way, shape, form, or manner to have any intercourse with Fred again." Ada then wrote to Alice's mother, telling Mrs. Mitchell of Alice's "intimacy" with Fred and about the engagement ring.[5]

Bereft of Fred, Alice felt betrayed. In the late afternoon of January 25, 1892, Alice hid their father's straightedge blade on their person and went for a ride in Memphis with Lillie Johnson, a friend. Alice had somehow learned that Freda and her sister Josephine Ward had spent a few days in town and were about to return to Gold Dust. Lillie steered her buggy toward the customs house near the riverbank, drawing to a halt when the Ward sisters, walking toward the steamer *Ora Lee*, came into view. "I have to see Fred again," Alice told Lillie. Bystanders later affirmed that they heard Alice yell "I'll fix her!" as they ran down the snow-slicked embankment. Alice caught Freda by the arm and slashed her across the face with the razor. Josephine threw herself between them and pushed Alice to the ground, jabbing Alice with an umbrella. Alice scrambled to their feet and stabbed Josephine with the blade. Freda, frantic and bleeding, tried to escape, but Alice caught up to her.

They cut Freda again across the face and then took a fist full of Freda's hair and yanked back her head for the final, fatal cut.

John Parry's butcher shop stood not far from the Mitchell household, and he had long teased Alice that they should have been born a boy. Parry saw them smoking cigarettes, playing ball, and riding a stick horse in the street. Alice did not mind being called a tomboy.[6]

Living as a boy—or, rather, a man—was by 1891 something Alice very much hoped to do. Like many people before them, Alice understood gender as something that could change during a person's lifetime—something that they themselves could change. Alice would not simply cross-dress to impersonate a man named Alvin; Alice would *be* Alvin, a husband to Freda, a married man traveling west with their new bride. Both Alice and Freda understood that they would each transform—Alice into Alvin J. Ward and Freda into Mrs. Alvin J. Ward.

The existence of people who wanted to move through gender—to live as a gender different from the one assigned to them at birth—was not novel when Alice Mitchell expressed a desire to become the husband of Freda Ward in the early 1890s. From Thomas/Thomasine Hall in the 1620s and the presence of two-spirit spirit people among Indigenous North Americans, through the gender-crossing figures that animated Thomas Jefferson ("Jeff") Withers's comments in the 1820s about his male friend's attractions to "she-males," gender-variant people circulate throughout this history. What was new were experts and psychiatrists who seized the opportunity to promote their own theories of sexual "perversion" and gender "inverts." According to theories of "sexual inversion," an insufficiently masculine male was at risk of becoming a homosexual; likewise, lesbian tendencies arose in the overly masculine female. An emerging science of sexual pathology shifted the conversation about sexuality and gender in the United States (as it was also shifting in Europe), promoting mental health experts and scientists as sexuality's foremost authorities. Alice Mitchell's trial contributed to

A two-spirit Zuni person named We'wha traveled to Washington, DC, in 1886, where she met President Grover Cleveland at the White House. Assigned male at birth, We'wha was one in a long line of revered two-spirit Native Americans.

a new conflation of "queer" desires and gender variance with mental illness and violence, a view that would endure for generations to come.

Gender-variant people formed relationships that often looked, to outsiders, to be heterosexual. Alices became Alvins and moved on foot, wagon, steamboat, or railroad to a place where they could reintroduce themselves. Cross-gender people were visible and recognized in the second half of the nineteenth century. Newspapers had covered the arrival of We'wha, a *lhamana* or two-spirit Zuni Pueblo person, in Washington, DC, in 1886. Deeply beloved by her people, this broad-shouldered, six-foot-tall "Indian princess" even visited President Grover Cleveland at the White House.[7]

Vaudeville theaters and concert saloons featured acts with female and male impersonators. Memphis residents in 1891 might have read about or seen a performance by famed male impersonator Annie Hindle, a fellow Memphian "who played male parts" and whose "inclination was altogether toward women." Five years earlier, Hindle had married her lover Annie Ryan in a ceremony officiated by a minister. He recognized the love the couple shared but did not notice that both were women. Ryan's death in December 1891 returned their story to newspapers mere weeks before Freda's murder. Such cases of "abnormal affection existing between persons of the same sex" made for good copy. The attorney general at Alice Mitchell's sanity inquest, arguing for the prosecution, in fact asked a defense witness about Hindle.[8]

A series of new laws made cross-gender self-expression far more dangerous than it had been earlier in the century when neighbors noted Charity Bryant's masculine habits but generally accepted her relationship with Sylvia Drake. Bans on cross-dressing passed state legislatures as early as 1843, but significant numbers of arrests occurred only when dozens of cities, especially in the South and West, passed separate local ordinances after the Civil War. As American cities grew and expanded their police forces, municipal leaders pledged to tamp down on "indecency" to rid neighborhoods of crime. Sex workers, vagrants, and cross-dressers were increasingly vulnerable. Anglo-American lawmakers had long worried that someone might cross-dress to evade identification while committing a crime or, if a woman dressed as a man, benefit from employment or other privileges to which she was not entitled. But the laws passed in U.S. cities in the mid-nineteenth century were specially focused on preventing "lewd" or "disorderly" public conduct.[9]

These laws proliferated despite ample evidence that many people arrested for "cross-dressing" were not doing so in commission of a crime or fraud but to express their authentic self. Charley Parkhurst was born in New England in the early 1800s but journeyed to Santa Cruz, California, by 1856, where he had a fifteen-year career as a stagecoach driver. Across routes that stretched from Oakland to San Jose, Parkhurst made a living in a man's occupation. Only upon his death in 1879 did neighbors discover that he did not have male sex organs. Most individuals who lived as a sex different from the one assigned to them at birth went about their daily routines without attracting any police response. Parkhurst would almost certainly have rejected any suggestion that he "cross-dressed."[10]

A white seventeen-year-old girl's murder in broad daylight by her lover captivated Americans and became grist for newspaper reports across the country. Violent deaths of white girls and young women from "good" families often grabbed headlines. The youth and gender of Freda Ward's killer, and the details of Alice and Freda's relationship, made this story a sensation. It was Alice, more than Freda, that distinguished the event, presented in newspaper stories as something of a novelty as a female suspect (as all the papers described Mitchell). In January 1892, Lizzie Borden was a relatively unknown single woman in her thirties living quietly at home with her father and stepmother in Fall River, Massachusetts, not yet famous for her hatchet.

Alice's murder of Freda drew attention to emerging theories about the relationship between gender, sexuality, and inherited criminality. Late-nineteenth-century Americans looking for explanations of illicit behavior often turned to theories of racial difference. Scientists examined cranial measurements to determine personal character, including the likelihood that an individual would commit a crime. Social scientists promulgated loose adaptations of Darwinian theories of evolution to argue that darker-skinned people resided lower on the evolutionary ladder, that both "lunacy" and poverty were inherited traits, and that "Anglo-Saxon" men occupied the highest strata of mental and moral attainment. Within twenty years, the emerging science of eugenics would be applied widely to understand all people's "fitness" and "traits."[11]

Neither criminality nor insanity were ever supposed to describe a graduate of a place such as Higbee's School for Young Ladies. Intense female friendships remained common at all-girls schools and colleges, much as they had for the students who climbed into Addie Brown's bed at Miss Porter's School in the 1860s. Classmates asked one another to dances (where one partner typically wore a man's suit), sent flowers, and wrote passionate love letters. A student scrapbook from the H. Sophie Newcomb College of Tulane University for "white girls and young women" included a photograph of a student's room, its two twin beds pushed together. "Smashing," as it was known in the northeast, or "chumming" as white Southerners called it, encouraged newer students to accept the attentions of an upper-class student. With rituals that closely mirrored heterosexual courtship, and even with few surviving records attesting to specific sex acts, the erotic possibilities remain obvious.[12]

The first generation of women to graduate from college in the 1870s and 1880s confronted outrage not because they had intimacies with one another but because of suspicions that their educations had damaged their reproductive systems. Psychologist G. Stanley Hall warned that female graduates would be "functionally castrated" and would "deplore the necessity of childbearing." Many graduates of women's colleges did indeed choose not to become mothers; 53 percent of Bryn Mawr students from 1889 to 1908 never married, and many college-educated women never had children. At a time when universities and many professional organizations refused to hire married women, remaining "single" (if possibly partnered to another woman) may have also been a strategy for employment and access to male privilege. In the early twentieth century, a study of unmarried college graduates found that 28 percent from women's colleges and 20 percent from coeducational institutions had had a queer sexual relationship.[13]

Freda's and Alice's parents sent them to Higbee's School for Young Ladies unconcerned with cross-dressed dance partners or Boston marriages. They fully expected their daughters to marry men after graduation. Alice was a distinguished student from a prominent family.

They won medals for their accomplishments in music and mathematics (although one of the psychiatrists who examined Alice insisted that they were "a slow pupil at school"). Newspapers identified Alice's father, George, as a "wealthy and honored citizen," a senior partner of a furniture company and brother to a "millionaire furniture manufacturer of Cincinnati." Freda's family was more tenuously middle-class; her father, Tom Ward, had been a machinist and now made his living by "planting and merchandizing" in Gold Dust.[14]

Freda's family responded to the discovery of Alice's love letters with fury but not with violence. They already knew that Alice and Freda hugged and kissed each other, because they had either seen or heard about it. Had Freda carried on an affair with an African American man, however, the response would likely have been assault, not an irate letter from Ada Volkmar. By the 1890s, reactions to sex across the color line were far more intense (and, often, vicious) than the disdain that met same-sex or queer relationships.

During the early days of Reconstruction (1865–1877), several Southern states, with new, Republican legislatures, repealed laws against interracial marriage. (Tennessee did not.) Once white-supremacist legislators succeeded in using terror and disenfranchisement to return the South to nearly all-white rule, these states reinstated their "anti-miscegenation" laws. Even mixed-race couples who married during Reconstruction in states that had briefly legalized interracial marriage faced the possibility of arrest. Western states like Oregon and Nevada added Chinese people (or, as California's law stipulated, persons with "Mongolian" blood) to their interracial marriage bans. By 1900, most U.S. states, including Indiana, Delaware, every Southern state, and most of the Mountain West, banned interracial marriage.[15]

That antipathy was pervasive. Newspapers in Memphis documented 81 murders of white women by white husbands and lovers in 1892, yet the papers more often portrayed unrelated Black men as the most lethal threats to white women's safety. They ran stories of white men like

Richard L. Johnson, who died defending his "charming daughter" from "the brutal blacks" who assaulted them. Time and again, whites across the South made allegations of attempted rape or rape against Black men who had achieved a modicum of economic or political power. Between 1882 and 1929, white mobs tortured and murdered more than 3,000 Americans of African descent accused or convicted of a crime.[16]

Just two months after Alice killed Freda, in March 1892, white men murdered three Black men whose store, the People's Grocery, competed with white-owned businesses. Judge Julius DuBose, who presided in this case as he did in Alice Mitchell's trial, believed that Black people were conspiring to incite violence in reaction to the murders and urged white Memphians to take up arms. Ida B. Wells was still a young woman at the time, a journalist who wrote for Memphis's Black newspaper, the *Free Speech*. Tommie Moss, one of the men lynched by the white mob, was her close friend.[17]

The deaths of Moss and two other Black men at the hands of a white mob inspired Wells to write one of the most incendiary editorials ever printed in the United States. Wells researched the circumstances surrounding the lynching of Black people and turned up multiple instances in which Black men accused of rape had been in consensual relationships with white women. Wells concluded that white families sometimes used rape allegations against Black men to allay gossip about what would otherwise constitute white women's scandalous sexual behaviors. As she wrote in an editorial printed on May 21, 1892, in the *Free Speech*, "If white men are not careful . . . a conclusion will then be reached which will be very damaging to the moral reputation of their women." She then left Memphis for a three-week trip to Philadelphia and New York City, where she had plans to meet with leading figures in the movement for African American civil rights.[18]

Wells never returned to Memphis, lifelong exile from her home city the price for daring to impugn the sexual reputations of Southern white women. Soon after her departure, a white mob ransacked the offices of the *Free Speech* and threatened to attack anyone who attempted to publish the paper again. Her former neighbors in Memphis sent word that white men were surveilling her home and threatening, she wrote, "to kill me on sight." Wells persisted, writing a series of essays about lynching for Black newspapers in the North, which she compiled into a pamphlet, *Southern Horrors* (1892). Lynchings of Black men for alleged rape, she argued, reflected not actual violence against women but the toxic sexual double standard of Southern "chivalry." Southern white men defend white women's "honor," Wells wrote, while doing nothing to prevent or hold anyone accountable for the rapes of Black women and girls. Racism, not sexual violence, thus motivated the vigilantes who attacked Tommie Moss and other Black victims of lynching.[19]

The white women of Memphis, meanwhile, were appalled by the murder of Freda Ward, one of their own, and clamored for justice. Alongside reports about Freda's murder, newspapers carried cautionary tales of young women whose boarding school or rooming house infatuations turned into dangerously passionate attachments. This was a dramatic departure from what had, until then, been presented as benign schoolgirl crushes. Financially secure white families expected women in their families to marry well, or, at the very least, cultivate domestic spinsterhood in the home of a married relative. They would reside among white people, socialize with members of their social class, and remain sexually virtuous. Now, however, the parents of such ladies had reason for concern.[20]

George Mitchell had the means to hire three attorneys to defend his daughter. They convinced the judge to forestall prosecution for murder until an inquest could determine if Alice was mentally competent to stand trial. That July, five months after the murder of Freda Ward, white Memphians packed the Shelby County Courthouse, where Judge DuBose presided over hearings to determine whether Alice Mitchell suffered from "present insanity."[21]

To prove that Alice was not competent to stand trial, the defense called on experts who connected Alice's erotic and gendered desires to a disordered mental state. F. L. Sim, an infectious-disease specialist at Memphis Hospital Medical College, explained that Alice's mental illness was hereditary. It had been passed down from their mother, who had experienced "puerperal insanity," today known as postpartum depression or psychosis, which had required a two-month hospitalization after the birth of her first child. The infant died soon after birth, and Mrs. Mitchell's "mind became unbalanced by the news," prompting a "mental aberration." Sim also cited the claim that masturbation could cause insanity, an idea that dated back at least as far as the physiology lectures of Sylvester Graham in the 1830s and 1840s. He speculated that "self-abuse or excessive sexual indulgence" would certainly have weakened Alice's nervous system. Another physician consulted for the insanity inquiry concluded that Alice suffered from an "unnatural and perverted passion" and, at the time of the murder, was afflicted by "hysterical mania."[22]

For some experts, it was Alice's stated interest in marrying Freda that proved their insanity. Distinguishing criminality from mental illness, these commentators explained that the presence of sexual depravity did not necessarily indicate insanity. Instead, Alice's confidence that they could marry Freda proved that Alice did not comprehend the mechanics of sexual intercourse: as the Medical Superintendent of the Central Hospital for the Insane of the State of Tennessee explained, the planned nuptials provided "evidence either of a gross delusion or the conception of a person imbecile or of a child" who lacked an understanding of "the connubial state" within marriage. The superintendent's statement erased the possibility of lesbian or queer desire, defining sex as *only* male-female vaginal intercourse.[23]

One physician concluded that Alice suffered from "erotomania," an aggressive female sexuality that these medical experts associated with darker-skinned people and sex workers. His statement reflected an emerging science of sexuality that drew from anthropologists' observations of "primitive" peoples in Africa and the Pacific Islands. Evolutionary theories about the progress of civilization placed Anglo-Saxons at the peak of racial maturity and sexual civility. American sexologists viewed their own presumptive gender norms—of feminine women and masculine men—as evidence of the triumph of a superior American culture over that of the Native peoples who originally populated those lands. A third-sex person such as We'wha symbolized a vanishing, inferior past.[24]

Sexological studies portrayed "savage" women as both physiologically distinct and threateningly sexual. F. E. Daniel, a physician in Austin, Texas, recommended "asexualizing" criminals because, he argued, "perversion" was not only hereditary but more common among "the lower classes, especially negroes." It's not certain how many Black women were subjected to clitorectomies in U.S. prisons or asylums. What's clear is that when physicians associated Black women with larger than average clitorises (and thus with intense sexual desires), they gave scientific authority to longstanding racist stereotypes.[25]

This logic led sexologists to conclude that queer desire was proof of a primitive sexuality. Dr. P. M. Wise at the Willard Asylum for the Insane in New York circulated a case study about one person whose queerness and gender nonconformity were especially well documented. Lucy Ann Lobdell wrote a memoir, *The Female Hunter*, in 1855, but they later dressed as a man, pursued men's labor, and sought relationships with women as a person named Joseph Lobdell. Wise attributed Lobdell's sexual aggression to an enlarged clitoris. In "A Case of Sexual Perversion" (1883), he described Lobdell as a "Lesbian," the first time an American publication used that word to describe a woman who sexually desired women. Such intense, atavistic sexual desires were out of place in a person such as Alice. By virtue of Alice's race and class status, their sexuality and gender nonconformity disrupted the South's social order. Alice was, to their contemporaries, an elite white woman displaying the sexual passion that medical elites believed was more often found among "savage" women and sex workers.[26]

An indication of Alice's supposed savagery was their "bisexuality," a newer term that connoted the presence of both male and female sexual characteristics. The American physician James G. Kiernan, Secretary of the Chicago Academy of Medicine and widely considered an expert on sexual science, explained in 1888 that bisexuality remained in some people as an evolutionary vestige from more primitive stages of development; the more civilized a group of people, the more they expressed distinct male/female gender differences and different-sex sexual attractions. Kiernan and others classified Native American, African, and lower-class women as hypersexual, a trait these scientists, like Wise, associated with an exceptionally large clitoris. They adopted the term "female inverts" for people like Alice (and Lobdell) and diagnosed both inverts and sex workers with degenerative nymphomania. Such people were more likely to masturbate, commit crimes, and go insane.[27]

Many contemporary theories about the psychology of queer desire and gender variance originated in Germany. The German lawyer Karl Heinrich Ulrichs coined the term "uranism" to describe a "contrary" sex drive in 1864. Ten years earlier he had been forced to resign a civil-service job after his supervisors learned that he had engaged in homosexual behavior. Ulrichs set out to prove that his erotic interest in men was natural, innate, and benign. "Urnings," he wrote, were people of an intermediate, third sex, their male bodies and female psyches leading them to desire same-gendered people. In an era when Germany and Britain enforced their anti-sodomy laws, Ulrichs and other physician-reformers explained that "contrary sexual feeling" was not criminal but natural. These traits were an individual inheritance, passed down through generations. Sexologists in the United States adapted ideas about "urnings," but when American medical journals discussed Alice Mitchell as an exemplar of sexual inversion or "urning," they did so to prove that Alice was a pervert.[28]

Lawyers in the Mitchell insanity trial could draw upon new theories about "normal" psychology—and the perverse manifestations of degeneracy. German physician Richard von Krafft-Ebing based his hugely influential book, *Psychopathia Sexualis*, on interviews with hundreds of clients from his private practice and of inmates in asylums. He concluded that people with underdeveloped nervous systems had uncontrollable sexual appetites. The book, which went through at least twelve editions following its initial publication in 1877, detailed perversions of "normal" sexuality, from sadism and fetishism to homosexuality. In his later years, Krafft-Ebing conceded that he had been in error when he labeled contrary sexual feeling a psychic degeneracy; same-sex desire, he now believed, was compatible with mental health. American psychiatry, still, did not agree.[29]

The defense lawyers for Alice Mitchell constructed their case for insanity by characterizing Alice as a person who had suffered throughout their life from a distorted gender identity, even if they didn't use those terms. As a young child, the lawyers explained in an account that appeared in a local paper and a medical journal, Alice "was fond of climbing" and preferred to spend time with their brother rather than their sisters. Men of Alice's cohort, the experts opined, recognized Alice's psychological impairment as the reason Alice turned them down: "[Alice] was regarded as mentally wrong by young men toward whom [they] had thus acted." Charles Mundinger knew Alice's family well and had always found Alice peculiar—especially after Alice "failed to pay as much attention to him as he expected." Lillie Johnson's brother, James, testified that when he asked Alice to dance with him, Alice refused; "[they] seemed to care nothing about young men."[30]

William Volkmar, by contrast, wanted Alice convicted of the murder of his sister-in-law. He said that Alice "never impressed him as being a crazy person" and, while "tomboyish," flirted relentlessly with men. This account was an outlier. It may have reflected Volkmar's personal motives more than a faithful recollection of Alice's behavior. Sexual interest in men would disprove the defense's insanity case and leave Alice vulnerable to murder charges. Other witnesses testified that Alice often purchased cigarettes, more proof of Alice's sexual or gender deviance; respectable, feminine women did not smoke, at least not in public, until the 1920s. Alice's "fondness for outdoor sports," their attorneys emphasized, was another consequence of "an unusual mind."[31]

It was thus Alice's notion that they could become Alvin, more than their presumably premeditated killing of Freda, that led an all-male jury to declare them insane. Alice and Freda's relationship had not led anyone to arrest or otherwise castigate them for sexual deviance, but Alice's criminal behavior ended up giving a boost to medical theories that stigmatized queer people. In the ensuing decades, those theories provided justifications for laws and policing strategies predicated on the idea that sexual "deviants" were also mentally unstable. The same physician who had ordered Alice's mother confined to an asylum after the death of her first child in St. Louis thirty years earlier also weighed in about the connections between sexuality and mental health. He wrote that the "unnatural affection existing between Alice Mitchell and Freda Ward" confirmed that Alice was "what is known in forensic medicine as a *sexual pervert*."[32]

On July 30, 1892, the jury declared Alice insane and remanded them to the care of an asylum in Bolivar, Tennessee. Before Alice left Memphis, they stopped at the cemetery, leaving flowers on Freda's grave. Newspapers now depicted Alice as consummately feminine, domesticated by their incarceration, playing the French harp from the asylum balcony.[33]

Alice lived only six years at Bolivar. They died there of tuberculosis in 1898, never having set foot outside the institution's grounds since their confinement. More than three decades later, one of Alice's attorneys provided a more sensational, if possibly true, cause of death: suicide by jumping into the Bolivar water tower.[34]

Had Alice's life worked out otherwise—if they had never found their father's knife or reached the mental health crisis that led them to commit murder—they would have entered adulthood in a world full of increasing danger but also increasing possibilities for trans and gender-nonconforming people. Some women and transmen who desired intimate relationships with women had started to take on what would many decades later be called "butch-femme" roles. In contrast to the Boston marriage, which presented a genteel, asexual image to the public, the "mannish" lesbian was a woman who did not conform to gender expectations and was assertively interested in sex with other women. Their masculine qualities became case studies of "inversion" for sexologists who interpreted homosexuality as a mismatch of gender identity and sexual desire. These lesbians renounced heterosexual expectations of their assigned sex or social station.[35]

Or Alice might have slipped out of her parents' house one night, boarded that steamship north from Memphis, and done what a truly unknowable number of people did: show up in a new town or city, where no one knew them, and introduce themselves, at last, as a man, hoping someday to marry and settle down. Towns, smaller cities, and even rural areas seem to have been particularly appealing places for transmen to reinvent themselves in the late nineteenth and early twentieth centuries. Perhaps Alice might have gravitated toward the androgynous style popular among middle-class and wealthier lesbians. Parodied in the press as unsexed women with overly active brains and irrational anger about their disenfranchisement, this "New" American woman had a solid education and the gall to defy expectations for delicacy or dependency.[36]

These possibilities had all been foreclosed for Alice, but Alice's case lived on. British sexologist Havelock Ellis discussed Alice Mitchell in the second volume of his famous book, *Studies in the Psychology of Sex*, entitled *Sexual Inversion* (1901). Alice was, Ellis wrote, "a typical invert of a very pronounced kind," and he described them as the prototype (in gender presentation, not in murderousness) of the masculine lesbian. He insisted that sexual desire and gender identity were inborn, or congenital, rather than traits acquired from bad habits like compulsive masturbation. Another physician studying the case wondered whether the theory of sexual inversion exculpated Alice Mitchell for the murder of Freda Ward: If Alice's desire for Freda reflected a "sexual condition" rather than a perpetually disordered mind, then they deserved the same clemency that judges and juries afforded to male defendants in heterosexual love murders who claimed temporary insanity. These theorists of sexual inversion insisted that homosexuality was a special but harmless trait, like synesthesia, and thus not a vice or weakness of character. Ellis had hoped to remove stigma from male and female homosexuality, but his concept of inversion helped popularize the argument that feminism reflected the interests of lesbians and mannish women.[37]

Ellis took issue with Krafft-Ebing's theory that homosexuality could be inherited or acquired, and he also disputed Sigmund Freud's argument that Eros's impulses resided within the subconscious. Freud, the founder of psychoanalysis, postulated that sexual "degeneracy" lurked within even the most educated, elite individuals from "good" families. All people, he explained, contained a "polymorphously perverse" sexuality in infancy, by which he meant that a person's innate sexuality had no predetermined object. Instead, children's experiences of maternal affection or rejection determined whether they would mature into well-adjusted heterosexual adults or develop sexual "neuroses." Freud theorized, for instance, that boys who were too attached to their mothers would identify too closely with feminine qualities and, like their mothers (presumably), seek male rather than female sexual partners. Heterosexual desire should be the result of an individual's subconscious resolution of adolescent bisexuality; homosexuals' psychological condition, in this theory, remained developmentally stunted. Freud and his colleagues argued for psychoanalysis, or talk therapy, rather than any surgical or endocrinological interventions, as the only way to help their patients become psychosexually mature.[38]

Theories abounded. The psychiatrist James Kiernan explained bisexuality to his professional colleagues as one of the consequences of "normal" women falling under the persuasion of the masculine women leading the suffrage movement. Sexologists, he wrote in 1914, do not "think every suffragette an invert," but "the very fact that women in general of today are more and more deeply invading man's sphere" was "indicative of a certain impelling force [sexual inversion] within them."[39]

Many of the leaders and rank-and-file of the suffrage movement in fact had intimate relationships with women, wore gender-nonconforming clothes or hairstyles, or otherwise rejected conventional femininity and heterosexuality. As the pressures of winning the right to vote intensified, movement leaders urged all suffrage women to conform to conventional expectations for their gender. Women who had led more openly gender-nonconforming or queer lives began to hide these aspects of themselves. They certainly faced relentless hostility from the broader public. J. W. Meagher, a physician, explained in 1929, "The driving force in many agitators and militant women . . . is often an unsatisfied sex impulse, with a homosexual aim." Importantly, Meagher was a supporter of "companionate marriage," an idea popular in the 1920s that emphasized the sexual pleasures of heterosexual love. The new configuration of identities treated same-sex desires as a threat to male-female relationships.[40]

What to do with the sexual pervert—lock them away, like Alice? Assume that insanity is hereditary and sterilize people such as Alice so that they would not give birth to anyone as "unfit" as they were? Educate other young people about the evils of lesbianism? Cleanse American bookstores and libraries of the sorts of salacious materials that might awaken depraved impulses in an impressionable mind? Or blame someone else—someone darker skinned, or poorer, or more marginal—for corrupting "American" morals? Nothing was off the table.

Chapter 9

Obscene and Immoral

In December 1872, a thirty-year-old man named Anthony Comstock boarded a train bound for the nation's capital with a suitcase full of porn. His dossier was a catalog of the images and texts that

Anthony Comstock devoted his adult life to battling obscenity. His endless crusade against all sexual subject matter is the subject of this satirical 1906 cartoon, "St. Anthony Comstock, the Village Nuisance," by L. M. Glackens, which portrays Comstock as a monk who cannot bear to undress himself for a bath and physically recoils from depictions of the female body. As suggested by the illustration in the bottom right, which shows a naked Comstock confronting the fires of hell, many Americans strongly rejected his views.

he believed proved the necessity of stronger federal anti-obscenity measures. Several states already had anti-obscenity laws on the books when Comstock, a devout Protestant, launched his pornographic road show, but federal laws were weak. The Tariff Act of 1842 permitted customs officials to seize "obscene or immoral" prints and pictures at the border but did nothing about interstate commerce. The anti-obscenity movement that Comstock led for fifty years was something entirely different: an unprecedented call for the federal government to regulate erotica produced and circulated within the United States.[1]

Comstock's train ride to Washington ended in victory. In 1873 Congress passed the "Act for the Suppression of Trade in, and Circulation of Obscene Literature and Articles of Immoral Use," soon known colloquially as the Comstock Act. The law prohibited sending "obscene, lewd, or lascivious" items through the U.S. mail. It contained the broadest definition yet of the kinds of materials that could be banned and seized by inspectors, including "any obscene book, pamphlet, paper, writing advertisement, circular, print, picture, drawing or other representation, figure, or image on or of paper or other material, or any cast, instrument, or other article of an immoral nature." Dildos and paintings of classical nudes hanging in art galleries were comparably forbidden. The law defined both pornography and physiological education guides as equally obscene. These offenses were misdemeanors, but a conviction could carry a sentence of six months of hard labor or a fine of $100 to $2,000.[2]

Comstock's definition of obscenity included not only erotica (broadly defined) but contraception and abortion too. The law banned from the U.S. mail "any drug or medicine, or any article whatever, for the prevention of conception, or for causing unlawful abortion" and made it illegal to write, print, or advertise "when, where, how, or of whom, or by what means" one could obtain them. It empowered government agents to search out and destroy condoms, pamphlets about contraception, or tonics to induce miscarriage, and to prosecute abortionists and sex educators. Comstock associated contraceptive devices and abortifacients with prostitution: all "decent" women would have sex only within marriage, and thus would have no reason to resort to measures more often found on the fringes of society, the demimonde of prostitutes, gamblers, and thieves. Prudish, sanctimonious, and cruel, Comstock succeeded in convincing the federal government to impose his values on all Americans' sexual behavior and speech.

Yet twenty years later, Comstock stormed out of the Egyptian Theater on Cairo Street, a destination at the 1893 World's Columbian Exposition in Chicago, appalled by what he considered an obscene performance that he was unable to shut down. Cairo Street was located on the "Midway Plaisance," a mile-long "bazaar of all nations" that boasted exhibits of "foreign" cultures as well as popular entertainments. Its reconstruction of an Egyptian thoroughfare attracted nearly as much excitement as the gigantic Ferris wheel nearby. Tourists came to look at men wearing turbans, fezzes, and tunics and lounging in front of stores.[3]

The Egyptian Theater on Cairo Street became especially famous (infamous, to some). The main show featured dancers named Fahrina and Nebowa, among a dozen other women wearing modest if flowing dresses, who tucked their pelvises and circled their hips as a few men accompanied them on castanets, tambourines, and flutes. Their performance was, according to a Chicago reporter, "weird and indescribable." In one act, a performer placed two champagne glasses on her bare midriff, contracting her abdominal muscles so precisely that the glasses clinked. Lifted skirts revealed a leg clothed in a loose pant, not bare, but the suggestion of nudity was enough to titillate. Middle Eastern women had a longstanding association in the American imagination with nonmonogamous, "exotic" sexuality; at the fair, they performed not just a dance but an erotic fantasy. Promoters advertised the dancers' "hootchy-kootchy" or "cootch" dance, also known as the *danse du ventre*, and soon it was the talk of both the fair and the national press.[4]

The dancers' demonstration of female sensuality, and the enjoyment of that display by men and women alike, encapsulated for many white Americans the essence of what made something "foreign" or "un-Christian." Anthony Comstock watched the dance not with fascination but in apparent horror. A sex radical and mystic named Ida Craddock, meanwhile, was enraptured. Their lives would soon intersect.

Comstock targeted people who sold contraceptives, provided abortions, and wrote about sexual health. He went after free lovers too. One of the least popular yet most influential figures in this book's history, Comstock was regularly ridiculed. A black market for contraceptives evaded the law's reach. Yet Comstock had an unquestioned influence over the way Americans spoke about, wrote about, and legislated sex. The people who defied him, including Craddock and birth-control reformer Margaret Sanger, often paid a steep price, but their insistence on the necessity of candor—its erotically liberating and even life-saving power—is one of his legacies.

Comstock was right about one thing: erotica was everywhere. Print editions of *Fanny Hill* and its saucy illustrations were only the start. Since the 1830s, advances in the vulcanization of rubber had enabled the mass production of condoms, cervical caps, dildos, and other sex toys. Improvements in printing and in mail delivery made it possible for rural residents to order contraceptive devices from circulars as niche as the *Grand Fancy Bijou Catalogue of the Sporting Man's Emporium*. The invention of photography soon created new categories of erotic images. Stereoscopes held two copies of an image at a fixed distance from the viewer, rendering a kind of three-dimensional visual experience. Such images often depicted famous buildings from European capitals, but many others showed sexual scenes. Timothy Osborn, a miner, discovered that a night out in Stockton, California, in the early 1850s included the opportunity to pay 2 cents to a Frenchman offering "*a vue de Paris.*" The view turned out to be "naked men and women in the *very act.*" Osborn noted in his diary that he had seen "*a very good view of Paris.*"[5]

Comstock had been attempting to sanctify his life by strenuously following God's laws. He believed that what one read or viewed had an immediate effect on one's soul. (How, precisely, he managed to spend his career looking at and reading the very materials he considered too dangerous to be in the public's hands was not something he addressed in public statements or writing.) "Good reading," he explained, "refines, elevates, ennobles, and stimulates the ambition to lofty purposes." Parents, teachers, and pastors needed to wake up to the pervasive threat of "*Evil Reading*," which controlled young people's minds and perverted their desires.[6]

His experiences as a soldier in the Union Army inspired him to launch a personal war against filth. Erotica was ubiquitous among his fellow soldiers, yet no one else seemed sufficiently concerned about the immoral items that soldiers and officers shared. After the war, Comstock settled in New York City, the center of American commercial erotica production and sale. From his rented room on Pearl Street in Lower Manhattan, he inventoried the brothels, saloons, dance houses, and gambling dens that operated nearby. Many booksellers and printers had successfully paid off police officers to protect their goods from seizure in the past, but rampant corruption was no match for Comstock's persistent intrusions.[7]

Business titans on the board of the Young Men's Christian Association (YMCA) admired Comstock's moxie. They paid him $100 a month, and individual donations added up to a salary of about $3,000 per year (approximately $75,000 in 2024). It was enough to allow him to fight vice full-time.[8]

After passage of the Comstock Act in 1873, the postmaster general appointed Comstock to be the Special Agent of the United States Post Office Department, responsible for overseeing the act's enforcement. When the Post Office hired only four additional inspectors, Comstock looked to other agencies for help. In his home state of New York, the legislature deputized members of the New York Society for the Suppression of Vice (NYSSV), an offshoot of the YMCA, to confiscate "obscene" materials.[9]

Comstock kept meticulous records of his arrests and raids. He proudly noted that he and his agents had destroyed more than 202,000 "pictures and photographs" by the end of 1876. During the same period, they seized 21,000 pounds of books. Comstock instigated the arrests of well-regarded photographers who printed erotic images or exhibited them through stereoscopes. New state-level anti-obscenity regulations were even more severe; "little Comstock laws" in thirty states banned or criminalized the sale, distribution, and possession of sexual materials. More than three-quarters of the arrests by 1900 were for violations of these state laws.[10]

Comstock and his agents did not wait for citizen complaints to root out obscenity. They sent decoy letters requesting sexually explicit materials and used false names to solicit contraceptive or abortion-related services, arguing in court (with imperfect success) that their deceptive methods nevertheless supported a conviction. They went undercover in brothels and other "vice resorts," sipping wine and playing poker until a formal solicitation justified an arrest. It was Comstock's belief that without the "vice" trades, the market for contraception would dry up.[11]

Comstock famously disguised his identity to implicate a well-known abortion provider, midwife, and contraception purveyor who went by the name of Madame Restell and whose real name was Ann Trow Summers Lohman (1811–1878). Restell was a veteran criminal defendant by the time Comstock set his sights on her in the 1870s. She had been charged with a misdemeanor in 1847 for the death of a fetus after performing an abortion on a woman whose pregnancy was not yet "quick." Restell was found guilty and spent a year in the bleak prison on Blackwell's Island, which was also the site of an almshouse and the New York Lunatic Asylum. Upon release, she almost immediately resumed her lucrative mail-order business, selling contraceptives and abortifacients, and reopened her lying-in hospital, where she delivered babies. She had a net worth in the millions and lived in a mansion on East Fifty-Second Street in Manhattan. All could agree that Restell was ubiquitous. Her advertisements appeared—with almost no innuendo—in newspapers and magazines. She rode through New York City in a lavish carriage, wearing "silks, satins, velvets, furs, and diamonds," generating controversy based on both her occupation and her refusal to apologize for it.[12]

Critics sneered that Restell's wealth derived from the outrageous price of silence. Perhaps wealthy clients were desperate enough to keep their own or their family's contraceptive emergencies out of the public eye that they paid Restell exorbitant fees. In the 1840s, the *National Police Gazette* and other local papers stepped up their criticism of Restell and her customers. These publications celebrated male sexual license but denigrated any woman who acquiesced to "an invasion of the course of nature."[13]

Restell provided abortion care amid a national movement to ban it. In 1857, the recently established American Medical Association (AMA) started a decades-long campaign to outlaw abortion at every stage of pregnancy. That effort reflected the moralism of some of the AMA's leaders as well as the organization's broader aim of replacing midwives with physicians in the care of pregnant and laboring patients. Prominent physicians such as Horatio Storer contravened centuries of common wisdom (and common law), which had marked quickening as the beginning of fetal life. Storer, instead, defined abortion at any stage of pregnancy as murder. The AMA demanded that only male doctors should diagnose a pregnancy—and never intervene to end one. Between 1880 and 1930, abortion was criminalized throughout all the individual states, often with exceptions only to save the life of the pregnant person.[14]

In the late 1870s, Comstock arrived at Restell's home and, without giving a name, claimed to be in search of medicine to help a woman end a pregnancy. Restell sold him two medications (a tonic and a pill) that, if taken according to her instructions, would likely cause a miscarriage. Comstock returned about a week later, still not identifying himself, and professed to now be in search of a "preventative" for his female friend. This time, Restell sold him a powder, instructing him to mix it into a contraceptive douche that the woman could inject deep within her vagina immediately after sexual intercourse. Local police accompanied the man when he returned for a third visit four days later, carrying a warrant to search her home. Only then did Restell recognize the man as Comstock. The officers walked out with armloads of contraceptive powders, condoms, syringes, written instructions, and pills.[15]

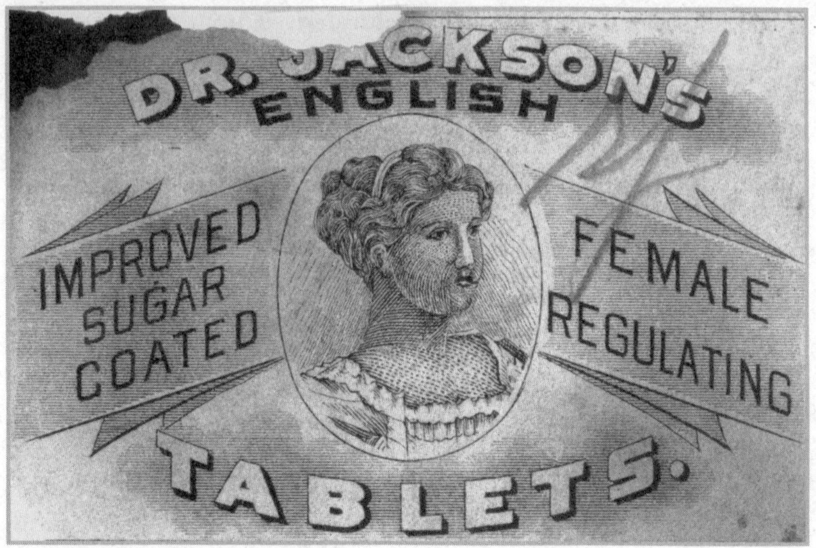

Purveyors of contraceptives and abortifacients, like Madame Restell (a pseudonym for Ann Trow Lohman), who operated out of New York City, advertised products like this box of "female regulating tablets" in newspapers and magazines. Dr. Jackson's Improved Sugar Coated English Tablets, 1880–1900, lithograph trade card, Bella C. Landauer Collection of Business and Advertising Ephemera, 96539d, New-York Historical Society.

After her arrest, Restell was held for several weeks in the Tombs, a detention center in Manhattan, until her lawyer pressured the police judge to accept an exorbitant $10,000 bail. A grand jury indicted Restell for selling and advertising items "for the prevention of conception," she was arraigned, and a trial date was set. Restell knew what awaited her on Blackwell's Island if she was found guilty. Rather than face another conviction, she undressed and climbed into her bathtub, where she slit her own throat. Restell was one of the first people, but not the last, who chose death over Comstock's persistent harassment.[16]

The scope of what Comstock considered "obscene" kept expanding, exceeding all reasonable limits. He and his agents seized postcards sold on the Bowery showing photographs of naked women, dime-store novels with steamy innuendo, and copies of Leo Tolstoy's *Kreutzer Sonata* (1889), which discussed prostitution. They targeted art schools in Philadelphia that employed living models and declared war on art high and low that featured nude female bodies. Comstock confiscated and destroyed tens of thousands of books, sexually explicit photographs and photograph negatives, sheet music, "rubber goods," advertising circulars, playing cards, stereotype plates, account books, and private letters, not to mention trick cigar cases that hid photographs of naked women and liquor bottles shaped like a penis and testicles.[17]

Only a small fraction of the cases Comstock brought were against providers of contraception and abortion services, and even fewer of those prosecutions ended in conviction. But he chose his targets strategically, arresting women with prominent businesses and attempting to silence them. Sarah Chase, a successful contraceptive entrepreneur and homeopathic physician, was arrested five times between 1878 and 1900 for distributing printed information about sex and contraceptive devices, such as a syringe that she said was intended as a hygienic aid, not a means of inducing abortion. Juries acquitted Chase all but once, when she received a ten-year sentence, for an abortion she performed that ended in the woman's death. Comstock brought most of his cases against individuals who printed, sold, or displayed anything that he considered obscene, but jurors and judges were skeptical of his methods and even less inclined to prosecute men and women for private sexual behaviors.[18]

The law was more effective in encouraging euphemism and omission. Dr. Edward Bliss Foote removed a discussion of condoms and womb veils from his marital guide after his 1874 conviction and fine. And Chase was unable to continue publication of her health journal, *The Physiologist and Family Physician*, after it was briefly banned from the U.S. mail in 1881.[19]

Raids on druggists and local proprietors frustrated people's efforts to access contraceptives, but clearly Americans found other ways. By 1900, the national fertility rate of white American women was 3.54 births, half of what it had been one hundred years prior. The decline was especially pronounced among urban, native-born, middle-class women whose husbands were employed in the professions or business.

One study in 1910 found that two-thirds of U.S. families did not have more than two children.[20]

Yet white women were prominent among the hundreds of thousands of volunteers who joined Comstock as "purity crusaders." These activists wanted to bring down the double standard—not by liberating women to enjoy the opportunities for sexual self-expression available to men, but by raising men to middle-class white women's assumed level of sexual decorum. Both prostitution and obscenity stood in the way of those goals. Purity crusaders likewise agreed with Comstock about the corrupting effects of "impure" images and words. While most of these activists were native-born white women, the middle-class members of African American women's clubs similarly resolved to discourage the presence of any "obscene literature" or uncouth songs in Black homes.[21]

Legions of Protestant women affiliated with the Woman's Christian Temperance Union (WCTU) argued that voluntary efforts—purity pledges, industry codes, and library committees—might rid the nation of sexual "filth" as effectively as any government action. Founded in 1872, the WCTU originally focused exclusively on ending the sale and consumption of alcohol. Under the leadership of Frances Willard, from 1879 to 1898 the WCTU grew into a formidable national organization with semi-independent state chapters. The WCTU also ventured into other causes that reflected a Protestant vision of moral purity. Willard and like-minded activists believed that external forces pushed some women into prostitution rather than it being entirely a matter of sin. They held men to account by promoting a "White Life for Two," which encouraged men to sign pledges to remain virgins until marriage and abstain from visiting sex workers.[22]

Unlike Comstock, the women of the WCTU did not simply destroy "obscene" literature but created "pure" alternatives. They established "purity libraries" purged of such salacious content as *Jane Eyre* and periodicals with advertisements that featured sexualized images of women. Their own magazine, *The Young Crusader,* aimed instead to provide wholesome content to impressionable younger readers. Over time, the WCTU's leadership came to see the women who participated in salacious cultural productions as victims of patriarchal degradation rather than purveyors of smut. They remained opposed to any public display of female nudity.[23]

Purity crusaders fought an uphill battle. No matter how many "rubber goods" Comstock and his agents confiscated, sex entrepreneurs found new outlets on a black market of unregulated, obliquely described contraceptives and sex toys. Proprietors small and large renamed condoms "capotes" and variously called pessaries "uterine elevators," ladies' shields, protectors, womb supporters, and "married women's friends." Some euphemisms pre-dated the Comstock Act, but by the 1870s, advertisements for contraceptives obscured the products' original purposes. Retailers mentioned only the vague benefits of "protection" and safety, noting that their goods provided "reliability" for married women. Even Comstock's name became a term for contraceptives; stores and circulars advertised postcoital douches as "Comstock syringes."[24]

The Egyptian women's performance at the 1893 World's Columbian Exposition seemed almost designed to provoke Comstock. In late July, he exited the Cairo Street theater full of righteous outrage. One member of his entourage pronounced that they had "been to the mouth of hell to-day." Comstock's subsequent decision to reenact the dance for a reporter, his rotund form hardly capturing the pelvic muscle flexions that belly dancing involved, provoked mirth rather than sympathetic outrage.[25]

Despite Comstock's protests, the fair's organizers refused to shut down the *danse du ventre*. Comstock had three "heathen" dancers arrested and fined when they came to New York City later that year to perform their "obscene & indecent exhibition." There was little else he could do, as the dance became a national sensation.[26]

If Comstock's anger was to be expected, few could have foreseen the rousing defense of the dance by an obscure, brilliant, and unconventional thinker named Ida Craddock. She was a free-love mystic and independent scholar who spent years as a "student of Phallic antiqui-

Ida Craddock (1857–1902) was a freethinker who applied to the University of Pennsylvania's graduate program in anthropology to study "phallic antiquities." Denied admission because she was a woman, Craddock instead patched together a living as an educator and marriage counselor. Committed to free speech and sexual candor, she was enthralled by the danse du ventre *at the 1893 World's Columbian Exposition in Chicago. She was hounded by Anthony Comstock to the point of suicide.*

ties." Craddock presented her research on phallic symbols in ancient religions to liberals and freethinkers in her hometown of Philadelphia who dared give her the podium; her topic was an audacious one for a female speaker. Hoping to continue her studies at the University of Pennsylvania, in 1882 she passed the grueling, four-day entrance examinations. Members of the university's board of trustees debated whether to admit her as their first female student, ultimately deciding against it. Seemingly undeterred, she drafted a book-length manuscript on the history of sex worship in which she argued that earlier cultures had worshiped male and female sexuality. In these initial years of academic anthropology, "primitive" religions were typically understood as inferior to Christianity or "Anglo-Saxon" cultures. Craddock instead found inspiration in ancient rituals that seemed to honor—rather than shame—women for their erotic power.[27]

Craddock eked out a living teaching stenography at Girard College in Philadelphia, and as a secretary for the American Secular Union, an organization fiercely opposed to the very sort of evangelical Christianity that drove Comstock's crusade against sexual speech. Unlike some of the freethinkers she associated with, Craddock did not oppose religion per se but rather wanted to untether spirituality from rigid doctrines.

She also agreed with other women's rights activists of the time that organized religion too often provided the rationale for women's oppression. Liberal and reform-minded, Craddock celebrated the somatic pleasures of a liberated spirit.[28]

A small but vocal free-speech movement shared many of Craddock's goals. The married couple Angela Fiducia Tilton Heywood and Ezra Hervey Heywood became notorious in the 1870s and 1880s for their radical demands for sexual frankness. Angela, in particular, pushed the limits of sexual speech. In an 1889 issue of *The Word,* the newspaper Ezra edited, Angela wrote, "As a girl, I used to say, in myself, 'When I grow up I shall deal with men's penises, write books about them; I mean to and I will do it.'" She especially wanted to expand women's vocabulary about their bodies. There was a profusion of vernacular expressions for the word "penis," she explained, but women had hardly any for the vulva. This linguistic inequality, she argued, disadvantaged women when they engaged in sexual conversation with men.[29]

When *The Word* advertised "the Comstock syringe for Preventing Conception" in 1882, Comstock had Ezra arrested. A sympathetic judge guided the jury to a not-guilty verdict, but Ezra was arrested again in 1890, when he was sixty-one years old. This time, he was found guilty of obscenity for publishing a letter in which a mother described how she had explained the meaning of "fuck" to her twelve-year-old daughter. For that offense, Ezra spent two years performing hard labor at Charlestown State Prison while Angela raised their four children on her own. Ezra died within one year of his release.[30]

Craddock found support among free lovers, but her advice about sexual pleasure was radical even by their standards. She based her philosophy on what she described as her ecstatic communions with a spiritual husband, a fantasy or dreamlike figure with whom she experienced, she wrote, deeply fulfilling sex. "My husband is in the world beyond the grave," she explained, "and had been for many years previous to our union, which took place in October, 1892."[31]

Plenty of post–Civil War Americans believed in the possibility for communion with the dead. Seances and spirit mediums grew only more popular in the wake of the war's enormous toll. While many Americans comfortably combined spiritualism with Christianity, Craddock drew upon her research in "eastern" religions for her theology of spiritual eroticism. Some of these religions, she thought, offered esoteric guidance on how to attain spiritual liberation through the correct practice of male-female sexual intercourse. Although never technically married, Craddock presented herself as an expert on marital intimacy, including the wedding night, based on her encounters with her spiritual husband.[32]

The *danse du ventre* in the Egyptian Theater thrilled Craddock. In the pages of the *New York World*, she praised the dancers for enacting "the apotheosis of female passion" and self-control, their pelvic movements mirroring the undulations of a woman's body in the throes of sexual ecstasy. The dance, she explained, "trains the muscles of the woman in the endurance desirable in the wife." Speaking directly to the possibilities for women's erotic pleasure, Craddock described this sexually liberated woman as an ideal sexual partner for a man, prepared "not only for receiving, but also for conferring pleasure."[33]

Where Craddock witnessed spiritual communion, Comstock saw the road to hell. That road, Comstock and his supporters believed, followed a steady descent from civilized "Anglo-Saxon" Christians to the depravity of darker-skinned "heathen" people. Some scandalized onlookers compared the performance on Cairo Street to Native American dances and pagan rites. Associating non-Christian cultures with sexual immorality was part of a larger effort in the late nineteenth and early twentieth centuries to argue for the superiority of white or "Anglo-Saxon" people. For Comstock and many others, Christianity alone promoted sexual morality.[34]

Craddock became one of Comstock's prime targets in the decade after the fair. She went to prison in 1898 for mailing pamphlets that provided explicit instructions to husbands about how to satisfy their wives. Comstock had Craddock arrested again in August 1899 for mailing another one of her pamphlets. This time, the lawyer Clarence Darrow, a well-known defender of free speech, paid her bail bond of $500 and took on the case pro bono. Darrow brokered a plea deal that gave Craddock a three-month suspended sentence, but only after she agreed to incinerate all the pamphlets she wrote.[35]

Then, in February of 1902, Comstock and three of his deputies raided Craddock's tiny apartment on West Twenty-Third Street in Manhattan. They arrested her for selling her new sexual guide, *The Wedding Night*, to an undercover detective. A jury returned a guilty verdict after a brief deliberation.[36]

What was it that Craddock wrote that so offended Anthony Comstock? She sold pamphlets and offered marriage counseling to teach men and women "an Oriental method of ideal coition," intended to ensure the woman's sexual gratification while "rejuvenating the entire being of both husband and wife." The man would learn how to achieve "prolonged coition, from at least a half hour to an hour after entrance." She presented this advice in *The Wedding Night* and *Right Marital Living*, which she mailed to people who signed up for her $10 correspondence course. Her students completed a lengthy self-assessment. In her questionnaire for men, after inquiring into the person's sources of sexual information and physical health, Craddock asked about the frequency of sexual intercourse with a wife or mistress, its duration "(three minutes, ten minutes, a half hour, one hour, or what?)," and the details of orgasmic experience. "Have you ever gone right through the orgasm (the final thrill), without spending semen, and with a certain heightened enjoyment of the orgiastic thrill which is impossible if the semen be expended in the usual way?" Such frank questions about sexual behavior, along with queries about erections, masturbation, and foreplay, put Craddock decades ahead of her time.[37]

Craddock's attentiveness to sexual consent was also extraordinary. She asked male students, "Are you accustomed to demand, or even to respectfully request the privilege of coition without previous lovemaking?" Yet her blunt questionnaires revealed a contradiction in the ways that she and nearly all free lovers and radicals celebrated sexual knowledge. Even as she insisted on a woman's consent and mutual pleasure during heterosexual intercourse, she offered unsparing denigration of same-sex sexuality. As Craddock queried on her questionnaire, "Do you practise homo-sexuality (that is, unnatural vice with your own sex)?"[38]

In October 1902, the night before she was to be sentenced on federal charges, Craddock closed her apartment windows, sealed off the crevices beneath the door, and turned on the gas. She was forty-five years old. Her mother and a police officer found her body the next morning, along with a letter in which she explained that she could not endure another prison sentence. She dreamed, she wrote, of a world free from "Anthony Comstocks and corrupt judges."[39]

In the 1910s, radicals took to the streets to challenge legal restrictions on sexual speech and contraception. Emma Goldman, a Russian-born anarchist, explained in 1911 that "Sex is the source of life [and] where sex is missing[,] everything is missing." She viewed sexual freedom, including equal access to safe contraceptives, as critical to class struggle, a way for working-class women to control the number of mouths they had to feed.[40]

Margaret Sanger, a nurse, free lover, and, at the time, socialist, made the expansion of contraceptive access her life's work. Sanger and other countercultural "Bohemians" of the era argued that the constraints of heterosexual monogamy were politically, spiritually, and sexually toxic. "Sexual modernity" emerged in socialist periodicals such as the *Masses*, in street-corner speeches, in literature and art, and in the cacophonous conversation of cafés and bars. Making the world anew required not only the toppling of industrial captains but also the dismantling of the conventions of monogamy and patriarchy. Sex need not have anything to do with procreation, and marriage need not require monogamy. In line with many of the sexual moderns inhabiting Greenwich Village apartments, working in Provincetown theater companies, writing for socialist magazines, and experimenting with art and romance, Sanger considered women's sexual autonomy—and thus reliable contraception—to be the foundation of their liberation.[41]

Margaret Sanger (1879–1966), a nurse who found a community among Greenwich Village's free-love "Bohemians," became the face of the American birth-control movement after she was arrested for distributing her pamphlet "Family Limitation." She opened the country's first birth-control clinic in Brooklyn, one year before this photo was taken.

That vision directly challenged Comstock's limitations on sexual speech. In 1914, Comstock told journalist Gertrude Marvin that "there is a personal Devil sitting in a real Hell tempting young and innocent children to look at obscene pictures and books." Published in the *Masses*, Marvin's interview with Comstock set the latter up for derision. His ideas seemed increasingly out of touch. That same year, Sanger's magazine, *The Woman Rebel*, popularized a new term, "birth control," and challenged restrictions on information-sharing. Later that year, Sanger was arrested for printing "Family Limitation," a pamphlet offering the type of detailed contraceptive information she had thus far omitted from *The Woman Rebel*. She briefly fled the country (and spent her time learning about contraceptive clinics in northern Europe).[42]

Sanger audaciously defied anti-obscenity laws by opening a birth-control clinic in 1916 in Brownsville, a working-class Brooklyn neighborhood of mostly first- and second-generation Jewish and Italian families. For nine days, Sanger and her sister Ethel Byrne met with hundreds of women who waited for an appointment in queues that stretched around the block. When one of these patients turned out to be an undercover police officer, Sanger and her colleagues were arrested.[43]

Sanger lost her case on appeal in January 1918 but won a small victory when the appellate judge carved out an exception for contraceptive devices intended to prevent disease (in other words, condoms), if prescribed by a physician. Druggists ignored the fine print, and corner pharmacies and other shops soon offered a growing assortment of condoms for sale, no longer shrouded in euphemism. Sanger made the most of the publicity that the trial generated. She fundraised, opened a research bureau, and founded the American Birth Control League. By the late 1920s, local birth-control groups operated clinics throughout the Northeast and Midwest United States.[44]

Mary Ware Dennett, who also lived among Greenwich Village freethinkers and activists, relentlessly fought federal and state Comstock laws, although hers was not a hedonistic celebration of sexual energies. "Sex relations belong to love, and love is never a *business*," Dennett concluded. In her pamphlet, *The Sex Side of Life* (1919), she wrote about sexual pleasure as a source of personal joy. "The physical side of love is the intensely intimate part of it, and the most critical for happiness . . . so it is the one side of us that we must be absolutely sure to keep in good order and perfect health, if we are going to make any one else happy or be happy ourselves." In the 1910s, while Sanger advocated for birth control as a necessity for women's freedom and workers' rights, Dennett spoke not only of pleasure but of health and survival.[45]

Dennett drew from her own experiences of terror and pain to become a fierce advocate for women's right to comprehensive information about sexuality and reproduction. She gave birth to three children near the turn of the twentieth century, one of whom died of starvation at three weeks old because she was too ill from his delivery to breastfeed him. After the birth of a third child, Dennett's doctor warned her to avoid another pregnancy at all costs, which in the absence of reliable contraception meant the cessation of sexual intimacy with her husband, Hartley. He responded that his "individual sovereignty" required that he have the freedom to have sex with other women. In particular, he wanted to spend more time with Margaret Chase, a married woman who was socially and financially prominent within the radical literary circles the Dennetts traveled in. Many of the Greenwich Village Bohemians had affairs with married and unmarried partners as part of their exploration of sexual pleasure disentangled from middle-class moralism. Mary's expectations of marriage were incompatible with Hartley's, and she obtained a divorce in 1913.[46]

Dennett wrote *The Sex Side of Life* because she knew that far too many women faced each pregnancy fearing death in childbirth and uncertain of what, if anything, they could do to protect their own health. The pamphlet contained basic information about male and female reproductive anatomy. With an emphasis on the naturalness of sex and its essential connections to romantic love, Dennett discussed ovulation, menstruation, sexual arousal, masturbation, and venereal diseases. Almost immediately, the postmaster general banned the pamphlet from the U.S. mail on the grounds that it violated anti-obscenity laws. Dennett was undeterred and filled 25,000 more orders. In 1928, she was indicted on federal charges after a postal inspector entrapped her by soliciting a copy under a false name. In a signal victory, New York's Second Circuit Court of Appeals in 1930 determined that her sex-education pamphlet did not constitute obscenity. The pamphlet's "decent language," the judge ruled, was precisely what young people needed lest they "grope about in mystery and morbid curiosity" for knowledge about sex.[47]

Comstock died in 1915, but his crusade against obscenity persisted. The Progressive Era of the early twentieth century was characterized by confidence in the ability of experts to solve social ills such as poverty and unwed pregnancy. Comstock had to drag police officers along with him to arrest purveyors of pornographic texts in the 1870s, but by the early twentieth century police departments embraced the idea that they should surveil sexual commerce. Anti-vice commissions in forty-three cities investigated the prevalence of prostitution and the conduct

The common association in the United States between Middle Eastern cultures and "exotic" sexuality inspired burlesque theater managers to add "Arabian" dance routines to their shows. In this poster from an 1888 production of the Imperial Burlesque Company, a sinister representation of Aladdin's lamp likely implied a titillating performance featuring a young woman threatened by insidious sexual dangers.

of young women at dance halls and gambling dens. Agents went undercover to "vice resorts" and tabulated the nature and quantity of the sexual services they offered. Plainclothes policewomen served as decoy patients in attempts to ensnare abortion providers and midwives.[48]

Definitions of obscenity continued to shift. Burlesque theater managers who already parlayed popular fantasies about exotic "foreign" women with acts that staged retellings of *1001 Arabian Nights* now adapted the "hootchy-kootchy dance" and its fantasy of "foreign" sensuality for their stages. Dancers at the 1893 World's Fair had worn folk dresses, but women doing the *danse du ventre* on burlesque stages wore translucent, loose-fitting costumes and shed scarves as they gyrated. In St. Louis, a performer named Omeena performed "the couchee-couchee or houchie-chouchie, or tootsie-wootsie . . . in the presence of men only,"

Fifty years after the danse du ventre *at the Egyptian Theater horrified Anthony Comstock, Sally Rand's "fan dance" drew crowds at the 1933 World's Fair in Chicago. This photo of Rand from 1934 shows how she used the fans, tricks of lighting, and a body stocking to give the audience the impression that she was naked onstage.*

her act concluding when she was nearly naked. Many burlesque entertainers wore flesh-toned bras and underpants, and the illusion of nudity they gave, aided by stage lighting and body makeup, was key to their popularity.[49]

Fahreda Mahzar, one of the women who captivated audiences with the *danse du ventre* at the 1893 fair, performed it once again at the 1933 Century of Progress International Exhibition in Chicago, wearing the same long skirts she had worn forty years earlier. But this time, the mere suggestion of exotic sexuality failed to stir the audience's imaginations. Mahzar, after all, did not take off her clothes.[50]

Instead, a dancer named Sally Rand drew the crowds at the 1933 fair. Taking the stage in a floor-length, translucent gown and high-heeled shoes, Rand carried two enormous, ostrich-feather fans. She twirled elegantly to a romantic instrumental tune, spinning herself until she was backlit behind a screen, her fans raised overhead to reveal the silhouette of her naked form. Assistants removed her gown so that when Rand spun herself out from behind the screen, she seemingly had only the fans to cover her—one held to the front of her body, one in back. Facing the audience, she raised up one fan, then swiftly lowered it while raising the other. Her routine coyly concealed her breasts, buttocks, and genitals, offering the audience tantalizing but inconclusive glimpses.[51]

Rand was technically never fully nude when she performed her fan dance (body stockings and pasties covered key parts of her anatomy), but she was arrested on obscenity charges several times. Throughout the United States, police carried on Anthony Comstock's mission to rid the public square of sexually exciting material. But in Rand's moves, and in the thrill of audience members, Ida Craddock's insistence on naming and expressing erotic pleasure claimed its place.

Chapter 10

Plays Too Stirring for a Boy Your Age

Howard Gan found himself in court in October of 1909 because he wanted to paint the town red. Howard was a young white man in his late teens living at home with his stepmother, Emma, his father, and three siblings. Emma expected Howard to con-

Moral-purity reformers worried that burlesque shows contributed to a culture of sexual permissiveness, especially among America's youth. This poster, printed in Oregon and likely from the 1930s, teased customers with the promise of a risqué event. From the perspective of many young people, though, seeking sexual pleasure by watching a burlesque show or reading a raunchy magazine was essential to the human experience.

tribute wages he earned as a clerk to the household budget, and they argued over how much he owed her. Howard thought $1 a week should suffice. Perhaps he reasoned that this would leave him with plenty of money for an evening out, when he would enjoy performances by comedians, jugglers, and chorus girls at one of the no-frills burlesque theaters in Cleveland, Ohio. A clerk's wages might not cover rent, but they afforded boys like Howard enough cash for a meal and a show, an opportunity to step out of his stepmother's household and imagine a life beyond it. Like the hundreds of thousands of other young people living and working in American cities in the early twentieth century, Howard recognized that cash could purchase access to sensual pleasure.

When Emma demanded that Howard give her $3 from his weekly wages, he balked. Maybe they shouted. Perhaps she threatened him. She was only eleven years older than him (and just six years older than Howard's sister Frances), and she may have struggled to gain his respect as an authority figure in the household. What is clear is that with a balled-up fist or the palm of his hand, Howard assaulted her. Neighbors may have heard the ruckus; someone brought a police officer to the scene. So it came to be that Howard stood before Police Judge Manuel Levine in a downtown Cleveland courthouse to answer for his crime.[1]

Judge Levine was committed to the progressive movement, which stressed the shaping force of social and economic circumstances on behavior and emphasized rehabilitation over punishment. In Howard Gan, the child of a German immigrant father, Levine saw a youth who would either mature into a stable adult or grow so enamored of base sexual pleasures that he would embark on a career of vice. "You will go home with your mother," Judge Levine ordered, stepping easily into his role as a surrogate father, "and behave yourself better."[2]

Judge Levine's authority within the courtroom represented but one small piece of the government's rapidly expanding authority over sexual behavior. These new developments included local policing mandates to round up "vagrants" and "sexual delinquents," expansive anti-prostitution measures that targeted immigrants and interstate travelers, and campaigns to raise the "age of consent" and enforce laws against statutory rape.[3]

At the time of his arrest, Howard was what psychologists had recently termed an "adolescent," a developmental stage halfway between childhood and adulthood that was considered pivotal to one's eventual progression to emotional and sexual maturity. Social reformers had already started to portray these years as fraught with confusion and danger. Judge Levine agreed that teens needed guidance. The sexual pitfalls he saw in Howard's path were all too apparent. "You must keep away from the burlesque houses," Levine concluded. "The plays are too stirring for a boy of your age—and keep out of saloons."[4]

All the elements of this otherwise obscure episode from a police court in Cleveland point to how differently Americans approached sex among younger people by the turn of the twentieth century. Few disagreed about the need to do something to address an apparent crisis of youthful sexual vulnerability. From the 1880s through the 1920s, reformers and legislators undertook new measures to protect children, and girls in particular, from the abuses they associated with commercialized sex. In doing so, they debated questions about the age at which a child became capable of giving consent, the culpability of teenage boys in these encounters, and whether the role of the state was to punish or reform "wayward" youth.

The notion that childhood extended past the age of ten, and that teens did not yet possess the maturity or resourcefulness of adults, gained traction in the nineteenth century. In the 1850s, some women's rights reformers began to warn against marriages between older men and "baby wives" who had not reached legal adulthood. Numerical age became a steadily more significant measure of a person's maturity—and, in tandem, of their sexual allure. By the late nineteenth and early twentieth centuries, popular culture portrayed young women as especially attractive, while new statutes and policing practices cast girls as sexually vulnerable. This combination of youthful allure and vulnerability drew the attention of psychologists and reformers.[5]

Among the most influential theorists of youthful sexual urges was

G. Stanley Hall, a psychologist who also served as president of Clark University in Worcester, Massachusetts. In his two-volume work, *Adolescence* (1904), Hall defined adolescence as a chaste interregnum between childhood and marriage. Much as Sylvester Graham and Sarah Mapps Douglass had in the first half of the nineteenth century, Hall characterized the young person's sexual awakening as a critical moment. But although Hall had been raised to see sexual desires and masturbation as religiously and physically dangerous, he wanted young people to understand that sexual pleasure was natural. At the same time, he warned that the capacity for sexual restraint was what distinguished "civilized" from "savage" races. These theories resonated with Freud's ideas about sexual degeneracy, though Hall emphasized biological inheritance rather than subconscious impulses.[6]

Hall shared with many leading American social scientists of the late nineteenth and early twentieth centuries an unabashed confidence in the evolutionary superiority of "Anglo-Saxon" people. British scientist Charles Darwin's theories of human evolution and "natural selection" changed the way Americans understood the origins of racial differences. Talk about "the race" suffused social movements and national politics: in 1904, President Theodore Roosevelt warned of "race suicide" if Japanese men could immigrate in greater numbers to the United States; he feared that Japan's supposedly less-civilized-but-still-manly men would take jobs from—and emasculate—American men. Although Darwin offered theories of evolution's biological effects, American and British social scientists saw these ideas about racial inheritance as a road map for social engineering.[7]

The popularity of Darwin's theories of survival of the fittest inspired what became known as the eugenics movement. Scientists, physicians, policymakers, and others believed they could improve the "fitness" of the American population by controlling who could reproduce with whom. State-wide eugenics programs sterilized vulnerable individuals whom physicians, prison wardens, mental health workers, or judges deemed hereditarily "unfit" (whether disabled or simply poor). Indiana passed the first eugenic sterilization law in 1907. All told, tens of thousands of men and women, most of them white residents of psychiatric hospitals or prisons, were surgically sterilized by the 1960s. Authorities had concluded that these people possessed physical or mental traits too detrimental to risk inheritance by the next generation. At the federal level, immigration laws passed in the 1910s and 1920s severely restricted arrivals from eastern and southern Europe, Asia, and other regions whose residents struck the all-white and mostly Protestant members of Congress as inferior to northern European "stock." A third effort, shorthanded as "pronatalism," developed premarital education and marital counseling programs to encourage native-born, educated, white citizens to marry at younger ages and produce larger families, thereby preserving "superior" white people's numerical dominance. By the early twentieth century, the eugenic idea that humans could "breed a better race" was mainstream.[8]

Hall's insight was a theory called "recapitulation," which described each individual's development as human evolution in miniature: a progression from the primitive impulses of childhood to the mature self-control of adulthood was akin to the progress of human societies. He argued that adults in "primitive" (non-white) cultures remained stuck in an earlier evolutionary stage and thus lacked the inhibitions that northern European cultures had achieved. Eastern and southern Europeans, who predominated among the new immigrants (and whom many white Americans did not consider fully white), lacked Anglo-Saxon maturity, as did the hundreds of thousands of African Americans migrating north to escape Jim Crow. Adolescence, then, served in this analogy as the critical stage at which a person learned to channel their impulsive drives into productive work and monogamous marriage, necessary milestones along the path to evolutionary improvement.[9]

What, then, of adolescent boys like Howard, who clearly lacked the maturity of adulthood but whose wages gave them access to a new world of cheap amusements? Young people pursued pleasure well beyond the mostly male or family-oriented pastimes of the nineteenth century. In the growing cities of the early twentieth-century United States, mixed-gender peer groups visited amusement parks and dance halls.

A few cents bought time at one of the peep shows cropping up on the margins of urban entertainment zones, sometimes viewed through a single-viewer kinetoscope. Nineteenth-century women who caroused in saloons and who walked without a chaperone in cities were often presumed to be sex workers; by the early twentieth century, working- and middle-class girls and women could safely enjoy urban entertainments without being associated with sexual commerce. Streetcars and, soon, automobiles moved courtship away from family parlors and front porches to dimly lit backseats far from parents' control.[10]

A new practice known as "treating" meant that the wages that Howard and boys like him earned were essential to their access to the company of girls of their social class. A teenage boy or young man might, for instance, pay for a teenage girl's dinner and tickets to an amusement park with the expectation that she would, in turn, provide companionship and possibly some degree of erotic play. A precursor to modern dating culture, "treating" offered women and girls a way to access public amusements—and to engage in premarital sexual acts ranging from kissing to intercourse—without damaging their reputations.[11]

Reformers emphasized that it was girls and young women whose virtue was imperiled by this new blend of youth, money, and sex, but that was not always the case. An investigation in Chicago in the 1920s found that some newsboys engaged in sex with older men in exchange for money that they then used to "treat" girls in their peer group. Sex work was prevalent in same-sex encounters between boys and men in the early twentieth century (a subject that the next chapter explores), but at least in the case of the Chicago newsboys, those exchanges helped male adolescents participate in a heterosexual peer culture that depended on access to cash.[12]

Racy vaudeville routines and movies contributed to a culture of sexual candor. Vaudeville was the most popular entertainment form in the United States at the time, with approximately 400 dedicated theaters throughout the United States and as many as 5,000 smaller venues in 1906. Vaudeville troupes promised wholesome entertainment for the whole family, but some of the jokes were suggestive enough that reform-

Bernarr McFadden (1868–1955) promoted bodybuilding and admiration for the male physique through his books and magazines in the late nineteenth and early twentieth centuries, often standing nearly nude in imitation of the muscular builds of men in Greek statues. This image, in which he is "posed as the modern Hercules," is one of dozens of similar photographs of him showing off his physique in his 1895 book, McFadden's System of Physical Training.

ers found them offensive. The nascent film industry gradually started with short films projected by the vitascope in the late 1890s. The invention of the nickelodeon in 1907 soon challenged vaudeville's dominance. Representations of female desire played across those screens. One of Thomas Edison's most famous early films, *What Demoralized the Barbershop,* centered on the flustered responses of male barbers and their customers at the sight of the stocking-covered legs of girls visible through the window of a street-level door. The film conveyed an increasingly common message. Physicians had begun to encourage girls and young women to exercise, and while bicycle riding was controversial, girls and young women learned that they should invest more time in the improvement of their bodies, the display of which would draw men's attention.[13]

Advertisers soon recognized the market potential of young people with cash and a desire to attract one another in a social world of their own making. Boys like Howard learned that they needed to become capable lovers with something called "sex appeal." Perhaps Howard read one of the new physique magazines published by Bernarr McFadden, a bodybuilder who had himself photographed nude, muscles flexed. Howard might have spent some of his wages on cologne. These combined pressures produced a novel American interest in heterosexuality: not simply in the existence of male-female pairings but in the idea that men's and women's desire for one another was necessary, normal, and important.[14]

New popular spectacles encouraged boys like Howard to gaze at respectable young women's bodies to an unprecedented extent. The Miss America competition debuted in 1921 with a revue of "bathing beauties" along the Atlantic City boardwalk, wearing suits that revealed far more flesh than previous fashions had allowed. Tourism boosters for Miami, Florida, portrayed their city as an oasis where "Miami Mermaids" (always depicted as white in the city's promotional materials) lounged on its beaches in one-piece bathing suits. Burlesque theaters introduced the strip tease and made their shows more sexually explicit, such as a Minneapolis act in which the women were "entirely nude with the exception of three ribbon rosettes," two of which, "about the size of a fifty-cent piece . . . were worn one on each breast," with a third rosette "worn over the pelvic region." The dancers paraded down a runway to cries of "Shake 'em up girls! Shake all you got for the boys!"[15]

Hall's fascination with adolescence as a crucial developmental stage, particularly for boys, avoided a question that women reformers had taken to heart: how could they protect girls from the sexual dangers that these youthful freedoms presented?

In the 1880s, across the United States, most state laws defined the legal age of consent for sex as either ten or twelve years old, norms established centuries earlier under English common law; in Delaware, the age of consent was seven. These laws defined sex with a female under that age as criminal conduct, regardless of the child's verbal consent or physical resistance. For social-purity reformers who saw girls and young women as sexually vulnerable, such standards no longer sufficed. Under

New York State law, they warned, a girl "is held by [the state's] criminal laws to be legally capable of giving 'consent' to her own corruption at the tender age of TEN YEARS!" Activists hoped to convince legislators to raise the age of consent and demanded enforcement of statutory rape laws. Because the laws applied to girls of ten as much as to teens of seventeen, prosecutions included cases of child rape as well as instances of consensual sexual experimentation among young people nearly old enough to marry.[16]

The energetic reformers in the WCTU added the reform of age of consent laws to their agenda for Christian morality in the late 1880s. At a time when public speech about adult women's sexuality remained taboo, this campaign allowed women to decry a double standard that too often blamed girls who had been abused of being unchaste. Their efforts were, by several measures, hugely successful: by 1920, the lowest age of consent in the United States stood at fourteen in Florida. Legislators in every other state had raised it to sixteen or eighteen. Revised criminal codes distinguished between rape (widely understood as forcible sexual intercourse during which the victim resisted and fought back with all of their strength) and statutory rape, in which the consent of the minor was immaterial to the perpetrator's guilt. Prosecutors brought charges against men who sexually assaulted children under the new laws. Because judges and juries often excused a certain degree of male aggression as a normal part of heterosexual relations, age-of-consent laws offered girls who did not consent to sex a new means of putting their assailants on trial. Successful prosecutions nevertheless often depended on presentations of girls and young women as helpless victims, with little understanding of sex.[17]

Sometimes it was parents who called the police for help when their attempts to turn their daughters away from older boyfriends failed, to force the father of a pregnant daughter's child to agree to marriage, or in the hope that the police could teach their daughters to respect authority. Virginia Zuniga contacted authorities in northern New Mexico in 1912 after her twelve-year-old daughter, Refugia Zuniga Torres, left home with Ricardo Alva, a twenty-five-year-old who boarded in their home. After police discovered Torres and Alva walking to a town where they said they planned to get married, Alva was arrested and charged with rape. (Since 1897, the age of consent in New Mexico had been fourteen.) Zuniga protested that she had no intention of charging Alva with a crime but rather wanted the police to bring her daughter home. Mexican parents expected young men to ask for permission to date their daughters, but their American daughters instead took advantage of what one Mexican mother described as the "terrible freedom" of American girls.[18]

Zuniga's concern was echoed in the comments of Black parents in New York City who invoked that state's delinquency statutes to discipline their daughters. Reformers tended to view Black, working-class, and immigrant families as the sources of girls' delinquency. Judges sentenced convicted Black girls to prison or to live hundreds of miles away with relatives in the South, where they would supposedly escape the moral turpitude of their urban environments and learn "traditional" values. Many parents nevertheless pleaded with prison staff to lessen their daughters' sentences or permit early parole, often because they needed the girls to contribute wages or labor to their households.[19]

The WCTU's emphasis on the innocence of vulnerable girls contrasted with new laws that treated girls as instigators of sexual crimes. In the 1880s, New York passed the first in a series of "wayward minor" and "incorrigibility" statutes that permitted the arrest and detention of girls who had not committed any crimes. Rather, a young person need only be considered "in danger of becoming morally depraved" to face arrest. (New York's wayward minors law targeted only girls until modifications in 1925 broadened its scope to include boys.)[20]

Courts often sent convicted wayward minors to private reform programs or, if pregnant, to privately run "maternity homes." By the 1920s, prisons such as New York's Bedford Hills Reformatory for Women increasingly handled these cases, housing sexually curious but inexperienced youth alongside the sex workers and petty criminals who comprised much of the prison population. Sexual behavior became the defining category for girls' criminality: in 1920 in the Los Angeles juvenile courts, 81 percent of the girls (under the age of eighteen) who were arrested were brought in for "morals" offenses, compared to only 5 percent of the boys. Boys were almost never charged with delinquency for consensual sex with girls.[21]

Black reformers concerned about the sexual morality of their youth had to contend with sexual stereotypes that presumed Black people's lasciviousness. In 1889, the white historian Philip Bruce argued that because Black people were innately promiscuous, they reverted to a pre-slavery state of licentiousness when Emancipation loosed them from the civilizing constraints of white paternalism. In that natural state, Bruce explained, Black women were perpetually sexually willing, and Black men, unaccustomed to any woman refusing their advances, became violent rapists. Bruce placed much of the blame on the failures of Black mothers to teach their daughters sexual modesty. Such viciously racist ideas were pervasive not only throughout much of the South but in the halls of academe.[22]

Black women such as Ida B. Wells and other advocates for "racial uplift" believed that sexual decorum, or "respectability," was both a moral imperative and a strategy for racial advancement. Wells made this argument despite some more conservative Black leaders' criticism: one prominent minister chastised Wells for speaking publicly about matters related to sexuality. Single women such as her, he warned, would better advance their race if they married and bore male children.[23]

She was undeterred, and she had good company. After the Civil War, Black women formed religious auxiliary clubs and local social-improvement societies devoted to "uplifting" other Black Americans through education, Christianity, and civic engagement. These Black women insisted that they were sexually respectable—and likewise insisted that other Black men, women, and young people demonstrate comparably virtuous behavior. Black clubwomen established sex-education programs and maternity homes for unmarried, pregnant girls. They created courses on social hygiene and marriage education at historically Black colleges and universities and urged the expansion of public health programs to reduce Black maternal and infant mortality rates, both of which far exceeded rates for whites (as they still do in 2024). Yet they also cultivated what one scholar termed a "culture of dissemblance": they presented themselves as beacons of bourgeois virtue, often at the expense of acknowledging their own sexual agency.[24]

"Respectable" behavior was also believed to be essential for the promotion of the next generation of healthy Black babies, amid a 50 percent decline in Black birth rates between 1880 and 1940. A Black educator named Ariel Serena Bowen spoke to the Negro Young People's Christian and Educational Congress in Atlanta in 1902 about the risks of "passions running riot," especially when they led to "child marriage." Bowen shared the popular belief that girls who became sexually active and pregnant at too young an age bore sickly children. Other reformers produced pamphlets that warned against promiscuity and "self-abuse," urging young African Americans to see sex not as simply an expression of physical passions but as a crucial decision with implications for the entire race. Acutely aware of the ways in which slavery and ongoing racial violence exposed Black girls and women to constant fears of sexual assault, Wells and Bowen emphasized individual morality and communal rectitude to guide their young people to a better future.[25]

The plight of Chinese sex workers living on the West Coast aroused a national panic over the existence of a new form of slavery, one that was fueled by immigration, and that exploited vulnerable girls and young women. Most people of Chinese origin then residing in the United States were male, having arrived after 1848 to labor for railroad companies with the intention of returning to their wives and children in China with the wages they earned. White Americans suspected all women arriving from China and Japan of being sex workers, and it is likely but impossible to verify how often this was the case. Chinese and Japanese women became sex workers in the United States because they had been sold by impoverished parents to procurers; had entered what they thought were licit marriages, only to have their supposed husbands sell them to brothels; or were kidnapped. They lived and worked under appalling conditions, suffering a high degree of violence and continual sex work.[26]

Reformers debated whether to rescue or expel foreign-born sex workers. The Page Act of 1875 specifically banned Chinese women who intended to work as prostitutes from entering the country. If a woman from China could not prove that she was the legal spouse of a man already residing in the United States, she was sent back.[27]

Yet the Page Act exacerbated the conditions it set out to resolve by ensuring the continuation of a "bachelor culture" among Chinese people in the United States. Their imbalanced gender ratio became, in turn, a further justification for the denigration of Chinese people's sexual morality. (In California, Chinese men outnumbered Chinese women 22 to 1 in 1890, and as late as 1920, there remained a 5 to 1 imbalance.) White Americans spread unsubstantiated rumors that Chinese bachelors lured white women and girls to their "opium dens" or laundries. A riot erupted in Milwaukee, Wisconsin, in 1889 after two "Chinese demons" were accused of "ruining" innocent white girls, ages eight to thirteen. (In fact, one of the thirteen-year-old girls may have been a street-gang leader who, in addition to experiencing abuse, acted as a procurer.) The very presence of Chinese men in the United States was portrayed as a threat to white women. Anti-Chinese press coverage and political cartoons contrasted scenes of exhausted Chinese laborers living in all-male, slovenly, and potentially queer spaces to scenes of orderly, heterosexual white families, where a male worker returned home to a wife and children.[28]

Reformers began to call the plight of coerced sex workers "white slavery": an international network that sent children and young women from eastern and southern Europe to the United States to work as prostitutes. (Some reformers included women from China in their description of white slavery's victims, but most did not.) They warned that single female immigrants might be intercepted as soon as they disembarked on U.S. shores by a deceitful procurer who promised respectable

This illustration by Thomas Nast, which appeared in Puck *magazine in 1878, contrasts the gender arrangements (and, implicitly, the morality) of Chinese and "American" workers. In the left-side image, a group of Chinese "bachelors" occupy a squalid, cramped dormitory in an opium den, where they subsist on rats. On the right, a healthy-looking white man returns home to a tidy domestic scene, with a dutiful wife and children. Images like these proliferated in anti-Chinese campaigns, and they often depicted Chinese people as socially and sexually chaotic.*

employment but corrupted the young woman into sexual servitude. Fundraisers supported Traveler's Aid and other groups that met single women at seaports and railway stations, directing them to "clean" forms of employment. Reformers presumed that immigrant women and girls who had moved to cities from the rural hinterlands and ended up selling sex did so against their wills.[29]

Yet few of the girls or women who earned a living as sex workers met the definition of white slaves. The cruelty that forced Chinese and Japanese women on the West Coast into brothels was unusual; most women engaged in prostitution in the 1910s chose to do so as a temporary means of survival. Katharine Bement Davis, the first superintendent at Bedford Hills, from 1901 to 1914, found that it was the *children* of immigrant women who turned to sex work in disproportionate numbers, learning from their native-born peers. Along with African Americans, immigrant women and their daughters faced poverty and social dislocation, not trafficking.[30]

By the 1910s, a new immigration policy allowed for the deportation of foreign-born sex workers. It was not always clear that a woman facing deportation for prostitution had been forced into sex work. Immigration officials and reformers tended to presume that *white* women had been coerced and that Asian, Black, or Mexican women willingly sought it out. Further defining prostitution as un-American, a clause in the 1917 Immigration Act stipulated that any woman convicted of prostitution was ineligible for naturalization, even if she married a U.S. citizen. And contrary to a stated concern with European girls who became white slaves, immigration officials deported women of Mexican origin at much higher rates than any other nationality between 1910 and 1920.[31]

The signature legislation designed to combat white slavery was the 1910 Mann Act, which prohibited the transport of female minors (younger than eighteen years old) across state lines for prostitution, "debauchery," or "any other immoral purpose." The law defined as a felony even the *intent* to bring a woman into the country or take a woman across state lines for "illicit purposes." The Bureau of Investigation (the precursor to the FBI) created a White Slavery Division and obtained approximately 2,300 convictions for trafficking between 1910 and 1918. Under the Mann Act, women were charged with conspiracy for arranging their own transportation to visit their boyfriends in other states. There was no similar constraint for men, whose solo travel was not subject to prosecution.[32]

The arrest of the African American boxer Jack Johnson became a notorious example of the law's selective enforcement. Johnson was a world champion, a powerfully built athlete famous for his dramatic victories in the ring against white men. He was also unapologetic about his relationships with white women. In 1913 police officers dredged up evidence that Johnson had traveled across state lines in 1909 with

Bell Schreiber, a sex worker with whom he had an affair. Johnson was found guilty and sentenced to a year in prison, despite the lack of any evidence that he had traveled across state lines to pay for sex or to force Schreiber to engage in sex for money. Those details appeared to be beside the point: he was a Black man who asserted his right to sexual pleasure with white women, and white law enforcement authorities wanted to punish him for his audacity. By the 1920s, the law targeted cases of adultery or interracial sex more often than cases of prostitution.[33]

How to handle adolescent girls who quite clearly chose to have sex outside of marriage was another matter. Raymond Fosdick, an attorney and reformer, testified before a congressional committee in September 1917 "that venereal disease was coming not from the prostitutes but from the type known in the military camps as the flapper—that is, the young girls who were not prostitutes, but who probably would be tomorrow, and who were diseased and promiscuous." Fosdick worked for the American Social Hygiene Association, funded by John D. Rockefeller Jr., which approached sexual vice in the United States less as a problem of "white slavery" than as a public health crisis.[34]

As U.S. soldiers began to assemble at military bases in preparation for the nation's entry into the Great War, government and military leaders discovered that an astonishingly high number of enlisted men—126 out of every 1,000—were infected with venereal disease. Infection rates among Black soldiers were even higher than the overall average. So prevalent was gonorrhea across the United States in the early twentieth century that some scientists speculated that *all* women might carry the germ in their genitourinary tract, where it stayed latent until it infected a male partner.[35]

The social-hygiene movement aimed to eradicate venereal diseases by eliminating prostitution but also by restricting the freedoms of girls and women. Far from the vulnerable girl in age-of-consent or white-slavery campaigns, sexually enthusiastic female adolescents now took the blame for endangering their male peers. Fosdick supported the formation of a wartime Committee for Protective Work for Girls, which sent out 150 women to patrol the streets surrounding military encampments, searching for wayward youth.[36]

Social hygienists working for the military produced a sixteen-page pamphlet, *Keeping Fit to Fight,* which was also made into a short film. These materials were remarkable at the time for their frankness about sexual function, commercialized sex, and disease. *Fit to Fight* portrays the adventures of five soldiers who go out for an evening of drinking and are propositioned by sex workers. Only one of the five demurs. Among those who assent, one man gets gonorrhea and two get some form of syphilis. Only one man who had sex with a prostitute escapes infection, because he uses a post-exposure prophylactic, a treatment that the army and navy had reluctantly begun to make available to servicemen. The abstinent man, teased for his rectitude, retorts that he is "not a coward because he won't go with a dirty slut." The American soldier, like the young man listening to a lecture by Sylvester Graham in the 1830s, heard messages about the need to practice self-restraint. Unlike Graham's lectures, the military's materials denigrated American women for their sexual immorality.[37]

Public displays of heterosexual pleasure were growing more common, however; Howard Gan and his contemporaries wore down the resistance of their stepmothers and the courts as the world of commercially available sex-related entertainments expanded. Here was sexual modernity, a celebration of the individual pursuit of pleasure amid experts' warnings about rebellious adolescents. The interplay of expressiveness, family concern, and state-sponsored attempts at control shaped Gan's life for at least a moment in 1909; it would prove dramatically more consequential for the lives of queer and gender-nonconforming people who experienced modern sexuality as a celebration of pleasure tempered by new fears of state repression.

Chapter 11

A Society of Queers

The Chinese servant at 2525 Baker Street in San Francisco watched a gathering of white gentlemen and their younger companions sip cocktails and wine on an evening in February 1918. Several of the carousing guests wore kimonos. The attire reflected "Japonisme," an elite, white fascination with Japanese arts and culture. A few of the men had met one another while pausing in front of stores

Members of the Bohemian Club relished the company of other educated, cultured men. Admission to the secret society, founded in 1872, cemented one's status as an elite man in late-nineteenth or early-twentieth-century San Francisco.

that displayed Japanese art. They might as well have announced to a stranger that they enjoyed the works of Irish playwright Oscar Wilde, another way for a man to signal his interest in queer sex.[1]

Japonisme was by no means limited to gay men, but it was often seen as feminine and thus, for men, abnormal. In 1914, guests at a men's party in a Venice Beach home each received a pair of slippers and a kimono upon arrival. Halfway across the country, weekend guests of Robert Allerton, heir to a Chicago stockyard fortune, attended lavish Saturday-night dinners "in costume," wearing robes and kimonos that Allerton collected during his travels throughout Asia. Of course, not all people enamored of these styles were gay, and not all gay men cared for Chinese or Japanese art. The "Latin" culture of Miami, a city marketed as a tourist destination, drew queer men attracted by a tropical aesthetic. Yet by demonstrating an interest in "the Orient," a man could indicate that he fit within an emerging understanding of "temperamental" men, who valued art and music, loved one another, and desired the company of other men. They may have agreed with a young man arrested in Long Beach in 1914 who explained that he belonged to a "society of queers," or a growing community of like-minded people who, among other things, adored the famous female impersonator Julian Eltinge and engaged in what local and state laws defined as deviant sex acts.[2]

We know very little about the "Chinese servant" who tended to the needs of the men at 2525 Baker Street, compared to what we know about the white men in this "society." Newspapers did not report his name. He may have been born in the United States and been a citizen, he might have had a white parent, and he might even have been a Japanese or Korean person misidentified in newspaper reports. He listened as the guests discussed plans to attend a party or perhaps stop by the Bohemian Club, an exclusive gathering place for "all gentlemen, and no ladies." He observed that some men left the first-floor living area for an upstairs bedroom. The gentlemen on Baker Street took little notice of him; they probably presumed, as white Americans often did, that, like most "Orientals," the Chinese man had more than a passing familiarity with sexual deviance and was paying them no mind.[3]

Unfortunately for the white men at 2525 Baker Street (and neighboring 2527, where the party continued), the servant was a plant, sent by the San Francisco Police Department's "morals squad." He gathered evidence of illegal "vice" at what became known in the press and in court as the Baker Street Club. In 1915, California had become the first state to criminalize fellatio and cunnilingus as felony "sex perversions," whether involving same-sex or male-female pairings, and it was under that statute that the men were charged in 1918. (Male-female pairs were hardly ever prosecuted under this or similar state statutes that criminalized oral sex.) The accused faced a maximum of fifteen years in prison. The case eventually implicated thirty-one men, including wealthier businessmen, clerks, and members of the U.S. military. After a police court dismissed several of the cases for lack of corroborating evidence, the district attorney called a grand jury to investigate. Four men fled before they could be arraigned; one went as far as Honduras.[4]

And yet at the end of a three-year ordeal, all the men involved were acquitted, and those who had been imprisoned were released. In a 1919 ruling that delved into the origins and scientific meanings of the word "fellatio," the California Supreme Court determined that its definition remained unsettled and vague. It was Latin rather than the plain English that the state constitution required of its laws. The justices consulted the works of sexologists Havelock Ellis and Richard von Krafft-Ebing, who described fellatio as a practice involving a man and a woman rather than one between two men. (The California assembly revised the relevant section of the state's criminal code in 1921 to define "oral copulation" between any two people as a felony.) Newspaper accounts about the Baker Street Club never mentioned the words "homosexuality" or "fellatio," writing instead about unspecified vice so vulgar that one judge dismissed women from the jury pool because he believed the "revolting character of the testimony" would upset them.[5]

The story of the kimono-clad white men of the Baker Street Club helps explain the emergence of the very idea of distinct sexual identities in the early twentieth-century United States. Nineteenth-century theories about the sexual "invert," as we saw in Chapter 8, defined certain men and women as members of a third sex, their masculine and feminine traits an "inversion" of what a "normal" person assigned male or female at birth presumably exhibited. Same-sex-desiring and queer people in the early twentieth-century United States created identities and communities that reflected this attention to gender, but they increasingly emphasized sexual desire as the defining aspect of their difference. They called themselves and one another queers, homosexuals, gay men, lesbians, bulldaggers, lady lovers, fairies, sissies, pansies, and a variety of other terms that emphasized an erotic interest that defied heterosexual norms. Several of these terms, such as "bulldagger" and "fairy," highlighted gender, and they also referenced differences of class and race.

The police who raided 2525 Baker Street and the judges who heard the resulting cases were often perplexed by what, exactly, had transpired there. But the evidence their intrusions revealed provides us with clues as we try to understand the past. Combined with first-person accounts of queer women's experiences, particularly Mabel Hampton's reminiscences of Harlem, the complex and vibrant queer subcultures of the early-twentieth-century United States come into view.

Urban police departments charged with cleaning up their city's "vice districts" began to search for evidence of "deviant" sexual activity. One arrest might expose an entire network of men seeking and having sex with other men—or, at times, those believed to belong to the "third sex." Police often targeted public or semi-public spaces, including migrant labor camps and shipping docks. The arrest of nineteen-year-old Benjamin Trout for petty crime in Portland, Oregon, in 1912 led to his disclosure that men purchased queer sexual pleasures in the city's parks, hotel restrooms, and downtown streets. Trout scratched out a living on the margins of Portland's economy, part of a transient labor force that extended from Alaska down the Canadian coast to Washington, Idaho, Oregon, and California and that drew wage-seekers from Europe, Mexico, Asia, and other parts of the United States. But many of the men he met for sex were white and middle-class, the kinds of people who were expected to call for "municipal reform" to "clean up" urban vice districts, not seek out sex there. The Portland Vice Scandal ultimately implicated about fifty men on charges ranging from "indecent acts" to sodomy and oral sex. Newspapers printed the accused men's names and home addresses, shaming them while offering a clear warning to others about the potential consequences of "degenerate practices." Dozens of suspects initially evaded arrest by fleeing the city until an international manhunt located them and returned them to Portland to stand trial. Several of them lived on the margins of Portland's economy, picking up work when they could and "tricking" (trading sexual favors for money or goods) when they couldn't. These men slept outdoors or rented inexpensive rooms. One of the arrested men, mortified that his sex life had been made public, died by suicide at the YMCA.[6]

These and other police investigations revealed the distinct vocabulary that characterized queer male sexual encounters in American cities and among migrant laborers. Some terms originated in the social world of male sex workers, while others indicated a person's gender presentation or preferred sex acts. Feminine men who performed oral sex on other men were called fairies in New York but were more derisively described as "cocksuckers" in California. A "pogue" was a man who wanted to be "browned," or anally penetrated, while "two-way artists" were men who enjoyed both oral and anal sex with men. (The second half of this chapter discusses the experiences of queer women in more detail.)[7]

Fairies developed their own lexicon: they called the men interested in a longer-term relationship with them "husbands" or "jockers." Their terminology distinguished normatively masculine men who had relationships with boys and adolescents as "wolves" and the youths they pursued as "punks" or "lambs," language that compared these sex partners to predators and prey. Yet outside of these specific subcultures, well into the twentieth century, Americans did not group all of the people involved in these sex acts as comparably "queer." They considered the people who had atypical gender presentations—mannish women and feminine men, like fairies—to be the "perverts." For a time, at least, the general public did not necessarily associate sexual deviance with normatively gendered women and men who engaged in queer sex.[8]

When newspapers reported on police raids, they also revealed that men of different classes preferred different forms of sex. In Portland, middle-class white men purchased oral sex from younger, laboring men, some of whom had immigrated from Greece. By contrast, when working-class men in Portland had sex with one another, they typically engaged in anal sex or in "interfemoral" or "thigh" sex, rubbing one person's penis between another person's thighs. Sailors were associated with sodomy and oral sex, especially after arrests and convictions brought the prevalence of sailors' sex with other men to public attention.[9]

As in other parts of the country, newspapers and attorneys in the Pacific Northwest nevertheless blamed working-class, foreign-born, and transient men for spreading their deviant "habits" to the white middle classes. The allegations did not describe any of these men as "homosexuals" with a particular sexual identity but rather associated sexual deviance with economic precarity, racial difference, and social dislocation. Most of the men arrested in the Portland Vice Scandal were found not guilty for lack of corroborating evidence. Guilty pleas and convictions still sent at least seven of the accused to prison.[10]

Vice squads exposed all men involved to public humiliation, but in an era rife with anti-immigrant fervor, men considered "foreign" by virtue of their country of origin or their religion (or both) seem to have received harsher sentences when convicted of criminal sexual conduct. Critics warned that sexual deviance was yet one more bad habit that foreigners were introducing into the country. Forty-four percent of the men arrested for queer sex in Portland between 1870 and 1921 were foreign-born, with a comparable percentage of foreign-born men convicted of queer sex in Washington State during that period.[11]

In California, local law enforcement led the charge against "sodomites" among the "Hindus," a term they applied to South Asian men regardless of their faith. Transient and otherwise indigent men were especially vulnerable to this intrusive policing; their "vagrancy" affirmed police associations of homosexuality with social outsiders, even as the very facts of their poverty left them with fewer options to have sex privately. One example was the case of Stanley Kurnick and Jamil Singh, both ranch hands in the Sacramento and San Joaquin valleys. On February 10, 1918, two police officers patrolling downtown Sacramento observed Kurnick, age nineteen, with the "Hindu" (Singh), who was forty years old, having a conversation on a street corner. Singh offered Kurnick 75 cents to go with him to a boardinghouse. Following a lead from an informant, the police located Kurnick's room later that night. An officer "looked through the keyhole and saw a boy lying face downward on the bed with his clothes partly off" and the "Hindu" also partially undressed, lying on top of the boy, "going through the motions . . . [of] having sexual intercourse." Officers broke open the door and arrested both men. Singh was sentenced to seven years in San Quentin, but the judge charged Kurnick, whom he considered "probably of low mentality," as "an accessory to the carnal act of the Hindu" and sent him to juvenile court, even though Kurnick was not a minor. "Hindus" and "Orientals" were presumed to be sexually immoral threats to white "Americans."[12]

Transmasculine people also suffered from the attention of these new vice squads. In 1913, police in Brooklyn arrested Elizabeth Trondle for "masquerading in men's clothes." While detained at the Raymond Street Jail, Trondle wrote to President Woodrow Wilson, a letter that newspapers throughout the United States reprinted. "I am a woman in trouble and I want my rights," Trondle wrote. "I want a permit from you or some one else to wear the costume I have adopted. I am tired of being kicked around and poorly paid." A judge explained that he sentenced Trondle to three years at the Bedford Hills Reformatory for Women "because I believe she is a moral pervert." Trondle was not accused of a criminal sex act, but the judge's words reveal the ways in which unconventional gender was increasingly associated with sexual deviance.[13]

All signs of gender nonconformity or displays of queer desire increased the risk of arrest for "lewd acts." New immigration policies were predicated on the idea that queerness was a visible trait, discernible from one's clothing, affect, and speech. At Ellis Island, immigration inspectors turned to psychiatrists working for the Public Health Service when they suspected that a prospective immigrant might be a degenerate. The psychiatrists were confident that they could *see* evidence of degeneracy on the person's body, conflating smaller-than-average male genitals or intersex bodies with perversion. Immigration officers believed that perverts would invariably lead a life of dissipation and crime, and that effeminate men were "prone to be moral perverts." They concluded that all such people were likely to become "public charges" (to depend on public welfare) and were thus ineligible for legal residency.[14]

An older man's affectionate interest in a younger man had occasioned little concern in decades past. Groups such as the YMCA and church ministries were premised on the idea that adult men formed close bonds with male youth to guide their personal development. The new visibility of "queer" communities, coupled with actual evidence from widely reported police raids that YMCAs could be sites of sex between men, cast those relationships in a different light. By the 1920s, tenderness toward a younger man or interest in the arts might each render a man vulnerable to suspicions of queerness.[15]

A new concept of sexual identity was gradually reshaping American life in the 1910s and 1920s. White, middle-class men who desired sex with men began to call themselves "queers," a term that they understood to designate their sexual interests but not their gender identity; a queer man might be primarily masculine or feminine. Queers differentiated themselves from "fairies," who were more often younger and less financially secure, and who were more likely to teasingly call one another by conventionally female names and assume a conventionally female affect. Fairies and queers generally celebrated the arts, paid attention to fashion, and valued refined manners. Some queer men tried on fairy effeminacy as part of their discovery of their sexuality, while others expressed anger at fairies for drawing attention to the desires that increasingly put them at risk of arrest or social ostracism. Queer men were more often able to pass for straight in their working lives (or in their marriages to women), leaving fairies to remain the most visible representatives of sexual nonconformity.[16]

Some queer women also began to understand themselves as a group apart. Middle-class and elite white women were the first to adopt a self-conscious identity as "queer" or "gay" women. Few used the word "lesbian" until the 1930s. (One study found that "lesbian" became a more common term of self-identification in San Francisco only in the 1960s.)[17]

But by the 1910s, groups of women began to recognize one another as members of a group defined by desire. Unlike the invert, whose sexual interest in women was explained by her masculinity, no particular gender presentation determined whether a woman was gay. In Chicago and New York, gay women lived in affordable rooming houses and studio apartments in lower-income neighborhoods, as well as in areas such as Greenwich Village in New York that were known for their sexual permissiveness.[18]

Lesbian identity was less appealing for Margaret Chung (1889–1959), the first American-born woman of Chinese descent to become a physician. Chung had intense romantic affairs with white writer Elsa Gidlow in the 1920s and with the white, Jewish actress Sophie Tucker in the 1940s. When Chung and Gidlow met in 1926, Chung wore "a dark tailored suit with felt hat and flat-heeled shoes," attire that helped her blend in with her overwhelmingly male colleagues but that she also enjoyed; she completed the look by carrying a "short sport cane." Gidlow, who was new to San Francisco, believed that she had found a "sister-lesbian" who was even more alluring because of "the ambiguity of this blend in her of East and West." She pursued Chung, bringing her flowers and poems, and they kissed and expressed their love for each other. Orientalist stereotypes infused Gidlow's attraction to Chung.[19]

Associations between gender nonconformity and queerness also transformed popular entertainments in the early twentieth century. In the mid-1920s, a "pansy and lesbian craze" attracted straight "slummers" to overtly queer performances in cabarets, tearooms, and speakeasies.

Chicago's Dill Pickle Club hosted lectures by a "guy named Theda Bara talking about his life as a homosexual" and a woman who presented a "paper from Lesbos" about the possibilities for women's domination over men. After Prohibition bankrupted many reputable restaurants, after-theater dinner clubs stocked with smuggled booze and operated by organized crime syndicates lit up Times Square in New York City and Chicago's Near North Side. Speakeasies featured female stripteases and queer lounge acts. Some slummers may have visited these venues as part of their own process of self-discovery: two young women spent the evening at a Chicago speakeasy popular with lesbians after one of them read *The Well of Loneliness* (1928), British author Radclyffe Hall's novel about a child named Stephen, assigned female at birth, who self-identifies as a masculine "invert" and falls in love with their neighbor's wife. By 1930, part of the point of going to see a female or male impersonator in one of the more mainstream theaters in Times Square, for instance, was to demonstrate a sophisticated appreciation for "queer" performances.[20]

These urban explorers observed a queer world amid transformation. Like the fairy, the pansy was a male-bodied person who exhibited feminine manners and interests, and both words were initially pejorative. But while a fairy was understood to be a feminine man who took the receptive role in sex, the pansy was a bit different: an atypically gendered man who, more importantly, had sex with other men. Small nuances in the meanings of these two words reveal a shift in how queer people were perceiving themselves and being described by others. It was the pansy's sexual desire for men, more than his feminine attributes, that defined him. The lesbian similarly emerged as a woman whose most salient character trait was her sexual interest in women.[21]

The idea that "normal" men were masculine and desired sex only with women (and vice versa) was a response to this understanding of queerness. "Heterosexual," a term coined in the 1860s by sexologists, still required a definition when it appeared in advice columns in the 1920s. It was a concept that came into focus for many Americans as they began to recognize pansies and lesbians as representatives of a seemingly opposite sexual type. Popular psychologists and advice columnists offered instruction about how to help children develop a "normal, heterosexual" disposition.[22]

The categories of homosexual and heterosexual represented a novel way of grouping people according to the sex of a person's object of desire. It was a binary that foreclosed older terms that had recognized gender-fluid and queer desires. Fairies and "mannish" lesbians bore the weight of intensifying American homophobia, their proudly public displays of alternative gender identity a visible marker of what was increasingly understood to be an intrinsic, fundamental difference.

Mabel Hampton, a Black Winston-Salem native, moved to West Twenty-Second Street in New York City in 1920, when she was in her late teens. The possibilities at first seemed limitless. An unprecedented number of single women lived apart from their parents in the early twentieth century. They moved to the furnished-room districts in Chicago and New York City or piled into shared apartments, as Hampton did. The privacy of these spaces provided young people with opportunities to socialize, have sex, and live independently. Factory and store owners paid women about half as much as they paid men; Hampton eked out a living in domestic service and as an occasional cabaret dancer. She already knew that she desired women—that she was a lady lover, as the Black press referred to women who were intimate with other women. By accident or design, her next-door neighbor was a lady lover, too, who threw parties in her four-room basement apartment.[23]

Hampton created a life for herself centered around Black women, their white friends, and the pleasures they made for themselves. Openly lesbian and gay characters appeared in theatrical productions and films in the 1920s (although voluntary "codes" imposed in the 1930s curtailed the representation of queer characters in film). Hampton went again and again to see the 1920s play *The Captive*, entranced and thrilled by its portrayal of two women in love. She attended drag balls in Harlem, perhaps the annual event at the Hamilton Lodge that drew about

1,500 spectators. Many of these balls included a "parade of fairies," a procession of transwomen and drag queens who competed for the most outrageous costume. Hampton saw fairies perform campy parodies of feminine behavior on and off Broadway. Vaudeville star Mae West staged a play called, simply, *Sex*, set in a Canadian brothel, about a sex worker, her pimp, and her sailor-client. The show opened in the spring of 1926 in New York City and ran until a police raid led to the arrests of twenty cast members in February 1927. West served a ten-day sentence at the Women's Workhouse on Welfare Island, but she was undeterred: her next theatrical undertaking was a play called *Drag*. Everywhere, the sexual innuendo Comstock had tried to eliminate from the public square now played across screens and stages.[24]

Hampton and her friends could not afford to go to most of the clubs that white men and women frequented. Nor would many of these clubs have admitted them even if they could have afforded the prices: the only Black people permitted in the Cotton Club and other popular venues were employees or were light-skinned enough to "pass" for white. Hampton and her friends gathered instead in one another's apartments. Sometimes these were "rent parties," where the hosts accepted a small amount of cash from each guest to raise money toward what they owed their landlord, as well as the cost of food and drink. (Residential segregation in American cities, including New York, pushed Black people into overcrowded tenements with high rents, usually collected by white landlords.) At parties that doubled as a form of mutual aid, Hampton and her friends danced the Charleston and "did a little bit of everything." Hampton learned the rules of sexual exclusivity as she sought dance partners and lovers. "The bulldykers used to come and bring their women with them, you know. And you wasn't supposed to jive with them, you know. You wasn't supposed to look over there at all. They danced up a breeze."[25]

One lover took Hampton to an apartment owned by A'Lelia Walker, one of the wealthiest Black women in the United States. A'Lelia's mother was Madam C. J. Walker, whose line of hair straighteners and face creams had made her the first Black female millionaire in the country. A celebrated hostess of Harlem Renaissance salons for queer writers and artists, A'Lelia Walker also threw sex parties that encouraged exploration. Hampton recalled a party at which all of the guests were naked. A'Lelia Walker had three marriages with men, and she may have also had an intimate relationship with her secretary, Mayme White, who lived with her for the last five years of her life. (A'Lelia Walker died in 1931 at the age of forty-six.)[26]

Hampton also attended gatherings known as "buffet flats," where illegal liquor, sex for hire, gambling, and dancing offered a "buffet" of options for the sexually curious. These hedonistic parties drew the attention of the "Committee of Fourteen," an influential citizens' association in New York City. Raymond Clymes, the only Black investigator on the Committee of Fourteen, located sixty-one apartments functioning as buffet flats in 1928. Clymes shared his findings with police. His 1929 report about the cabarets, speakeasies, and buffet flats he visited may have led to an uptick in arrests of Black women in Harlem for prostitution that year.[27]

The audacious gender nonconformity and sexual assertiveness of Black blues singers captivated Hampton. Song lyrics teased "sissy" men and masculine women. Some Blues songs warned that a "natural" man who failed to satisfy his woman would lose her to the more gratifying charms of a mannish lesbian or "bulldagger." Gertrude "Ma" Rainey, the "Mother of the Blues," teasingly hinted at her desire for women in her song lyrics (especially in her 1928 hit, "Prove It on Me Blues"), and she privately dated women throughout her two marriages to men. Ethel Waters, the star of Black Swan Records, the first Black recording label, lived in Harlem with her girlfriend Ethel Williams, where they were known to entertain other same-sex couples. Williams toured with Waters as one of her dancers, but Black Swan's promotional materials portrayed Waters as a single woman too busy with her career to search for a husband. Bessie Smith, the "Empress of the Blues," had numerous affairs with women in her touring company.[28]

One of Hampton's older companions introduced her to the famous singer Gladys Bentley, who performed in a tuxedo and flirted with

Gladys Bentley (1907–1960) performed blues songs in a top hat and tails and flirted with women in the audience. Known as a "lady lover" in the Black community, Bentley was an inspiration to Mabel Hampton and other Black women who adopted a more masculine self-presentation.

women in the audience. Hampton admired Bentley and other masculine-presenting "butch" Black women who wore trousers not only onstage but in the streets. Hampton "dressed nicely" in trousers, a tie, and a Panama hat and wore her hair short. Later in life, she referred to herself as a "stud," an affectionate term for masculine-presenting women after World War II, at a time when "butch" and "femme" became the identifiers of choice among many working-class lesbians.[29]

An arrest in 1924 interrupted Hampton's enjoyment of those pleasures. She insisted at the time and afterward that the situation had been a setup. She and a female friend, she claimed, were chatting in an apartment while they waited for their male dates to take them to a cabaret. No sooner did the men arrive than two white police officers loomed in the doorway and announced that they were raiding the home on suspicion of prostitution. "I couldn't figure it out," Hampton later said. "I didn't have time to get clothes or nothing." Hampton was attracted only to women, but she stuck to her story. A year later, when attempting to negotiate parole, she told prison officials that the date she had been waiting for on the night of her arrest was someone she had been seeing for a month and that he had marriage on his mind.[30]

That may have been true. Or maybe she was helping her friend use the house for the "purposes of prostitution." She herself was possibly involved in an exchange of sex for cash. The refusals of landlords to lease decent properties to Black people forced many Southern migrants to live in urban neighborhoods that were also home to gambling dens and brothels. White entrepreneurs moved their "vice resorts" to these neighborhoods, confident that law enforcement would not follow them there. But once police officers understood certain neighborhoods to be "vice districts," they started arresting Black teens and women for solicitation on flimsy premises, such as observing the teen or woman walking down a city street alone or entering a building with a man. In Hampton's case, she might have engaged in occasional sex work, participating in an underground economy to supplement the meager wages that a working-class woman could otherwise earn. Whatever the reason for Hampton's presence in the apartment that evening, she was charged with being an accessory to sexual solicitation. The court gave Hampton the same sentence Trondle had received: three years at the Bedford Hills Reformatory for Women.[31]

Hampton stayed in one of two cottages at Bedford designated for Black women. The prison had formally instituted racial segregation in 1917 after a State Board of Charities investigative committee discovered "harmful intimacy" between Black and white female prisoners. The study was but one of several reports about interracial sex in women's reformatories and prisons during the 1910s. White social scientists portrayed Black women as the masculine aggressors in these relationships, with white women as the passive, feminine objects of their attention. These stereotypes characterized Black women as unfeminine, primitive, and dangerously seductive, yet another example of the long and terrible history of stigmatizing Black women as undeserving of respect.[32]

At Bedford, Hampton found comfort in the beds of Black women. "It was summertime," she later recalled about one fellow inmate, "and we went back out there and sat down. She says 'I like you.' 'I like you too.' . . . We went to bed and she took me in her arms and I went to sleep." Hampton was released on parole after thirteen months, on the condition that she live with her aunt in New Jersey and stay away from New York City. Such arrangements were common in delinquency cases, which approached rehabilitation as a project requiring family support and gainful employment. Hampton's aunt complained to the parole board that her niece continued to attend parties in the city. Unable to tolerate her aunt's criticisms and unwilling to stop enjoying nights out on the town, Hampton voluntarily served out the final five months of her sentence at Bedford.[33]

Mabel Hampton may have lied about her "date" on the night of her arrest, but among friends and neighbors, her identity as a lady lover was well known. She and her friends understood themselves as part of a community defined by their own understandings of queer desire. They accepted gender nonconformity, shared experiences of same-sex attraction, and pursued pleasure—sexual and otherwise—as an expression of their inner selves.

Hundreds of speakeasies and illicit entertainment venues flourished in New York City throughout the 1920s. Civic reformers soon blamed queer performers and clubs for much of the city's sexualized culture. A pushback against the pansy craze in New York began in 1931, as police shut down Times Square venues that featured female impersonators or drag balls, which they blamed for crime and "disorderly" conduct. Police raided even more clubs with queer acts and patrons following the repeal of Prohibition in 1933. The State Liquor Authority (SLA) in New York, one of many new state-level liquor-control boards across the United States, authorized its agents to revoke the liquor license of any "disorderly" establishment. The mere presence of gender-nonconforming people, sex workers, lesbians, gay men, or gambling was enough to force a bar to close. Between the 1930s and 1950s, the SLA shut down hundreds of New York City bars that welcomed (or simply ignored the presence of) gay and lesbian patrons. In Chicago, a mayor cracked down on female impersonators and striptease acts as he ran for reelection in 1934. As the relative openness of queer nightlife in New York and other northern cities declined in the 1930s, new leisure markets expanded in places farther south and west, where visible queer cultures flourished.[34]

In San Francisco and Miami, the repeal of Prohibition created conditions ripe for the expansion of bars that accepted queer patrons and for nightclubs that featured queer acts. The cities' economies depended on tourism, and each had a reputation for being a "wide-open town," where anything was possible. (Miami also competed for tourists with Caribbean cities, especially Havana, that had vibrant nightlife scenes.) One important shift in San Francisco was the end of organized crime's control of the city's clubs and bars after repeal. Gender-transgressive nightclubs like Mona's and Finocchio's opened near the central theater district. Police in San Francisco could still harass gay and lesbian patrons and bar owners, but there was no analogue there to the powerful SLA in New York. Rather than a liquor-control board, California established a fiscal agency that could accept fees for liquor licenses but had no enforcement powers to take away licenses from "disorderly" establishments.[35]

Hampton and other queer Black people, meanwhile, confronted overt hostility from Black leaders. Adam Clayton Powell Sr., the pastor of the Abyssinian Baptist Church in Harlem and one of the most influential Black men of his day, preached in 1929 that "Homo-sexuality and sex perversion among women" had become "one of the most horrible, debasing, alarming and damning vices of present day civilization." Worse, he continued, it spread by "contract and association" and "is increasing day by day." Powell concluded that a decline in sexual morality was decimating the Black population. In the mid-1920s, Marcus Garvey, a dynamic Jamaican immigrant who led the Universal Negro Improvement Association (UNIA), condemned both birth control and same-sex sexuality as forms of genocide. Powell's and Garvey's condemnation of homosexuality added a new layer to middle-class Black warnings about the effects of undisciplined sexual behaviors on the survival of the Black population.[36]

By the mid-1930s, queer people relied upon longstanding strategies to hide their desires from the broader public. In a scene reminiscent of Alice Mitchell's plans with Freda Ward, two Black women in New York City got married in 1938 when one of them put on trousers so that they could pass as straight at City Hall, filling out forms and getting their premarital blood test without anyone the wiser. The officiating minister was the only man present at a private ceremony at the couple's home. And while he asked the partners to state whether they "took this woman" and "took this man" to be their lawfully wedded wife and husband, he knew that two women kissed when he proclaimed that it was time to "kiss the bride." Hampton, who attended the wedding, presumed that the minister was gay as well. In her reminiscences about the wedding, Hampton recalled a ceremony between lesbians, and it's very possible that the marriage partners also understood themselves that way. It is equally possible that the partner dressed as a groom was what eighteenth- and nineteenth-century people called a female husband or what we more recently describe as a transman.[37]

Hampton's own domestic life changed after she received a flyer from a Black woman named Lillian Foster in 1932. It announced Foster's upcoming rent party, "A Sunday Matinee given by Lillian," at her apartment on West 130th Street. The flyer promised: "Hard times are here, but not [to] stay. So come, sing and dance your blues away." Hampton went, entranced by Foster, who "always looked like a fashion plate." She stayed for the next forty-six years, until Foster's death in 1978 parted them.

Mabel Hampton's defiant assertion of sexual selfhood illuminates Black women's contributions to "modern" sexuality, a sense that sexual desire constitutes an essential part of one's being, and that seeking sexual pleasure is necessary for one's full humanity. Like the white men of the Baker Street Club, she belonged to a community centered on queer

Mabel Hampton (1902–1989) moved to New York in 1920 when she was seventeen years old, finding a home among other "lady lovers," first in Greenwich Village and later in Harlem. A flyer advertising a rent party in the home of Lillian Foster in 1932 changed Hampton's life. They were lovers and partners until Lillian Foster's death in 1978. In this undated photo, Lillian Foster drapes her arm over Mabel Hampton's shoulder.

desire and accepting of gender nonconformity. These early decades of the twentieth century enabled queer communities to cohere in many American cities, even as police began to target homosexuality as a perverse source of urban vice. But Hampton described same-sex love and erotic expression in ecstatic terms. "Joan," she told her friend Joan Nestle years later, "there are some women I can't touch because the desire burns my hand like a blue flame, those women, those women!"[38]

PART THREE

SOLVING SEXUAL PROBLEMS

1938–2024

Chapter 12

Scientific Methods

How long does it take you to come to climax in masturbation? What would you say was the main source of your early knowledge about sex?

The project staff of the Institute for Sex Research at Indiana University assembled and interpreted thousands of interviews about human sexual behavior, carefully tabulating the frequency of various desires, behaviors, and pleasures. Staff members pictured in this 1953 photo include: Cornelia V. Christenson; Mrs. Leser; Clyde E. Martin; Mrs. Brown; Paul H. Gebhard; William Dellenback; Alfred C. Kinsey; Wardell B. Pomeroy; Dr. Davis; Eleanor Roehr; and Dorothy Collins.

To males: How often do you wake up in the morning with an erection?

To females: When you are sexually excited, does the vagina become slightly wet, moderately wet, or enough to wet the bed?

Do you dream of sex with an animal?[1]

A white man wearing a button-down shirt and tie asks these questions in a hotel room, a corner booth at a local dive, or a college lounge. The person sitting across from him may answer immediately or may prevaricate, but he waits patiently for a response. He has practiced how to exude empathy and to make assurances of confidentiality in exchange for complete candor. Certain answers lead to additional questions—about preadolescent petting, sex with prostitutes, or extramarital affairs. These interviews often take two hours to complete.

The man—either biologist Alfred C. Kinsey or one of his trusted associates, Clyde Martin or Wardell Pomeroy—jots down the person's answers using a coded system of circles, lines, and numbers on a single sheet of paper. He is tallying up when, where, how often, and in what contexts the person being interviewed has had an orgasm, or "outlet," "a sudden release which produces local spasms or more extensive or all-consuming convolutions." Back at their offices at the Institute for Sex Research at Indiana University, a member of the research team will spend over an hour transferring that data onto thirteen punched cards. Those cards will be fed into a Hollerith computational machine the size of an upright piano, and it will cross-tabulate each interviewee's responses against an ever-growing data set.[2]

Science, data, and statistics, Kinsey believed, would reveal the vast diversity of human sexual behavior. He designed two major studies—one of men, one of women—to investigate how often Americans engaged in marital sex, premarital sex, extramarital sex, masturbation, homosexual contact, or sex with animals. The published analyses became known as the "Kinsey Reports": more specifically, a 1948 book, *Sexual Behavior in the Human Male (SBHM)*, and its 1953 follow-up, *Sexual Behavior in the Human Female* (*SBHF*). Funding from the Rockefeller Foundation supported the Institute for Sex Research, enabling Kinsey and his team to assemble and interpret thousands of interviews, each one comprised of answers to between three hundred and five hundred questions.[3]

Kinsey insisted that sex research must be impartial rather than moralistic. It should calculate means and modes but not prescribe norms. Yet his research's emphasis on statistical range created a new public awareness of what was sexually "normal," if not necessarily generally accepted. His studies' evidence about the frequency of male homosexuality and of female nonmarital sexual activity reverberated across American culture for decades. Whether interpreted as promising acceptance for people who previously thought their desires were strange or as a dire warning about the decline of more traditional values, the Kinsey Reports marked a "before and after" moment in America's sexual history. This chapter thus brings us to Part Three, as Kinsey's evidence of human sexual variety inaugurated a new era, one in which sexuality emerged fully as a defining feature of the human experience, and one that saw more and more people insist that sex was a discrete, immutable aspect of their identities.

It began with a college course about marriage. At least, that was how Alfred Kinsey explained his growing interest in the science of sex. Kinsey grew up in a strict Protestant home, where he learned that sexual desires outside of marriage were sinful. Virgins on their wedding night, Kinsey and his wife, Clara, quickly realized that they lacked the information they needed to enjoy sexual intimacy with each other. Learning about sexuality and developing a pleasurable erotic partnership drew them closer. Sex also became one of Alfred's professional preoccupations as he pursued his research into the genetic variations—the taxonomy—of the gall wasp.[4]

Kinsey became a zoology professor at Indiana University, but human sexuality and its variability continued to pique his interest. As it turned out, thousands of college students across the country—and their professors—agreed that sexuality was a crucial element in students' education. Several predominantly white and historically Black colleges had already introduced marriage education into their curricula. In 1938, when students at Indiana University clamored for a marriage course, Kinsey was prepared to teach it.[5]

The students needed the course. Even relatively well-educated young people remained largely ignorant about sexual matters. As high school education expanded across the United States in the early twentieth century, few institutions offered any instruction in human sexual anatomy, reproduction, contraception, or function. A brief experiment with sexual education in the Chicago public schools in 1913 ended disastrously when local Roman Catholic leaders mobilized to oppose it. Sex education was limited to "social hygiene" programs that slowly developed within mainline Protestant churches and church-adjacent organizations such as the YMCA. Social hygiene programs covered the dangers of venereal disease, the benefits of avoiding premarital sex, and the evils of prostitution.[6]

Kinsey wanted to know where he or his students might go to find scientifically based information about human sexuality. Books with facts about sexual anatomy and human reproduction circulated legally in the United States by the 1930s, thanks to very recent changes in obscenity rules under the Tariff Act in 1931. It became legal to import, sell, and possess the 1918 book by British educator and physician Marie Stopes entitled *Married Love: A New Contribution to the Solution of Sex Differences*, which was a guide to "the joys of marriage," and an English translation of a sexually explicit marriage guide from 1926 by the Dutch physician Theodore H. van de Velde, *Ideal Marriage: Its Physiology and Technique*. Van de Velde urged physicians and a presumptively male reader to recognize that "sex is the foundation of marriage," and that a marriage's success depended upon education about male and female physiology, anatomy, hygiene, male-female sexual intercourse, and various sexual "attitudes" or positions. For Stopes and Van de Velde, "normal" sex meant male-female sexual intercourse within marriage. And what was "normal" was "healthy." Domestic and imported texts about human sexuality proliferated in the 1930s as additional American laws permitted the "scientific" discussion of sex in print. By 1962, van de Velde's book was in its forty-second printing.[7]

The idea that erotic satisfaction was necessary for a marriage to succeed was becoming axiomatic. In the pages of *Reader's Digest,* a Protestant minister named Oliver M. Butterfield counseled that "nothing in marriage will contribute more to the growth of love and spiritual oneness than sex fellowship," but that the absence of pleasurable sex could doom a relationship. Butterfield reiterated this idea in *Marriage and Sexual Harmony* (1936), which for decades was one of the most frequently recommended marriage guides. Dozens of other sex guides published in the first half of the twentieth century in the United States echoed this warning.[8]

Sociologists, physicians, and clergy who wrote these manuals were particularly troubled by evidence from recent studies that between 25 and 40 percent of married women were sexually *un*-satisfied. The authors claimed that many marriages fell apart because husbands failed to learn enough about either female anatomy or their wives' desires. They encouraged men and women to find erotic satisfaction within their marriages during "normal" (penis-in-vagina) intercourse, but they chastised men for rushing or being too rough. Premarital sex was still discouraged, but at least the female partner's sexual pleasure was considered relevant.[9]

Kinsey wanted to discuss sexuality of all varieties and contexts. He taught that when it came to sex, there was no normal to be found. Except when sex harmed a person, he explained, it was never deviant. Instead, erotic desires found expression along a continuum of behaviors.[10]

The available research on human sexuality mostly disappointed him. Some physicians had collected information from patient histories, and others sought data by circulating questionnaires. These sources confirmed that human sexual behavior did not conform to any particular set of moral precepts. George V. Hamilton, a physician, interviewed two hundred married people (all white and college-educated) and discovered that they had engaged in a wide range of sexual practices before and during their marriages. Kinsey eventually found somewhat similar results but distrusted Hamilton's research because the sample was so small and unrepresentative. Too many sex researchers, Kinsey complained, relied on anecdotes or case records for their data.[11]

One of the few sex researchers Kinsey admired was Katharine Bement Davis. She had become the superintendent of the women's reformatory in Bedford Hills after earning a PhD in economics in 1900, at age forty. In 1914, she was appointed to serve as the commissioner of corrections for New York City, and in 1917 she was named the general secretary of the Bureau of Social Hygiene, an organization founded and funded by John D. Rockefeller Jr., who bankrolled much of the social-hygiene movement. Money flowed from the bureau and other private organizations into sex research, mostly small-scale surveys that focused on qualitative rather than quantitative data, or studies of physiology, psychology, or reproductive biology. Aside from Davis's work, Kinsey found none of it compelling.[12]

With the Rockefeller Foundation's financial support, Davis led a pioneering effort to document "the sex life of the normal woman," who in Davis's study was white and middle-class. The resulting report was *Factors in the Sex Life of Twenty-Two Hundred Women* (1922). Davis sent detailed questionnaires to unmarried and married white women whose names she had gathered from the General Federation of Women's Clubs and the alumnae lists of women's colleges and coed universities. The surveys asked about autoeroticism, contraception, sexual pleasure, and same-sex desires. One of her key findings was that large percentages of married and unmarried women had intense relationships with other women, many but not all of which were erotic, and that these relationships in no way diminished their relative degrees of personal health or happiness. Her team also noted that women they classified as "highly erotic" (who enjoyed the most active and pleasurable sex life) were more likely to have received "responsible" sex education during their childhoods.[13]

Sex research by the 1930s reflected a divide between those who argued that sexuality was biological and those who thought it had a psy-

A well-regarded prison reformer and sociologist, Katherine Bement Davis (1860–1935), pictured here in 1910, served as the first superintendent of the New York State Reformatory for Women at Bedford. With support from the Rockefeller Foundation, she conducted two especially influential studies on female sexuality—one of incarcerated women and one of college women.

chogenic origin. Many researchers assumed that all people had an innate bisexuality, meaning that each person had elements of both male and female psychologies. European scientists in the late nineteenth and early twentieth centuries made the case that embryonic humans contained male and female biological traits, and they explained that it was relative hormonal differences that determined which sex characteristics were expressed after birth. They viewed the discovery in the 1920s and 1930s that both men and women had some degree of androgen and estrogen as a validation of their theory. If everyone was "bisexual," then "transvestism" (what we might today call transgender identity), homosexuality, and other gender or sexual expressions were just matters of degree. By contrast, psychiatrists and psychoanalysts located gender identities and sexual drives within the psyche, seeing them as the manifestations of neuroses that originated in early childhood or in psychological trauma. Kinsey rejected both models: humans were not innately comprised of male and female qualities, nor could early childhood experiences lead to what psychoanalysts described as pathological sexual desires. Instead Kinsey observed varieties of sexual fantasy and behavior.[14]

Neither did Kinsey agree with the presumption in much of the existing research on sexuality that same-sex desire was inferior to different-sex desire. Even researchers sympathetic to the challenges facing gay men and lesbians tended to presume that homosexuality was a disease that needed to be cured. In the 1930s, Harvard researcher George Henry's study of "Sex Variants" had observed a range of homosexual desires and concluded that some homosexuals resisted attempts at a cure. Henry was considered sympathetic to the plight of gay men and disagreed with the criminalization of consensual queer sex. Similarly, while many "homophile" psychiatrists pathologized homosexuality as a form of illness, they nevertheless warned against trying to transform all homosexuals into heterosexuals. Many psychiatrists believed that once a homosexual individual reached adulthood, his or her chances for marital happiness depended upon the depth of the homosexual desire and thus the prospects for treatment. Kinsey insisted that these conclusions rested on assumptions that had not been proved. He refused to assume that any sexual behavior was inherently disordered or deviant.[15]

The famous anthropologist Ruth Benedict's approach to sexual variation hewed closer to Kinsey's. Both rejected the concept of "normal" sexuality. Social circumstances, far more than sexual interests, they believed, influenced whether a homosexual person experienced psychological distress. As Benedict put it, many homosexuals in the United States suffered because "the culture asks adjustments of them that would strain any man's vitality." Benedict, who was married, had sexual affairs with several women, eventually separating from her husband and identifying as a lesbian. She theorized that people were "plastic to the moulding force of the society into which they are born," their sexual behaviors a reflection of social conditioning. In a society in which heterosexuality was the norm, most people would be heterosexual, but strongly homosexual people would appear "incompetent."[16]

Kinsey wrote his lectures for his marriage course using the little he had learned from other sex researchers, but the material did not satisfy his students' curiosity. They flocked to his office hours with questions ranging from the basics of sexual anatomy to queries about fetishes and fantasies. Kinsey began to turn these meetings on their head by asking questions of the students. Their answers formed his first data set on human sexuality and inspired him to redirect his career toward the study of sexual behavior.

Kinsey won the support of the Rockefeller Foundation for a bold proposal: He would conduct thousands of such interviews, not only with college students and university faculty but with medical professionals, elementary and secondary students and educators, imprisoned people, civic groups, and local communities. By asking complex yet open-ended questions and tabulating the responses, Kinsey would create a taxonomy of human sexuality much as he had for the gall wasp—a descriptive analysis of behaviors and desires as they existed within the population. The results fundamentally changed the way Americans talked about sex.[17]

As far as we know, no one had ever asked so many people about their sexual desires or behaviors as Kinsey and his research team did in the 1940s and early 1950s. Their data set was larger than any previously amassed, although, as in the study directed by Katherine Davis, the subjects of Kinsey's studies were primarily white. (Kinsey appeared to think that white, native-born Protestants were so normative as to be ethnically unmarked.) He and his team gathered interviews across the United States, but the Northeast and Midwest predominated. Over 5,000 interviews supplied data for the male volume, published in 1948, and nearly 6,000 interviews informed the female volume (which, unlike *SBHM*, included data from the histories of African Americans), published five years later.[18]

The dryly written scientific reports created a national sensation. The publishing house W. B. Saunders, which specialized in medical texts, had anticipated sales of 10,000 copies of the male volume. Instead *SBHM* sold 185,000 copies in the first two months after publication. It spent dozens of weeks on various national bestseller lists. A 25-cent condensed paperback edition sold a million copies. The Institute for Sex

Research collected approximately 25,000 press clippings about *SBHM*. The second volume, *SBHF*, sold fewer copies but still far exceeded expectations for a scholarly work.[19]

In turgid prose illuminated by charts and graphs, Kinsey and his research team documented the surprising prevalence of male sexual contacts with animals, of premarital sex, and of same-sex sexual behavior. The last subject drew the most attention. From the thousands of sexual histories they collected and tabulated, the researchers calculated that 37 percent of American men had at least one sexual contact with another man that resulted in an orgasm.[20]

A combination of scientific observation and his own life experience convinced Kinsey that the terms "homosexuality" and "heterosexuality" were inadequate to describe human sexual behaviors. Kinsey was attracted to both men and women throughout his life, and he observed that hundreds of people he interviewed similarly expressed a variety of desires. Kinsey's personal life was its own critique of assumptions about the predominance of marital heterosexuality. Alfred and Clara had an open marriage. For Alfred, this openness included sex with men. The core research team at the Kinsey Institute engaged in a web of sexual encounters. Wardell Pomeroy, Paul Gebhard, and Clyde Martin had sex with one another's wives, and Martin additionally had sex with both Alfred and Clara Kinsey.[21]

Seeking an alternative to the heterosexual/homosexual binary, Kinsey developed a seven-point scale, from 0 to 6, with 0 indicating someone whose sexual experiences were exclusively heterosexual and 6 for those whose sexual experiences were exclusively homosexual. The "Kinsey scale" encapsulated his core argument: too often, definitions of sexual "health" reflected what people thought sex *should* be rather than what, for the vast majority of people, sex actually was.[22]

This notion of variation contradicted all other mainstream ideas about sex. Psychiatrists were some of Kinsey's fiercest critics, accusing him of normalizing pathology as a benign variation. In mental health practice of the time, homosexuality was understood as a pathological impulse. The psychiatric understanding of homosexuality as a symp-

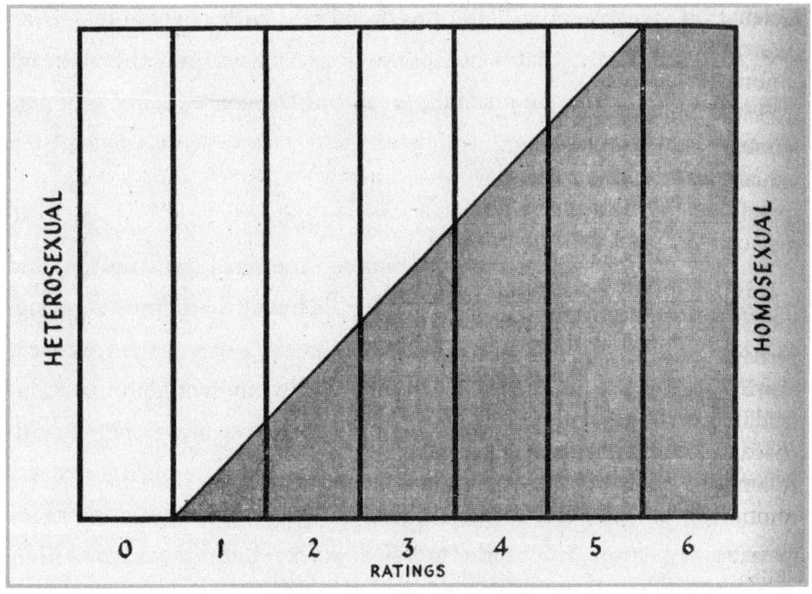

Based on data collected from thousands of interviews for SBHM, Alfred Kinsey developed a seven-point scale of human sexual behavior. With 0 indicating someone whose sexual experiences were exclusively heterosexual and 6 indicating those whose sexual experiences were exclusively homosexual, the breadth of the "Kinsey scale" reflected his core argument: that individuals' sexual desires and experiences were far more diverse and complex than previously thought.

tom of psychological impairment became official U.S. military policy during World War II after psychiatrists convinced the military to consider mental illness—and thus homosexuality—a disqualifying medical condition. After the Selective Service Act of 1940 called up tens of thousands of American men, the federal government hired thirty thousand psychologists and psychiatrists as local board examiners to screen inductees for evidence of psychological impairment. At induction physicals, draft-board workers and military doctors asked men if they had homosexual feelings or experiences, soon developing a standard questionnaire. Many draftees were turned away; "neuropsychiatric" cases represented 38 percent of all rejections. By 1941, the army surgeon general included homosexuality on his list of disqualifying "deviations."

All of this investment in detecting homosexuality contributed to an emerging consensus: that a homosexual sex act was not the aberrant behavior of an otherwise normal person but the consequence of a person's fundamental nature.[23]

The 1948 report's findings that American men had sex so often, and in so many ways, was shocking in its details but still affirmed the long-standing presumption that men had stronger sex drives than women. The 1953 report's findings that women (and white women in particular) had rich and varied sex lives was something else altogether: a challenge to a double standard that taught women that premarital sex was a lifelong stain on their souls but that men could seek forgiveness for a temporary lapse. Among the married women interviewed for *SBHF*, a staggering 50 percent reported engaging in coitus prior to marriage. Roughly 64 percent had experienced orgasm prior to marriage. While only 17 percent of those orgasms occurred as a result of coitus, the data suggested a level of premarital sexual activity that alarmed many readers. By age forty, 19 percent of women in the total sample had had sexual contact with other women, and 26 percent had engaged in extramarital sex. Kinsey's data indicated that sexual permissiveness was increasing; women born after 1900—regardless of class status or geographic region—were twice as likely as women born earlier to have had sexual intercourse with a man prior to marriage.[24]

Kinsey debunked an idea popular among psychiatrists and others that a woman can have a "mature" experience of orgasm only during vaginal intercourse. Instead, his study documented that the prevailing female experience of orgasm was through other forms of sexual stimulation. Women who had sex with other women said that they had orgasms much more often than women who had sex with men. The female report also clearly showed that women who engaged in premarital sex found greater sexual satisfaction in their marriages. (Kinsey was nevertheless somewhat conservative in his own gender politics. He did

During World War II, the U.S. government launched a public health campaign that warned American men to avoid "pick ups," a term for sexually eager unmarried women, and sex workers, decrying both groups as vectors of sexually transmitted infections. This poster suggested that even a young woman who appeared innocent or "clean" might, by transmitting disease, impair a patriotic man's ability to fight against the Axis powers.

not hire women as sex researchers because he believed that women's primary responsibilities were in the home.)[25]

Kinsey's statistics about the erotic experiences of American women shocked an American public that was more conflicted than ever about the sexualization of white women's bodies. World War II–era advertisements and wartime propaganda mixed paeans to the chaste, wholesome (white) girl next door with anxiety over dangerous vixens. Public health officials and the press portrayed girls and young women who sought out soldiers for sexual adventure as "victory girls," "khaki-wackies," and even "patriotutes," who all too often infected their soldier boys with a venereal disease. Police moved aggressively to curtail white women's nonmarital sexuality; a woman out at a bar with a man other than her husband risked arrest for disorderly conduct. In the name of public health, these regulations subjected American women to a new wave of sexual surveillance.[26]

At the same time, the U.S. Army distributed millions of pinup posters and permitted flight crews to paint sexually suggestive "nose art" on their planes. The pinups that the army sent to American soldiers included images of Hollywood sirens like Jean Harlow, but the most popular by far was a leggy photograph of Betty Grable, Hollywood's "girl next door." Nose art combined drawings of suggestively posed women with cheeky double entendre: "Miss Please" promised to satisfy her sexual companion while expressing the crew members' fears about enemy fire. In *Esquire* magazine, an illustrator named Alberto Vargas found fame with his depictions of USO hostesses and members of the Women's Auxiliary Army Corps in uniforms so tight they might as well have been literally painted on. These "Vargas Girls" added to an unprecedented quantity of images of nude or semi-clad women circulating among American men.[27]

In other words, the Kinsey Reports exploded into American culture at a time of both greater sexual candor and persistent moral conservatism. Suggestively posed female bodies populated magazine art and advertisements while public health workers and social-hygiene educators warned that "loose" women endangered the health and happiness of American homes. Marriage guides and social-hygiene programs provided increasingly candid information about sexual pleasure and human reproduction, emphasizing the significance of orgasm to marital success. Yet from military policy to local policing to psychiatric practice, representations and views of homosexuality were almost universally negative, even as World War II–related migration and military service allowed many same-sex-desiring people to form relationships and build communities. Information alone could not settle these debates.

American women and girls responded to Kinsey's 1953 report in ways that reflected the era's conflicted attitudes toward female sexuality. In letters to the editor and to Kinsey himself, many women expressed a conservative concern that the study would confuse young people unable to distinguish between statistical and moral normality. A woman in Kentucky bemoaned that "all our years of patient upbringing . . . will be torn down by this one man." But others cheered the report on women as a "liberatory force." Many of the women who publicly aired their opinions about the 1953 report challenged the idea that Kinsey's findings were dirty, unrepresentative, or immoral. Instead, these women wrote, Kinsey was finally showing the public the otherwise hidden truth about women's sexual experiences. "It's about time things like this were brought out into the open, instead of having people approach it in a 'sneaky' way," a woman from Bridgeport, Connecticut, told a reporter in 1953. The report's evidence of high rates of premarital sex among women prompted a teenager identified as Kathy to write to *Personal Romances* magazine that she and her girlfriends were "all mixed up" because "girls all over the country are doing things that my folks say are bad," yet Kinsey's evidence suggested that premarital sex helped women have more satisfying sex during marriage.[28]

Toleration of women's premarital sexual activity—often accompanied by support for sex education in schools, contraceptive access, and legal abortion—became a point of disagreement between liberal religious promoters of a reformed sexual ethics and conservative advocates for sexual "tradition." Catholic and evangelical Protestant leaders detested Kinsey as a supposed purveyor of smut. Liberal Protestant ministers were cautiously optimistic that the reports would offer them an opportunity to reassert their moral authority over sexual values. Kinsey's attention to human sexual diversity meanwhile inspired a new generation of liberal Protestant ministers and educators to reconsider their ethical positions on contraception, abortion, premarital sex, and homosexuality.[29]

Billy Graham was a rising star among conservative evangelical Protestants in the 1940s and 1950s. His revivals galvanized a cultural movement that combined a fundamentalist interpretation of the Bible with a rejection of liberalizing racial and sexual norms. On ABC radio, Graham sermonized about "The Bible and Dr. Kinsey." Born-again women, the tall, blond evangelist promised, rejected premarital sex. Instead, they "put the highest price on virtue, decency, and modesty." Decades before "purity culture" became a byword among American evangelicals, Graham portrayed female chastity as a defining difference between secular hedonism and biblical morality. Conservative religious criticism of Kinsey's second report was sufficiently intense to spur the Rockefeller Foundation to drop its financial support of the Institute for Sex Research in 1954.[30]

Kinsey turned next to a study of the effects of laws that criminalized certain sexual behaviors. He opposed laws against consensual sex between adults, and even was critical of prohibitions on sex between adults and adolescents. For all his assertions of scientific disinterest, Kinsey was an ardent crusader against a legal system that treated most forms of nonmarital sexuality as criminal conduct. He believed the pervasive sense of crisis over Americans' sexuality reflected a disconnect between conventional morality and the manifest variety of human sexual desires.[31]

Public fear about criminal sex acts was increasing. A wave of new laws and commissions emerged between the 1930s and the 1960s that focused public outrage on the crimes of the "sexual psychopath." This new criminal category originated in panics over sexual crimes against girls and young women. The "sexual psychopath" was characterized as a man whose sexual drive was so excessive that it led him to violent acts. Overly masculine and mentally ill, this criminal was typically antisocial and possibly a vagrant, and he needed psychiatric care. (Black men were rarely labeled as sexual psychopaths and confined to a psychiatric facility. They were more often convicted of sex crimes and sent to prison.) The new sex-crime laws also targeted men who had sex with men. Lawmakers used Kinsey's statistics on the prevalence of homosexual sex to bolster their argument that homosexuality was spreading and posed a growing threat to American families.[32]

Kinsey did not live to see this third major study completed; he died from heart failure in 1956, just three years after his report on female sexuality was published. His tireless research nevertheless did augur changes to criminal law. Between 1951 and 1965, nine states liberalized their sodomy laws, although only Illinois completely decriminalized consensual homosexual sodomy.[33]

In a shift of even greater legal importance, the American Law Institute (ALI), an influential association of lawyers, judges, and law professors, drafted a model penal code in 1961 that recommended the elimination of all criminal statutes that outlawed consensual homosexual behavior among adults. Presented as part of the ALI's broader critique of American criminal law, the model code sought to legalize private sexual acts between consenting adults. This theory of privacy as a fundamental right would shape subsequent Supreme Court decisions about contraception (*Griswold v. Connecticut*, 1965) and abortion (*Roe v. Wade*, 1973). Kinsey's passionate crusade to legitimate all private sex between consenting adults was hardly realized during his lifetime or the decades that followed, but his research was foundational to subsequent legal strategies.[34]

The Kinsey Reports remained controversial, their messages of toleration and of the naturalness of human sexual variety cited in debates over sex education in public schools, gay rights, and public assistance programs. "Kinsey" became, in conservative political circles, a shorthand for hedonism, "situation ethics," the decline of the traditional family, and child endangerment. False allegations that Kinsey was a pedophile provided a rhetorical link, for critics, between non-heterosexual sexualities and child molestation.[35]

But the reports also gave people hope. In 1950, a gay man living in Los Angeles named Harry Hay read the first Kinsey Report and quickly realized he wanted to discuss it with as many other gay men as he could. The report spoke to two of Hay's animating beliefs: that sexual desire was a core part of each person's essential identity, and that homosexuals constituted a rights-bearing minority group. Fortified with Kinsey's findings and outraged by growing anti-gay animus across the country, Hay set out to challenge anti-gay discrimination. The group he established in the winter of 1950–1951, the Mattachine Society, was the first gay rights organization in the United States in nearly three decades. (In 1924, an army veteran named Henry Gerber founded the Society for Human Rights in Chicago, which published the first U.S. gay periodical, *Friendship and Freedom*. Gerber and several other members of the group were arrested in 1925. Although Gerber was never charged with a crime, the negative publicity and stress of the ordeal led the group to disband.) Within two years, hundreds of men in Southern California belonged to one of the dozens of independently run Mattachine groups, with dozens more forming over the next ten years.[36]

A group of women in the San Francisco area similarly embraced Kinsey's 1953 report. The lesbian partners Del Martin and Phyllis Lyon started the Daughters of Bilitis in 1955, originally intending the organization to function as a social club for lesbians, "an alternative to the gay bar scene." Within just a few months, Martin and Lyon realized that their private social group needed to confront urgent public matters. They reached out to the Mattachine Society in Los Angeles. Together, those groups formed the nucleus of a new "homophile" movement dedicated to educating the public about the naturalness of homosexuality. Martin and Lyon urged members of the Daughters of Bilitis to participate in sex research in order to demonstrate that their desires were not pathological at all, contrary to all of mainstream psychiatry.[37]

Sixty miles inland from the Malibu beaches where Harry Hay first drummed up interest in the Mattachine Society, a boy of ten thought his sexual interest in other boys was an aberration. Steven Kiyoshi Kuromiya had no knowledge of the Mattachine Society, but he found a library that permitted him to read the Kinsey Report on male sexual behavior. It was for him, as for so many others, a revelation.

Chapter 13

Revolutionary Love

Steve was still a kid in the early 1950s, but he had matured early. Among other signs of puberty, his ten-year-old's voice had dropped. With changes in his body came the knowledge that he was attracted to other boys. He had never heard the word "homo-

Frank Kameny and Barbara Gittings held the first homophile demonstration in front of Independence Hall in Philadelphia on July 4, 1965. This photo captures some participants in a similar protest one year later, in what the organizers decided to call the "Annual Reminder." Here, Gittings leads a line of well-dressed activists carrying signs calling for equal rights for "Homosexual Citizens." Kiyoshi Kuromiya is at the end of the line, wearing a dark suit.

sexual," but, he later recalled, "I knew . . . what was important to me." These sexual interests set him apart from nearly everyone he knew in suburban Los Angeles. Ceaselessly curious and creative, he looked for information to explain his difference.[1]

The public library in his hometown of Monrovia, California, barred him from an adults-only section that held books about sexuality. Undeterred, he tried the county library in Duarte, one town over. There he found a copy of Alfred Kinsey's *Sexual Behavior in the Human Male* and, like Harry Hay and thousands of others, he read it cover to cover. Kinsey's study was the first book that told Steve about the sexual feelings he had. He sat in the library for hours, thumbing through hundreds of pages dense with data, charts, and statistical analysis. He found the book dry, but it confirmed that he was not the only boy who orgasmed with other boys. Quite the contrary.

Hiroshi and Emiko Kuromiya, Steve's parents, may have been amused or startled by their son's precocious puberty; a ten-year-old baritone turned heads. An unexpected knock on the door by Monrovia police officers, their son in tow, forced them to see Steve's sexuality as a problem to be solved. A vice squad had staked out a local park, one of the places where Steve had started to meet a sixteen-year-old male acquaintance for sex. Officers warned Steve's stunned parents that he "was in danger of leading a lewd and immoral life." Such arrests were increasingly common by the 1950s in Los Angeles. The police department's "sex bureau" defined working-class, non-white, and queer neighborhoods as hot spots for "degenerates."[2]

Steve did not know what "lewd" meant, but three days of incarceration in a juvenile hall left him with a profound sense of his pariah status. Exposed to the worst of postwar treatment of people with same-sex desires—for the first time, commonly described as "homosexuals"—he quickly understood that who he was and what he desired put his freedom at risk.

Steve Kiyoshi Kuromiya was arrested dozens of times over the next fifty years, most often not for clandestine sexual acts but for public protests against injustice. Across his dramatic but too-brief life, Kiyoshi (as he was later known) insisted upon the connections among civil rights, the antiwar movement, and sexual equality. His own life reflected the intersections of those radical movements. Born in a place that represented one of the greatest failures of American justice, he envisioned a world freed from oppression of all kinds, a liberation that would depend on a radically new approach to sexuality and gender.

Steve Kuromiya was born in 1943 at the Heart Mountain, Wyoming, incarceration site. Following Japan's attack on the U.S. naval base at Pearl Harbor in December 1941, President Franklin D. Roosevelt issued Executive Order 9066. Unfounded fears of domestic subversion among Japanese people living in the United States persuaded FDR to order 120,000 Japanese and Japanese American residents, two-thirds of whom were U.S. citizens, to abandon their homes and property. They were assigned to one of ten "relocation centers" on the West Coast, in the Mountain West, and in the South. Elderly, infant, and adult alike had to leave their farms, furniture, apartments, and businesses, bringing only what they could carry to the converted horse tracks, barren desert encampments, and other miserably outfitted sites that the War Relocation Authority had hastily prepared.

Emiko and Hiroshi, both of whom were birthright U.S. citizens, "assembled" in Pomona before traveling by train to Heart Mountain in 1942. In their mid-twenties and newly married, they were assigned to one of the crowded, poorly ventilated wood-and-tar-paper barracks, each of which housed six families, on arid land surrounded by manned machine-gun towers and barbed wire. Bulldozers had ripped through the native grasses and sagebrush to build the barracks, stirring up continual clouds of dust. Medical care was rudimentary; "we were giving baths in fire buckets," a nurse who worked there recalled. Illness spread among the inmates of the camp. Emiko was soon pregnant. Perhaps, surrounded by other Japanese-descended women at Heart Mountain, she wore the *hari oba*, a pregnancy sash. When she went into labor in May 1943, she would have had reason to doubt the proficiency of the chronically short-staffed Heart Mountain Hospital; inmates with serious medical conditions were usually sent to hospitals in nearby towns. Had Emiko not been forced to leave Los Angeles, a Japanese American midwife, or *sanba*, might have delivered her child at home.[3]

The Kuromiya family left Heart Mountain in 1945 after Japan's surrender, moving first to Ohio (possibly because the War Relocation Authority resettled them there) and then back to Southern California. They started over in suburban Monrovia. By 1950, Hiroshi and Emiko operated a produce business that they built from scratch. According to a 1983 federal study, Japanese Americans lost approximately $6 billion (in 1983 dollars) in property and investments because of their incarceration during the war.[4]

As he grew up, Kuromiya knew he was different not only because he was taunted by white classmates for being Japanese American but also because of his sexual interest in boys, which he tried to conceal. Secrecy did not translate to celibacy, for Kuromiya or for countless other queer youth. Instead, in response to new law enforcement mandates that defined queer desire as pathological and criminal, they snuck around in ways that would have shocked Rebecca Primus or Alonzo Choate. These patterns carried significant risks: vice squads prided themselves on learning the cruising habits of gay men, setting up stakeouts and surveillance cameras in public restrooms, parks, and highway rest stops. Stretching the bounds of legal law enforcement, officers used decoys to entrap men on solicitation charges. They believed themselves to be experts in knowing how to spot a homosexual. Lesbians, too, contended with heightened policing. Butch women, transmen, lesbians and transmen of color, and women and transmen in interracial relationships were especially vulnerable to police harassment and arrest.[5]

Church choirs, single-sex schools, dance troupes, haylofts, and city parks: all provided trapdoors in the postwar closet for sexually curious young people (and their elders). Queer people living outside the city during the mid-twentieth century lacked the sense of community that emerged in certain urban neighborhoods, but they enjoyed a surprising degree of freedom. From the rural South to small towns and farm country, adolescent boys who experimented with various kinds of queer erotic play got into trouble only when censorious adults discovered that they had been "carrying on" with other boys. Nor did sexologists' warnings about single-sex institutions eliminate the erotic possibilities of those spaces. Laurie Barron, born in 1948, had erotic relationships with other students at Girls' High in Philadelphia, which she called "a hotbed of lesbianism."[6]

Kuromiya was too young to know about or connect with Harry Hay's Mattachine Society in Los Angeles, which had taken up the cause of police harassment following the arrest of Dale Jennings, a member of Mattachine, in the spring of 1952. A man Jennings later described as a "big, rough-looking character" from the Los Angeles Vice Squad had followed Jennings through Westlake Park, a known cruising spot, all the way to his apartment, at which point the officer arrested Jennings for lewd conduct. Jennings admitted that he was a homosexual but denied any basis for the morals charge and demanded a jury trial. Mattachine raised money for his defense, and the charges were dropped after the jury deadlocked. Inspired by this unprecedented legal victory, gay men organized Mattachine groups throughout California.[7]

The judge who presided over Kuromiya's case sentenced him to three days in a juvenile detention center, amid a resurgence of popular concern about "juvenile delinquency" in the 1940s and 1950s. Kuromiya did not recount his experiences in detail, but he looked back on his arrest and detention as the moments when he first felt "that somehow I was a criminal without knowing it." He carried into adulthood "this level of shame" about his sexual desires—that whenever he expressed his sexuality he was "misbehaving or maybe even living on the wild side or being on the wrong side of the law." In interviews and extensive oral histories, Kuromiya described no other experience in such wretched terms.[8]

More punishment followed Kuromiya's release, when he was ordered to receive testosterone injections. Endocrinologists had only recently begun to understand how androgens and estrogen affected sex differences. This knowledge challenged the older concept of homosexuality as a disorder of gender. Even though research into hormonal therapies yielded no changed behaviors, Dr. Charles Posner, an endocrinologist with a practice in Pasadena, believed that pumping Kuromiya's body full of androgens would "cure" his homosexuality.[9]

The injections were meant to increase Kuromiya's sex drive, "supposedly to make me into a real man," Kuromiya recalled, even though a precocious libido is what had landed him in trouble in the first place. He remarked in the early 1980s, "I recall that as a rather traumatic experience." It was an understatement.

Physicians recommended "treatments" for same-sex desires because they considered homosexuality a form of mental illness or physiological inadequacy. The providers of these interventions interpreted Alfred Kinsey's studies not to mean that queer desire was normal but that pathology was more widespread than they had formerly realized. In addition to hormone therapy, gay men and lesbians were subjected to shock or aversion therapy, counseling to help the person achieve an appropriate "adjustment" to either heterosexuality or celibacy, and psychoanalysis to resolve what were thought to be neurotic behaviors rooted in infantile or childhood experiences. Kuromiya seems to have avoided all other attempts to "cure" his same-sex desires, but countless queer people—pressured by family members, ordered by courts or other government organizations, or compelled by internalized shame—were not so fortunate.[10]

More than ever before, the entire apparatus of the American government agreed with mental health professionals that homosexuality was a pathology. In 1947, President Harry Truman signed an executive order that required loyalty oaths and security screening for federal employees and contractors. The authors of this policy believed that a U.S. citizen could not both sympathize with Communism and be loyal to the Constitution, and that homosexuals were "security risks"—weak-willed deviants susceptible to blackmail by enemy agents. Almost immediately, the State Department began firing all employees known or suspected to be homosexual. A few years later, the 1952 McCarran–Walter Immigration Act excluded any person with a diagnosis of "psychopathic personality"—by which lawmakers meant homosexuality—from entering the country. That terminology echoed the language in the American Psychiatric Association's *Diagnostic and Statistical Manual* (DSM), first published in 1952, which classified homosexuality as a mental illness.[11]

In 1953, the same year that vice squad officers picked up Kuromiya in a Monrovia park, President Dwight Eisenhower banned homosexuals from federal employment with Executive Order 10450, part of what historians have labeled the Cold War's "Lavender Scare." Eisenhower's action accelerated what the Truman administration began. The Lavender Scare cost thousands of people their livelihoods: the State Department alone fired 1,000 suspected gay men and lesbians between 1947 and the early 1960s, with approximately 5,000 people fired throughout the federal government. Many other people resigned to avoid an investigation into their sexuality, and untold numbers of state and local government workers and private-sector employees were dismissed on suspicion of homosexuality. The U.S. military led an especially aggressive purge of suspected lesbians from the armed forces. Numbers are difficult to come by because so much secrecy and shame surrounded the investigations. The anti-Communist purges of the same period cost an estimated 10,000 Americans their jobs, but historians estimate that the Lavender Scare was even worse.[12]

In that environment, Kuromiya would not have encountered many positive portrayals of queer people. Gay and lesbian characters, when they appeared at all in fiction or film, were almost invariably tragic or malevolent figures whose character arcs ended in their deaths by suicide or murder. Members of Congress nevertheless considered these representations dangerous; they held hearings about the possibility of coded inducements to male homosexuality within comic books, while public health campaigns warned boys as well as girls to be suspicious of male strangers who wanted to make their acquaintance.[13]

Kuromiya was undeterred. As a high schooler, he bought a subscription to the *Village Voice*, an alternative newspaper based in New York City that was not overtly "gay" and thus did not arouse his parents' suspicions. He learned how to do something we might describe as "reading queerly": in film reviews, pulp novels, gossip columns, and elsewhere, a

Physique magazines were popular in the 1950s and 1960s among queer men who enjoyed the illustrated and photographed images of shirtless, muscular men. In addition to illustrations such as this one from the Spring 1955 issue, Physique Pictorial *included photographs shot by the iconic physique photographer Bob Mizer, who also published and edited the magazine.*

character's style of dress or mannerisms, or a critic's reference to "temperament" or "queer" interests, signaled a great deal to the attentive reader. Men's physique magazines, small-circulation newsletters, and gay-themed book services represented other sources of homoerotic and otherwise queer content.[14]

Lesbians were among the most avid consumers of the pulp fiction that increasingly appeared in tabloid magazines and paperback form after World War II. Publishers targeted what they presumed to be a heterosexual male reading audience with "pulp" or mass-market paperbacks that featured lurid tales of sinister older lesbians and their innocent female prey. With sensational titles and voyeuristic cover art depicting "twilight women," these books were a sort of soft-core pornography. Eager to find anything that described their experiences, many lesbians made do with homophobic pulp novels that at the very least put the word "lesbian" into the mainstream book market. A few clever authors realized they could disguise more sympathetic accounts of lesbians so long as they conformed to the conventions of the pulp novel, and lesbian readers looked for these titles especially.[15]

Perhaps Kuromiya also read the L.A.-based *ONE Magazine*, which put out its first issue in January 1953. The magazine was the creation of ONE, Inc., founded in October 1952 by former members of a West Hollywood Mattachine group and other activists, including a Japanese American who had been incarcerated at Manzanar Relocation Camp. *ONE Magazine* raised awareness of police harassment, offered legal advice, and created a forum for otherwise marginalized readers, who bought 5,000 copies a month through newsstand sales and subscriptions throughout the United States. The U.S. Post Office seized the October 1954 issue because of a fairly tame short story, "Sappho Remembered," about a lesbian couple. *ONE*'s lawyer challenged the obscenity charge all the way to the Supreme Court, which ruled in 1958 that a magazine about homosexuality was not obscene.[16]

Somehow, teenage Kuromiya heard about the League for Civil Education, a San Francisco–based organization founded in 1961 by two influential gay activists, José Sarria (who ran for city supervisor in 1962) and Guy Strait. Fed up with incessant police harassment, Sarria and Strait hoped that their organization would increase the power of bar owners and bartenders, protect men from entrapment, and buttress the gay community's political clout. Kuromiya received the group's newsletter, the *LCE News*, which included warnings about hot spots for police surveillance, as well as gossip and entertainment. Strait became a prolific publisher, producing a bar-and-nightlife guide in 1963. In 1964 he helped found the Society for Individual Rights (SIR), a gay rights organization modeled on direct-action civil rights groups like the Student Nonviolent Coordinating Committee (SNCC). Like thousands of others, Kuromiya had found a way to connect to a larger community of gay and lesbian people through these publications. From *LCE News*, he also learned about the early drumbeats of gay collective action.[17]

Around the time of his detention in juvenile hall, Kuromiya wrote about Philadelphia for a school paper. The idea that there existed a "city of brotherly love" stuck in his mind like a pin on a cork board. By the time he was a senior in high school, he also knew that the University of Pennsylvania had a cutting-edge architecture program, a discipline that he associated with utopian visions of harmonious living. He applied and was accepted with a prestigious scholarship that covered his expenses. As he boarded the flight out of Los Angeles in the fall of 1961, he could hardly have guessed at the adventures, dangers, and tragedies that awaited him in Love City.

Philadelphia did not disappoint. If the Penn campus itself was not a welcoming place for openly gay or lesbian people, nearby Rittenhouse Square was a spot not only to meet men for sex but to gather and talk. Center City as a whole, Steve Kiyoshi Kuromiya later recalled, was "quite gay."

Kuromiya's interest in activism drew him beyond the city and into the heart of the civil rights movement. In January 1962, during his freshman year, he joined the Freedom Rides and participated in a sit-in. He met Martin Luther King Jr., John Lewis, and other movement leaders at the 1963 March on Washington. In March 1965, as part of the voting-rights march from Selma to Montgomery, Kuromiya led a group of high school students to the Capitol Building, where a mounted sheriff's deputy beat him so badly that civil rights leaders announced to crowds of supporters that he might not survive the night. More committed to activism than coursework, Kuromiya left college without a degree but with a thick surveillance file at the FBI. He was a "security risk," the FBI feared, and a leftist anarchist.[18]

Kuromiya was slower to connect with the "homophile" movement, which sought social acceptance and equal protection for homosexuals as American citizens. It was a daring proposition amid the profoundly anti-gay culture of the postwar decades. A New York City conference hosted by the East Coast Homophile Organizations (ECHO) in 1964 was his introduction to the group. Attendees listened to presentations on homosexuality by "experts" from the fields of medicine, law, and psychology. Some members of the homophile movement insisted that participants dress conservatively; they shared a broader middle-class gay frustration with men derogatively called "swishes" and with butch women. Even so, anyone who publicly identified as gay or lesbian, "respectably" attired or not, faced the very real possibility of losing their jobs and being rejected by their families.[19]

Kuromiya wanted to push for civil rights without conforming to normative gender roles. Along with other homophile activists, he drew inspiration from the direct-action strategies of the Black civil rights movement. Kuromiya's assessment of the ECHO meeting was therefore mixed: "I thought, 'These are the activists and they're really courageous and everything, but they were accountants and librarians.' It was a little bit of a surprise. There were no flaming radicals." Short and slightly built, his trim haircut not yet grown out into a ponytail, Kuromiya himself could still pass for a moderate. Harder to miss was that he was usually one of very few nonwhite people at homophile gatherings.[20]

By the summer of 1965, Kuromiya was not exactly "in the closet," but he did not publicly identify as gay either. That changed when he heard about plans for a Fourth of July protest at Independence Hall in Philadelphia. The members of ECHO who led the picket urged gay men and lesbians to demand equal rights rather than politely ask for acceptance. The decision to launch a protest at government buildings was controversial. Among the activists hungry for a more militant strategy was Barbara Gittings, a devoted member of the Daughters of Bilitis (DOB), the homophile lesbian organization founded in 1955 in San Francisco. Gittings had grown increasingly frustrated with the group's official deference to professionals, rather than seeing lesbians and gay men themselves as the experts on homosexuality. As editor of DOB's magazine, *The Ladder*, she published an article by Frank Kameny, another leader of the pickets. Kameny was a former astronomer for the U.S. Army Maps Service who had been fired in the Lavender Scare purges. The Fourth of July event announced a new militancy among a cohort of gay and lesbian activists who nevertheless sought change within the existing political system, not a social revolution.[21]

Kuromiya met up with Clark Polak, an outspoken publisher, who joined the protest but refused to separate homoeroticism from gay activism. Polak complained that homophile leaders were "concerned with the rights of homosexuals as long as they somehow appear to be heterosexual, whatever that is." As the elected leader of the Philadelphia-based Janus Society, a homophile group that was part of ECHO, Polak transformed the group's newsletter into a ribald magazine, *DRUM*, with "news for 'queers' and fiction for 'perverts.'" Starting in 1964, in addition to substantive articles about the homophile movement, the magazine contained personal ads, comics, and parodies; Polak boasted that he had created a "gay *Playboy*." (Hugh Hefner's decidedly straight *Playboy* magazine had started publication in 1953.) By 1966, Polak, ever the savvy businessman, also operated the Trojan Book Service, which distributed gay pornography.[22]

Polak used the profits from his publishing ventures to establish the Homosexual Law Reform Society, which supported lawsuits against anti-gay policing and immigration policies. When the U.S. Immigration and Naturalization Service initiated deportation proceedings against Canadian citizen Clive Michael Boutilier, who was gay, the Homosexual Law Reform Society funded litigation challenging that deportation order all the way to the Supreme Court. In 1967, the court upheld the deportation as consistent with the 1952 McCarren–Walter Immigration and Naturalization Act's ban on people with a "psychopathic personality." Hounded by FBI agents and postal inspectors who had started to monitor homophile groups around the country, Polak was arrested on obscenity charges in 1967 and again in 1969. He fought the charges up to a 1972 plea-bargain that shuttered his pornography business.[23]

On July 4, 1965, Kuromiya helped Polak load picket signs into the back of Polak's Ford Falcon. They drove to Philadelphia's historic district, joining about ten other demonstrators at Independence Hall. Those present included Ernestine Eckstein, a Black woman who, like Kuromiya, came to the homophile movement as a seasoned civil rights activist, and Frank Kameny. On a day when temperatures peaked at

88 degrees, Kameny insisted that the men wear suits, the women wear dresses and pumps, and no one hold hands. Kuromiya understood this tactic as part of Kameny's message to the heterosexual majority that "we aren't monsters," but rather a respectable, persecuted minority demanding equal protection under the law. When they gathered again at Independence Hall in 1966, they called the event the "Annual Reminder"—a reminder that "homosexual citizens" lacked the liberties promised to all Americans. Kameny, Gittings, and others also demonstrated in front of the Civil Service Administration Building in Washington, DC, to protest federal employment discrimination.[24]

Genderqueer people who would not have been welcome at the Annual Reminders demanded respect from the establishments they patronized. In the spring of 1965, a small group of teenagers staged a sit-in at Dewey's, a restaurant in Philadelphia's Center City neighborhood, after staff refused to serve about 150 young people, apparently because some were "masculine women" and "feminine men" "wearing non-conformist clothing." To the protesters' delight, police instructed Dewey's owner to serve them. Their success was one small part of an upsurge in civil rights agitation across the country, which slowly but undeniably encompassed the demands of lesbian, gay, and transgender people. One year after Dewey's, transgender women, drag queens, and sex workers in San Francisco's Tenderloin district fought back against police who attempted to expel them from Compton's Cafeteria, a twenty-four-hour restaurant that served as their regular gathering place. Hurling purses, sugar shakers, and coffee cups, they forced the police to back down. The episode led to a landmark coalition of clergy, transwomen, sex workers, and police officers who agreed on reforms to local policing and expanded access to medical care.[25]

Since 1965, Kuromiya had accepted that the homophile-rights movement would occupy some of his time but that he would focus more on pursuing racial justice and protesting the American war in Vietnam. By the end of the 1960s and into the early 1970s, a new wave of gay activism opened up possibilities for a transnational, anticapitalist, and multiracial liberation project that united all of his political commitments. Kuromiya hoped that he could realize the utopian revolution he had long pursued.

The mood at the final "annual reminder" picket on July 4, 1969, was starkly different from how it had been at the first. Just a week earlier, gay, lesbian, and transgender patrons of the Stonewall Inn in New York City put up a fight when officers from the New York Police Department's Morals Squad raided the bar. (Two undercover policewomen were already inside.) The Stonewall Inn was a popular neighborhood bar, known for drawing white, Black, and Latinx queer people, including sex workers, drag queens, office workers, and artists. Police raids of bars that catered to queer customers were less frequent by the late 1960s; in 1966 the New York Court of Appeals ruled that drinking establishments had to serve homosexuals. The "Inn," however, did not have a liquor license. It instead operated as a "private club," an obvious ruse. The police decided it was time to shut it down.

The raid on June 28, 1969, turned into a riot after the police dragged a butch lesbian out of the bar, in handcuffs, and shoved her into a squad car. She escaped the car several times, trying to get back inside the Inn. Witnesses heard her yell, "Why don't you guys do something?" Infuriated patrons threw debris at the officers. Marsha P. ("Pay It No Mind") Johnson, a Black transwoman and street activist wearing a dress and high heels, climbed a lamppost holding a bag full of bricks, which she threw onto an officer's car, shattering the windshield. One eyewitness described "screaming queens forming chorus lines and kicking" in defiance of police with batons.[26]

The uprising quickly intensified. Police officers called for backup, and hundreds of queer New Yorkers rushed to Greenwich Village to join the protest. At one point, about one thousand protesters fought against eight officers, who blockaded themselves inside the bar. The arrival of additional police, on buses, enabled the officers to exit safely, but the standoff lasted three days. Someone spray painted "Gay Power" on a brick

The Gay Liberation Front originated in New York City in response to the uprising at the Stonewall Inn in June 1969. Kiyoshi Kuromiya cofounded the Philadelphia GLF, which was notably interracial and committed to liberating all people from sexism and homophobia.

wall. The activists who participated in the Stonewall rebellion refused the politics of respectability. They demanded immediate freedom to gather, carouse, and express themselves without fear of police harassment. A new organization, the Gay Liberation Front (GLF), emerged in Stonewall's wake and dramatically changed the tenor of gay politics.[27]

Many homophile activists at the "Annual Reminder" in July 1969 were therefore frustrated by Kameny's insistence on respectability and gender conformity, which seemed increasingly out of touch. Young people across the United States were experimenting with drugs, sexual liberation, and countercultural self-expression. The play *Oh! Calcutta!*, which featured full-frontal nudity, had opened off-Broadway just the month before. Mainstream films featured scenes with simulated sex and otherwise sexual themes. "Free love" in the nineteenth century often meant the ability to get a divorce or otherwise leave an unloving marriage to forge a fulfilling heterosexual relationship, but in the 1960s it connoted a defiant celebration of nonmarital, commitment-free consensual sex. That July 4 in Philadelphia, activists flouted Kameny's rules against hand-holding and casual attire, embracing an androgynous style that was increasingly popular among hippies and political radicals. By the summer of 1970, rather than another Annual Reminder, activists gathered for commemorations of the Stonewall rebellion, which became "gay pride" parades.[28]

Inspired by Black Power, militant feminism, and antiwar radicalism, the GLF announced a new vision of liberation rooted in multiracial solidarity and invested in individual freedoms rather than social acceptance. Stonewall was not the first queer riot, and the Gay Liberation Front was all but defunct within a few years. In the summer of 1969, the events at Stonewall generated a very modest amount of media coverage. But the fact that the Stonewall uprising inspired an annual commemoration with "pride" marches in New York, San Francisco, and other cities meant that it assumed a mythic quality as the event that transformed queer politics.[29]

Kuromiya was only too eager to abandon the homophile movement's defense of the "homosexual citizen" and endorse the GLF's vision of a revolution in sex roles and politics. "Out of the Closet, Into the Streets!" became GLF's exuberant mantra, not simply a call to make the sheer number of gay and lesbian people visible to straight society but to take up space and reimagine the boundaries of sexual identity. Kuromiya cofounded the Gay Liberation Front in Philadelphia. A predominantly nonwhite group of gay activists produced a written statement of the group's aims but had no official structure or leaders. With his broad network of antiwar and civil rights activist colleagues, Kuromiya likely influenced the composition of GLF Philly, attracting working-class, nonwhite queer people who were far less likely to feel comfortable in a majority-white group such as ECHO. Also unlike ECHO, GLF Philly

When activists staged the first "Annual Reminder" demonstration outside Independence Hall in Philadelphia in 1965, the decision to picket at government buildings was controversial within the homophile movement. But by the 1970s, the movement for gay rights had moved beyond respectful demonstrations, favoring radical, liberatory action instead. Activists like the man pictured here, identified by the photographer as "Alex," were no longer asking for rights but demanding them. Photographed at a Philadelphia Pride March on Independence Mall in 1973, Alex holds a large sign that reads GAY RIGHTS NOW*!*

did not present gay people as an oppressed minority fighting for rights. Instead, it envisioned a society where everyone could express themselves openly. Voicing the erotic ethos of the sexual revolution, the GLF statement declared, "Homosexual love is the most complete form of expression between two members of the same sex." Their meetings encouraged a form of consciousness raising (CR)—a tenet and practice of the feminist movement—so that all men could recognize how a world built around assumed heterosexuality had limited their self-expression and led them to look down on openly gay people.[30]

Kuromiya believed (as did many other radicals) that nearly all men, if freed from cultural inhibitions, would experience same-sex desires; sexism and homophobia constrained their sexuality and taught them a very narrow norm of masculinity. He likened his philosophy of universal male desire to the vision of the "Woman-Identified Woman," a manifesto created by a group called the Radicalesbians. The women in Radicalesbians had split off from the GLF in New York City in response to the misogyny of the group's gay male leaders. Radicalesbians crafted the "Woman-Identified Woman" as a declaration of woman-centered values, relationships, and politics. They pledged that their primary allegiances and affections were with other women. In this way, they shared with other radical gay men and lesbians an understanding of their sexual desire not as the thing that defined them but as the foundation of their freedom.[31]

Gay and lesbian radicals of the 1970s pursued not only liberation but solidarity with oppressed people everywhere. Kuromiya and other members of GLF Philadelphia showed up at Welfare Rights Organization meetings, protested alongside the Puerto Rican Young Lords Party, and voiced solidarity with the Black Panther Party, solidarity that not all GLF members embraced. (Gay liberationists also dealt with homophobia among members of the New Left, many of whom considered homosexuality a distraction from or even antithetical to their dreams of a worldwide communist revolution.) It was a way of viewing the world, as a web of interconnected identities and politics. Kuromiya had viscerally experienced this notion. After all, the U.S. government had imprisoned him in a camp because of his race and the state of California incarcerated him in a juvenile detention center because of his sexuality. Through GLF Philadelphia, Kuromiya and others connected the cause of gay and lesbian liberation to the emancipation of oppressed people across the globe.[32]

A movement for gay rights emerged in these years too. A new organization, the Gay Activists Alliance (GAA), originated in New York in 1969 as a GLF splinter group and soon had a Philadelphia chapter. GAA was committed to political organizing; it was almost entirely male and predominantly white. GAA's focus on securing legal rights for homosexuals, and its antipathy to the Black Panthers, succeeded in alienating Kuromiya. He wanted no part of any campaign to expand legal definitions of "consenting adults" or of the phrase "in private" to include same-sex sexual acts; he believed the government should have no role in defining which sex acts were legal.

Kuromiya may have been more sympathetic to the GAA's efforts to end professional psychiatry's brutal treatment of gay men and lesbians. At the 1970 and 1971 meetings of the American Psychiatric Association (APA), members of GLF and GAA interrupted a talk by Dr. Irving Bieber, whose 1962 book, *Homosexuals: A Psychoanalytic Study of Male Homosexuals,* had solidified the prevailing psychiatric view that all homosexuals were mentally ill. Behind the scenes, an underground group of closeted psychiatrists calling itself GayPA met to discuss how to change their profession's understanding of same-sex desires. Sustained pressure from activists shifted the culture within the APA and led the board of trustees to declassify homosexuality as a pathological condition in the revised edition of the *DSM* in 1973, a decision upheld by nearly 60 percent of the APA's membership.[33]

It was the beginning of a dramatic transformation in the possibilities for queer advocacy in the United States (and beyond, as many groups built international coalitions to support LGBT rights). The National Gay Task Force, a pivotal advocacy organization in the APA campaign, was soon joined in 1972 by Lambda Legal Defense and Education Fund. Together with the new Sexual Privacy Project at the American Civil Liberties Union (ACLU) and the Sexuality and Lesbianism Task Force at the National Organization for Women (NOW), they launched lawsuits against discriminatory policies. Fourteen college and university student groups used the courts to win recognition from their institutions during the 1970s, often by challenging the idea that universities would be complicit in abetting sex crimes if they legitimated an LGBT student group.[34]

One issue that became central to the gay rights movement—lifting the ban on gay and lesbians from military service—failed to inspire radical activists like Kuromiya. For him and other revolutionaries, the goal was not acceptance within what they viewed as an institution of imperial violence. The draft that remained in effect in the early 1970s put gay men at risk: they would likely be excluded from the military—and outed publicly—if they self-disclosed or were discovered to be gay at induction. (That said, plenty of straight men pretended to be gay to avoid military service.) Selective Service officials occasionally ignored such revelations and either allowed a gay man into the military or wrote down a less-stigmatizing reason for his disqualifications to serve. More typically, the man's homosexuality was noted on his selective service record, an action that disqualified him from civil service employment and led the FBI to open a file on a potentially "subversive" citizen.[35]

The results of the new gay rights movement were decidedly mixed. In 1975, the U.S. Civil Service Commission (CSC) dropped its ban on gay and lesbian employees. The ban on gay and lesbian servicemembers remained (replaced, in 1993, by the highly problematic "Don't Ask, Don't Tell" policy), as did a rule prohibiting the issuance of security clearances to gays and lesbians (until 1997). Across the 1970s and 1980s, twenty-one states decriminalized sodomy (joining Illinois, which had decriminalized male same-sex activity in 1961), and several municipalities passed gay rights ordinances. Harvey Milk won election to the San Francisco Board of Supervisors in 1977 as one of the first openly gay public officials in the United States. His leadership helped defeat a statewide measure, known as the Briggs Initiative, that would have barred gay men and lesbians from employment in public schools. These dramatic developments remained exceptional. Most gay and lesbian public figures remained deeply closeted. Civil Service reforms did not apply to the FBI or CIA, an indication of the lasting associations between homosexuality and security risks.[36]

Opponents of these reforms insisted that homosexuality was a contagion and a learned behavior. Just months after an anti-discrimination law was passed in Florida's Miami-Dade County in 1977, voters returned to the polls to vote on a referendum to reverse those protections for gay and lesbian public employees. A former beauty queen and gospel singer named Anita Bryant led the repeal campaign with the slogan "Save Our Children." Anti-gay activists presented open homosexuality as a pernicious threat to the nation's youth; "because [homosexuals] can't reproduce, they recruit," Bryant blared. Her campaign portrayed gay men as indefatigable sex fiends who wanted to abolish age-of-consent laws and, if they were teachers, lure their students into homosexuality. That June, a majority of voters heeded Bryant's warning and passed the referendum, repealing the months-old anti-discrimination statute. Activists elsewhere in the country who opposed gay rights took note. Many leaders of these reactionary efforts adopted the strategies of white supremacists, who had warned that school integration would lead to interracial sex; often the same people who supported segregation now opposed gay rights.[37]

Community building by gay, lesbian, and transgender people flourished in spite of those setbacks. Choirs, coffee klatches (including a Gay Coffee Hour that Kuromiya started at Penn), softball teams, professional caucuses, political clubs, religious gatherings, record labels, music festivals, and bookstores—a far from exhaustive list—opened the door to a more expansive kind of openly gay or lesbian life. Small numbers of lesbians and gay men started communes in both cities and the countryside, utopian experiments in which they hoped to express their sexuality in ways that reflected a radically egalitarian, feminist, anticapitalist, and antiracist politics. Others moved into party politics, ran for office, and lobbied their elected officials on behalf of LGBT rights. After decades of viewing police officers as adversaries, middle-class and mostly white gay men built partnerships with their local police departments; rather than fearing vice squads, they looked to the cops to protect them and their property from anti-gay attacks and vandalism. (Those alliances profoundly alienated queer people of color and street youth.) Activists founded health clinics for LGBT people in Boston; Washington, DC; and San Francisco, among other cities. Gay workers formed alliances within their unions and professional organizations. The aims and activities of these new communities and organizations were manifold, from the grand (revolution) to the prosaic (meeting potential sexual or romantic partners).[38]

Kuromiya moved in and out of the gay liberation movement in the 1970s and 1980s. He was taking psychedelics, living communally, and practicing yoga. Somewhat incongruously, he made a living as a restaurant critic and occasional editorial assistant to futurist architect Buckminster Fuller, with whom he shared visions of a world transformed by revolutionary design.

It was a life rich with friendships and ideas. No one experiencing the exhilarating freedoms of gay liberation in the 1970s knew what lay ahead. They were survivors already, of Cold War–era homophobia and of an entire state apparatus that had decided to single out gay men and lesbians as dangers to civil society. They were finally, forcefully claiming their citizenship and defying attempts to limit their full personhood. The entitlement of all people to the pleasures of sex remained an argument far too many Americans still needed to defend.

Chapter 14

Public Masturbator Number One

"We celebrated Groundhog Day with a small sex party."

In the annals of the history of sexuality, there is perhaps but one enthusiast who would think to commemorate the minor holiday in those terms. But Betty Dodson was no ordinary chronicler of sexual behaviors and information. Describ-

Betty Dodson (1929–2020) moved to New York City to become an artist. Following a six-year marriage, she immersed herself in the city's sex scene, enjoying group sex, pornography, and erotic painting. In 1968 she had a successful gallery show in Manhattan that featured life-size drawings of couples having sex.

ing herself as "America's Public Masturbator Number One," Dodson devoted her adult life to experiencing, teaching about, and advocating for the pleasures of solo and partnered orgasm.[1]

Dodson's career spanned decades and cultural eras. In the late 1960s, she resolved to liberate women to enjoy masturbation. Her advice was a radical departure from even previously boundary-pushing works. *Sex and the Single Girl,* the 1962 bestseller by *Cosmopolitan* editor Helen Gurley Brown, encouraged single women to see sex with men as a pleasure they were entitled to enjoy, and also, when strategically arranged, a means to career advancement. Dodson wanted women to view solo sex as the foundation of their sexual, spiritual, and political emancipation, not as a means to an end. She stripped sex of its contexts, idealizing instead an erotic experience unaffected by race, class, gender, or other identities. Hers was, in many ways, an especially privileged white, middle-class argument for sex's singular importance to human liberation. As a call for women to name, own, and celebrate their orgasmic capacity, it was also more than a bit revolutionary.[2]

At lectures and at the all-female, completely nude workshops she hosted in her apartment living room, Dodson taught women to appreciate and admire their genitals, to prioritize the erotic importance of the clitoris, and to embrace the satisfactions of a good vibrator. Always more than a bit outside the mainstream, even as the mainstream shifted, she was an adult-film devotee during the "golden age of porn" in the 1970s, promoted women's sex-toy companies, enjoyed group sex and kink, and became embroiled in the "sex wars" among anti-porn and pro-sex feminists in the 1980s. Not long before her death at the age of ninety-one in 2020, Dodson shared her lifetime of orgasmic knowledge with actor and entrepreneur Gwyneth Paltrow for a *Goop Lab* (Netflix) episode about women's sexuality, perhaps hoping to reach the affluent but erotically underinformed female audience that Paltrow attracted to her "lifestyle" company.[3]

The arc of Dodson's wild career illuminates the radicalism as well as the limitations of sex-positive feminism. She glossed over the class dimensions of sex equality and was oblivious to its racial complexities.

In denouncing erotic inhibition, she minimized the risks of assault and the effects of abuse. Reducing women's liberation to orgasmic independence oversimplified the reasons for gendered power differences and women's subordination.

What endeared Dodson to multiple generations of women—and what has remained controversial—was her adamant refusal to shroud women's erotic pleasures in shame. In the late 1960s and 1970s, Dodson envisioned an erotic insurgency on the horizon, in which women would claim pleasure for themselves. What seemed self-explanatory to her instead drove a wedge into the women's liberation movement and provided an easy target for defenders of sexual conservatism.

A 1960 *Cosmopolitan* magazine article answered the question posed by its title, "Do Women Provoke Sex Attack?" with a resounding "yes." Women should scrupulously monitor their own behavior, lest they arouse a man "past the point of no return" after which, "when the girl resists, he seeks gratification by force." Staying "chaste" until marriage was, the dominant narrative insisted, a young woman's responsibility.[4]

Dodson rejected that advice wholesale. She grew up in Wichita, Kansas, where her mother, Bess, ignored the repressive politics of Wichita's evangelical Christian culture. In 1934, when a five-year-old Betty masturbated in the backseat of the family car during a long road trip, Bess did not interrupt her because "that was such a long trip and we were so short of money and you kids weren't having that much fun." Bess's nonchalance about her daughter's autoeroticism was extremely unusual. Although health experts in the 1930s had largely jettisoned more than a century of warnings about masturbation as a disease, the idea that solitary sex was both physically injurious and psychologically damaging persisted.[5]

Betty likewise refused to view premarital sex as a precursor to a life of pain and degradation. "First intercourse (sexual) at 20 yrs old[.] It was good," she noted matter-of-factly in the margins of a personal narrative she drafted years later as she was launching her sex workshops.[6]

Television shows and film later portrayed the 1950s as the wholesome era of June Cleaver and suburban tranquility, but young women in the United States did not universally conform to that image. Like the "Victory Girls" who unabashedly pursued sex with U.S. servicemen during World War II, Dodson owned her sexual desires. Her sexual adventures exposed her to far less risk than unmarried white women had faced even a decade earlier. Victory Girls were periodically rounded up as threats to the morals and health of U.S. servicemen, but Dodson benefitted from being at the leading edge of white women's heterosexual liberation. Civil libertarians and sex educators advocated toleration of nonmarital heterosexual sex, to distinguish private and therefore protected acts from truly criminal behaviors, such as prostitution and rape. (As Chapter 16 explores, this shift coincided with stepped-up policing of Black women's sexuality.)[7]

Dodson arrived in New York City in 1950 after one year of college and several years' experience creating art and advertising copy for a local newspaper and department stores. She was already unusual for not marrying directly out of high school. Dodson wanted to live the life of the successful, sexually uninhibited artist. She spent five years studying classical drawing and painting, paying her way with a combination of scholarships and freelance fashion-illustration gigs. Although her art and self-presentation initially remained somewhat conventional (she wore dresses and kept her hair long), Dodson had a series of boyfriends and casual sex partners with whom she explored her enthusiasms. She pursued the sort of libidinal freedom that a new magazine, *Playboy*, promised urbane American men from its first issue in 1953. With partially naked women posed for its centerfolds, celebrity interviews, and advice about hi-fi stereos and sophisticated cocktails, *Playboy* presented a fantasy world of sensual gratification. Publisher Hugh Hefner envisioned a sexual playground for straight men, but Dodson saw no reason why she couldn't have as much fun as the boys were having.[8]

Contraception made it possible for Dodson to enjoy sex without fear of pregnancy. Before she left Wichita for New York, the spermicidal jelly she used during sex failed her and led her to seek what turned out to be an unanesthetized illegal abortion "on a dingy kitchen table." After that harrowing experience, Dodson borrowed a friend's engagement ring to convince a gynecologist to prescribe her a diaphragm. That woman-directed method of birth control, which Margaret Sanger had touted since she opened her first clinic in Brooklyn in 1916, was typically available only to married women—or engaged women who could convince a sympathetic physician that they were *almost* married. Legal impediments remained even after the Food and Drug Administration (FDA) authorized the first oral contraceptive for women in 1960. Enovid, manufactured by the G. D. Searle company, was nearly 100 percent effective; by 1962, 1.2 million American women were taking it daily. Women like Dodson who were already sexually active were the ones most likely to ask their physicians for a prescription (contrary to complaints that "the Pill" inspired young women to rush out and initiate premarital sex). Dodson stayed loyal to her diaphragm for the duration of her fertile years. Given that early iterations of the Pill had such high doses of hormones that many women experienced blood clots and other painful side effects, Dodson was wise to avoid it.[9]

A 1965 Supreme Court case, *Griswold v. Connecticut*, protected the right of married people to access contraception as a matter of privacy, if not of women's sexual liberation. The *Griswold* decision occurred amid a wave of efforts throughout the United States to decriminalize private sexual acts involving consenting adults. Unmarried women's access to physician-prescribed contraception was not protected until 1972, in *Eisenstadt v. Baird*.[10]

Still, fear of becoming an "old maid" spurred Dodson to get married, in 1959, when she was twenty-nine years old. Her husband, an advertising executive, was a kind person but an unsatisfying lover, and they soon ceased to have much of a sex life together. Masturbating in secret was her only way to experience the pleasures that popular culture had led her to think she would find in the marriage bed. Dodson and her spouse never managed to reconcile their divergent erotic needs.[11]

An amicable divorce after about six years of marriage left Dodson in possession of a rent-controlled apartment, some financial security, and a burning desire to find more compatible sexual partners. She "cut loose." "I want to be a pervert," she told her friends—a daring if privileged aspiration at a time when the idea of queer people's "psychopathic personality" continued to shape immigration policies, civil rights law, and policing. "I want to be one of those sex fiends." Her erotic encounters proliferated and grew more satisfying. Petite and fit, Dodson cut her hair shorter, started a regular yoga practice, and launched into her new life's work.[12]

Her companion in many of these adventures was a former professor named Grant Taylor, a longtime (if never exclusive) partner who was as willing as Dodson was to experiment. They dove headfirst into the group-sex scene. By the late 1960s, the growing popularity of "spouse swapping" and group sex had attracted the attention of academic researchers and prompted occasional (and, naturally, sensationalistic) press coverage. Unlike most "swappers," Dodson and Taylor were unmarried, but they fit the profile of the white, middle-class individual who predominated in the American swinging subculture and in films such as *Bob and Carol and Ted and Alice* (1969), which was nominated for four Academy Awards. Dodson expanded her relationship with Taylor into a committed group that included his new girlfriend, Sheila Shea, and another couple.[13]

She also mounted gallery exhibits of her drawings of nudes, some featuring pairs having sex, some of individuals masturbating. Negative reactions to her life-size masturbation drawings convinced her that the world was more sexually repressed than she had realized: "I called every woman I knew and asked if she was masturbating. If she wasn't, I suggested she start immediately." She even called her mother, who was sixty-eight and a widow. (After initial reticence, Bess reported two weeks later to her daughter that she was having solo orgasms.)[14]

Dodson belonged to a new wave of sex educators who argued that autonomous sexual pleasure was normal and even essential. They argued that, far from being physically or mentally damaging, masturbation improved a person's bodily and emotional health, much as Kinsey had noted in his 1953 study of female sexuality. But Dodson's celebration of masturbation for its own sake was unusual. Even the sex researchers William Masters and Virginia Johnson, authors of the famed study *Human Sexual Response* (1966), extolled masturbation principally as a way to improve marital sex, a view echoed in much of the sex therapy of the 1960s and 1970s. The pursuit of sexual pleasure for oneself became Dodson's obsessive goal. She pieced together a living by "creating erotic wallpaper," "running commercial sex parties," and more.[15]

Dodson's desire to tell the world about the power of masturbation and orgasm quickly ran afoul of anti-obscenity laws, a thorn still deep in the side of free-speech advocates, sex educators, and pornographers nearly a hundred years after Anthony Comstock went to Washington to plead his case before Congress. The offending item was "The Fine Art of Lovemaking," a long-form interview with Dodson published in the February 1971 issue of the *Evergreen Review,* a highbrow literary magazine. Amply illustrated with sixteen of Dodson's sex drawings, the interview gave the "woman painter of erotic art" an international platform to present her theories. She proudly described herself as both a feminist and a pornographer.[16]

The definition of legal obscenity was far from clear. *Roth v. United States* (1957) defined obscenity as whatever "the average person, applying contemporary community standards," would consider to be something that principally "appeals to prurient interest." Although the *Roth* test created a First Amendment protection for anything understood to express "even the slightest redeeming social importance," it offered censors a basis for restricting sexually explicit films, magazines, and books as violations of "community standards." Homophile magazines like *ONE*, which contained no nudity, were thus especially vulnerable to prosecution. Both American culture and U.S. law had grown significantly more tolerant of explicit sexual material, but law enforcement continued to single out "perverse" forms of sexual expression, particularly anything relating to homosexuality, for harsher restrictions.[17]

Defining obscenity—and determining how, if at all, to limit it—confounded the Supreme Court, which issued a series of contradictory decisions between the mid-1960s and the early 1970s. *Memoirs v. Massachusetts* (1966) held that John Cleland's infamous novel was not obscene and strengthened First Amendment protections for sexually explicit work. Just a few years later, however, the Supreme Court reversed course in *Miller v. California* (1973) and made it easier for material to be found obscene, so long as the "average person, applying contemporary community standards," would conclude that the material lacked "serious literary, artistic, political, or scientific value." *Paris Adult Theatre v. Slaton* (1973), handed down the same day, likewise permitted governments to ban obscene materials for the sake of maintaining "a decent society." Dramatic shifts in those "community standards" made successful obscenity prosecutions increasingly rare, but the possibility for government censorship endured. Dodson's aim was to set sex free from all limitations.[18]

The "obscene" art that Dodson showed in galleries paled in comparison to the "hard-core" pornography on screens in an increasing number of American movie theaters in the late 1960s and early 1970s. For years, short pornographic films, often called "stags," had played in arcades, peep shows, and private homes. In the 1960s, loosely plotted films with female nudity and simulated heterosexual intercourse were introduced to small urban theaters and rural drive-ins—about six hundred venues by 1969. Feature-length pornographic films became fashionable—and commercially feasible—after the Motion Picture Association of America (MPAA) abandoned its production code in 1968, which had forbidden the discussion of sexual topics, not to mention overt representations of sex, in American films. (In 1973, the MPAA adopted the age-based rating system.) In the early 1970s, straight, hardcore pornographic films moved from the backrooms of sex clubs and porn houses to neighborhood theaters, a phenomenon that became known as "porno chic."[19]

Deep Throat and *Behind the Green Door,* both released in 1972, were two of the most popular feature-length pornos, each depicting explicit male-female oral and vaginal sex. Although it played on fewer theatrical screens, *Nights in Black Leather* (1973) was a popular gay adult film. During the 1960s, men cruised for sex with other men in theaters screening softcore pornography. Hardcore gay films in the early 1970s became an important form of gay male popular culture, even as they popularized a new stereotype of the macho, denim- and cowboy-boot-clad gay "clone."[20]

The unexpected popularity of *Deep Throat* and *Behind the Green Door* normalized conversations about explicit sex acts and helped make straight porn acceptable for heterosexual middle-class Americans. *Deep Throat* earned an estimated $100 million worldwide, and its star, Linda Boreman (acting under the name Linda Lovelace), appeared on late-night talk shows and in mainstream magazines. The film featured Boreman as a woman whose clitoris was rather anomalously located in her throat. Adult film star Harry Reems played the physician who explained to Lovelace's character why she found penis-vagina sex disappointing—news that led her to "deep-throat" a series of men, with orgasmic results for all involved. It was a premise that might be credited for acknowledging the importance of the female orgasm, albeit within a straight male fantasy that a man receiving fellatio had simultaneously satisfied his female partner.[21]

Behind the Green Door, a film about an extremely kinky orgy, included a trapeze scene in which white actor Marilyn Chambers simultaneously had intercourse with a Black actor named Johnnie Keyes, gave another man a blowjob, and manually stimulated two more men. The fetishized portrayal of Keyes as a "savage" African, wearing a bone necklace and face paint, epitomized a racialized fantasy common in pornography. (Interracial pornography more often featured scenes of white men dominating Black women and typically included both implied and overt violence.)[22]

The mainstreaming of hardcore pornography fired the political imaginations of Dodson and like-minded sex radicals. Pornography's "fantasy dreams of expanded sexuality," Dodson explained, were not only arousing but politically explosive. Her main inspiration on this point was the Austrian American psychoanalyst Wilhelm Reich. He had studied with Freud, who believed that sexual desires were natural, and that repression led to a debilitated, neurotic, and impotent society. Too much repression, Freud explained in 1908, was the cause of such "perversions" as homosexuality and compulsive masturbation. Reich went several steps further. In *The Function of Orgasm: Sex-Economic Problems of Biological Energy* (1942), he warned that sexual repression was dangerous. Orgasm, by contrast, prepared the individual psyche for liberation. Even better known than Reich was his contemporary, Herbert Marcuse, another psychoanalyst. Marcuse argued that sexual repression fed authoritarianism, and that capitalism drained libidinous energies necessary for individuals to pursue the "Pleasure Principle." The mantra that people should "Make Love, Not War" was not merely philosophical, then, but a plan to achieve global peace. Dodson interpreted these theories as more evidence that sex was the driving force in the human experience. Alluding to the Soviet Union's economic plans, she added that in any revolution, "Those five-year plans have got to include orgasms."[23]

In the fall of 1971, she traveled to the second Wet Dreams Film Festival in Amsterdam, a gathering of about four hundred people who watched the latest adult films during the day and gathered for drugs and group sex at night. Dodson was one of the invited judges, and she celebrated the festival's hedonism, which culminated in a "superorgy" of about fifty people. "I was making love to people and I didn't know their names and it didn't matter you know," she recalled. The parties at the festival affirmed an idea Dodson shared with contemporary sex liberationists: sex is social, a way of knowing a person and building a community. More often associated with some queer men's sexual sociability, this relational view of sex inspired Dodson to seek erotic encounters with as many different people as possible.[24]

Back in the United States, Dodson created an especially interactive form of sex education: her "Bodysex" workshops, in which she helped other women learn about their bodies and practice masturbation techniques. She hosted the workshops in her apartment, greeting each woman at the door fully naked and inviting them to leave their clothes on hooks in her entryway. Nudity was part of Dodson's method for helping women move past any shame or ignorance they had about their bodies. Dell Williams, who attended a workshop in 1972, initially recoiled: "since I had never been conditioned to feel comfortable with anyone in the nude, I was not prepared to be nude among complete strangers, all women or no." But Dodson set her at ease: "To be with her was to share her sense of joy and aliveness, her environment, her sexuality, HERSELF." Dodson reinforced the idea that her workshops offered women the opportunity to shed a lifetime of learned inhibitions. It was a scene that Angela Heywood, in her late-nineteenth-century quest for sexual candor, could only have imagined.[25]

Participants in Bodysex workshops discussed how they felt about

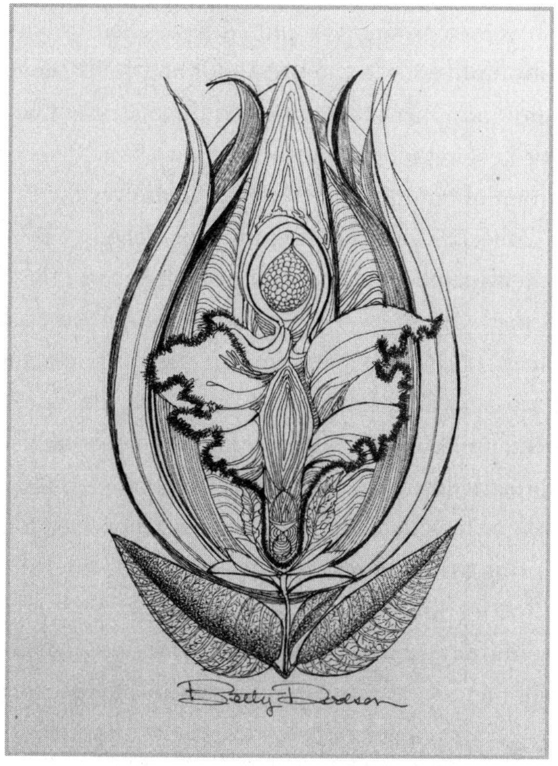

Dodson's self-published booklet, Liberating Masturbation, *was her manifesto about the necessity of sexual self-pleasure for women's liberation. This cover art captured Dodson's artistic sensibility and humor: an ornately detailed flower blossom that represents female genitals.*

their bodies, their degrees of satisfaction with their orgasms, and their fantasies. The workshops had several standard elements. "Genital show and tell" asked each woman to hold up a mirror to her genitals, which were illuminated by a desk lamp for everyone else in the room to view and appreciate. Williams admitted that she was initially shy about showing her vulva to strangers: "But Betty made it easy by commencing to show her own genitals first in such a matter-of-fact manner that you would think she was demonstrating a new coffee pot." Dodson and Sheila Shea, who helped run the workshops, masturbated with vibrators in front of the group. Dodson expanded on these ideas in *Liberating Masturbation*, her self-published guide for women, which sold thousands of copies.[26]

Groups of women around the United States had begun to perform cervical self-examinations in the late 1960s and 1970s, an element of a women's health movement that criticized the male-dominated medical profession for keeping most women ignorant about their own bodies. In 1971, a group of feminists who called themselves the Boston Women's Health Collective distributed a mimeographed guide to women's health that their members had written, which became the blockbuster book *Our Bodies, Ourselves* (1973). Across the United States, women in consciousness-raising groups examined their cervices and educated each other about gynecological conditions. Dodson was not passing around a speculum, but her call for women to know their own bodies echoed the broader women's liberation movement.[27]

Over the next four decades, Bodysex workshop fees supplemented the modest living that Dodson made as a lecturer, writer, and educator. News about the workshops circulated in feminist newsletters. She did not keep records of the participants in her workshops, but the most outspoken fans of them were white, pro-sex feminists like Dodson.[28]

Betty Dodson was in her early forties when she joined the resurgent feminist movement, fully convinced that orgasm was the foundation of a better world. Drawing on Reich, she explained that "the economic and political control of women is based on sexual repression." That argument appealed to many women, but Dodson's insistence that orgasm

Betty Dodson's presentation at the NOW Sexuality Conference in New York City in 1973 introduced her to an influential cohort of feminist women committed to including sexual liberation within the women's movement. Here, Dodson demonstrates how she masturbated using a Hitachi Magic Wand vibrator.

was a *catalyst* for revolution offended activists who prioritized class-, race-, and gender-based analyses of their oppression.[29]

Dodson's philosophy found a warm welcome among the feminists who gathered for NOW's "Sexuality Conference" in June 1973 in New York City. NOW had been founded in 1966 to advance gender equality, and by 1973, it addressed a range of feminist issues. Judy Wenning, the president of NOW's New York chapter, explained that the conference's goal was to "encourage women to see themselves not as heterosexual or homosexual or bisexual, but as sexual." Among the more than one thousand women who attended the conference's lectures and workshops, Dodson's Sunday-morning presentation became legendary.[30]

She showed slides of her artwork, images of genitals in medical texts and pamphlets, and then "huge, full-color, extreme-closeup slides of the individual genitals of about ten women who'd taken her workshops." With her trained eye, she invited her audience to see each vulva as a work of art, describing one with elaborate folds as "baroque," another one with a narrow, elongated shape as a "Classical Cunt," and a hairless one as

In this additional image from the NOW Sexuality Conference, Dodson seems to have turned on the vibrator, demonstrating its movement against her hand. Her matter-of-fact presentation, with photographs of female genitals and frank descriptions of masturbatory techniques, inspired women such as Dell Williams, who subsequently opened Eve's Garden, the first sex shop for women, in New York City.

"Danish modern." (All of her examples drew from European art styles.) "Betty emphasized the special beauty of each woman's skin texture and hair color," one attendee recalled, "and the unique shape of each clitoris, vagina, and anus . . . When she finished, the women applauded and whistled triumphantly." The crowd rewarded her with a standing ovation.[31]

Williams was so inspired by Dodson that she opened Eve's Garden, the first women-only sex store in the United States. Williams envisioned Eve's Garden as "a comfortable place where women would be able to buy vibrators without embarrassment, harassment, or hassle." Williams's store was one of a host of new businesses and organizations created by and for women in the 1970s. Many of these enterprises operated on a collectivist ethos, eschewing a drive for profits in favor of free educational workshops and community-building.[32]

Dodson lived an increasingly bicoastal life, splitting her time between her Bodysex workshops in New York and a group of sexual iconoclasts in San Francisco. She earned a PhD in sexology from the Institute for the Advanced Study of Sexuality, an unconventional (and unaccredited) graduate program that operated out of a "seedy" San Francisco storefront. The Institute's signature instructional tool, Sexual Attitude Restructuring (SAR), entailed watching hours upon hours of commercial porn to "desensitize" participants to the choreographed erotic configurations the films portrayed. SAR continued with "sensitization," as they watched verité sex films, non-commercial productions featuring individuals, couples, and groups having sex without the artificial elements of studio lighting or professional camera work. Students were encouraged to express their own sexual desires as they watched, with the event invariably resulting in what participants affectionately called the "Fuckorama."[33]

This was a far cry from the priorities of sex researchers of the time. In the 1970s, sexologists named two new categories of sexual disorder: inhibited sexual desire and sex addiction. While a later generation of activists would name asexuality as a category of identity (especially after the 2014 publication of Julie Decker's book, *The Invisible Orientation: An Introduction to Asexuality*), sex therapists and researchers in the 1970s viewed it as one of several diagnoses of disordered sexual desire they observed in their patients. To Dodson, lack of interest in sex was a hang-up, and something to be gotten over as quickly as possible.[34]

Such sexual hedonism deeply offended some feminists, who found it not simply tangential but antithetical to the movement's aims. "There's a danger," an editorial in a feminist newsletter noted, "of confusing self-gratification with liberation." In 1975, feminist Ti-Grace Atkinson forcefully argued that the women's movement was never about sexual liberation, an idea that merely reproduced "an old Left-Establishment joke on feminism: that feminists were just women who needed to get properly laid." Atkinson blamed the patriarchy for making sex appear to be far more important than she believed it truly was. Valerie Solanas, a like-minded radical, described sex as "a gross waste of time." Dodson, of course, did not want simply to "get laid" but to give other women the knowledge and skills they needed to enjoy orgasm whenever and wherever they wanted to.[35]

Nor could many feminists ignore sexual violence to the extent that Dodson had. In consciousness-raising groups and "rap sessions," many women divulged their personal experiences with intimate-partner violence and sexual assault. Awareness of violence against women as a social and political matter, rather than merely an individual one, motivated thousands of women to become anti-rape activists. Helping women escape domestic violence and heal from rape became a unifying cause within an otherwise fractious feminist movement. By 1976, four hundred feminist-led rape crisis centers existed across the country.[36]

Yet even approaches to sexual violence revealed divisions among women. In Susan Brownmiller's landmark treatise about rape and gender, *Against Our Will* (1975), she argued that rape was an expression of male power over women, of the desire of "*all men* to keep *all women* in a state of fear." Brownmiller's refusal to concede that some people, especially nonwhite men, suffered under a different set of assumptions—that, for instance, there was a long history of false rape accusations against Black men—dismayed Black women who insisted on a politics that foregrounded race as well as sex.[37]

What became known as the "sex wars" pitted "pro-sex" feminists like Dodson against "anti-porn" feminists. Anti-porn activists argued that all pornography abused women and that sadomasochistic (SM) erotic role-play reproduced women's subordination. According to Robin Morgan, a prominent radical feminist, "pornography is the theory, and rape is the practice." Pro-sex feminists countered that these distinctions between "good" and "bad" sex were simply new ways to control and shame women. As the sex-radical feminist Ellen Willis asserted, the sexual revolution for women entailed not "the simple absence of external restrictions—laws and overt social taboos" but the "social and psychological conditions that foster satisfying sexual relations."[38]

The exuberantly public sexuality that Dodson and other sex liberationists celebrated struck anti-pornography feminists as evidence of women's ongoing subjugation, especially when children were involved. They were quick to point to such films as *Pretty Baby* (1978), in which a preadolescent Brooke Shields played a child prostitute in a New Orleans brothel, and *Taxi Driver* (1976), in which Jodi Foster portrayed a teen sex worker. Shields's seductive ads for Calvin Klein jeans in the 1980s similarly registered with these critics as attempts to transform female children into objects of desire. Black feminists, meanwhile, pointed out that anti-pornography feminists, in their outrage over the sexualization of female minors, ignored how vulnerable girls and women of color were to sexual exploitation and to abuse by police officers. Stepped-up law enforcement and morals reforms, they knew, had never made Black women or men safer.[39]

Dodson was undeterred. She explored her affinity for "kink," and by 1982 she was experimenting with SM, which involved consent-based submission and punishment. Dodson now identified as a "bisexual lesbian" who acted as the dominant, or "Domme," partner during SM. Adopting an androgynous style, she reveled in her self-presentation as "a leather dyke" for whom leather harnesses and toys were major turn-ons. Lesbian SM practitioners rejected the idea that role-playing was inherently oppressive, a mere mimicry of heterosexual power relations. Far from a re-creation of violence, they argued, SM provided a safe opportunity for women to experiment with partners they trusted. Some even described SM as a way for women to heal from patriarchy.[40]

Gayle Rubin, a leading feminist theorist and founding member of the lesbian SM group Samois in San Francisco, assailed the idea that sexual pleasure was "a male value and activity." Rubin was dismayed by lesbian feminists who attempted to create a sexuality free of power dynamics. These women, Rubin argued, treated sex as "something that good/nice women do not especially like." A strain of lesbian feminism that focused on intimacy more than orgasm, she warned, threatened to derail women's liberation. She and other members of Samois also rose to the defense of "gay lovers of youth." Boldly rejecting the idea of an "age of consent," Samois supported "young people's right to complete

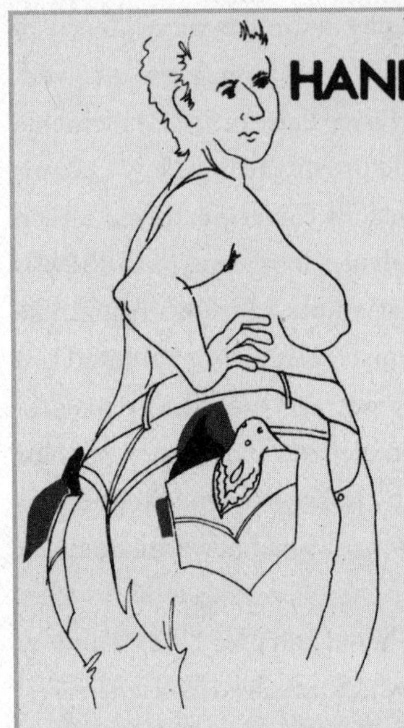

HANKERCHIEF COLOR CODE FOR LESBIANS

a project of

samois

SAN FRANCISCO BAY AREA'S LESBIAN-FEMINIST S/M SUPPORT GROUP

1978

Women's Press Project

COLOR	LEFT SIDE	RIGHT SIDE
Red	Fist Fucker	Fist Fuckee
Dark Blue	Gives Anal Sex	Wants Anal Sex
Light Blue	Gives Oral Sex	Wants Oral Sex
Robins Egg Blue	Light S/M, Top	Light S/M, Bottom
Mustard	Food Fetish, Top	Food Fetish, Bottom
Orange	Anything Goes, Top	Anything Goes, Bottom
Yellow	Gives Golden Showers	Wants Golden Showers
Green	Hustler, Selling	Hustler, Buying
Olive Drab	Uniforms/Military, Top	Uniforms/Military, Bottom
White	Likes Novices, Chickenhawk	Novice (or Virgin)
White Lace	Victorian Scenes, Top	Victorian Scenes, Bottom
Gray	Does Bondage	Wants To Be Put In Bondage
Brown	Shit Scenes, Top	Shit Scenes, Bottom
Black	Top, Heavy S/M & Whipping	Bottom, Heavy S/M & Whipping
Purple	Piercer	Piercee
Maroon	Likes Menstruating Women	Is Menstruating
Lavender	Group Sex, Top	Group Sex, Bottom
Pink	Breast Fondler	Breast Fondlee

Lesbian feminists interested in sadomasochism, bondage, and kink created a group called Samois in San Francisco during the late 1970s. This "Handkerchief Color Code" was both playful and informative, offering women interested in SM sex a way to communicate their erotic preferences to potential partners.

Some feminists considered SM, pornography, and a more general emphasis on orgasm as frivolous distractions from the sexual perils that women faced. The activist group Women Against Pornography became the face of this opposition in the "feminist sex wars" of the early 1980s. Eugene Gordon, Women Against Pornography, Greenwich Village, New York City, 1985, Eugene Gordon Photograph Collection, 87652d, New-York Historical Society.

autonomy, including sexual freedom and the right to have sexual partners of any age that they wish." The enforcement of statutory rape laws, Rubin argued, simplistically defined "a fully consensual love affair" between an adult and a minor as assault.[41]

Conflicts over SM and pornography moved from the pages of feminist publications to the streets of New York City in 1982, when protests erupted at the *Scholar and the Feminist IX* conference at Barnard College on the theme, "Towards a Politics of Sexuality." As attendees gathered for lectures and workshops, demonstrators massed outside the building. Days earlier, college administrators had seized 1,500 copies of the conference "diary," a sixty-page booklet with abstracts of the talks. Members of a group that called itself the Coalition of Women for a Feminist Sexuality and Against Sadomasochism handed out leaflets denouncing the conference for promoting sadomasochism and seeking "an end to laws that protect children from sexual abuse by adults." They made these claims even though the conference was not remotely devoted to those topics—it instead broadly considered the tension between sexual pleasure and danger from a feminist perspective. This animosity soured relationships among American feminists. Southern novelist Dorothy Allison, who was named in the protestors' pamphlet as the founder of the Lesbian Sex Mafia (which she was), subsequently published a poetry volume titled *The Women Who Hate Me.*[42]

Support for Dodson's erotic vision emerged not from mainstream white or women-of-color feminism but a small network of pro-sex feminists. This included not only Samois but also a group of San Francisco lesbians who launched *On Our Backs*, a magazine whose title poked fun at *off our backs*, a redoubtable lesbian separatist publication. Articles and pictorials in *On Our Backs* celebrated sex play with dildos, strap-ons, nipple clamps, pornography, group sex, and SM. Sex writer Susie Bright, who considered Dodson a personal and professional inspiration, had first learned about sex toys as an employee of Good Vibrations, the first sex shop for women in San Francisco. Her column in *On Our Backs*, "Toys for Us," often included reviews of sex toys written with unapologetic enthusiasm for erotic adventure. Bright soon had a regular column in *Penthouse Forum*, a hardcore pornographic magazine for men.[43]

Dodson and other pro-sex feminists similarly supported pornographic videos written and directed by and for women. The invention of the VCR in the mid-1970s made the production of pornographic films much cheaper, opening the market to female directors and producers whose movies would never have turned a profit in a traditional theater. After a slow start, an estimated 26 million VCRs had been sold in the United States by 1985, and there were approximately 22,000 video rental stores across the country. As many as half of all videotapes sold in the mid-1980s were adult films. In December 1991, Dodson proudly presented *Selfloving*, a candid video recording of one of her Bodysex workshops, including the "genital show and tell" and demonstrations of Dodson's masturbation techniques. It premiered at Eve's Garden.[44]

The anti-pornography movement meanwhile tried to ban the sale and distribution of pornography. Catharine MacKinnon, an attorney who advocated for local anti-porn regulations in the 1980s, argued that porn "sexualizes women's inequality" and "increases attitudes and behaviors of aggression and discrimination, specifically by men against women." A New York–based group that Dodson loathed, Women Against Pornography (WAP), looked to the federal government to suppress porn. A coalition of odd bedfellows, WAP included marquee feminists such as Gloria Steinem, the anti-pornography zealot Andrea Dworkin, and a cohort of Catholic and evangelical Protestant women.[45]

In 1985, when Attorney General Edwin Meese announced the formation of a Commission on Pornography, WAP provided the commission with a list of potential witnesses, each prepared to testify at federal hearings that pornography had hurt them personally. (Many of these activists were still angry about the Presidential Commission on Obscenity and Pornography appointed by President Lyndon Johnson in 1967. That commission's 1970 report declared that it had found no evidence that pornography caused harm and recommended the repeal of all laws that restricted adults' access to sexually explicit materials.) Several women testifying before the Meese Commission described years of sexual, emotional, and physical abuse from husbands "addicted" to pornography. The 1,960-page *Final Report* (1986) concluded unequivocally that pornography instigated violence against women. This view persisted on the political right for decades; the 2006 GOP platform declared pornography a "public health crisis" that was "destroying the lives of millions." The idea that pornography is fundamentally harmful, especially to children, remains a contentious policy issue across the political spectrum.[46]

Government censors singled out homoerotic art for special criticism. In 1989, new federal legislation barred the National Endowment for the Arts (NEA), a federal agency, from supporting "obscene" projects "including but not limited to sadomasochism [and] homoeroticism." The NEA pulled its funding from artists who created sexually explicit work, including the photographer Robert Mapplethorpe, who often portrayed scenes of male homoeroticism and sadomasochism. In 1990, Dennis Barrie, the director of the Contemporary Arts Center in Cincinnati, was indicted on obscenity charges for mounting a Mapplethorpe exhibit. Artists' representations of queer pleasure were far more vulnerable to claims of "obscenity" and to censorship than were productions focused on heterosexuality.[47]

Outcries over masturbation in the 1980s revealed how dramatically the boundaries of acceptable sexual speech had narrowed since the heyday of sexual liberation in the 1970s. Joycelyn Elders, President Bill Clinton's surgeon general and the first Black woman to hold that position, was forced out in 1994 after she spoke in favor of sex-education programs that included information about the benign effects of masturbation. Even sex therapists warned that masturbation, if it became a "compulsion," indicated that an individual suffered from "sex addiction." Dodson's boast that she spent two hours a day masturbating "and designing sex rituals" remained a challenge to the status quo.[48]

Dodson's message about the centrality of sexual pleasure to human fulfillment nevertheless survived. Four lesbian sex magazines started publication in the mid-1980s. Their success reflected the increasing confidence of queer women and inspired new experiments with feminist erotica. "Sex-positive" feminism laid the foundation for "third wave" feminism in the 1990s, which viewed female erotic pleasure as the cornerstone of women's equality. In homegrown "zines" and punk-rock "Riot Grrrl" bands, girls and women proclaimed their erotic autonomy.[49]

Dodson championed extraordinary sexual candor throughout her life, but she never seemed to grasp the importance of race for American sexual norms. She ignored the significance of racial stereotypes to sexual fantasies, even as she fetishized the ideal of the well-endowed Black man. As Dodson critiqued American prudishness, she overlooked the disparate ways in which ideals of white female purity depended on contrasting assumptions about Black and Asian women's sexual availability. A cringeworthy moment of racial obliviousness occurred during the "genital show and tell" of a video-recorded workshop she hosted in the 2010s. On this occasion, Dodson attempted to tease the only non-white participant, a woman of Asian descent, by quipping that everyone assumed that her vagina opened "sideways." Although Dodson likely believed that invoking this racist trope about Asian women's bodies demonstrated her disdain for stereotypes, the woman in question was clearly uncomfortable.[50]

Dodson's mission to educate women about their bodies remained relevant. On *Goop Lab*'s episode with Dodson in 2020, host Gwyneth Paltrow squealed about their opportunity to talk about "vaginas!" Dodson met Paltrow's gaze with an unamused stare. "The vagina is the birth canal only," she corrected. "You want to talk about the vulva."[51]

Chapter 15

Irresponsible Intercourse

The fire that tore through the Blue Mountain Clinic (BMC) in Missoula, Montana, in March 1993, fed by gasoline poured over the building's interior that ignited and blew out the building's windows and collapsed its floors and walls, was the worst in a series of attacks on one of only two abortion clinics in the state. Picketers with

Members of WHAM! (Women's Health Action and Mobilization) counter--protested when members of Operation Rescue demonstrated outside the home of abortion provider Dr. Bernard Luck in Monroe County, New York, in 1992. Luck and other providers were the targets of constant harassment and, in some cases, murder, by anti-abortion extremists.

signs calling abortion "murder" had regularly gathered outside the clinic since the late 1970s. They accosted women walking in and tried to persuade them to change their minds. Patients struggled to make their way to the clinic's doors through a gauntlet of abortion opponents.[1]

Over the years, the protests became more intrusive, with demonstrators attempting to storm the clinic. Local members of Right to Life and other anti-abortion groups denied culpability after the firebombing that destroyed the BMC in 1993. They repeated an argument that major anti-abortion groups had been making since the 1970s: it was abortion, not the protests against it, that was violent.[2]

Conspicuously absent from the local conversation about the 1993 fire was a Catholic woman named Suzanne Pennypacker Morris, who was Missoula's most vocal and influential opponent of abortion. She led the first picket of the Blue Mountain Clinic in 1978 as head of the local chapter of the national organization Right to Life (RTL). The anti-abortion movement she joined had mobilized in the late 1960s, and it was a force in American life by the time the Supreme Court's decision in *Roe v. Wade* (1973) ensured a constitutional right to an abortion as a matter of privacy.[3]

Morris played no part in the 1993 attack, but she helped build the ideological foundation for anti-abortion protests in her state. Although newspapers identified Morris as a "homemaker," she was also a seasoned activist and political operative. To Morris and her allies, abortion threatened the lives of "unborn humans" and it undermined the very meaning of male and female, of heterosexuality, and of Christian virtue. Betty Dodson's celebrations of sexual liberation and Kiyoshi Kuromiya's organizing for gay liberation struck these activists as not only hedonistic but immoral. In 1979 Morris challenged a reporter with a rhetorical question: "Are women really asking to be as sexually irresponsible as men are? It would be much nicer if we could make men more responsible." That argument echoed the slogans of purity reformers in the late nineteenth century, who advocated for "a white life for two" to make premarital chastity the norm for men as well as women. Women in the anti-abortion movement often portrayed abortion-seeking women as victims of callous men, desperately seeking the protection and support that dutiful husbands should have provided. Morris's comments reflected another strain in the movement, one that construed abortion as the craven choice of promiscuous women.[4]

In step with the National Right to Life leadership, Morris called for a constitutional amendment to ban abortion and in the meantime supported incremental changes to impede access. She lobbied elected officials and even ran for Congress, twice, as an anti-abortion Republican, losing in the primaries in 1980 and 1982. Her opposition to abortion was rooted in her Catholic faith, which taught her that life began at conception and that the quest for sexual freedom was irresponsible. But Morris's zeal also flowed from her combative temperament. She loved the fight.[5]

It has become common to describe abortion supporters and opponents as "single-issue voters" in U.S. elections. That framing overlooks how the abortion issue became a referendum on the sexual revolution, gay rights, and feminism. Abortion opponents described the procedure as an assault on the "American family" because, they argued, it untethered reproductive sex from marriage, women from men, and men from their responsibilities as family breadwinners. Abortion struck at their beliefs that the conventionally gendered, heterosexual family held the nation together. It was a threat on par with new "no-fault" divorce laws (first in California, and soon in many other states); increasingly visible gay and lesbian communities; and the feminist demand for an end to conventional gender roles. As such, an individual's sexual decisions were matters of public concern, requiring community vigilance and, when necessary, state intervention. This worldview rejected the modern understanding of desire as a discrete aspect of human experience, arguing instead that sexual behaviors indicated how well a person understood and followed Christian values.[6]

Anti-abortion activists depicted the fetus as the brutalized victim of sexual excess. They also attacked the abortion rights movement as a feminist plot to undermine male-female reproductive marriage. The combination of these two images—slaughtered infants and promiscuous women—provoked righteous fury on the right. Casting abortion as murder riled up rank-and-file activists and extremists alike. Their crusade was—and remains—an ardent critique not only of women's sexual liberation but of the legitimacy of all sexualities and genders other than a heterosexual, marital, reproductive norm.

Montana's legislature first restricted abortion in 1895, just six years after the territory became a state. The state of Montana existed because of wars against local Indigenous nations. With the support of the federal government, white settlers pushed Crow, Blackfeet, Northern Cheyenne, and other Native people onto reservations and carved up tribal lands into small "allotments." Native leaders agreed to land cessions that they hoped would allow them to live in peace, but the allotment process strained their kinship networks and further impoverished them.[7]

The 1895 law punished not only the abortion provider but also the woman who agreed to "any operation, or to the use of any means whatever, with intent thereby to procure a miscarriage." (In practice, Montana providers were probably prosecuted more often than their patients, as was the case elsewhere.) Montana's anti-abortion law was part of a wave of new state-level restrictions on abortion throughout the United States. Inspired by the likes of Horatio Storer, who defined abortion at any stage in a pregnancy as murder, state legislators rejected the idea that no "life" existed until quickening.[8]

Little had changed in the state's abortion laws by the time of Suzanne Pennypacker's birth in 1944 in Missoula. Montana's revised criminal code of 1947 permitted abortion only when the procedure would save the life of the pregnant person. Initially, the determination of whether a pregnancy endangered a life was left to the attending physician's discretion. Contraindications included everything from cardiovascular disease to diabetes or psychiatric conditions. Over time, such "therapeutic abortions" in hospitals became increasingly rare. Dr. James Armstrong, a family physician who provided women with reproductive healthcare, recalled only one therapeutic hospital abortion in the 1960s in north-western Montana, where he practiced, "and that was done as a hysterectomy, [on] a married woman with a brain tumor." Improved surgical techniques and medical interventions weakened the case that an abortion was necessary to save a woman's life. Hospital administrators instituted new "therapeutic abortion committees" to ensure that only the direst cases met their criteria.[9]

Maternity homes and illegal abortions were the alternatives for a Montana woman who did not want to continue a pregnancy. Maternity homes were privately operated residences and training schools, run by religious or social welfare organizations. The homes promised to provide an unmarried pregnant woman with a discreet residence, teach her basic domestic skills, and facilitate the child's adoption. Other people simply broke the law. At least thirty physicians, midwives, and untrained practitioners performed abortions in Montana between 1882 and 1973. Some of them undertook this illegal work to help desperate women. Other abortion providers exploited women for financial gain. During his medical residency in the 1950s, Armstrong cared for a woman who became fatally septic after a botched abortion. Decades later, after a long career providing abortions to women in Montana, he remembered every detail of that patient's suffering and his inability to prevent her death.[10]

Armstrong's harrowing experience was unfortunately common among medical providers of his generation. Thousands of women died each year from illegal abortions in the United States. Lower-income women who had little access to medical care or to reliable contraceptives were among the most vulnerable, taking terrible risks to end unwanted pregnancies. A physician at a family planning program in Louisiana described patients who were "very carved up—[from] very crude abortions—knitting needles, cloth packing," he recalled. "And we see them coming in highly febrile, puerperal discharge in the vagina, germs in their blood, blood poisoning, septicemia, and those who survive have a very high probability of being reproductive cripples."[11]

That misery prompted efforts to refer and transport women to safe abortion providers. Volunteers in Missoula helped women pay for travel to places where abortion was legal, initially to Colorado, which passed a narrow therapeutic abortion law in 1967, and soon to Washington state, which in 1970 repealed its abortion ban by popular referendum. Joan McCracken, a nurse and mother of five who ran the women's health clinic in Billings, Montana, found additional support from the Clergy Consultation Service (CCS), a network of Protestant ministers, Reform rabbis, and even a few Catholic nuns who created a national abortion referral service and travel fund that aided hundreds of thousands of women between 1967 and 1972.[12]

Access to safe, legal abortions across the United States arrived with the Supreme Court's majority opinion in *Roe v. Wade,* issued in January 1973. The opinion emphasized the importance of both competent healthcare and privacy; the justices did not defend access to abortion using the language or arguments of women's liberation. *Roe* prohibited state-level restrictions on abortions in the first trimester of pregnancy (up to twelve weeks after the onset of the person's most recent menstrual period) and allowed states to regulate second-trimester abortions only under limited circumstances. After *Roe,* many states, including Montana, mandated that second-trimester abortions, typically achieved through saline installation, be performed in hospitals. In fact, *anyone* who needed an abortion in Montana, even very early in a pregnancy, was sent to a hospital in the years immediately following *Roe,* because the state had no freestanding clinics for abortion care.[13]

The Blue Mountain Women's Clinic, named after the mountain peak that was visible from downtown Missoula, opened its doors in February 1977 after members of a feminist collective, the Women's Place, decided to expand reproductive healthcare options for Montana women. Clients came in for pap smears, prescriptions for contraception, and vasectomies. (Within a few years, the name was changed to Blue Mountain Clinic to reflect that it served people of all genders.) The clinic hosted workshops on topics ranging from fibromyalgia to herpes to menopause. And once a week, a physician at the clinic performed abortions for people in the first trimester of a pregnancy. Across the country, activists surveyed similar challenges and established hundreds of freestanding clinics.[14]

Over 650 women had abortions at the Blue Mountain Clinic during its first year. Patients ranged in age from fourteen to forty-eight, and they sought first-trimester abortions for a variety of personal reasons. The BMC kept costs low, charging $165 for an abortion that would cost $500 at Deaconess Hospital in Billings. Patients at the BMC received local anesthesia before undergoing a five-minute procedure known as vacuum aspiration, which removed all fetal tissue from the uterus.[15]

Suzanne Pennypacker Morris was paying attention to news about the clinic, nicknaming it, disparagingly, "the Blue Mountain Abortion Clinic." For her and thousands of other Americans, no matter what else the clinic did to provide healthcare, its abortion services tarnished the entire enterprise. She and other anti-abortion activists were intent on making "abortion" a dirty word that bore no relation to women's well-being.

Catholic women such as Suzanne Pennypacker grew to adulthood learning that abortion was singularly evil. Pope Pius XI's 1930 encyclical, *Casti Connubii,* asserted the Church's belief that both contraception and abortion were sinful violations of God's "natural law," a position sustained in Pope Paul VI's *Humanae Vitae* in 1968. Still, most American Catholics at the time practiced some form of contraception. In 1968, when she was twenty-four, Suzanne married Patrick Morris, and they soon had three daughters. Patrick worked for the National Forest Service, and his job took them from DC to Dayton, Ohio. Caring for three young children, Suzanne was not in the paid workforce. That said, she found her calling outside of her home. Six years into her marriage and about a year after the *Roe v. Wade* decision, Morris first appeared in a local Ohio paper as a fierce opponent of "the slaughter of babies" in area hospitals that performed abortions.[16]

Morris joined thousands of other American Catholic women who supported crisis pregnancy centers (CPCs). A group called Birthright operated many of these centers; Morris encouraged pregnant women in distress to call Birthright rather than Planned Parenthood. These centers looked like women's health clinics but functioned primarily to discourage women from seeking abortion care. CPCs typically offered free pregnancy tests and presented clients with extensive print, photographic, and eventually video evidence of fetal development while they waited for their results. For the sake of "saving babies," CPC volunteers rented or used donated space in high-poverty urban neighborhoods; women there were more likely to need a free pregnancy test. CPC activists believed that they could teach one woman at a time that life began at conception. Initially, Catholic women led most CPCs in the United States. These centers eventually became places for Catholics and evangelical Protestants to join forces.[17]

Morris led pickets in October 1975 and January 1976 at the Dayton Women's Health Center, where protesters carried signs that read "Ten Babies Will Die Here Today." She churned out letters to the editors of local newspapers in which she defended the civil rights of "preborn human beings." "A totally unique human being exists at conception," she argued, comparing *Roe* to the infamous 1850s Supreme Court opinion in *Dred Scott v. Sandford*, which argued that African Americans could not be citizens because they were not "people" in the eyes of the Constitution's framers. Morris parroted the national anti-abortion movement's rhetoric when she maintained that it was just as wrong in the 1970s to deny that the fetus was a rights-bearing person as it had been in the 1850s to deny Black humanity.[18]

It was a provocative thesis: if abortion violated the civil rights of a fetus, then the movement to stop it was an extension of the civil rights cause. Starting in the late 1960s, Catholic leaders had appealed to the social justice wing of American Catholicism and to Protestants (few of whom, at the time, opposed abortion on religious grounds) to view abortion as a matter of civil rights. They described abortion as a singularly violent violation of individual rights rather than as disobedience to papal decrees. As Morris wrote in one 1976 letter, "Hopefully, it will not take as long to extend civil rights to the unborn as it has to our black brothers." Morris seems not to have written publicly about civil rights aside from her defenses of the unborn. In another letter to the editor, she analogized aborted fetuses to European Jews killed in the Holocaust, already a common rhetorical gambit among abortion opponents, as it remains today.[19]

Rights language that appeared in anti-abortion campaigns, however, did not lead anti-abortion activists into actual civil rights work. Some leaders in the anti-abortion movement had participated in civil rights and antiwar demonstrations, but many others were the same people who had recently lost the battle over racial segregation. In the abortion battle, they cast themselves as latter-day abolitionists, not segregationists, who defended Black people by seeking to protect unborn Black children.[20]

In doing so, some white conservatives forged alliances with Black nationalists who considered abortion a form of "genocide." Those arguments echoed the pronatalism of Black nationalist Marcus Garvey in the 1910s and early 1920s. In the late 1960s, Black nationalist organizations, including the Black Panther Party, described birth control as a tool of white supremacists to kill off Black people. Even some male leaders of the National Association for the Advancement of Colored People (NAACP) and the Urban League, both mainstream civil rights organizations, reversed their earlier support for women's access to safe contraceptives and to abortion. Black people who supported birth-control clinics, and Black women in particular, rejected those criticisms. In Pittsburgh, Black women opened a birth-control clinic over the opposition of a local Black minister. Confrontations erupted among the Puerto Rican Young Lords in New York City when male leaders opposed birth control and abortion access. Women in the movement successfully pushed the group to recognize the value of contraception for their liberation.[21]

What many anti-abortion activists shared—and what remained consistent across their involvement in various causes—was sexual conservatism. They largely opposed the Equal Rights Amendment (ERA), gay rights, and other movements for sexual equality. As the newsletters of a Catholic anti-abortion group in Michigan put it in 1972, abortion was "a symbol of addiction to unrestrained sexual license and an abdication to [*sic*] personal responsibility in the sphere of reproductive conduct."

Those political priorities contributed to the socially conservative tilt of the Republican Party in the 1970s, as it persuaded many white Catholic voters, long-standing supporters of the Democratic Party, to see their cultural values reflected in the GOP's battle against socially "permissive" liberalism. Rights talk also secularized the abortion issue, shifting it more decisively from a matter of Catholic theology to a referendum on universal human dignity. These shifts—of large numbers of Catholics into the Republican Party and of evangelical Protestants into the anti-abortion cause—originated at the grassroots, as voters responded to the anti-abortion movement's portrayal of abortion as the murderous denial of the fetus's civil rights.[22]

Morris was something of an exception. She joined International Feminists for Life, a group of white Catholic women who simultaneously opposed abortion and supported the ERA. She seems to have desired sexual equality without sexual liberation. A leader of Feminists for Life described abortion as a tool of men's exploitation of women, manifesting "the idea that a man can use a woman, vacuum her out, and she's ready to be used again." Whatever her feminist inclinations, Morris remained adamantly opposed to abortion. At a rally in Dayton, she called out the National Organization for Women for "deceiving women into thinking that their equality can only be achieved over the dead bodies of unborn children." Feminists for Life mocked the idea of a woman's right to reproductive self-determination, characterizing it as a specious justification for immoral behavior. "Abortion—A Woman's Right to Choose to Kill," a protester's sign read.[23]

The Morris family relocated to Missoula in 1977 to further Patrick's career with the Forest Service. Suzanne soon took the helm of both the Missoula and the Montana Right to Life chapters. She served in leadership roles from 1977 to 1984, increasing the relatively small membership of Missoula RTL from 50 or 60 people in 1974 to about 100 people in 1979. Morris claimed to speak for a majority of women in her state and across the country, but national polls suggested otherwise. In a February 1976 CBS/*New York Times* poll, 67 percent of respondents supported legal abortion.[24]

At that first picket of the Blue Mountain Clinic, in December 1978, Morris hosted a "pray-in" for fetuses aborted there "and all others who die in abortion." By mourning outside of women's health clinics, Morris and other members of RTL gave visible expression to the belief that pre-viability fetuses were rights-bearing people. In 1979 she led a Montana Right to Life rally that included posters displaying what one reporter described as "gruesome pictures of aborted babies." It was a familiar tactic of the movement. Advances in ultrasound technology by then allowed abortion opponents to display images of fetuses in utero, a way to drive home their argument that fetuses were people. That visual evidence has remained central to the movement's strategies ever since.[25]

Sexual restraint remained the anti-abortion movement's primary advice for women who did not want to get pregnant (a view that, among other things, does not account for non-consensual sex). Planned Parenthood's sex-education curriculum appeared to preach the opposite. As it stood, comprehensive sex education was relatively new, incorporated into middle and high school curricula in the 1960s and thereafter thanks

The Planned Parenthood Federation of America and its state branches created sex-education curricula that included information about human reproduction, contraception, and masturbation, among other topics. For anti-abortion activists like Suzanne Pennypacker Morris, Planned Parenthood's associations with abortion provision overshadowed all other aspects of the group's work. This PPFA poster was printed some time between 1965 and 1980.

to organizations such as the Sexuality Information and Education Council of the United States (SIECUS). Shaped by the moderate ethos of its founder, Mary Steichen Calderone, SIECUS emphasized the importance of helping young people become sexually responsible adults capable of a healthy marriage. Typically provided in health classes, sex education followed a carefully designed curriculum. Middle schoolers learned about menstruation and nocturnal emissions, and high school students discussed contraception and sexually transmitted infections. These programs redefined sexual health, previously understood as the absence of disease, as "preventive medicine" that might help individuals build sexually fulfilling lives. Yet from the earliest iterations of SIECUS and other progressive curricula, sex education lesson plans infuriated certain parents—usually but not always conservative Christians. These opponents argued variously that sex education programs were Communist, taught their children to be gay, sexualized very young children, exposed youth to pornography, and contributed to rising teen pregnancy rates.[26]

Sex education was a new venture for Planned Parenthood Federation of America (PPFA). Throughout the 1960s and 1970s, PPFA had focused its resources on educating women about the birth-control pill and other contraceptive methods. Local chapters operated health clinics. The PPFA also advocated for "population control" around the world. Then, in 1979, PPFA created an education division, and some of the local affiliates launched sex-education programs of their own. Many of these curricula borrowed from a popular program created in 1971 by the Unitarian Universalist Association, *About Your Sexuality*, which found broad support among liberal Protestants. Intended for twelve-to-fourteen-year-olds, *About Your Sexuality* taught that sexuality was natural. Program facilitators led conversations about "Lovemaking, Birth Control and Abortion, Same Sex Friendships, Masturbation" and a range of other topics. Morris assailed her local and state Planned Parenthood offices for distributing sexual health and education materials that, she said, taught that "if it feels good, do it." As another Montana woman explained, rather than teaching birth control, schools should seek to "cut down the rate of irresponsible intercourse." Morris maintained that

Planned Parenthood promoted sex outside of marriage and contributed to the rising rate of teen pregnancy.[27]

Heterosexual hedonism, Morris and others argued, was but one piece of a broader decline in sexual morality that included the new visibility of homosexuality. She echoed the anti-gay critique made by Phyllis Schlafly, a Catholic firebrand and political operative. From her home in St. Louis, Schlafly produced a widely circulated newsletter, the *Phyllis Schlafly Report*, which promoted her pet causes of anti-communism and opposition to women's equal rights. In *The Power of the Positive Woman* (1977), Schlafly attacked NOW for stripping men and women of their distinct gender roles and transforming them into homosexuals. (In fact, NOW had not initially welcomed lesbians into its membership; in 1969, NOW's president, Betty Friedan, disparaged lesbians as the "lavender menace" whose visibility might torpedo the feminist movement's chances of success. Lesbian feminists successfully demanded that NOW represent their interests, whatever the cost to the organization's public image.)[28]

Schlafly insisted that sex equality would lead lesbians and gay men to demand "special rights," a phrase that she and other social conservatives increasingly applied to efforts to achieve equal rights: "NOW is for pro-lesbian legislation giving perverts the same legal rights as husbands and wives—such as the rights to get marriage licenses, to file joint income tax returns, and to adopt children," she wrote. Women would find fulfillment, Schlafly argued, only when they embraced their unique reproductive capacities. (The mother of five children herself, Schlafly benefitted from both paid and unpaid childcare and housekeeping assistance; she was unsalaried but put in long days writing and organizing.) Morris similarly complained that Planned Parenthood, "teaches people to be gay, perverted . . . to be promiscuous. It teaches everything but the sanctity of sex." Social conservatives like Schlafly and Morris portrayed secular sex education curricula as dangerously libidinous indoctrination.[29]

Sexual conservatism was the bridge that linked evangelical Protestants and Catholics across deep waters of theological and cultural difference. (It would ultimately also bring Mormon women into conservative politics.) In 1961, the evangelical megastar preacher Billy Graham answered a question in his newspaper advice column from a young woman who confessed, "through a young and foolish sin, I had an abortion. . . . How can I ever know forgiveness?" Graham responded by describing abortion as "violent" and "a sin against God, nature, and one's self," and urged the young woman to pray for God's forgiveness. Evangelicals did not yet equate abortion with murder, though. In 1970, the evangelical magazine *Christianity Today* denounced the "War on the Womb" and campaigned against abortion reform, but no single position on abortion had yet cohered among conservative Christians.[30]

Instead, Protestants teamed up with Catholics to oppose pornography and stop comprehensive sex education in public schools. Thousands of evangelical Protestant women joined Schlafly's campaign against the ERA in the early 1970s. It was through these organized protests against feminism, gay rights, and sexual liberation that many evangelical women became anti-abortion activists. By mid-decade, leading evangelical theologians and organizers unambiguously described abortion as evil. While Protestant men took over as leaders of national "pro-life" groups, evangelical Protestant women were the movement's fiercest and most effective organizers at the grassroots level, just as Catholic women had been for years.[31]

Descriptions of abortion as the violent murder of innocent babies—descriptions often accompanied by graphic photographs of fetal remains—aroused the fury of activists who decided to stop abortion by any means necessary. Women like Suzanne Pennypacker Morris did not instigate firebombing, arson, bomb threats, clinic invasions, death threats, or assaults of abortion providers. They did, however, construct a narrative in which abortion providers were callous criminals, plying their obscene trade with the government's consent. That narrative empowered some radical extremists to retaliate.[32]

In 1984, when Patrick's job brought his family back to Washington, DC, Morris resigned her leadership position in Montana RTL. She does not appear to have assumed a comparable role in the nation's capital. Five years later, Suzanne was featured in a "Where Are They Now?" roundup in the local Missoula newspaper. She and her teenage daughters had recently returned to Missoula without Patrick; the marriage had ended. Six months after she relocated to Missoula, perhaps seeking a new start after her divorce, she had her name legally changed back to Suzanne Pennypacker.[33]

The employees and clients of the Blue Mountain Clinic had, in the meantime, faced unprecedented threats. An especially relentless group, Operation Rescue (OR), founded in 1987 by a previously obscure zealot named Randall Terry, protested outside the clinic every Saturday. Anti-abortion activists had first launched what they called "rescues" in 1977: women activists would secretively enter and hide within clinics, barricade the doors, and then storm through the facility, destroying equipment and records. By 1985, thirty clinics had been bombed or set on fire.[34]

Willa Craig, who served as the executive director for the Blue Mountain Clinic during the late 1980s and early 1990s, recalled that OR activists "would stand in front of that person and try to get in the way of her actually entering the clinic." On a few occasions, OR activists blocked the clinic's doors. While OR attracted both Catholic and Protestant participants, Terry was an evangelical. Craig and other abortion providers began to describe their opponents as "fundamentalist" Christians.[35]

Blue Mountain trained a cohort of volunteer escorts, who created pathways for patients to walk in and out of the clinic and to their cars. Local police often arrested protesters who were trespassing or physically harassing patients, but the protesters returned to the picket lines as soon as they were able. Over 60,000 people were arrested at OR events across the United States. Many clinics suffered financially, if they managed to stay open at all, because potential clients were afraid to face a hostile gauntlet.[36]

Harassment of the Blue Mountain Clinic escalated. In November 1991, seventy-five anti-abortion protesters swarmed the building. Some used bicycle locks to chain themselves to one another's necks. Others waved Bibles. Protesters threw their bodies against the doors and heckled patients trying to enter the clinic. A man and a woman pretending to be patients succeeded in having clinic employees bring them to the back entrance, which the couple then tried to hold open so that other protesters could get inside. Those protesters trampled several clinic workers who tried to stop them. Missoula firefighters and police responded quickly. They read aloud from a court order that prohibited protesters from blocking the clinic's entrance, cut bicycle locks off a dozen necks, and corralled violent extremists into a school bus and a van, which took them to a holding cell at city hall.[37]

Supporters of abortion access turned to the government for help. A class-action lawsuit brought by NOW convinced federal prosecutors that Operation Rescue had violated the 1970 Racketeer Influenced and Corrupt Organization Act, better-known by its acronym, RICO, which prohibited coordinated efforts to interfere with legitimate business operations. Appellate courts upheld RICO convictions against anti-abortion organizations and leaders, prompting most of those groups to distance themselves officially from violence at clinics. Operation Rescue was soon more or less defunct.[38]

Individual fanatics nevertheless continued to harass and threaten physicians and other clinic employees. In 1993, during the three months prior to the fire at the Blue Mountain Clinic, anti-abortion extremists threatened to kill at least thirty-one abortion providers. On March 10 of that year, an anti-abortion activist murdered Dr. David Gunn as he entered a clinic in Pensacola, Florida. It was the first, but not the last, murder of an abortion provider in the United States. Jane Snyder, the office manager at the Blue Mountain Clinic at the time, saw trouble on the horizon. Abortions represented just 20 percent of the clinic's services by 1993. Yet to abortion opponents, that procedure defined the clinic's existence. "I think the violence will pick up," Snyder worried.[39]

Rain was falling in Missoula in the cold predawn hours of Monday, March 29, 1993, when an individual broke windows at the Blue Mountain Clinic, poured gasoline over the floors, and lit a match. That person's movements or smoke from the flames tripped the security system. When an alert reached the fire department six minutes later, it was already too late. As the firefighters' trucks pulled out of stations several blocks away, they saw a blaze touching the sky. Flames billowed out of the clinic. Fire Chief Chuck Gibson was apologetic when he explained, "By the time our crews got here, the building was totally engulfed." Water and soot saturated what remained of patient records, and the roof over the reception area fell in. The fire was already the third arson of an abortion clinic that year.[40]

Local and federal investigators immediately suspected arson. Willa Craig blamed anti-abortion activists "and some local fundamentalist Christian churches." Local evangelical, Catholic, and RTL leaders rejected the suggestion that they had anything to do with the fire. Instead, they suggested that it was the work of "out-of-control or deranged individuals." A Republican in the Montana legislature suggested that the clinic's employees might have set the blaze themselves to get an insurance payout. When arson destroyed the Women's Health Center in Boise, Idaho, two months later, its director shared Craig's assumptions about the culprit: "Religious fanaticism is a very scary thing, and if they can get away with what they're doing now, then what's next?"[41]

Craig insisted that the attack would not stop the BMC from providing care. They rented space from a sympathetic medical practice near the site of their former building, but there was no way that the clinic could continue as before. By August 1993, the staff had been reduced from thirty-eight to eight or ten people, a fourfold reduction, and the remaining employees were unable to meet the needs of what previously had been 7,000 patients per year. Missoula's Planned Parenthood did not provide abortion services, only referrals. An abortion provider in eastern Montana, Dr. Susan Wicklund, was receiving death threats, and the fire in Missoula intensified her dread. Fear of violence deterred many physicians from entering this line of work at all. Nearly one-fifth of the budget for a new freestanding BMC, built after two years of fundraising, went toward a fence that encircled the building and parking lot, security cameras, and other precautionary measures.[42]

Clinics across the nation soon received some additional support. The 1994 Freedom of Access to Clinic Entrances (FACE) Act made it a federal crime to create barriers at the entrance to a clinic or otherwise interfere in a clinic's normal operations. President Bill Clinton's attorney general, Janet Reno, additionally authorized the FBI to investigate some clinic arsons and designated federal marshals to provide protection to clinics after an anti-abortion extremist murdered two more physicians in 1994. Within five years, fewer than one-quarter of U.S clinics reported incidents of violence, compared to one-half of all clinics in 1994.[43]

Abortion providers remained vulnerable to vigilantism. In October 1994, a fire caused structural damage to the roof of the clinic where Dr. James Armstrong worked in Kalispell, Montana; he was the community's only abortion provider. The suspect was a man named Richard Andrews, who led an Operation Rescue group in Washington state during the 1980s. By 1997 Andrews had also been indicted on three counts of arson against abortion clinics in California.[44]

Andrews initially denied all wrongdoing. His attorney, Thomas S. Olmstead, blamed a coordinated political effort by "powerful . . . vindictive" abortion rights supporters, who targeted Andrews and other pro-life activists to win support for their cause. For Olmstead, the campaign to normalize abortion was insidious because it diverted attention from that movement's ultimate goal: consequence-free nonreproductive, nonmarital sex that elevated the rights of gay people and, he argued, oppressed heterosexuals. "[Pro-choice forces] are mostly feminists, lesbians," he explained, "and they don't want to see the product of a normal relationship between a man and a woman, which is a child." Phyllis Schlafly and Suzanne Pennypacker Morris had made much the same argument in the 1970s.[45]

Federal investigators eventually collected so much evidence that Andrews confessed. In February 1998, in a federal court room where the judge described Andrews as a "terrorist," Andrews pleaded guilty to eight counts of arson at clinics in Montana, California, Idaho, and Wyoming, the Blue Mountain Clinic among them. He was sentenced to eighty-one months in prison.[46]

Pro-choice activists took to the streets in cities across the United States in 1992 as the Supreme Court deliberated in Planned Parenthood v. Casey. *The decision ultimately upheld the constitutional right to an abortion but permitted states to impose new restrictions.*

Legal remedies failed to deter radicals who believed they were on a hero's mission to save innocent babies from murder. In 2007, anti-abortion activists in Wichita, Kansas, began to attend the Lutheran church that abortion provider Dr. George Tiller and his wife had joined. They sent postcards with images of dismembered fetuses to everyone in the church's directory. On Sunday, May 31, 2009, one of those activists, Scott Roeder, fatally shot Tiller in the head in the church foyer.[47]

A protective fence encircled the rebuilt Blue Mountain Clinic in June 2022 when the Supreme Court issued its decision in *Dobbs v. Jackson Women's Health*. In the majority opinion, Supreme Court Justice Samuel Alito issued a sweeping (and scathing) indictment of abortion and explicitly overturned *Roe*. Leaving the terms of legal abortion entirely to the states, *Dobbs* put abortion-seekers in limbo. The Blue Mountain

Clinic stayed open because Montana, unlike many other states, did not have a "trigger law" ready to ban abortion the moment *Roe* was overturned. While legal access to abortion in Montana remained imperiled, it was something of a haven, relatively speaking. Abortion rights supporters helped Idaho residents journey to Montana for the medical care now outlawed in their state.[48]

Suzanne Pennypacker did not live to see *Roe*'s fall, having died in 2006 at the age of sixty-two. Her final letter to the editor appeared in 1994 in a dispute not over abortion but regarding her pet Dobermans. A neighboring woman had complained that Pennypacker allowed her three large and aggressive dogs to roam off-leash. One of the dogs had jumped on her several times, and all were a menace to the neighborhood, the neighbor claimed. Pennypacker called the woman a weakling who should simply spray the dogs with a little water if they got too close. She offered no apologies.[49]

Chapter 16

Sexual Advances

The Irvine Auditorium at the University of Pennsylvania was filled to capacity on the afternoon of Wednesday, October 10, 2018, a little more than a month after Brett Kavanaugh's contentious Supreme Court confirmation hearings thrust debates over

The nomination of Clarence Thomas for associate justice of the Supreme Court in 1991 motivated Anita Hill, a law professor, to send a confidential letter to the Senate Judiciary Committee describing Thomas's sexual harassment of her while he was her supervisor at the Labor Department in the early 1980s. After that letter leaked, the committee asked Hill to testify on the record, which she did. At that time, no women or people of color served on the committee.

sexual consent, male privilege, and the concept of "rape culture"—the casual acceptance of male sexual coercion in law and culture—into the national spotlight. Hundreds of people registered in advance for a conversation among three of the most influential law professors of the late twentieth and early twenty-first centuries: Anita Hill, Kimberlé Crenshaw, and Dorothy Roberts.[1]

Nearly thirty years earlier, in 1991, Hill's testimony in the confirmation hearings for Supreme Court associate justice Clarence Thomas made her name synonymous with women's experiences of workplace sexual harassment. Thomas, a Black arch-conservative, had been nominated by Republican president George H. W. Bush to fill the seat left vacant by the death of Thurgood Marshall, a liberal and the first African American to serve on the court. Thomas's nomination prompted Hill to send a confidential statement to the Senate Judiciary Committee. In it, she reported that Thomas had made sexually explicit jokes, propositioned her, and otherwise subjected her to a hostile work environment when he was her supervisor at the Department of Education and at the Equal Employment Opportunity Commission (EEOC) in the early 1980s.[2]

The 2018 event with Hill, Crenshaw, and Roberts had been planned for months, but they confronted the rhyme of history: allegations of sexual misconduct against the latest nominee to the highest court. When psychologist Christine Blasey Ford learned of Kavanaugh's nomination, she informed the Senate Judiciary Committee that he had attempted to rape her in the 1980s when they were both in their teens in the Washington, DC, suburbs. (Thomas's harassment of Hill also occurred in the early 1980s, when Hill was in her twenties.) Blasey Ford testified before the committee, and several other people who knew Kavanaugh in his younger years shared additional details about his sexually aggressive treatment of women. Kavanaugh erupted into furious denials of these allegations under questioning from the committee, shouting red-faced that while he "liked beer," he had never behaved in the ways Blasey Ford described. The Senate confirmed Kavanaugh by a razor-thin margin of 50 to 48, with Sen. Joe Manchin of West Virginia breaking from the rest of the Democratic caucus to supply the crucial fiftieth vote. Almost immediately, Blasey Ford went into hiding in response to death threats.[3]

Anita Hill could sympathize with Blasey Ford's ordeal. Since her testimony she had become a scholar of some renown. Crenshaw and Roberts—who, like Hill, are Black—also brought deep intellectual and philosophical expertise to the issue. Crenshaw authored a pathbreaking 1989 article that put forth a legal theory of "intersectionality," arguing that laws against sex discrimination failed to account for Black women's experiences of racism, while laws against racial discrimination likewise could not accommodate the ways that sexism shaped the experiences of Black women. Roberts was a leading figure in a movement for "reproductive justice." Her work argued that women of color's sexual autonomy depended on their access to contraception and abortion, protection from coercive sterilization (a practice affecting nonwhite and lower-income women well into the 1970s), and public policies that supported the rights of parents and children regardless of income or marital status.[4]

Together, Crenshaw, Roberts, and Hill tackled a question at the heart of the history of sexuality in the United States: to what extent could women possess sexual autonomy so long as law and custom at once maligned sexually independent women and forgave men for using force?

"Few colored girls reach the age of sixteen without receiving advances from [a Southern white man]," a black woman wrote in 1904, "often from a man old enough to be their father, a white haired veteran of sin." Even if a Black woman carefully avoided walking too close to a red-light district, she might be teased or derided. In New Orleans during the 1930s and 1940s, a Black woman or girl strolling down South Rampart Street to meet a friend for a drink at the Tick Tock Tavern or to hear a band play at the Dew Drop Inn, might brace herself for insult. Black women and girls learned to navigate their cities according to a mental map of sexual insult and danger. Sexual violence in the South was one of the principal motivators for Black women who moved north or west in the first half of the twentieth century as part of the Great Migration, but assumptions about Black women's sexual immorality followed them there. In the 1960s, Black women in Los Angeles brought cases to the ACLU and NAACP after police arrested them for prostitution when they had simply been walking down the street.[5]

Sexual harassment and assault were persistent burdens in Black women's lives and drove their agitation for justice. On September 3, 1944, six white boys and men viciously gang raped Recy Taylor, a Black married woman, while Taylor was walking home from church in Abbeville, Alabama. News of the assault reached the Montgomery branch of the NAACP, whose secretary, Rosa Parks, launched an investigation and established the Committee for Equal Justice for Taylor. Those efforts drew international attention to the sexual violence Black women in the South faced, comparing the attack on Taylor to the brutality of Hitler's Nazi soldiers. Ten years later, Parks became an icon of Black respectability when she refused to give up her seat on a Montgomery bus, an event that sparked the yearlong Montgomery Bus Boycott. Less remembered is that she devoted much of her civil rights advocacy to defending Black women who had been sexually abused by white men.[6]

Racist stereotypes about Black people's sexual immorality even informed the mundane details of government assistance programs. Throughout the United States, low-income mothers with dependent children relied on monthly support from the Aid to Dependent Children (ADC) program, known as "welfare," which originated with the Social Security Act of 1935. While nothing in the language of the law treated Black women differently, discrimination was rife in practice. The law gave social workers the authority to determine if a home was "unsuitable," which was cause for denying benefits and even removing children from the home. Louisiana passed a law in 1960 that revoked welfare benefits for the children of a woman who had ever borne a child out of wedlock; the law even barred such women from *voting*. Of the 22,501 children Louisiana dropped from its welfare rolls in July 1960 when the law was implemented, 22,000 were Black, a number equivalent to nearly every Black family receiving ADC in the state. Only months of protest by poor Black women, eventually represented by the ACLU, pressured the federal government to end states' use of "suitable-home" rules.[7]

Other exclusionary policies followed. In the 1960s, twenty-one states implemented "man of the house" or "substitute father" laws, which reduced or eliminated welfare benefits to families if caseworkers discovered that the mother was involved in a nonmarital sexual relationship. In effect, the laws required that any man who "cohabited" with the welfare recipient—if he lived in the home or if "he visits frequently for the purpose of cohabiting"—was responsible for at least a portion of the children's support. The meaning of cohabitation was explicitly sexual: Alabama lawmakers determined that a man was cohabiting if he and the children's mother had " 'frequent' or 'continuous' sexual relations," such that the man enjoyed "the privileges of a husband." Social workers interpreted the law to mean that they should directly ask women, "Do you have sexual intercourse?" and even query the children about "whether their mother was sleeping around." Approximately 98 percent of the women and children who lost their benefits under "substitute father" laws in Louisiana and Alabama were Black. The lawmakers who supported these measures disingenuously explained that they wanted to limit welfare disbursements to protect taxpayers. Both the laws' implementation and lawmakers' own words about Black people's sexuality make clear that anti-Black racism informed their votes.[8]

The Black women who challenged these laws refused to trade their sexual autonomy and privacy for government benefits. In 1966, Mrs. Sylvester Smith's caseworker warned her that, under Alabama's "substitute father" law, she would lose the meager ADC benefits she relied on to support her four children and one grandchild unless she ended her sexual affair with a married man, who was himself the father of nine children. Smith needed the ADC support—her eight-hour-a-day job as a cook in Selma paid only $20 per week—but she was outraged at the caseworker's intrusions into her intimate life. "I told [the caseworker] it was none of her business," Smith asserted. So long as she was able, she added, she would enjoy "going with" whichever men she pleased. The court ruled in Smith's favor by invalidating Alabama's substitute-father law, but it affirmed the right of states to use their power to promote marriage and to penalize certain sexual relationships.[9]

Black women and their allies filed dozens of lawsuits in the late 1960s against a variety of laws that penalized "illegitimate" children and their mothers, targeting Social Security regulations that excluded such children from benefits, policies that disinherited nonmarital children, and workplaces that discriminated against unmarried women who became pregnant or raised children born out of wedlock. Even when their efforts succeeded, the rulings often reinforced a traditional view of sexual morality. In a 1972 case over whether Louisiana could deny workers' compensation to nonmarital children, Supreme Court Justice Lewis F. Powell wrote in the majority opinion that such distinctions were unfair to the "hapless" children who should not suffer for the "irresponsible liaisons" of their parents.[10]

Stereotypes of poor and nonwhite women's "excessive" sexuality—and of their male partners' sexual irresponsibility—also propelled coercive sterilization programs across the United States, the worst of which provoked national outrage in the early 1970s. Accusations of precocious fertility were increasingly hurled at nonwhite women in the United States. During the economic crisis of the 1930s, public health officials in Los Angeles castigated Mexicans as both disease-carrying and exceptionally fertile. Newspaper reports featured stories of Mexican women with five or more children. This racism shaped public health policies. White physicians and policymakers argued that Mexicans' high rates of infant mortality indicated cultural inferiority rather than the consequences of poverty and inadequate housing.[11]

The idea that certain groups of people (almost always nonwhite and poor) were having "too many" children motivated wealthy donors and policymakers to propose a global push for "family planning" as a solution to poverty. Margaret Sanger had promoted birth control as the most important means of liberating women sexually when she launched her cause in the 1910s, but amid the conservative political climate of the 1920s, she teamed up with physicians and eugenicists who touted contraceptives as a solution to the growing global population. In 1942, the American Birth Control League became the Planned Parenthood Federation of America, an organization that pursued legally available contraception as a method of population control.[12]

President Lyndon Johnson's ambitious War on Poverty directed hundreds of millions of dollars to "family planning" programs. In 1967, Congress appropriated funds to provide family planning services to welfare recipients. For the first time, the federal government made grants to nonprofits like Planned Parenthood to help them distribute birth control to low-income women. In 1971, Medicaid, the government health insurance program for lower-income Americans, began to pay 90 percent of the cost of a sterilization procedure. Problems arose almost immediately: the National Welfare Rights Organization (NWRO) successfully lobbied against a bill in Tennessee that would have required women to be sterilized after the birth of "one or more" children out of wedlock or lose their welfare benefits.[13]

National outrage escalated after revelations about the Relf sisters in Alabama. Caseworkers had sent fourteen-year-old Minnie Lee Relf and her twelve-year-old sister Mary Alice to the Montgomery Family Planning Clinic. Minnie had at first gone to the clinic to get shots of Depo-Provera, a new form of long-acting hormonal contraception hailed as a way to prevent pregnancy without needing to remember to take—or get access to—a daily oral contraceptive pill. When research showed that Depo-Provera caused cancer in lab rats, the clinic discontinued its use. Caseworkers then approached Minnie's mother, a sharecropper who was illiterate, about finding an alternative contraceptive for Minnie, whom they had determined to be "mentally incompetent." The state of Alabama permitted eugenic sterilizations for individuals with that diagnosis. When Mrs. Relf signed the consent form, she later explained, she thought she was agreeing to a different kind of injection, not tubal ligation. Mary Alice was also sterilized.[14]

Another scandal involved coercive sterilizations of Mexican women at the University of Southern California–Los Angeles County Medical Center (LACMC). Women and outraged healthcare workers relayed stories of a physician at LACMC holding up a syringe filled with anesthesia and telling a woman in advanced labor that she would receive pain relief only when she consented to be sterilized. Some women were threatened with deportation. LACMC's often callous approach to women's reproductive options fell especially hard on Mexican women. Very few of these migrants received any welfare benefits, but, as in the 1930s, newspaper articles cast Mexican women as hyperfertile threats to taxpayer resources. These articles repeated the stereotype of the "pregnant pilgrim," the Mexican woman who crossed the border for the purpose of giving birth to an American citizen, her hospital expenses covered by taxpayer-supported public hospitals. In response to a class-action lawsuit, *Madrigal v. Quilligan,* a federal judge ruled that the doctors' behavior did not violate the women's civil rights, but activists heralded the case for pushing LACMC to enforce federal guidelines to prevent sterilization abuses.[15]

A movement of "Third World" women rallied in defense of the victims of coercive sterilization and demanded that the reproductive rights movement consider the "choices" available to women of color. Abortion access highlighted the inequalities they faced. The 1977 Hyde Amendment, an addendum to federal welfare legislation, had eliminated federal funding for most abortions, directly limiting abortion access for women on Medicaid and for Native women dependent on the Indian Health Service. Coupled with the recent infusion of federal funds for "family planning" services, the situation belied any pretext of choice for less privileged people. As Brenda Joyner, a member of the Committee for Abortion Rights and Against Sterilization Abuse (CARASA) explained, "The government will not pay for a $200 or $300 abortion for a poor woman on Medicaid. But it will pay for a $2,000 or $3,000 sterilization procedure for the same poor woman." Founded in 1977, CARASA reframed the cause as "the right to decide if and when to have children and the right to be respected and accepted no matter what decisions we make." That approach eventually became the philosophy of an international feminist movement that sought to expand all women's access to reproductive healthcare.[16]

Reproductive health and survival motivated women of color to organize collectively and push for change. Byllye Avery was already known among fellow African Americans in her Gainesville, Florida, community as the person to call for help finding a safe abortion provider in the days before abortion was legal in Florida. A few years after the *Roe* decision, she cofounded the Gainesville Women's Health Clinic and opened a birthing center to serve Black women. In 1983 she joined with other health activists and established the National Black Women's Health Project (NBWHP), the first reproductive-freedom organization led by and for women of color. Similar organizations soon followed: the National Latina Health Organization (1986), the Native American Women's Health Education Resource Center (1988), and the National Asian Women's Health Organization (1993).[17]

When an influential group of twelve Black feminists coined the phrase "reproductive justice" at a 1994 abortion rights conference, they named a movement many decades in the making. "Reproductive justice activists," Dorothy Roberts explained, "treat abortion and other reproductive health services as akin to the resources all human beings are entitled to, such as health care, education, housing, and food—in an equitable, democratic society." The National LGBT Task Force and the National Center for Lesbian Rights joined the movement for reproductive justice, forging new alliances with organizations centered on race. The language of reproductive justice, unlike "choice," demonstrated the impossibility of separating questions of sexual autonomy from broader social issues or their histories. The vulnerability of a single woman speaking out against powerful men, however, remained.

Laws concerning sexual harassment were relatively new in 1991 when Anita Hill sent her memo to the Senate Judiciary Committee, but sexual harassment, of course, was not. A 1976 *Redbook* survey about "Sex on the Job" concluded from its readers' responses that harassment was "not epidemic, it is pandemic—an everyday, everywhere occurrence." A scandal that same year revealed pervasive sexual harassment on Capitol Hill when it came to light that some congressional secretaries were traded, sexually, among members of Congress in exchange for votes. Only slowly did media coverage of such practices shift its focus away from the sexual peccadilloes of the men to consider the consequences of coercive workplace sexualization for women.[18]

The EEOC brought the first successful federal sexual harassment suit that same year, winning a case on behalf of a woman employed at a federal agency who was fired after repeatedly refusing her married supervisor's advances. Over the next several years, the EEOC and women's advocates developed a legal standard for sexual harassment as "unwelcome sexual advances, requests for sexual favors, and other verbal or physical conduct of a sexual nature" related to a person's employment. This definition explained that actions constituted sexual harassment if they had "the purpose or effect of substantially interfering with an individual's work performance or creating an intimidating, hostile, or offensive working environment."[19]

Hill's statement about the harassment she endured from Clarence Thomas was leaked to the press two days before the confirmation hearings were scheduled to start. As Hill testified when called before the committee, Thomas had repeatedly asked her on dates while she worked as his assistant at the Department of Education. He "began to use work situations to discuss sex," always doing so in the privacy of his office or hers. "On several occasions," she continued, "Thomas told me graphically of his own sexual prowess."[20]

Supporters of Thomas asserted that Hill was delusional and had fantasized his interest due to her own "erotomania." One of the diagnoses given to Alice Mitchell to prove their insanity in the 1890s, erotomania evoked theories of racial degeneracy—in Mitchell's case, evidence of their immature sexual psychology as an "invert." Allegations that Hill suffered from this disease recalled descriptions dating back hundreds of years that women of African origin were physically primitive and sexually voracious. The very act of speaking out in defense of her sexual respectability cast Hill into old stereotypes of the "loose" Black woman. Millions of people watched the live broadcast as Hill sat alone, facing a row of all white, male senators, several of whom asked her intrusive questions about her own sexual attitudes. (Two women served in the Senate in 1991, but neither sat on the Judiciary Committee.)[21]

Testifying in response to Hill's statement, Thomas denied that he "had any personal sexual interest in her" and described her testimony as "sleaze." Most provocatively, he accused Hill and her supporters of being agents of a "high-tech lynching for uppity Blacks" who had reached higher levels of professional achievement. Thomas's comparison of Hill's testimony to a lynching recalled an especially horrific chapter in the history of anti-Black violence in the United States, albeit one in which white men and women, not Black women, had victimized Black men. Black activists had long decried false accusations of rape against Black men by white girls and women, portraying them as perpetrators of the "rape lie," but Thomas and his supporters turned that aspersion against Hill.[22]

White conservatives welcomed the support of the many Black men who rallied to Thomas's defense and made their own endorsement of an anti-affirmative-action far-right justice appear less extreme. Despite Hill's testimony, the Senate confirmed Thomas, 52 to 48, one of the narrowest margins in the court's history. Black support for Thomas rose from 54 percent before the hearings to 80 percent after them, as many Black people saw Hill as "a vindictive sister trying to discredit a fun-loving brother."[23]

Thomas's Black defenders blamed Hill for exhibiting a prudish incomprehension. Harvard sociologist Orlando Patterson argued that the hearings revealed the weakness of a "neo-Puritan" white feminism that failed to appreciate that Thomas's behavior was typical of both "Rabelaisian humor" and a Southern Black "down-home style of courting." Patterson cited his "post-feminist" daughter's frustration with the very idea of legally prohibiting sexual harassment. Even if "Judge Thomas did say those raunchy things" in the early 1980s, Hill should have told him then "what a 'dog' he was and reported to the authorities . . . if his advances had continued to annoy her." It is up to women to shed their sexual inhibitions, Patterson concluded, if they truly want to break through the glass ceiling. Patterson, like Thomas, appeared to confuse workplace conduct with private sexual banter. Nor did he appear cognizant of what Kimberlé Crenshaw described as the "race-specific dimensions of black women's sexual empowerment." Many Black women hesitated to speak out when harmed by Black men for fear of reinforcing white stereotypes of Black men as sexual predators.[24]

A generation of Black women who had been fighting for sex- and race-based justice begged to differ. A full-page advertisement signed by more than 1,600 Black women, "African American Women in Defense of Ourselves," ran in the *New York Times* on Sunday, November 11, 1991. The statement argued that Hill's experiences epitomized how sexism and racism shaped Black women's sexual reputations and exposed them to violence. "Throughout U.S. history," the signers wrote, "Black women have been sexually stereotyped as immoral, insatiable, perverse; the initiators in all sexual contacts—abusive or otherwise." Black women confronted those stereotypes whenever they brought charges of rape or sexual abuse of any kind. "As Anita Hill's experience demonstrates," the authors wrote, "Black women who speak of these matters are not likely to be believed." The fact that Thomas had previously disparaged his older sister, Emma Mae Martin, for depending on public assistance (which she did, in part, to help raise her siblings while seeking employment), compounded their anger about Thomas's seeming disregard for Black women.[25]

Hill's testimony at the Thomas hearings subjected her to a torrent of verbal abuse and threats to her safety that lasted for decades, but it may have improved the legal options available to other women. Hill became a hero to many Black women for teaching the world about the struggles they faced. "All America's consciousness has been raised on this issue," wrote Nellie Y. McKay, a noted scholar of Black literature. The hearings seem to have shifted the tenor of some legislative debates too. Shortly after the hearings concluded, Congress voted on a civil rights bill that would allow victims of sexual harassment to receive monetary damages. After the Hill-Thomas hearings, Senators who had previously spoken out against the law suddenly had no comment. It passed both houses of Congress, and President Bush did not veto it. Subsequent Supreme Court cases strengthened the rights of women bringing sexual-harassment charges against school districts and clarified the legal consequences of forcing employees to work in an "intimidating, hostile, or offensive working environment." Women won class-action lawsuits that accused employers of exposing women, as a group, to unwelcome sexual taunts and hostility.[26]

Perhaps the most direct result of the Judiciary Committee's cavalier response to Hill's reports of sexual harassment was the determination of an unprecedented number of women to run for office. Patty Murray, a state senator in Washington, watched the Hill-Thomas hearings and wondered, "Who's saying what I would say if I were there?" before launching a successful campaign for the U.S. Senate in 1992. In Illinois, Carol Moseley Braun, an attorney with years of experience in local politics, defeated the incumbent, Sen. John Dixon, in the Democratic Primary. Dixon's service on the Judiciary Committee became a mark against him among women voters, Republican and Democratic alike, who propelled Moseley Braun to victory that November, enabling her to become the first Black woman to serve in the U.S. Senate.[27]

Anita Hill's public tribulations motivated Black feminists to pursue not only legal protections from abuse but also how to express their desires apart from historically denigrating stereotypes. Scholars of Black women's experiences discussed the ways in which the "politics of silence" that Black women adopted as strategies for survival under slavery and freedom had produced "a very narrow view of black women's sexuality," theorist Evelyn Hammonds wrote, which largely omitted Black women's "pleasure, exploration, and agency." The influential writer bell hooks described at length her efforts to express a deeply felt erotic longing on her own terms. She called on Black women to define themselves *for* themselves: "When black women relate to our bodies, our sexuality, in ways that place erotic recognition, desire, pleasure, and fulfillment at the center of our efforts to create radical black female subjectivity, we can make new and different representations of ourselves as sexual subjects." Surveying popular culture, hooks found few films that "explore issues of black female sexuality in ways that intervene and disrupt conventional representations." The few that did, she noted, gave Black women a way to write themselves into a different erotic narrative.[28]

Legal definitions of "unwanted" sexual behavior became the stuff of late-night talk shows and tabloids when news broke in 1997 that President Bill Clinton, an Arkansas Democrat, had had an extramarital affair with Monica Lewinsky, who had interned and worked in the White House before taking a job at the Pentagon. Lewinsky confided to a work friend, Linda Tripp, that she and the president had conducted an affair from November 1995, when she was twenty-two, until May 1997. Tripp disliked the president, and unbeknownst to Lewinsky, she recorded their phone calls.

Clinton was meanwhile under investigation by a congressionally appointed special prosecutor, Kenneth Starr, for alleged illegal real estate dealings and corruption. He was also being sued by Paula Jones, formerly employed by the state of Arkansas. Jones gave sworn statements alleging that in 1991 she had gone to then-Governor Clinton's hotel room at his invitation, where he exposed himself and asked her to "kiss" his penis, a request that Jones said caused her emotional and psychological injury. Knowing that sexual harassment cases often hinged on whether lawyers could establish a pattern of behavior, Tripp alerted Jones's lawyers to Lewinsky's relationship with the president. Starr then convened a grand jury to investigate Clinton's behavior. The grand jury weighed allegations that Clinton had perjured himself when he denied an affair with Lewinsky while under oath in a deposition for the Jones suit.[29]

In a televised address, Clinton famously refused to concede that he had had "sexual relations" with "that woman." To the contrary, in her sworn statements, Lewinsky asserted that she performed oral sex on the president on multiple occasions. He touched her breasts, and he digitally penetrated her several times (once with a cigar) to orgasm. The legal definition of harassment included that the "inappropriate intimate contact" occurred with the "intent to arouse or gratify." Clinton insisted that no harassment occurred because even if Lewinsky fellated him, it was his pleasure, not hers, that was involved. Lewinsky was adamant that their encounters were mutual; she had orgasmed during them more often than the president had. But the president's denials, however absurd they became (with Clinton arguing over "what the meaning of 'is' is," at one point), portrayed Lewinsky as deluded, slutty, and unimportant. Clinton was impeached in the Republican-controlled House of Representatives for committing perjury and then acquitted in the Senate. By the time the impeachment trial had ended, Clinton's approval ratings had gone up. Lewinsky, meanwhile, was ridiculed by much of the nation as a bimbo. In a 2001 HBO documentary, she was asked about her role as "America's premier blowjob queen." She later divulged that she had become suicidal in the aftermath of her public humiliation, an experience that inspired her to become an anti-bullying advocate in the 2010s.[30]

Lewinsky and Jones appeared to epitomize two sides of the feminist sex wars. Lewinsky reached adulthood expecting to benefit from feminism's gains, while Paula Jones sought restitution from a legal system that was supposed to identify and punish sexual harassers in a world dominated by men and their interests. Years later, Lewinsky reconsidered her youthful sense of sexual agency, of "owning desire" in her sexual encounters with the former president. Perhaps, she reflected in 2018, the issue was better framed not so much as a matter of consent as one of power.[31]

Kavanaugh's confirmation hearings in the fall of 2018 occurred amid a national outpouring of concern about sexual assault that arose largely out of the resurgent #MeToo movement. Initiated a decade earlier by a

Black activist named Tarana Burke, #MeToo caught fire across American life in 2017 when white celebrities spoke out on social media against powerful men such as Hollywood producer Harvey Weinstein, comedian Louis C. K., and television personality Matt Lauer, among dozens of others. Personal testimonials about sexual harassment and assault flooded social media and made headlines. People sharing these stories, encompassing all genders and sexual orientations, were often disclosing painful details from their past for the first time. For several months, #MeToo was *the* story. Investigative reporters from the *New York Times* and the *New Yorker* who covered the Weinstein allegations would ultimately share a Pulitzer Prize.[32]

The fact that more than two dozen women had accused President Donald Trump of sexual assault, including allegations of rape, amplified the sense that powerful men (powerful white men, in particular) evaded repercussions for their actions. A month before the 2016 election, someone had leaked to the press an audio recording of a 2005 *Access Hollywood* interview in which Trump boasted that because he was a "star," he could "do anything" he wanted to women, even "grab them by the pussy." At a presidential election debate two days later with Secretary Hillary Clinton, the Democratic nominee, Trump scoffed that "that was locker-room talk," typical when (heterosexual) men joked with one another. By the time the Kavanaugh hearings began two years later, waves of revelations about sexual harassment and assault in media companies, governments, literary circles, professional organizations, private schools, and social clubs, not to mention among members of Trump's cabinet and advisors, left little doubt that the president's attitudes and behaviors were, in fact, typical—and not just boastful talk.[33]

Blasey Ford's testimony was harrowing. She described how another boy held her down while Kavanaugh assaulted her. An expert on the psychology of trauma, Blasey Ford explained that while she could not recall every detail of the evening, the part of the brain responsible for storing memories preserved certain things clearly: "Indelible in the hippocampus is the laughter, the uproarious laughter between the two [men], and their having fun at my expense." In the days surrounding the hearings, women's advocates unequivocally backed Blasey Ford while Republican elected officials and their media allies reaffirmed their allegiance to Kavanaugh.[34]

From boardrooms to coffee shops, Americans engaged in acrimonious debates over whether rape culture existed and whether too great an emphasis on consent drained the erotic charge from sexual encounters. Some pro-sex feminists warned of a "neo-Puritan" embrace of sexual censoriousness that negated their efforts to empower women's and queer sexualities. ("Neo-Puritan" was a phrase Orlando Patterson had used to describe Anita Hill and her defenders' attitudes toward sex.) College administrators huddled with legal counsel to determine how best to revise their codes of student conduct and disciplinary procedures when one student accused another of sexual assault. Advocates for "men's rights," a movement premised on the belief that American men suffer significant sex discrimination, warned that false accusations could ruin a man's reputation or livelihood, a concern shared by some pro-sex feminists.[35]

Members of the audience in the Irvine Auditorium that October afternoon in 2018 looked to the women seated on the stage—each, in her own way, an expert on women's historical and legal struggle for sexual rights and bodily autonomy—for reassurance and clarity. Hill noted that the circumstances of Blasey Ford's testimony revealed the advances women had made in the intervening years. Four women served on the Judiciary Committee in 2018, and two members of the committee were Black.[36]

Yet the Senate had failed to put in place a process for receiving complaints about judicial nominees, which resulted in considerable confusion when Sen. Dianne Feinstein (D-CA) received but did not disclose Blasey Ford's complaint until pressured to do so. Still, there was no question that Blasey Ford had more social support than Hill had (even though she had needed it too). Blasey Ford joined a wider movement of people of all genders speaking out about their experiences of nonconsensual sex and demanding that abusers face consequences for their actions. It was a movement that Hill helped accelerate decades before, its ultimate aims still unrealized. There was another concern, as well: that plenty of people believed that Kavanaugh, as a drunk teenager, attempted to rape Blasey Ford with such violence that she feared he was going to kill her, and they nonetheless concluded that his conduct did not disqualify him for public office because it was perfectly normal adolescent male behavior.[37]

If nothing else, the experts at the Irvine Auditorium conveyed the power of collective action and the advances in the legal options available to women since Hill testified in 1991. Blasey Ford's testimony validated the voices of untold numbers of people speaking publicly about sexual abuse and demanding justice. But so long as powerful state actors willfully dismissed these voices and diminished the salience of sexual abuse, the cause remained a pressing one.

Chapter 17

Family's Value

Anthony R. G. Hardaway felt called to help HIV-positive, "same-gender-loving" (SGL) Black men. ("SGL" is a preferred designation among some Black men who connect with other Black men but who do not identify as "gay" or "queer" because they asso-

When the federal government failed to address the rising toll of HIV/AIDS, protestors organized dramatic expressions of anger, grief, and resolve. Public funerals were one way of drawing attention to the epidemic's devastating impact.

ciate those identities with white people, a subject this chapter explores.) Spirit-filled and outgoing, Hardaway modeled his attire on expressions of Black elegance that he encountered in church. But he was moved as well by the sorrow that soaked the ground he walked on. "He feels a part of himself is buried" with each community member lost to HIV/AIDS, a reporter explained in 2004, "and thinks it is not normal that gay men his age, 34, should feel such hurt, pain, fear and numbness to death." More than 581,000 Americans were diagnosed with acquired immune deficiency syndrome (AIDS), the cluster of diseases caused by HIV infection, between 1980 and 1996; approximately 362,000 of those people died, a horrific 62 percent mortality rate. Lower-income and nonwhite people perished with the most alarming frequency. Even after antiretroviral therapies introduced in the mid-1990s extended the life expectancies of many people with AIDS, HIV-positive Black men remained three times more likely to die than HIV-positive white men. Rates for HIV-positive Black women were comparably dire.[1]

Among countless acts of resistance to the epidemic, Hardaway forged a family-like community of Black men who celebrated their collective beauty. Starting in the late 1990s, he led the Memphis chapter of Brothers United in Support, an education-oriented community group for Black SGL men. (It also served, Hardaway noted, as an alternative gathering spot to the only Memphis club that welcomed queer Black people.) His efforts contributed to an international movement in response to HIV/AIDS. In Philadelphia, Kiyoshi Kuromiya cofounded that city's branch of the AIDS Coalition to Unleash Power (ACT UP) in the 1980s, created an internet communications platform for HIV/AIDS treatment information in the 1990s, and shaped the agendas of health policy organizations as an openly gay and HIV-positive person of color. Activists invented new forms of protest to save and improve as many lives as they could. A "people with AIDS" (PWA) movement coalesced in the early 1980s that championed self-love, community engagement, and safer sex. In 1983, PWA activists distributed the first-ever safer-sex manual, "How to Have Sex in an Epidemic: One Approach" and then stormed a medical conference on AIDS to present their demands for an end to medical homophobia. Community members ran errands and cared for the pets of the chronically ill, celebrities fundraised for medical research foundations, and advocacy organizations lobbied elected officials. They channeled their collective fury and grief into transforming healthcare systems, advocating for what was now more often abbreviated as "GLBT" or "LGBT" rights. Hardaway was born about twenty-five years after Kiyoshi Kuromiya, but both of their stories remind us that while we might think of HIV/AIDS as a story that ended in the 1990s, for many people, and people of color in particular, the epidemic continues and remains a threat.[2]

HIV/AIDS also accelerated a reimagining of what it meant to be a family. A 2001 "Family Album" of the Memphis chapter of Brothers United included a photograph of two men embracing and depicted several members wearing elaborate drag, each image in its own way evidence of the love, acceptance, and joy that the group fostered. Such a vision of family was more than affectionate: it was a political statement about a community's survival.[3]

Hardaway was in his early teens when reports began to circulate of young men falling suddenly and gravely ill. In June 1981, the Centers for Disease Control (CDC)'s *Morbidity and Mortality Weekly* reported five cases of a rare illness, pneumocystis carinii pneumonia, among previously healthy young men, "all active homosexuals," in Los Angeles. Two of the men had died. A month later, an article in the *New York Times* described the appearance in New York and California of a "rare and often rapidly fatal" cancer called Karposi's sarcoma among "41 homosexuals." Eight of those men had died.[4]

No one knew at first why or how previously healthy and often quite young people were getting sick. Already by 1979, young gay men in New York and California were terminally ill with diseases uncommon in otherwise healthy younger people. Hospital workers in New York began to refer to the "wrath of God syndrome" (WOGS). Some "bewildered" physicians concluded that male homosexuality was the common denominator in the problematically named condition, "gay-related immune deficiency" (GRID). Once it became obvious that people who did not engage in queer male sex were also getting sick, medical professionals in 1982 adopted the now-standard name for AIDS. Scientists in 1984 identified a novel retrovirus that destroyed previously healthy immune systems as the culprit. Two years later, the international medical community agreed to call it the human immunodeficiency virus (HIV). Spread through semen, vaginal mucus, and blood, HIV attacks the immune systems of infected people of all ages and genders. Behaviors such as unprotected sex or intravenous drug use, and medical experiences such as a blood plasma transfusion, are the conduits of HIV transmission.[5]

HIV/AIDS was falsely termed the "gay plague," but communities with large concentrations of gay and SGL men were initially the hardest hit. During and after World War II, large numbers of LGBT people had relocated to San Francisco, Los Angeles, Chicago, Miami, Boston, Philadelphia, New York, and other cities because they wanted to live among other LGBT people—to find more gay and lesbian bars, social networks, lovers, and organizations. Those same residential concentrations abetted the spread of HIV. Gay men and lesbians living through the HIV/AIDS epidemic in its early years recalled spending every weekend at funerals. "I began to live in this world where you got to know people, and you got to love them, and you laughed with them and found out how beautiful they were, and they were going to die," one lesbian activist recalled. "In some cases you watched them fucking die . . . In sort of a naive way, it's like, 'You've got to be kidding.'" Lesbians and gay men had not always agreed about the priorities or internal dynamics of queer activism, but the exigencies of HIV/AIDS created a new sense of common purpose.[6]

Gay health clinics established in the 1970s became vital resources. Like the women's health movement, the LGBT healthcare movement centered the patient's experience. Clinicians focused not only on disease treatment and prevention but on a more holistic understanding of sexual health. In the early 1980s, clinics provided compassionate care for HIV-positive patients, but they did so in the absence of any viable treatments. The data about HIV/AIDS that they collected and shared with other medical centers was nonetheless invaluable.[7]

Larry Kramer, a white gay writer who lived in New York City, founded the Gay Men's Health Crisis (GMHC) in New York City in the summer of 1982. GHMC connected volunteers, affectionately called "buddies," with seriously ill gay men and their loved ones to ensure that their needs were met. Buddies delivered meals, fetched prescriptions, cleaned apartments, or simply offered a hand to hold. Lawyers volunteering with GMHC donated their time to prevent the evictions of men too sick to earn rent money. PWAs and their partners attended group therapy sessions or called in to the twenty-four-hour crisis hotline staffed by GMHC volunteers. Similar organizations soon operated in Los Angeles and San Francisco, including Gay and Lesbian Latinos Unidos (GLLU), which advocated for gay men and lesbians within the Latino community.[8]

Safer-sex workshops—or "playshops," as one group called them—were considered a crucial means of public health outreach and education, but they also affirmed the desires of HIV-positive people. One of the most popular was the "Hot, Horny and Healthy!" playshop. It originated as a project of white men who volunteered at GMHC in 1985 and was later adapted by the National Task Force on AIDS Prevention for Black, Latino, Asian-American, and Native American gay men. The playshop included discussions about sex before and during the AIDS epidemic, erotic play, condom use, and role-playing exercises. This sex-positive approach to HIV/AIDS urged gay men to change their behaviors while avoiding calls from Larry Kramer and other LGBT advocates to blame bathhouses and "promiscuity" for the suffering of gay male PWAs.[9]

In the rush to bring education and assistance to reeling communities, some advocates overlooked the racial divides that marked nearly all aspects of American life. A predominantly white gay organization might develop an HIV/AIDS prevention program for bars, clubs, and bathhouses where white, gay men were most likely to congregate. Yet

Safer-sex workshops were key aspects of the response to HIV/AIDS. The "Hot, Horny, and Healthy" program was tailored to address the concerns of HIV-positive Black men, encouraging them to seek pleasure while protecting their own and their partners' health.

as Kuromiya had observed since the 1970s, many of these hangouts either excluded people of color or treated them with sufficient hostility that they felt unwelcome. This discrimination occasionally included a policy against queer women. Locals in Greensboro, North Carolina, in the 1970s knew that one gay bar had a tacit policy of "no dykes and no blacks allowed."[10]

Adding to this problem, many Black men saw HIV/AIDS as a primarily white, gay disease and considered AIDS service organizations to be tools of a racist healthcare system. In language that echoed some Black nationalists' critique of "family planning" and contraception, they suspected that HIV/AIDS was a white conspiracy to rid the Earth of Black people. The scientific theory that HIV originated in Africa further alienated many Americans of African descent, who rejected that idea as the product of anti-Black animus. Native Americans were similarly suspicious about a "white man's disease," a skepticism based on centuries of medical abuse. That combination of inequitable medical care and cultural antagonism contributed to devastatingly high rates of infection. In 1992, the rate of infection among Native Americans was ten times the rate for Black or Latinx people.[11]

The Reagan administration and its conservative religious allies abetted those fears by blaming HIV/AIDS on homosexuality and utterly abandoning LGBT Americans. On the floor of the U.S. Senate, Jesse Helms (R-NC) held up a copy of GMHC's *Safer Sex Comix* and insisted that what appeared at first blush to be a sex-positive presentation of condom use was instead a subversive attempt to lure unsuspecting innocents into gay sexuality. He succeeded in passing the 1987 Helms Amendment, which prohibited the CDC from spending federal dollars on AIDS education or prevention materials that, the legislation explained, "promote, encourage, and condone homosexual sexual activities or the intravenous use of illegal drugs." Helms and other anti-gay legislators and activists warned that information about the transmission of HIV between men was equivalent to an endorsement of homosexuality.[12]

HIV/AIDS stirred up the fervid imaginations of some religious and political conservatives. Jerry Falwell, a fundamentalist Protestant minister and leader of the Moral Majority, a national political organization of far-right Christians, argued in 1983 for the quarantine of everyone with AIDS. The president of the Christian American Family Association, Daniel Villanueva, took the idea a step further and demanded that the United States government "QUARANTINE ALL HOMOSEXUAL ESTABLISHMENTS." Conspiracy theorist Lyndon LaRouche and his supporters put ballot measures before California voters in 1986 and 1988 that called for quarantining all "suspected AIDS carriers."

Both measures failed, as did executive and legislative efforts in Florida to incarcerate PWAs, but the idea of quarantine persisted. The U.S. government banned HIV-positive immigrants from entering the country from 1987 to 2009.[13]

A vast network of "family values" publications, think tanks, advocacy organizations, and political action committees blamed HIV/AIDS on feminism, sexual liberation, legal abortion, gay and lesbian rights, and no-fault divorce. Deep-pocketed organizations like Focus on the Family, the Moral Majority, and the Family Research Council portrayed homosexuality as a sign of civilization's imminent downfall. In 1987, Falwell proclaimed that "AIDS is the lethal judgment of God on the sin of homosexuality, and it is also the judgment of God on America for endorsing this vulgar, perverted, and reprobate lifestyle." Such cruel statements were not confined to the family values movement. The Reagan administration shaped a national response to HIV/AIDS that appeared to treat gay men as disposable.[14]

The Reagan administration, closely tied to the family values movement, initially failed to respond to the HIV/AIDS epidemic at all. Surgeon General C. Everett Koop recommended a public health campaign to prevent HIV transmission and was vocal about the importance of practicing safe sex, but by 1987 the Reagan administration had done little beyond creating an "AIDS Commission" to study prevention methods. Many conservatives, including two of Reagan's chief domestic policy advisers, Gary Bauer and William Bennett, ridiculed Koop for his views, particularly his insistence on the importance of using condoms. The Supreme Court's majority opinion in *Bowers v. Hardwick* (1986), upholding a Georgia law that banned male sodomy, only reinforced the sense that the U.S. government considered homosexuality immoral and threatening.[15]

That antigay bias prevented the federal government from allocating resources to lessen the suffering of PWAs. In 1987, outraged and grief-stricken activists in New York City called a meeting that ultimately led

ACT UP Philadelphia, which Kiyoshi Kuromiya helped establish, emphasized that the high price of prescription drugs—and inequitable access to treatment—were crises that transcended national borders. At this protest in 2000, demonstrators reminded presidential candidate Al Gore about their voting priorities.

to the creation of ACT UP—the AIDS Coalition to Unleash Power. The radical, leaderless organization became one of the most effective single-issue pressure groups in U.S. history. Through direct actions, members of ACT UP demanded that the federal government appropriate millions of dollars for HIV/AIDS treatment and prevention research, lower the cost of medications, and loosen the criteria for drug-trial participation. Even radicals like Kiyoshi, who had spent decades protesting the incursions of state power into intimate life, now called upon the federal government for help.

ACT UP's tactics were intentionally dramatic and disruptive. Activists stormed the stages of professional meetings, hung banners from the headquarters of the FDA, interrupted mass at St. Patrick's Cathedral, staged a "die-in" on Wall Street to draw attention to the exorbitant price of potentially lifesaving drugs, and protested repeatedly at government agencies. Anger mixed with grief when activists marched coffins through the street in public funerals and even cast the ashes of AIDS victims on the White House lawn. "It's so hard to remember what it was like then, with people just getting sick and dying," a lesbian and ACT UP participant named Amy Bauer recalled years later. "There were no drugs available, and there was a lot of blame—blaming gay men for having the disease, for promiscuity, for anal sex." Bauer found that ACT UP "gave people a place to be with other people who were as angry as they were." That anger fueled ACT UP's incessant efforts to save the lives of PWAs.[16]

It was a style of protest that Kiyoshi Kuromiya understood well. Kuromiya had been working as an editor and a writer for about a decade when the existential crisis of HIV/AIDS became the focus of his wide-ranging attention. In ACT UP Philadelphia, he pursued the twin goals of disseminating evidence-based information about treatments and pushing for more equitable healthcare access. ACT UP Philadelphia was notable for its emphasis on the interconnections among illness, economic inequality, global migration, and the capitalistic motives of the healthcare industry—pharmaceutical companies in particular. It was also notably interracial, far more so than other ACT UP groups. As he had when he connected the gay liberation movement in the United States to the human rights struggles of "Third World people" everywhere, Kuromiya recognized that any effort to expand healthcare access for people with HIV/AIDS must prioritize "global treatment access." ACT UP Philadelphia approached the challenges facing people with HIV/AIDS in the United States as symptoms of a worldwide struggle against corporations that put profits over people.[17]

The association between HIV/AIDS and gay men, however, drew attention away from the epidemic's prevalence among incarcerated women and sex workers. Katrina Haslip, a Black Muslim, learned that she was HIV-positive while incarcerated at Bedford Hills Correctional Facility, the updated name for the same institution that had housed Mabel Hampton fifty years earlier. As she educated other HIV-positive women at Bedford Hills about available treatments, she learned that the federal government based its definition of AIDS on criteria gleaned from the medical records of HIV-positive men. As a result, the definition excluded illnesses specific to female bodies, which prevented many extremely ill people from qualifying for healthcare and other services designated for people with AIDS. Compounding the problem, the Food and Drug Administration (FDA) had excluded women from HIV/AIDS clinical trials based on their potential for pregnancy, which meant that healthcare providers lacked any data about the appropriate dosages of experimental medications for female-bodied people, not to mention the potential side effects. After her release from Bedford, Haslip testified about the government's failure to acknowledge HIV-positive women's suffering. In response to a 1991 lawsuit, federal agencies expanded the definition of AIDS to include additional symptomatic illnesses. Haslip died in December 1992, at the age of thirty-three, shortly before the FDA speeded up the protocols for drug trials in cases of fatal illness and opened clinical trials to women.[18]

Anthony Hardaway's efforts within Brothers United in Support reflected a somewhat different activist tradition, one that connected Black SGL people's survival not only to medical and legal resources but to pride in their culture. Gay Men of African Descent (GMAD) in New York City, established in 1986, was among the first groups for Black gay men. GMAD and Brothers United filled a critical void left by established Black institutions, which initially directed few resources toward PWAs, and by the exclusions of majority-white gay service organizations. Brothers United's programs emphasized the multiple risk factors in Black men's lives: low self-esteem, inadequate access to healthcare, entrenched homophobia within Black churches in the United States and sub-Saharan Africa, and economic inequality. Those circumstances compounded the threat that HIV/AIDS posed to Black men. A breakthrough antiretroviral therapy discovered in 1996 suppressed the presence of HIV in many patients' bodies, allowing their immune systems to function once again (some dubbed it a "Lazarus effect"), but Hardaway knew that isolated or despondent SGL men might never know about or seek medical care.[19]

Hardaway believed that Black literature and art, combined with public health outreach, could improve Black SGL men's sense of pride and thus encourage them to take better care of themselves and their partners. He was inspired by an outpouring of anthologies, zines, essays, poetry, and theatrical productions by queer Black people in the 1980s and 1990s. (Essays and poetry that Black lesbian feminists published in the 1970s provided a model for much of this queer-of-color creative work.) Brothers United in Memphis sponsored a raft of events devoted to Black writers and artists. Art provided opportunities for connection. The Memphis group also hosted a support group and safer-sex workshops.[20]

"It was an extended family," Hardaway commented after a weekend retreat with Brothers United of Tennessee in the early 2000s. "(It was a time) for all of us to come to one arena to encourage each other, as well as to support one another." In his call for familial love, Hardaway and other HIV/AIDS activists invoked not the nuclear patriarchal ideal championed by "family values" conservatives nor the marital equality that would soon preoccupy centrist LGBTQ activism. He instead called upon long-standing traditions, among Black and queer people, of fictive kin, found family, and expansive networks of caring.[21]

Just what it was that made people family to one another had engaged the imaginations of LGBTQ people for decades. For some, the normative family and its associated sex roles were antithetical to gay liberation. "Homosexuals have burst their chains and abandoned their closets," Kuromiya declared in 1970 in the *Philadelphia Free Press*, an alternative newspaper. "We came to challenge the incredible hypocrisy of your serial monogamy, your oppressive sexual role-playing, your nuclear family, your Protestant ethic, apple pie and Mother." Feminist theorist Shulamith Firestone shared Kuromiya's disdain for the patriarchal nuclear family. In *The Dialectic of Sex: The Case for Feminist Revolution* (1970), she argued that sex roles created pathological forms of heterosexuality and homosexuality that merely reproduced the power imbalances of the patriarchal family. Only the complete eradication of "sex roles," Firestone added, offered hope for liberation. Radical activist Carl Wittman's widely circulated essay, "A Gay Manifesto," envisioned the creation of communes and the dismantling of the traditional family.[22]

One alternative to the normative heterosexual family was queer kinship, comprised of fluid yet intentional networks of "found" or chosen family members that defied legal or biological definitions. Anthropologist Kath Weston, who studied queer kinship among gay men and lesbians in the San Francisco area in the 1980s, noted that biological and adoptive relatives did not automatically merit inclusion in this kinship network. A lesbian might consider her birth or adoptive parents her family only if they accepted her sexuality and welcomed her lover into their home. Queer kinship was premised on actions: the people who accepted you and showed up for you—emotionally and materially—were your family. For queer people whose biological or adoptive parents had disowned or otherwise rejected them, chosen family filled a void.[23]

Chosen family became a crucial lifeline as HIV/AIDS transformed previously healthy young people into critically ill patients with complex healthcare needs more often associated with the elderly. Queer kin sat at hospital bedsides, checked in with an ailing patient's doctors, and memorialized the dead. As the next chapter explores, such caregiving was one facet of a larger effort by LGBT advocates to protect the custody rights of lesbian and gay parents and formalize the legal relationships between same-sex partners.

An AIDS diagnosis was often how biological family members learned that a child or sibling was gay, using intravenous drugs, or having sex with HIV-infected people. Parents might hide the truth about their child's illness, telling neighbors (and writing in obituaries) that their child had died from cancer or another disease. Others became advocates for PWAs and allies of the LGBTQ community, such as one Jewish mother who left her synagogue after the president of the congregation treated her son's gay identity as something shameful. Many parents, and especially mothers, became the primary caregivers for their ailing adult children.[24]

Hardaway wanted young SGL Black men to experience love and affirmation. Even while in his early thirties, often going by his nickname "Ladybug," he surrounded himself with "the children," younger people for whom he was more than a mentor; he was family. As a friend observed, "People see God in Anthony. He touches them." Survival depended on healthcare, housing, and other material assistance; Hardaway insisted that SGL Black men such as himself also needed to have their souls and spirits uplifted.[25]

Hardaway grew up singing in his church choir, a space filled with gender-nonconforming men but also significant hostility toward homosexuality. "I heard what other church people said," he recalled. "'It's a shame all them sissies in the church,' but it wasn't directed toward me. I never heard the word 'gay' in church, or 'homosexual'; it was always 'sissy.'" None of those experiences offered Hardaway a positive role model. "Nobody wanted to be gay," he added. "My parents didn't want a gay child . . . You were lower than the devil if you were gay in the church. You could be the biggest ho in the church and get respect. [But not] being gay." Gay men and lesbians participated in their churches only by masking or silencing their desires. Rev. Renee McCoy, who led the gay Harlem Metropolitan Community Church, explained, "If Black lesbians and gay men are willing to check their sexuality at the door of the church, and come bearing gifts of talent, there are relatively few problems."[26]

Yet within those silences, many queer people sang in their congregations' choirs, fooled around with same-sex partners in church basements, and otherwise participated in a religious community. Particularly in parts of the South and within subcultures where the church dominated much of the community's social life and politics, the adaptations were manifold. Hardaway gradually came out by inviting his family members to events with gay themes; they took the hint.[27]

The Black church's culture of silence around homosexuality did not diminish Hardaway's faith, but he knew that he needed to protect his reputation—even in death. "I don't want a funeral," Hardaway noted in the early 2000s. "I want to be taken straight to my grave. I can't stand the lies. If you really want to honor what I've done, teach someone who's black and gay. Teach them about their history. That's how you eulogize me." Hardaway's concern about how to eulogize the dying—how to mourn—has preoccupied generations of people affected by HIV/AIDS. The hostility of many major U.S. religious organizations, particularly the Roman Catholic Church and many evangelical Protestant congregations, pushed some people out of organized religious life while ushering others into alternative spaces for spiritual community.[28]

Gay- and lesbian-friendly churches and synagogues, the first of which opened during the 1970s, meanwhile became havens for PWAs and their loved ones. Parents and lovers who had been excluded from mourning rituals within anti-gay religious spaces (Orthodox Judaism, many Roman Catholic parishes, and much of evangelical Protestantism) sought out queer-friendly congregations. In the years before domestic partnership laws, not to mention marriage equality, these religious groups recognized bonds among same-sex friends and lovers that the state did not. AIDS thrust these congregations to the front lines of the epidemic. Half of the men active in New York City's Congregation Beit Simchat Torah, the first gay and lesbian synagogue in the United States, died during the early 1980s. The nondenominational, gay-friendly Metropolitan Community Church of San Francisco similarly watched as AIDS devastated its community. Over the ensuing decades, mainstream religious organizations with more liberal philosophies became accepting of LGBTQ people, but culturally conservative religions remain hostile spaces for many queer people.[29]

Kiyoshi Kuromiya was diagnosed with AIDS in 1989. At one point, his T-cell count, which hovers around 1,000 per cubic millimeter of blood in a healthy person, dropped to 36, leaving him dangerously vul-

Kiyoshi Kuromiya devoted the last fifteen years of his life to healthcare activism on behalf of PWAs. Here, he joins other members of ACT UP Philadelphia in opposing mandatory HIV testing programs and urging comprehensive safer sex awareness instead.

nerable to infections. He took AZT, a drug with noxious side effects, to raise that count to 53. All told, he took nearly thirty pills a day. Kuromiya was determined to live "25 years with a T-cell count in the single figures," but his appetite and strength declined.[30]

In addition to his work with ACT UP, Kuromiya created the Critical Path Project, an initiative to get free internet access to people with HIV/AIDS and to circulate the latest information about new drugs and clinical trials. Spending hours at his computer in his cramped apartment, Kuromiya connected patients with advocates, caregivers, researchers, and policymakers. He ran a hotline and published a newsletter. By 1994, he even ran a small buyers' club, "Transcendental Medication," providing marijuana to about twenty people with AIDS and other illnesses. Kuromiya defended marijuana as an essential means of easing the nausea and appetite loss he experienced due to AIDS: "I can smoke a joint, and five minutes later, I can eat every last drop of food." Ever the activist, in 1999 Kuromiya was a lead plaintiff in an unsuccessful case to legalize medical marijuana use.[31]

In early May of 2000, as Kuromiya's mind and body reached their end, a rotation of friends kept vigil at his bedside at Pennsylvania Hospital in Philadelphia. Several of these friends—Jeff Maskovsky, J. D. Davids, and Jane Shull—had been overseeing his care for months already as he declined. Most knew Kuromiya through activism with ACT UP or other HIV/AIDS advocacy groups. Maskovsky was completing a PhD in anthropology at Temple University about We the People, a coalition of PWAs made up almost entirely of low-income people from racial minorities. Maskovsky was not one of Kuromiya's closest friends, but he and others undertook this incredibly difficult role out of respect and love. They scrupulously recorded Kuromiya's vitals, pain levels, and medications in a spiral-bound notebook. One person would arrive for the night shift, relieving someone who had been there throughout the day. Emiko Kuromiya was there, too, massaging her son's hand.[32]

Kuromiya briefly woke one night and "even sang a refrain of the Univ. of PA cheerleading song." Cathy, his night nurse, gave him morphine a few minutes later, and he fell asleep. Kuromiya's blood pressure was normal, but he was bleeding from his rectum and had a fever. He trembled occasionally. When awake, his conversation straddled delusion and reality. He held his fingers to his ears as if speaking into an imaginary phone. "I was just trying to get some information across," he told Scott Tucker, a friend. Knowing time was precious, Tucker seized this moment of quasi-lucidity.

"Kiyoshi, I never asked you what your name means in Japanese."

"Kiyoshi means 'to make clear.' "

Tucker and other friends noted every shift in Kuromiya's affect. The night of May 1, Kuromiya's pain intensified. The nurse switched from morphine to Demerol. By the following morning, Kuromiya had started to vomit blood.

Maskovsky took over from Tucker a little after three a.m. on May 2. "5:30 a.m. Temp. 101." Maskovsky kept careful notes but worried that he did not know the names of all of Kuromiya's caregivers. "5:45 Senior Surgical Resident, Dr. Shannon Gehr—check spelling!—visits room. Heart 130." Tucker had not yet gone home; perhaps he napped while Maskovsky took notes. By morning, Shull, the executive director of Philadelphia FIGHT, an AIDS organization, was recording Kuromiya's condition in the notebook.

Kuromiya moved through states of being asleep, awake, and somewhere in between.

"Where should I be?" he asked Shull.

"Right here?" she offered.

"No," he countered. "Where-should-I-be?"

"Physically?"

"Yes, I know I'm here for now, but I'm in the [San Francisco] bay area [without] a map, on foot somewhere [east] of Presidio—not sure where that is—like a desert, 5 or 20 or 30 miles from where I should be . . . People are climbing giant trees."

"That sounds nice," Shull said.

Pain medications allowed Kuromiya to hallucinate. "It's amusing since otherwise I'm just laying here. Somewhere I lost my shirt and I'm not even in Reno!" His sense of humor was intact.

Another friend arrived a little after six that evening. Kuromiya's condition was worsening. The nurse paged the doctor on call after Kuromiya had a bowel movement: "blood is just pouring out of him." They gave him two units of platelets, and the doctor arrived. The plan, a friend explained, was "pumping blood into him as needed and monitoring blood loss." Kuromiya woke occasionally and asked questions about his condition. His friends offered what reassurance they could. He coughed up what one friend estimated to be half a cup of blood.

"Kiyoshi sleeps," David Acosta wrote on May 3, after Ativan eased Kuromiya's mind. As had other friends, Acosta noted when Kuromiya was in pain and the relief that he felt after another dose of Demerol.

The friends were incessantly attentive. Had the nurses given Kuromiya enough pain medicine? Were they rotating him every four hours to protect his fragile skin from tearing? When Kuromiya had episodes of labored breathing, they insisted that nurses call a resident. They questioned recommendations for certain medications that could improve breathing but risked causing cardiac distress.

By the afternoon of May 5, the doctors were "cautiously optimistic," but that feeling was short-lived. Kuromiya was soon vomiting a mix of blood and phlegm. He was becoming increasingly delusional.

The twelve or thirteen friends who rotated shifts by Kiyoshi Kuromiya's bedside cared for one another too—and for Emiko. "Chuck just took Mrs. K. to dinner," one of the friends noted. "Jackie [Jacqueline Ambrosini] took Jeff home. Rita A., Judith P. [Peters] and Heshie [Zinman] here. 5:15 Demerol. Dr. Lobo—here—advises Demerol 3x hrly."

Human touch and presence bound Kuromiya to the members of his found and natal family. "Foot massages help K feet very cold. Mom makes K smile."

Kiyoshi Kuromiya died on May 10, 2000, the day after his fifty-seventh birthday, surrounded by family. A few friends recited Jewish and Christian prayers at his bedside. They read aloud the Buddhist Heart Sutra: "Gone, gone, gone beyond, gone altogether beyond: all hail the Awakened One!"[33]

Perhaps Kuromiya had experienced his vision of mapless wandering as a kind of relief, liberated from pain, time, and distance. He was shirtless yet mobile, amused by people climbing "giant trees." He was also vulnerable, "somewhere" in the desert, exposed.

Anthony Hardaway sauntered through a 2022 Instagram reel for the Haven, a community-based testing, counseling, and referral organization in Memphis, as a three-decades (and counting) HIV/AIDS survivor. He smiled and twirled to advertise the Haven's upcoming competition and fundraiser, the "Triple Threat Ball." In the tradition of queer-of-color ballroom, contestants between the ages of eighteen and twenty-five competed for prizes that recognized the "realness" of their performances of dance, attire, and attitude.[34]

Escalating police harassment in the 1930s and 1940s shuttered most queer ballroom events, but queer performances persisted. *Ebony* magazine reported in 1953 on "the world's most unusual fashion show" in Harlem, where "men who like to dress in women's clothing parade before judges." The article mocked drag, but it also testified to drag's persistence. In the 1960s, a new circuit of gay beauty pageants created alternative spaces for drag performance and helped bring about ballroom's renaissance.[35]

The 1967 "Miss All-America Camp Beauty" competition in New York City became legendary for the outraged reaction of Crystal LaBeija (Miss Manhattan) following the announcement that she was the third runner-up. Crystal, who was Black, accused the winner, a white queen from Philadelphia named Rachel Harlow, of benefitting from a "rigged" process. Crystal's verbal evisceration of Harlow and the pageant's organizer, memorialized in the documentary *The Queen*, epitomized the practice of "reading," an artful and often vicious form of verbal insult. Another legendary ballroom mother, Dorian Corey, explained in the 1991 documentary *Paris Is Burning* that a person who gives a reading "found a flaw and exaggerated it." The related art of "shade" takes the insult a step further. "Shade is, I don't tell you you're ugly," Corey noted while applying her makeup at her elaborate vanity. "But, I don't have to tell you, because you know you're ugly."[36]

Crystal LaBeija vowed never to compete in a white-run pageant again and instead cofounded the first ballroom "house," the House of LaBeija. Other ballroom houses, often named for a fashion designer or drag icon, soon followed: House of Corey (1972), House of Dior (1974), House of Wong (1975), and House of Dupree (1975), among others. The House of Xtravaganza (1982) was the first Latinx house. By the early 1980s, houses based in Harlem and Brooklyn competed for which one could bring home the most trophies for a series of established categories, such as "femme realness," "butch realness," "voguing," and "executive realness." Ballroom houses gradually emerged in U.S. cities from Detroit to

Miami to Los Angeles, with some rural and Southern communities also creating regional "scenes."[37]

Familial terms suffuse the world of queer ballroom, with contestants performing on behalf of particular "houses," each of which has a "mother" or "father," a queer man or transwoman who looks out for their "children." House mothers take in kids who have been kicked out of their homes or disowned because of their sexuality or gender expression; many are HIV-positive. Ballroom serves as a lifeline for young people who hustle drugs or sex to sustain themselves, and who depend on their "street families" for their survival. "If they join a house, they can belong somewhere," a DJ who spun records at a club in the Bronx noted in 2000. Ballroom participants celebrate survival despite unfathomable loss, and they do so while giving shade, reading, and voguing, a dance that combines defiantly glamorous poses with acrobatic spins and falls.[38]

Too many of Hardaway's friends died too soon, but he has held on to joy. "We were such a rarity, so powerful and magnificent, the common people don't know how to take it," he once boasted about queer Black people. "Anything that is so beautiful, too beautiful to be touched or expressed, we tend to destroy." He wanted that beauty to endure. In 2019 Hardaway partnered with local LGBT organizations and faculty at the University of Memphis to establish an archive that would gather and interpret records of Memphis's queer past. He continues to work in HIV/AIDS outreach and education, and he celebrates the beauty of queer drag and LGBTQ love.[39]

And really, what *is* the danger in that?

Chapter 18

Save the Children

More than one hundred children and adults walked through metal detectors and past bomb-sniffing dogs to attend Drag Queen Story Hour at a community church in northeastern Ohio in December 2022. Drag Queen Story Hour began in San Francisco in 2015 as an effort to encourage literacy and provide children

Activists in the United States continued to pursue sexual liberation and freedom of gender expression in the early twenty-first century. In this undated photograph, participants in a "Gay Freedom Day" event wear the colors of the rainbow, symbolic of LGBTQ+ people in all their diversity.

with queer role models. Libraries and bookstores across the United States began to host the story hours, some of which drew many times the usual number of people who typically came to library events. But protests against it also grew more frequent.[1]

The Ohio church's pastor, Jess Peacock, had fielded "accusations of pedophilia, grooming, and horrible things being done to kids" in the days leading up to the December 2022 story hour. Violent threats prompted her to spend $20,000 on security measures. Just the day before the story hour, federal authorities arrested Aimenn D. Penny, a neo-Nazi, for attempting to "burn . . . the entire church to the ground" with Molotov cocktails. Penny told authorities that he had targeted the church "to protect children and stop the drag show event." Penny belonged to "White Lives Matter, Ohio" and had distributed white nationalist literature. Peacock's fears were well founded: on the night of March 25, 2023, about a week before the church was scheduled to host a drag show and another drag story hour, Penny hit the church with Molotov cocktails in a failed attempt to set it on fire. (The shows went on as planned, and in January 2024, Penny received an eighteen-year sentence in federal prison.)[2]

Anti-LGBTQ protests in the name of child protection have flared up across the country. Also in December 2022, New York City Council member Erik Bottcher filmed anti-drag protesters outside of a public library in the Chelsea neighborhood of Manhattan, an area known for its substantial LGBTQ community. One man held up a sign that said "Stop Grooming Kids for Sex" and asked Bottcher if he was a member of "NAMBLA," the largely defunct North American Man/Boy Love Association, whose stated aim was to legitimize relationships between older men and much younger ones. A woman raised her own smart phone to film Bottcher as he filmed her. She flung expletives at him and asked, "What are you, a pedophile?"[3]

Far too many children and adolescents in the United States face very real sexual danger. Starting in the 1990s, and steadily ever since, new revelations have surfaced about the extent of clerical sex abuse in the Roman Catholic Church, with diocesan leaders hiding accusations of pedophile priests and placing tens of thousands of children, of all genders, in harm's way. Similar scandals have rocked the Southern Baptist Convention, the Boy Scouts of America, and other civic and religious organizations. No evidence supports the assertion that drag queens or queer people more generally are uniquely dangerous threats to children. Scholars who research hate crimes argue that not only are people in sexual or gender minorities not more likely to perpetrate sex crimes, but they are far more likely to be the *victims* of assault, harassment, and bullying.[4]

The allegation that homosexuality endangers children is an old one, taking shape initially in the 1910s and 1920s when vice squads arrested men for having sex with minors. As we have seen, campaigns in the 1930s against the "sexual psychopath" circulated warnings about predatory queer people who lured unsuspecting adolescent boys into their criminal perversions. Using nearly the same logic, Florida's legislature systematically investigated and fired lesbian and gay public school teachers and university professors in the 1950s and 1960s. An unsuccessful 1978 effort in California known as the Briggs Initiative, inspired by Anita Bryant's "Save Our Children" campaign in Miami-Dade County, would have allowed school districts to fire anyone "advocating, imposing, encouraging or promoting" homosexuality. Anti-gay statutes defined queer people as criminals, and many mental health professionals continued to treat homosexuality as a psychological disorder.[5]

These damaging stereotypes affected the ability of queer people to retain their parental rights. Judges and juries construed the simple fact of *being* queer as a disqualification for safe parenting. In an infamous case from California in 1967, Ellen Nadler's petition for custody of her child was denied based on what the judge described as her "psychological problems." Only if Nadler agreed to psychiatric treatment for her lesbianism, the judge determined, would she be permitted unsupervised visits with her child. Lesbian mothers from New York City to Portland, Oregon, contributed to legal defense funds. The Daughters of Bilitis created a legal resource center for lesbians worried about losing custody of their children. Del Martin, one of the group's founders, had given up custody of her only child when she and her husband divorced in the 1940s, feeling immense shame about her sexual desires for women and hopeless about her chances of winning a favorable decision in family court. The lesbian and gay rights movement of the 1970s hoped to shift those attitudes. Even so, many queer people stayed closeted within unhappy heterosexual marriages for fear of losing custody of their children or went through excruciating legal ordeals to try to remain part of their children's lives. In the decades before the Supreme Court issued its decision in *Obergefell v. Hodges* (2015), formally recognizing same-sex marriage equality, advocates for queer partners, parents, and children first had to convince the courts—and the broader public—that queer people conformed to, rather than undermined, the conventionally understood American family.[6]

Family court judges stood in the way of queer parents' rights. For decades, they ruled that LGBT people were unsuitable parents. Relying on a medical definition of queer sexuality as pathological and contagious, judges warned that the presence in the home of a loving same-sex relationship put children at risk of sexual harm. That logic ultimately denied Sharon Bottoms custody of the son she bore during a brief marriage to a man, more than twenty years after Ellen Nadler's unsuccessful custody petition. Bottoms had started to date women in 1991, when her son was still very young. She soon formed an intimate partnership with April Wade. Bottoms and Wade could not marry legally, nor could Wade adopt the boy under Virginia law. A custody battle with Bottoms's ex-husband resulted in the court terminating her parental rights and placing the child in the custody of his paternal grandmother. The judge decided that, by kissing and hugging in front of the child, Bottoms and Wade had endangered the child's safety, as if their display of affection was a noxious gas contaminating innocent lungs.[7]

The persistent belief that homosexuality was a kind of contagion inspired conservatives to compare LGBT anti-discrimination laws to sexual indoctrination. An unsuccessful 1992 ballot initiative in Oregon, for instance, would have made it illegal to use state, regional, or local funds to "promote, encourage, or facilitate homosexuality." (The lesbian feminist attorney and activist Nan D. Hunter wryly nicknamed this legislative agenda "No Promo Homo.") The idea that gay men and lesbians "recruited" children to become homosexuals mirrored the anti-porn movement's notions that sexually explicit words and images could cause violent behavior. Both campaigns likewise characterized sexual desires as forces that required vigilant supervision. Granting even the most basic antidiscrimination protections to LGBT Americans was controversial. The same year that Oregon's initiative failed, Colorado adopted a constitutional amendment that made it illegal for local governments or the state to ban discrimination against gay men and lesbians. With clear echoes of earlier arguments against civil rights for Black Americans, the amendment's supporters derided the LGBT equality movement as a plea for "special rights" that disadvantaged straight people. Taken together, these arguments warned that queer people were sex deviants intent on pushing heterosexuals to the margins of American life.[8]

These anti-LGBTQ measures coincided with headline-grabbing child abductions in the late 1970s and 1980s, which in turn spawned a new era of child safety advocacy. Reports of child abductions and assaults had not increased demonstrably, but sensationalist news coverage gave the appearance of an escalating crisis. By the middle of the 1980s, innumerable cardboard milk cartons for sale in the United States featured a photograph of one of these "missing children." Television networks launched programs devoted to cracking cold cases. While not all these cases involved evidence of sexual assault, fears of sexually deviant criminals fueled a widening panic over "stranger danger" and child abuse. The overwhelming majority of child sex abuse was still committed—as it had been for centuries—by family members and acquaintances, not strangers.[9]

Conservatives blamed the apparent rise in sexual crimes against children on feminism, gay rights, and the expansion of sexual freedoms during the previous decades. The anti-tax, pro-military right won support from religious traditionalists by making "family values" a cornerstone of the emerging Republican coalition. As President Ronald Reagan signed into law the Missing Children's Act of 1982, he and his allies argued that sexual liberation had created a culture that encouraged child abuse. Arguments against the sexual revolution associated it with other left-leaning causes, grouping Black nationalist and antiwar protesters with feminists and gay liberationists as stokers of social chaos. Sexual conservatism once again served the interests of white privilege. Vocal supporters of the Missing Children's Act sought more funding for the juvenile justice system, which disproportionately affected nonwhite children, and argued for longer sentences for convicted minors. As in the past, these measures to restrict gay and lesbian rights brought more police into nonwhite communities; both populations, conservatives argued, posed threats to public safety.[10]

In the 1990s, amid a wave of unfounded allegations of abuse and even Satanism at daycare centers and preschools, a related panic spread myths about sex-education curricula that allegedly encouraged students to strip naked and explore one another's bodies, as if Betty Dodson herself was standing in front of kindergarteners with a Hitachi Magic Wand. Opponents argued for "abstinence-only" curricula instead, and such plans received government support in the 2000s. Concerns about sex education in the public schools helped motivate many previously apolitical people, and married women with children in particular, to get involved and even run for school board and other public offices. The prevalence of porn on the internet convinced these activists that all sexual content damaged their children.[11]

Child sex abuse became something of a national obsession. In 2004, MSNBC debuted *To Catch a Predator*, a show in which reporters and private investigators used entrapment to ensnare men who solicited sex from minors. Its formula mimicked the aims and methods of earlier anti-vice crusades: Anthony Comstock sent decoy letters to abortionists, and police on the vice patrol went undercover to entrap men interested in sex with other men. On *To Catch a Predator*, men in an extralegal group called "Perverted Justice" impersonated young and almost always white girls in online chat rooms, luring adult men to a house where camera crews (and sometimes, but not always, actual police officers) intercepted them. The show, which ran until 2007, led to the arrests of three hundred men.[12]

Anti-drag protesters in the 2020s speak of perverse dangers. Drag, they claim, is a form of pornography that attempts to lure unsuspecting children into a life of gender and sexual deviance. Multiple surveys of trans youth meanwhile demonstrate a connection between anti-trans rhetoric and incidences of self-harm and suicidality. LGBTQ+ advocates insist that while drag does not harm young people, efforts to impede LGBTQ+ people's rights and freedoms do.[13]

This politicized national preoccupation with child sex abuse has upended the unrelated provision of medical care to transgender youth. Advocates for and recipients of gender-affirming care (GAC) describe it as life-saving, especially for young people struggling through adolescence. GAC is a catchall term for medical and nonmedical interventions for transgender people who wish to socially and/or physically transition their gender. Supporting a person's adoption of pronouns or clothing appropriate for their gender; psychological counseling; and medical services such as endocrinological or surgical care all fall under the GAC umbrella. Transgender young people may be prescribed hormone therapies to pause the progression of puberty (puberty blockers) or, later in adolescence, hormone-replacement therapies to encourage the development of the secondary sex characteristics common to their gender identity. Adult patients can seek operations such as "top" surgery to reduce or augment breast tissue or "bottom" surgery to remove or reconstruct internal or external genitals. Hospitals very rarely provide surgical GAC to legal minors, despite what anti-trans activists claim.[14]

Of the thousands of bills introduced in state legislatures during 2023, nearly 550 targeted transgender people, whether to limit access to GAC, ban trans athletes from school sports, or prohibit schools from using a student's preferred pronouns. By the end of 2023, twenty-three states had restricted or outlawed GAC care for minors, and several others tried, unsuccessfully, to ban drag performances on the premise that drag was a pornographic violation of children's safety. Civil libertarian and LGBTQ+ legal advocacy groups challenged all these measures as unconstitutional infringements on sex equality, but as of this writing, state legislatures continue to debate additional restrictions on GAC, athletics participation, and social affirmation.[15]

The letter of these laws reveal their authors' intention: the imposition of distinct male/female gender differences and exclusive heterosexuality on the entire U.S. population. Laws limiting GAC for minors include carve-outs for intersex infants and children, referred to in these bills as "children with a medically verifiable disorder of sex development" or "DSD." (Intersex activists have long rejected the language of "disorder" as pejorative.) "Intersex" is a general term for any person with a "difference of sexual development," whether due to chromosomal, anatomical, or gonadal anomalies, some of which result in atypical genital development. The category encompasses androgen insensitivity syndrome, congenital adrenal hyperplasia, Klinefelter syndrome (XXY), Turner syndrome (XO), and Rokitansky syndrome (a body that is XX but at birth lacks a uterus and/or a cervix), among other conditions. Intersex advocates and major medical associations, including the American Academy of Pediatrics, argue strenuously against any nonconsensual genital surgeries unless they are medically necessary. The presence of an enlarged clitoris or a micro-penis, they argue, does not constitute a medical emergency in a child, who should be allowed to make their own decisions, in adulthood, about any possible surgical alterations to their genitals. Bills targeting trans minors ignore that nuance, instead suggesting that while GAC for transgender minors is abusive, surgical interventions on the genitals of otherwise healthy intersex infants is a healthcare priority. These policies reflect not medical best practices but a political vision that seeks to legislate a binary concept of gender and sex.[16]

Proposed bans on GAC and drag are often accompanied by efforts to restrict discussions of sex and sexuality in schools and to eliminate books with LGBTQ+ themes from public and school libraries. For centuries, people have spoken out against such restrictions, whether through lectures, newspaper editorials, or information shared via radio, television, video, or the internet. Opponents of reform have often thus turned to censorship, branding anything they consider offensive as "obscenity." Censorship is about stopping communication. As both supporters and opponents of LGBTQ+ rights understand, communication allows for connection. But whereas anti-gay and anti-trans activists see information related to gender and sexuality as a form of contagion, advocates for queer people's rights recognize the value of opportunities to affirm or clarify previously inchoate desires. Historical evidence supports only one of these interpretations. Opponents of LGBTQ+ rights deny that sexuality and gender nonconformity have histories at all because recognition of a past populated by gender-nonconforming people, non-scandalous expressions of queer desire, and multiple (rather than homogenous) ideas about sexual morality would undermine their cause entirely.

Could younger Americans take sex back from the naysayers and fearmongers? In a 2012 issue of *The Atlantic*, reporter Hanna Rosin wrote admiringly about young American women who had embraced casual sex, or "hook-up culture," and used it for their own ends. Unbothered by pornography or crass humor, these women recognized their value in a sexual marketplace and took advantage of opportunities to have the kinds of sex they wanted, when they wanted it, all without any apparent desire for long-term commitments at that stage of their lives. Contrary to reports lamenting the dangers that girls and young women faced in this new sexual frontier, Rosin remarked that "for college girls these days, an overly serious suitor fills the same role an accidental pregnancy did in the 19th century: a danger to be avoided at all costs, lest it get in the way of a promising future." I would amend Rosin's timeline, because fears of plan-derailing pregnancies persisted well into the twentieth century, but I otherwise find her statement striking: young American women who want to enjoy sex and pursue their educations and careers have decided that casual sex is far preferable to a committed relationship.[17]

That said, this casual sexual culture has not translated to equitable sexual pleasure; men experienced orgasm during hook-ups at nearly twice the rate of women. Men and women describing shared sexual encounters also came away with different understandings of what had occurred, with men reporting that their female partners had orgasms at two to three times the rate of the women's self-report of orgasm. Nor did Rosin's relatively sunny picture of commitment-free heterosexual sex account for a growing awareness of pervasive sexual harassment, assault, and "rape culture."[18]

Far from a hedonist hook-up bonanza, since the 1990s Americans have been living through what sociologists have called a "sex recession." Several studies from the early 2000s and 2010s found that about one-fifth of college seniors had not engaged in any form of sexual intercourse, and that only about 40 percent of "hooking-up" events included sexual intercourse. Teens and adults are having less sex, with fewer partners across their lifetimes, and with fewer sexual encounters each year.

Another *Atlantic* story, this one in 2018, captured a sense of dismay about these changes. Although a steady decline in the U.S. teen pregnancy rate might appear to be "an unambiguously good thing," there was reason to fear that "the delay in teen sex may have been the first indication of a broader withdrawal from physical intimacy that extends well into adulthood." The causes of the American sex recession appear manifold, and it mirrors trends in Japan, Sweden, and the Netherlands. Americans in 2018 were masturbating more often than they had in the 1990s, often while consuming video or internet pornography. Teens and college students were less likely to be in committed relationships, but they were not having all that much casual sex compared to prior generations. Some young women were avoiding hook-ups because of past experiences with or fear of being pressured by their male peers to engage in rough sex acts that the men had seen in pornography, especially anal sex and choking. As people become more isolated and fixated on solitary pleasures, the opportunities to meet potential partners face-to-face have apparently declined. Dating apps hardly substitute for in-person sociability because they so heavily favor physical appearance over other traits.[19]

Particularly as the #MeToo movement exposed the pervasiveness of coercion in Americans' sexual experiences, many observers concluded that the future of sex looked grim. Scholar Asa Seresin coined the term "heteropessimism" to characterize the gloom that had descended over heterosexuality by the late 2010s. Many young people either viewed heterosexuality as a pathetic concession to normative expectations, or they surveyed the cascade of evidence of men's abuses of women and concluded that such relationships could never incorporate respect, desire, and fulfillment. One manifestation of heteropessimism, Seresin notes, is the "incel" movement: virginal men who justify hatred of or even violence against women who refuse their advances. In this light, the sex recession may not simply be the result of many people making a calculated decision to delay sexual initiation but a hostile landscape in which heterosexuality, at least, appears pathetic, impossible, or obsolete.[20]

Is the situation really so dismal? Perhaps we might consider younger people's hesitation to initiate sex, amid a profusion of information about sexuality, as a hopeful sign. Better prepared than many previous generations to understand both the mechanics and the possible consequences of sexual intimacy, they are making decisions on their own timelines. A movement for "pleasure activism," rooted in Black queer/women's liberation politics, offers another pathway, one that connects sexuality to social justice. Pleasure activists honor the words of the poet Audre Lorde, a Black lesbian and feminist who wrote in the early 1980s about "the erotic as a resource . . . that can provide energy for change." They seek to empower themselves and their communities through a recognition of their sexualities.[21]

As I write this paragraph in early 2024, "ethical non-monogamy" has burst into mainstream news coverage, which vacillates from outrage to titillation. Proponents reject what they view as the oppressive trappings of traditional sexuality, while critics point to the persistence of jealousy, gender inequality, and unexamined class privilege in some of the most widely circulated narratives of nonmonogamous relationships. The practice of polyamory is not, of course, new. It has long been well established within many queer communities, flourished in Betty Dodson's countercultural social circles, and might well describe Complex Marriage at Oneida. In the early 2000s, groups like the National Coalition for Sexual Freedom and the more niche Unitarian Universalists for Responsible Multi-Partnering began to host conferences and offer resources for people exploring "romantic love with more than one person, honestly, ethically, and with full knowledge and consent of all involved." The practice's actual popularity is difficult to gauge; most of the renewed attention to polyamory highlights a cohort of affluent and mostly white heterosexuals pursuing personal fulfillment.[22]

These seemingly contradictory trends—toward erotic liberation or sexual avoidance—expose the limitations of trying to treat sexuality as a static force in our lives. Instead, if we find ourselves struggling to understand the erotic fantasies or fears of a rising generation, we should think historically. We should recall the myriad moments in this book's narrative when broad currents of social change—regarding enslavement, women's rights, obscenity, religion, social justice, policing, and so on—enabled or foreclosed sexual conduct. We might then acknowledge the salience of sexual identities (today, more manifold than ever), even as we recall how differently people in the past described their genders, desires, and relationships.

This history does not point toward liberation, however much some of us might wish that it did. Never could I have imagined that my long-scheduled plan to spend June 2022 writing a chapter about the battle over legal abortion would coincide with *Roe*'s demise. American politics today reverberates with debates over abortion access, GAC, and the alleged obscenity of books about queer teens. And I am confident that whenever it is that you are reading this book, sex will be no less relevant to the political arguments that affect your freedoms. But if the history recounted in this book is any guide, both individual identities and collective activism will continue to shape the possibilities for sexual pleasures—and the manifold meanings of those fierce desires—for the foreseeable future. History is at the heart of Americans' arguments about sex; resolutions to many of these issues depend on whether we deny or affirm that history's existence.

Coda

The Ghost of Anthony Comstock

In 2023, a federal judge in Oklahoma, Matthew Kacsmaryk, justified his decision to outlaw the practice of mailing mifepristone, a common abortion medication, by citing the Comstock Act. Since the early twentieth century, court cases had slowly chipped away at Comstock's rigid definition of "obscenity," and Congress repealed the law's restrictions on contraception in 1971. Surely the controversial 1873 legislation was dead and gone.[1]

Yet the Comstock Act rose again. In 1996, U.S. Congresswoman Pat Schroeder (D-CO) warned fellow members of the House of Representatives about the consequences of their failure to repeal the law in its entirety. At issue was the Communications Decency Act (CDA), the first congressional effort to keep sex-related content off the internet. The CDA criminalized "indecent" or "patently offensive" speech that a minor could access from an online computer. Republican congressman Henry Hyde had authored an additional provision within the CDA that explicitly revived those portions of the Comstock Act related to abortion. Schroeder said that the CDA resuscitated "Comstockery" by "making it a crime to use the internet to provide or receive information which directly or indirectly tells where, how, of whom, or by what means an abortion may be obtained." At stake, Schroeder emphasized, were both reproductive choice and free speech.[2]

Kiyoshi Kuromiya understood this idea intimately when he challenged government restrictions on what he could tell adolescents about sex and HIV/AIDS. Because the CDA made it a crime to use the internet to show minors any "patently offensive" material "as measured by contemporary community standards," Kuromiya faced prosecution for including sexually explicit information about preventing the spread of HIV on the Critical Path website. Along with about forty other plaintiffs, he sued the federal government. "I don't know what 'indecent' means," he noted before a panel of three federal judges in Philadelphia, his wry self-composure mixed with an advocate's intensity. "I don't know what 'patently offensive' means in terms of providing life-saving information to people with AIDS, including teenagers." Material that was legal to circulate in print would, under the CDA, be illegal to post on the internet.[3]

Initially, Schroeder's concerns seemed overblown. Although the law passed, the ACLU won a preliminary injunction in federal district court, blocking enforcement of bans on "indecent" and "patently offensive" content on the internet. Kuromiya's arguments had won the day. When the Justice Department pledged not to enforce the CDA's abortion restrictions, rendering them moot, the judge allowed that portion of the CDA to stand. Two subsequent efforts to limit sexual content on the internet, the Child Pornography Prevention Act of 1996 and the 1998 Child Online Protection Act, were struck down in 2002 and 2009, respectively.[4]

But Schroeder was right: anti-abortion activists remembered those dormant clauses. Their moment arrived in June 2022 when the Supreme Court's decision in *Dobbs v. Jackson Women's Health Organization* overturned *Roe v. Wade* (1973), which had guaranteed a constitutional right to abortion. "Zombie" laws that were never stricken from state statutes, such as a total abortion ban passed in the 1840s in Wisconsin, lurched to life, enforceable once again in the absence of *Roe*'s constitutional protections. (A county circuit judge subsequently ruled in 2023 that the 173-year-old law did not prohibit consensual medical abortions, only the murder of fetuses, but abortion access in Wisconsin remains heavily restricted.) The Comstock Act, preserved and expanded under the CDA, joined the ranks of the legislative undead. In early 2023, state legislators in Texas and Iowa introduced bills that allowed private citizens to sue internet service providers "for distribution of abortion-inducing drugs," those Comstockian relics of the CDA reanimated for the *Dobbs* era.[5]

As I write these concluding pages, several otherwise conservative states have approved ballot measures to protect abortion rights; elsewhere, abortion is illegal under virtually any circumstance. In addition to restrictions on GAC and drag shows at the state level, the Supreme Court in *303 Creative LLC* (2023) ruled that it was not unconstitutional for a business owner to refuse to provide services to a gay person, in a decision that prioritized commerce as "freedom of speech," protected by the First Amendment, over claims of sex-based discrimination.[6]

Today's fights over sex and sexuality play out in a world far different from the one Comstock inhabited. In the 2020s, attempts at sexual censorship must contend with movements grounded in a sense of sexuality's essential importance to a person's self-conception, diverse and well-established support for women's and LGBTQ+ rights, and a popular appreciation that sexual pleasure and bodily autonomy are rights widely shared. Comstock's ghost may haunt our halls of government, but it has never faced as much organized opposition.

Acknowledgments

"You're writing a history of sex? The whole of it?" Many people asked me some version of this question over the years that I have worked on this book, and each time, my heart briefly stopped beating. That I have managed to complete it is a testament to the support I received from friends, family, and colleagues near and far.

Kathleen Brown, Joanne Meyerowitz, and Nicholas Syrett were the first people to read a complete draft of the book. They were generous with their time and expertise, not least during a three-hour Zoom conversation to discuss the manuscript's path forward. I am enormously grateful for their wise counsel. Anne Boylan, Richard Godbeer, Christine Heyrman, and Dael Norwood each read several chapter drafts. I have endeavored to follow the advice of these deeply learned—and gracious—scholars at every turn. Stephanie Coontz read multiple drafts of the introduction; her many years of encouragement and advice are priceless gifts. For reading and critiquing chapters aligned with their areas of expertise, I additionally thank Kimberly Blockett, Julio Capó, Rachel Hope Cleves, Jayatri Das, Gillian Frank, April Haynes, Ronni Hayon, Cheryl Hicks, Emily Hobson, Lauren Gutterman, Regina Kunzel, Amanda Littauer, Serena Mayeri, Bethany Moreton, Julia Ott, Dan Royles, Leigh Eric Schmidt, Emily Skidmore, Marc Stein, and Cookie Woolner. Their feedback helped me see the bigger picture emerging from the book's details, sharpened my analysis, and reminded me that collegiality is at the heart of good scholarship. Any remaining errors or omissions are mine alone. Anya Jabour, Cindy Ott, and Lauren Hunley shared their knowledge about Montana and Indigenous history with me. Anthony R. G. Hardaway generously gave his time to speak with me about his life and work, and Diane Sands shared her memories about abortion politics in Montana. Jeff Maskofsky recalled key details about his experience of caring for Kiyoshi Kuromiya during his final illness.

Independent scholars, community organizations, and academic faculty and institutions have gathered crucial information about the history of sexuality through the collection of oral histories. For work that is not only priceless but publicly available, I want especially to thank Joan Nestle and the Lesbian Herstory Archives; Marc Stein and Jonathan Ned Katz at OutHistory.org; Tommi Avicolli Mecca; Carlin Ross; and the historians who created the Illegal Abortion in Montana Oral History Project and the Montana Feminist History Oral History Collection at the University of Montana's Mansfield Library.

For excellent research assistance, I thank Peyton Cleary, Madeline Price, Helen Siers, Andrea Spencer, and Natalie Walton. Peyton deserves a medal for her extraordinary contributions to this project, double-checking page numbers, organizing the images and permissions, locating elusive documents, and remaining a steadfast voice of calm competence.

A twelve-month Public Scholar Award from the National Endowment for the Humanities, Grant FZ-280071–21, was exactly what I needed to complete this book. The views expressed here do not necessarily reflect those of the NEH. My thanks as well to the College of Arts and Sciences at the University of Delaware, and Associate Dean Wendy Bellion in particular, for providing a subvention for costs associated with image reproduction and permissions, and to Alison Parker, chair of the Department of History, for unflagging support.

Opportunities to present early versions of this research to the Herbert D. Katz Center for Judaic Studies at the University of Pennsylvania and the Colloquium of Religion and Sexuality (CORAH) at the University of Notre Dame generated the perfect combination of enthusiasm and critical feedback. Special thanks to Steven Weitzman at Penn and Darren Dochuk at Notre Dame for organizing those talks.

Librarians are the historian's secret weapon. Special thanks to John Anderies, archivist extraordinaire at the John J. Wilcox, Jr. Archives of the William Way LGBT Community Center in Philadelphia, for pointing me in the direction of Kiyoshi Kuromiya and sharing his deep knowledge of Philadelphia's queer history, and to Molly M. Wolf at the Widener Sexuality Archives, who made space for me to explore their library's excellent collection. My gratitude as well to the staffs of the Human Sexuality Collection at Cornell University, the Library Company of Philadelphia, and the resplendent Interlibrary Loan Department at the University of Delaware (who I hope at least found some enjoyment in sourcing all the erotica I requested). I am indebted to Kaitlyn Tanis, the history librarian at the University of Delaware, who helped me navigate the vast landscape of digital resources.

Special thanks to Lila Berman, Kimberly Blockett, Eve Buckley, Jennifer Gallo-Fox, Serena Mayeri, Bethany Moreton, Julia Ott, and Dael Norwood, as well as Roxanne Donovan and the community she nurtures at WellAcademic, for company while writing and the extraordinary gift of their friendship. Samira Mehta, Jayatri Das, Sara Bressi, Leah Hart Tennen, Abby Sipress, Ronni Hayon, Deborah Kahn, Whitney and David Posternack, Kate Tejada, Melissa Crawford, and Natalie Tronson cheered me on when I needed encouragement most, and I love them for it.

Dan Gerstle has sharpened my thinking, my writing, and my appreciation for the revision process. It is to his endless credit that he saw the need for this book, and I am indebted to him for believing that I could write it. I cannot imagine developing this book in partnership with any other editor. The pros in Norton's editorial, production, and marketing teams are a pleasure to work with. My thanks especially to Zeba Arora and Rebecca Munro. I am indebted to Rachelle Mandik for her copy edits and to Ingsu Liu for the book's stunning cover. Matthew Avery Sutton's kind words connected me to Sandra Dijkstra, and I remain grateful for that opportunity.

To my parents, Nancy and Charles Davis; my sister, Sarah Davis; my mother-in-law, Sandra Hoffman, and her partner, Donald Lustig; and all my sisters- and brothers-in-law, nieces, and nephews, thank you for love that endures and grows.

I promised my children that I would not dedicate a book about sex to them. But that doesn't mean I can't say here that Jonathan and Hannah are my life's greatest joys. Once again, Mark, thank you for all the things that you know, and I know, that matter most of all.

Notes

Introduction

1. In two updated editions, in 1997 and 2012, D'Emilio and Freedman sustained their original thesis while bringing the book's timeline up to date. John D'Emilio and Estelle B. Freedman, *Intimate Matters: A History of Sexuality in America* (New York: Harper & Row, 1988); John D'Emilio and Estelle B. Freedman, "Since Intimate Matters: Recent Developments in the History of Sexuality in the United States," *Journal of Women's History* 25, no. 4 (2013): 88–100.
2. For overviews and anthologies, see Kevin P. Murphy, Jason Ruiz, and David Serlin, eds., *The Routledge History of American Sexuality* (New York: Routledge, 2020); Daina Ramey Berry and Leslie M. Harris, eds., *Sexuality and Slavery: Reclaiming Intimate Histories in the Americas* (Athens: University of Georgia Press, 2018); Don Romesburg, ed., *The Routledge History of Queer America* (New York: Routledge, 2018); Susan Stryker, *Transgender History: The Roots of Today's Revolution*, 2nd ed. (New York: Seal Press, 2017); Jennifer Brier, Jim Downs, and Jennifer L. Morgan, eds., *Connexions: Histories of Race and Sex in North America* (Urbana: University of Illinois Press, 2016); Lillian Faderman, *The Gay Revolution: The Story of the Struggle* (New York: Simon & Schuster, 2015); Kathleen Kennedy and Sharon R. Ullman, *Sexual Borderlands: Constructing an American Sexual Past* (Columbus: Ohio State University Press, 2003); Michael Bronski, *A Queer History of the United States* (Boston: Beacon Press, 2011); Kathy Lee Peiss, ed., *Major Problems in the History of American Sexuality: Documents and Essays* (Boston: Houghton Mifflin Co., 2002); Elizabeth Reis, ed., *American Sexual Histories* (Oxford: Blackwell, 2001); Leila J. Rupp, *A Desired Past: A Short History of Same-Sex Love in America* (Chicago: University of Chicago Press, 1999); Martha Hodes, ed., *Sex, Love, Race: Crossing Boundaries in North American History* (New York: New York University Press, 1999).
3. Susan Stryker, "Transgender Studies: Queer Theory's Evil Twin," and David Valentine,

"The Categories Themselves," in Annamarie Jagose and Don Kulick, eds., "Thinking Sex/Thinking Gender (GLQ Forum)," *GLQ: A Journal of Lesbian and Gay Studies* 10, no. 2 (2004): 211–313; Joanne Meyerowitz, *How Sex Changed: A History of Transsexuality in the United States* (Cambridge, MA: Harvard University Press, 2005); Gayle Rubin, "Thinking Sex: Notes for a Radical Theory of the Politics of Sexuality," in *Pleasure and Danger: Exploring Female Sexuality*, ed. Carole S. Vance (London: Pandora, 1992), 267–319; Marlon M. Bailey, *Butch Queens Up in Pumps: Gender, Performance, and Ballroom Culture in Detroit* (Ann Arbor: University of Michigan Press, 2013); Kit Heyam, *Before We Were Trans: A New History of Gender* (New York: Seal Press, 2023); Jonathan Ned Katz, *The Invention of Heterosexuality* (Chicago: University of Chicago Press, 1995); Rebecca L. Davis and Michele Mitchell, eds., *Heterosexual Histories* (New York: New York University Press, 2021); Peter Cryle and Elizabeth Stephens, *Normality: A Critical Genealogy* (Chicago: University of Chicago Press, 2017); Julian B. Carter, *The Heart of Whiteness: Normal Sexuality and Race in America, 1880–1940* (Durham: Duke University Press, 2007); Regina Kunzel, *Criminal Intimacy: Prison and the Uneven History of Modern American Sexuality* (Chicago: University of Chicago Press, 2008); Rebecca L. Davis, *More Perfect Unions: The American Search for Marital Bliss* (Cambridge, MA: Harvard University Press, 2010).

4. Stephen Valocchi, "'Where Did Gender Go?' Same-Sex Desire and the Persistence of Gender in Gay Male Historiography," *GLQ: A Journal of Lesbian and Gay Studies* 18, no. 4 (2012): 453–479.

A Note on Language

1. P. Gabrielle Foreman et al., "Writing About Slavery? This Might Help," community-sourced document, May 17, 2023, 4:40 p.m., https://docs.google.com/document/d/1A4TEdDgYslX-hlKezLodMIM71My3KTN0zxRv0IQTOQs/mobilebasic; "The Impact of Words and Tips for Using Appropriate Terminology: Am I Using the Right Word?" National Museum of the American Indian, Smithsonian, https://americanindian.si.edu/nk360/informational/impact-words-tips; "Editorial Guide," Bureau of Indian Affairs, U.S. Department of the Interior, https://www.bia.gov/guide/editorial-guide. See also "A Note About Language" in Gregory D. Smithers, *Reclaiming Two-Spirits* (Boston: Beacon Press, 2022), xiii–xiv, and the National Congress of American Indians, https://www.ncai.org/.

Chapter 1: To Confound the Course of Nature

1. Depositions and testimony from H. R. McIlwaine, *Minutes of the Council and General Court of Colonial Virginia, 1622–1632, 1670–1676, with Notes and Excerpts from Original Council and General Court Records, into 1683, Now Lost* (Richmond, VA: [The Colonial Press, Everett Waddey Co.], 1924), 194–195. For historical discussions of the case, see Kathleen M. Brown, *Good Wives, Nasty Wenches, and Anxious Patriarchs: Gender, Race, and Power in Colonial Virginia* (Chapel Hill: University of North Carolina Press, 1996), 75–80; Kathleen M. Brown, "Thomas/Thomasine Court Case (1629)," *Global Encyclopedia of LGBTQ History*, forthcoming; Mary Beth Norton, *Founding Mothers and Fathers: Gendered Power and the Forming of American Society*

(New York: Alfred A. Knopf, 1996), 183–202; Kathryn Wichelns, "From *The Scarlet Letter* to Stonewall: Reading the 1629 Thomas(ine) Hall Case, 1978–2009," *Early American Studies: An Interdisciplinary Journal* 12, no. 3 (2014): 500–523. For a discussion of Hall as intersex, see Elizabeth Reis, *Bodies in Doubt: An American History of Intersex* (Baltimore: Johns Hopkins University Press, 2009), 10–15.

2. Richard Godbeer, "Toward a Cultural Poetics of Desire in a World Before Heterosexuality," in *Heterosexual Histories*, eds. Rebecca L. Davis and Michele Mitchell (New York: New York University Press, 2021), 37–68; Laurel Thatcher Ulrich, *Good Wives: Image and Reality in the Lives of Women in Northern New England* (New York: Oxford University Press, 1980).
3. Richard Godbeer, *Sexual Revolution in Early America* (Baltimore: Johns Hopkins University Press, 2002), 52–56, 71–82; Charles L. Cohen, *God's Caress: The Psychology of Puritan Religious Experience* (New York: Oxford University Press, 1986), 223; Elizabeth Maddock Dillon, "Nursing Fathers and Brides of Christ: The Feminized Body of the Puritan Convert," in *A Centre of Wonders: The Body in Early America*, eds. Janet Moore Lindman and Michelle Lise Tarter (Ithaca: Cornell University Press, 2001), 129–143; John Cotton, "Sermon III," *Christ the Fountaine of Life* (London: Robert Ibbitson, [1651]), 36–37, Text Creation Partnership/University of Michigan Library, https://quod.lib.umich.edu/e/eebogroup/.
4. Kelly A. Ryan, *Regulating Passion: Sexuality and Patriarchal Rule in Massachusetts, 1700–1830* (New York: Oxford University Press, 2014), 18–19; Elizabeth Reis, *Damned Women: Sinners and Witches in Puritan New England* (Ithaca: Cornell University Press, 1997), chapter 3.
5. Wendy Warren, *New England Bound: Slavery and Colonization in Early America* (New York: Liveright, 2016), 159; John Ruston Pagan, *Anne Orthwood's Bastard: Sex and Law in Early Virginia* (New York: Oxford University Press), 50; Godbeer, *Sexual Revolution in Early America*, 124; Susan Dwyer Amussen, *An Ordered Society: Gender and Class in Early Modern England* (New York: Columbia University Press, 1993), 98–100.
6. Jennifer L. Morgan, *Laboring Women: Reproduction and Gender in the Making of New World Slavery* (Philadelphia: University of Pennsylvania Press, 2004), chapter 1, quoted at 27; Sharon Block, *Colonial Complexions: Race and Bodies in Eighteenth-Century America* (Philadelphia: University of Pennsylvania Press, 2018); Stephanie M. H. Camp, "Early European Views of African Bodies: Beauty," in *Sexuality and Slavery: Reclaiming Intimate Histories in the Americas*, eds. Daina Ramey Berry and Leslie M. Harris (Athens: University of Georgia Press, 2018), 9–32.
7. Daina Ramey Berry and Kali Nicole Gross, *A Black Women's History of the United States* (Boston: Beacon Press, 2020), 12; Lisa Brooks, *Our Beloved Kin: A New History of King Philip's War* (New Haven: Yale University Press, 2018), 80; Stephanie E. Smallwood, *Saltwater Slavery: A Middle Passage from Africa to American Diaspora* (Cambridge, MA: Harvard University Press, 2007), chapter 1; Brown, *Good Wives, Nasty Wenches*, chapter 4; Alan Scot Willis, "Abusing Hugh Davis: Determining the Crime in a Seventeenth-Century American Morality Case," *Journal of the History of Sexuality* 28, no. 1 (2019): 126.
8. Theda Perdue, "Columbus Meets Pocahontas in the American South," *Southern Cultures* 3, no. 1 (1997): 5, 8; Godbeer, *Sexual Revolution in Early America*, 154–156, 174–175; Stephanie Wood, "Sexual Violation in the Conquest of the Americas," in *Sex and*

Sexuality in Early America, ed. Merril D. Smith (New York: New York University Press, 1998), 11; Gordon Sayre, "Indigenous American Sexuality in the Eyes of the Beholders, 1535–1710," in Smith, *Sex and Sexuality in Early America*, 35.

9. Brown, *Good Wives, Nasty Wenches*, 33–37, chapter 2; Godbeer, *Sexual Revolution in Early America*, chapter 6.
10. David D. Smits, "'Abominable Mixture': Toward Repudiation of Anglo-Indian Intermarriage in Seventeenth-Century Virginia," *Virginia Magazine of History and Biography* 95, no. 2 (1987): 157–192; Camilla Townsend, *Pocahontas and the Powhatan Dilemma* (New York: Hill and Wang, 2004), 52–60; Karen Ordahl Kupperman, *Pocahontas and the English Boys: Caught Between Cultures in Early Virginia* (New York: New York University Press, 2019); Godbeer, *Sexual Revolution in Early America*, 159–163.
11. Brown, *Good Wives, Nasty Wenches*, 82–85.
12. Scholars describe this phenomenon as "settler colonialism," a form of imperial conquest that seeks to establish permanent communities dominated by the colonizers, as compared to colonial projects focused on resource extraction by itinerant colonizers. For English women shipped to seventeenth-century North America, see David R. Ransome, "Wives for Virginia, 1621," *William and Mary Quarterly* 48, no. 1 (1991): 3–18; Brown, *Good Wives, Nasty Wenches*, 81–83; Morgan, *Laboring Women*, 74–75; Richard B. Sheridan, *Sugar and Slavery: An Economic History of the British West Indies, 1623–1775* (Baltimore: Johns Hopkins University Press, 1973), 237; Leslie M. Harris, *In the Shadow of Slavery: African Americans in New York City, 1626–1863* (Chicago: University of Chicago Press, 2003), 21, 26–27; Laurel Clark Shire, *The Threshold of Manifest Destiny: Gender and National Expansion in Florida* (Philadelphia: University of Pennsylvania Press, 2016).
13. Brown, *Good Wives, Nasty Wenches*, 13–14.
14. Brown, *Good Wives, Nasty Wenches*, 97.
15. Brown, *Good Wives, Nasty Wenches*, 89.
16. Wichelns, "From *The Scarlet Letter* to Stonewall," 503–504.
17. Leah DeVun, *The Shape of Sex: Nonbinary Gender from Genesis to the Renaissance* (New York: Columbia University Press, 2021); Reis, *Bodies in Doubt*, chapter 1.
18. On women's surveillance of other women's bodies, including obtaining confessions of paternity, see Norton, *Founding Mothers and Fathers*, 222–239.
19. Godbeer, *Sexual Revolution in Early America*, 28–29; Helena M. Wall, *Fierce Communion: Family and Community in Early America* (Cambridge, MA: Harvard University Press, 1990), 63; Terri L. Snyder, *Brabbling Women: Disorderly Speech and the Law in Early Virginia* (Ithaca: Cornell University Press, 2003), chapter 2.
20. Godbeer, *Sexual Revolution in Early America*, chapter 1.
21. Norton, *Founding Mothers and Fathers*, 40, 101–105; M. Michelle Jarrett Morris, *Under Household Government: Sex and Family in Puritan Massachusetts* (Cambridge, MA: Harvard University Press, 2013); Carole Shammas, *A History of Household Government in America* (Charlottesville: University of Virginia Press, 2002); Brown, *Good Wives, Nasty Wenches*, chapter 1.
22. Else L. Hambleton, "The Regulation of Sex in Seventeenth-Century Massachusetts: The Quarterly Court of Essex County vs. Priscilla Wilson and Mr. Samuel Appleton," in Smith, *Sex and Sexuality in Early America*, 89–115; Angus McLaren, *Reproductive Rituals: The Perception of Fertility in England from the Sixteenth Century to the Nineteenth Century* (London: Methuen, 1984), 20.

23. Ryan, *Regulating Passion*, 22–24; Brown, *Good Wives, Nasty Wenches*, 130–131; Norton, *Founding Mothers and Fathers*, 336; Godbeer, *Sexual Revolution in Early America*, 124–125; Kirsten Fischer, *Suspect Relations: Sex, Race, and Resistance in Colonial North Carolina* (Ithaca: Cornell University Press, 2002), 101–103; Pagan, *Anne Orthwood's Bastard*, 106–108, 128–129.
24. Brown, "Thomas/Thomasine Court Case (1629)"; Norton, *Founding Mothers and Fathers*, 193, 444n18, n19.
25. Brown, *Good Wives, Nasty Wenches*, chapter 4.
26. Ryan, *Regulating Passion*, 15; Morris, *Under Household Government*, chapter 1; Warren, *New England Bound*, 161–174; Gloria McCahon Whiting, "Power, Patriarchy, and Provision: African Families Negotiate Gender and Slavery in New England," *Journal of American History* 103, no. 3 (2016): 593–594; Rebecca Anne Goetz, *The Baptism of Early Virginia: How Christianity Created Race* (Baltimore: Johns Hopkins University Press, 2012), 71.
27. Peter W. Bardaglio, "'Shamefull Matches': The Regulation of Interracial Sex and Marriage in the South before 1900," in *Sex, Love, Race: Crossing Boundaries in North American History*, ed. Martha Hodes (New York: New York University Press, 1999), 114–115; Martha Hodes, *White Women, Black Men: Illicit Sex in the Nineteenth-Century South* (New Haven: Yale University Press, 1997), chapter 1.
28. Jessica Marie Johnson, *Wicked Flesh: Black Women, Intimacy, and Freedom in the Atlantic World* (Philadelphia: University of Pennsylvania Press, 2020), 105–106; Brown, *Good Wives, Nasty Wenches*, 194–211; Jennifer L. Morgan, "Partus Sequitur Ventrem: Law, Race, and Reproduction in Colonial Slavery," *Small Axe* 22, no. 1 (2018): 1–17.
29. Godbeer, *Sexual Revolution in Early America*, 105–106, 363n42; Robert F. Oaks, "'Things Fearful to Name': Sodomy and Buggery in Seventeenth-Century New England," *Journal of Social History* 12, no. 2 (1978): 268–271; Anne G. Myles, "Queering the Study of Early American Sexuality," *William and Mary Quarterly* 60, no. 1 (2003): 201.
30. Oaks, "Things Fearful," 269–270; Colin L. Talley, "Gender and Male Same-Sex Erotic Behavior in British North America in the Seventeenth Century," *Journal of the History of Sexuality* 6, no. 3 (1996): 385–408. The colony of New Netherland, under Dutch control, enforced its anti-sodomy laws with more vigor than other colonies did, a reflection of the stricter enforcement of anti-sodomy statutes in the Netherlands. See John M. Murrin, "'Things Fearful to Name': Bestiality in Early America," *Pennsylvania History: A Journal of Mid-Atlantic Studies* 65 (1998): 15–16, 20; Oaks, "Things Fearful," 273.
31. Godbeer, *Sexual Revolution in Early America*, 45–50; Richard Godbeer and Douglas L. Winiarski, "The Sodomy Trial of Nicholas Sension, 1677: Documents and Teaching Guide," *Early American Studies: An Interdisciplinary Journal* 12, no. 2 (2014): 402–443.
32. Godbeer, *Sexual Revolution in Early America*, 202–203; Brown, *Good Wives, Nasty Wenches*, 197–201. On opposition to interracial sex elsewhere in British North America, see Emily Jeannine Clark, "'Their Negro Nanny Was with Child by a White Man': Gossip, Sex, and Slavery in an Eighteenth-Century New England Town," *William and Mary Quarterly* 79, no. 4 (2022): 544n37; Thomas A. Foster, *Sex and the Eighteenth-Century Man: Massachusetts and the History of Sexuality in America* (Boston: Beacon

Press, 2006), 129; *Acts and Resolves of the Massachusetts Bay* (Boston: Wright & Potter, 1869), 1:578–580.

33. Ann M. Little, *Abraham in Arms: War and Gender in Colonial New England* (Philadelphia: University of Pennsylvania Press, 2007), 62–63.

Chapter 2: Sacred Possessions

1. Juliana Barr, *Peace Came in the Form of a Woman: Indians and Spaniards in the Texas Borderlands* (Chapel Hill: University of North Carolina Press, 2007), 13.
2. Charles W. Hackett, trans. and ed., *Historical Documents Relating to New Mexico, Nueva Vizcaya and Approaches Thereto, to 1773* (Washington, DC: Carnegie Institution, 1937), 3:404–405; James F. Brooks, *Captives and Cousins: Slavery, Kinship, and Community in the Southwest Borderlands* (Chapel Hill: University of North Carolina Press, 2002), 99–103; James F. Brooks, "'This Evil Extends Especially . . . to the Feminine Sex': Negotiating Captivity in the New Mexico Borderlands," *Feminist Studies* 22, no. 2 (1996): 285–288.
3. Ramón A. Gutiérrez, *When Jesus Came, the Corn Mothers Went Away: Marriage, Sexuality, and Power in New Mexico, 1500–1846* (Stanford: Stanford University Press, 1991), 15.
4. Ramón A. Gutiérrez, "Documents in Hopi Indian Sexuality: Imperialism, Culture and Resistance," *Radical History Review* 20 (1979): 124.
5. Gutiérrez, *When Jesus Came*, 17–18.
6. Gutiérrez, *When Jesus Came*, 20; Gregory D. Smithers, *Reclaiming Two-Spirits* (Boston: Beacon Press, 2022), 13, 43.
7. Gutiérrez, *When Jesus Came*, 10–11; Will Roscoe, *The Zuni Man-Woman* (Albuquerque: University of New Mexico Press, 1991), 19–20; Theda Perdue, *Cherokee Women: Gender and Culture Change, 1700–1835* (Lincoln: University of Nebraska Press, 1998), 44–45; Ann Marie Plane, *Colonial Intimacies: Indian Marriage in Early New England* (Ithaca: Cornell University Press, 2000), 20–21, 98; Don Francisco de Valverde, "Investigation of Conditions in New Mexico, 1601," in *Don Juan De Oñate: Colonizer of New Mexico, 1595–1628* (Albuquerque: University of New Mexico Press, 1953), 2, 627.
8. Albert L. Hurtado, "When Strangers Met: Sex and Gender on Three Frontiers," *Frontiers* 17, no. 3 (1996): 52–75; Theda Perdue, "Columbus Meets Pocahontas in the American South," *Southern Cultures* 3, no. 1 (1997): 11.
9. Gutiérrez, *When Jesus Came*, 32–33; Roscoe, *Zuni Man-Woman*, 18–22.
10. Jacques Marquette, "Of the First Voyage Made by Father Marquette Toward New Mexico, and How the Idea Thereof Was Conceived," in *The Jesuit Relations and Allied Documents: Travels and Explorations of the Jesuit Missionaries in New France, 1610–1791*, ed. Reuben Gold Thwaites (Cleveland: The Burrows Brothers Company, 1900), 39:129; Deborah A. Miranda, "Extermination of the Joyas: Gendercide in Spanish California," *GLQ: A Journal of Gay and Lesbian Studies* 16, nos. 1–2 (2010): 253–284; Smithers, *Reclaiming*, chapter 6; Will Roscoe, "Was We'wha a Homosexual?: Native American Survivance and the Two-Spirit Tradition," *GLQ: A Journal of Lesbian and Gay Studies* 2, no. 3 (1995): 193–235; Will Roscoe, *Changing Ones: Third and Fourth Genders in Native North America* (New York: St. Martin's Press, 1998), chapter 1; Walter L. Williams, *The Spirit and the Flesh: Sexual Diversity in American Indian Culture*, 2nd ed.

(Boston: Beacon Press, 1992), xi–xii; Ramón A. Gutiérrez, "Warfare, Homosexuality, and Gender Status Among American Indian Men in the Southwest," in *Long Before Stonewall: Histories of Same-Sex Sexuality in Early America*, ed. Thomas A. Foster (New York: New York University Press, 2007), 19–31; Sandra Slater, "'Nought but Women': Constructions of Masculinities and Modes of Emasculation in the New World," in *Gender and Sexuality in Indigenous North America*, eds. Sandra Slater and Fay A. Yarbrough (Columbia: University of South Carolina Press, 2011), 46–49.

11. Williams, *Spirit and the Flesh*, chapter 11; Sabine Lang, *Men as Women, Women as Men: Changing Gender in Native American Cultures*, trans. John L. Vantine (Austin: University of Texas Press, 1998), chapter 14; Roger M. Carpenter, "Womanish Men and Manlike Women: The Native American Two-Spirit as Warrior," in Slater and Yarbrough, *Gender and Sexuality in Indigenous North America*, 158–161.
12. Pekka Hämäläinen, *Lakota America: A New History of Indigenous Power* (New Haven: Yale University Press, 2019), 46; Barr, *Peace Came in the Form of a Woman*, 289; Emma Hart, *Trading Spaces: The Colonial Marketplace and the Foundations of American Capitalism* (Chicago: University of Chicago Press, 2019).
13. Barr, *Peace Came in the Form of a Woman*, 80–81.
14. Sylvia Van Kirk, *Many Tender Ties: Women in Fur-Trade Society, 1670–1870* (Norman: University of Oklahoma Press, 1983), chapter 2; Susan Sleeper-Smith, *Indian Women and French Men: Rethinking Cultural Encounter in the Western Great Lakes* (Amherst: University of Massachusetts Press, 2001); Tiya Miles, *The Dawn of Detroit: A Chronicle of Slavery and Freedom in the City of the Straits* (New York: The New Press, 2017), 47–48; Plane, *Colonial Intimacies*, 146–151; Jennifer M. Spear, *Race, Sex, and Social Order in Early New Orleans* (Baltimore: Johns Hopkins University Press, 2009), chapter 1.
15. Daniel Richter, *Before the Revolution: America's Ancient Pasts* (Cambridge, MA: The Belknap Press of Harvard University Press, 2011), 227; Perdue, *Cherokee Women*, 174–76; Plane, *Colonial Intimacies*, 22, 27–28; Sarah M. S. Pearsall, *Polygamy: An Early American History* (New Haven: Yale University Press, 2019), chapters 1 and 2; Sleeper-Smith, *Indian Women and French Men*, 35.
16. Gutiérrez, *When Jesus Came*, 72–73; Ramón A. Gutiérrez, "Women on Top: The Love Magic of the Indian Witches of New Mexico," *Journal of the History of Sexuality* 16, no. 3 (2007): 373–390.
17. Gutiérrez, *When Jesus Came*, 114.
18. Brooks, *Captives and Cousins*, 86–87, 101.
19. Gutiérrez, *When Jesus Came*, 130–140; Richter, *Before the Revolution*, 215–216, 228–230.
20. Richter, *Before the Revolution*, 30–35, 51–52; Christina Snyder, *Slavery in Indian Country: The Changing Face of Captivity in Early America* (Cambridge, MA: Harvard University Press, 2010), 5–6, 42–45; Christina Snyder, "The South," in *The Oxford Handbook of American Indian History*, ed. Frederick E. Hoxie (New York: Oxford University Press, 2016), 315–334.
21. George P. Hammond, ed., *First Expedition of Vargas Into New Mexico, 1692*, in Coronado Cuarto Centennial Publications, 1540–1940 (Albuquerque: University of New Mexico Press, 1940), 10:237; Brooks, *Captives and Cousins*, 100–101.
22. "Declaration of Fray Miguel de Menchero, Santa Bárbara," May 10, 1744, in Hackett, *Historical Documents Relating to New Mexico*, 3:404–405; Brooks, *Captives and Cous-*

ins, 99–102, "favored" quoted on 102; Ralph Emerson Twitchell, *The Spanish Archives of New Mexico: Compiled and Chronologically Arranged with Historical, Genealogical, Geographical, and Other Annotations, by Authority of the State of New Mexico* (New York: Arno Press, 1976), 2:524–541.

23. Quincy Newell, "'The Indians Generally Love Their Wives and Children': Native American Marriage and Sexual Practices in Missions San Francisco, Santa Clara, and San Jose," *The Catholic Historical Review* 91, no. 1 (2005): 61; Junípero Serra, "Report to Antonio María de Bucareli y Ursúa," in *Lands of Promise and Despair: Chronicles of Early California, 1535–1846*, eds. Rose Marie Beebe and Robert M. Senkewicz (Norman: University of Oklahoma Press, 2015), 169.

24. Yolanda Venegas, "The Erotics of Racialization: Gender and Sexuality in the Making of California," *Frontiers* 25, no. 3 (2004): 66; Ann Twinam, *Public Lives, Private Secrets: Gender, Honor, Sexuality, and Illegitimacy in Colonial Spanish America* (Stanford: Stanford University Press, 1999), chapter 3; Patricia Seed, *To Love, Honor, and Obey in Colonial Mexico: Conflicts over Marriage Choice, 1574–1821* (Stanford: Stanford University Press, 1988); Gutiérrez, *When Jesus Came*, chapter 7.

25. Fr. Luis Jayme, Letter to Fr. Rafael Verger, in Beebe and Senkewicz, *Lands of Promise and Despair*, 158.

26. Jayme to Verger, Letter, 156–157; Pearsall, *Polygamy*, 218–220; Antonia I. Castañeda, "Sexual Violence and the Politics and Policies of Conquest: Amerindian Women and the Spanish Conquest of Alta California," in *Building with Our Hands: New Directions in Chicana Studies*, eds. Adela de la Torre and Beatríz M. Pesquera (Berkeley: University of California Press, 1993), 15; Albert L. Hurtado, *Intimate Frontiers: Sex, Gender, and Culture in Old California* (Albuquerque: University of New Mexico Press, 1999), chapter 1; Miroslava Chávez-García, *Negotiating Conquest: Gender and Power in California, 1770s to 1880s* (Tucson: University of Arizona Press, 2004), chapter 1; Richard Godbeer, *Sexual Revolution in Early America* (Baltimore: Johns Hopkins University Press, 2002), 180.

27. Castañeda, "Sexual Violence," 15–16; Pearsall, *Polygamy*, 224–225.

28. Junípero Serra, "To Felipe de Neve, Written at Monterey, January 7, 1780," in *Writings of Junípero Serra*, ed. Antonine Tibesar (Washington, DC: Academy of American Franciscan History, 1956), 3:411; Hurtado, *Intimate Frontiers*, 17–19; Steven W. Hackel, *Children of Coyote, Missionaries of Saint Francis: Indian-Spanish Relations in Colonial California, 1769–1850* (Chapel Hill: Omohundro Institute of Early American History and Culture, by the University of North Carolina Press, 2005), 200–201; Virginia Marie Bouvier, *Women and the Conquest of California, 1542–1840: Codes of Silence* (Tucson: University of Arizona Press, 2001), chapter 6.

29. William S. Simmons, "Indian Peoples of California," in *Contested Eden: California Before the Gold Rush, Published in Association with the California Historical Society*, eds. Richard J. Orsi and Ramón A. Gutiérrez (Berkeley: University of California Press, 1998), 52.

30. Hackel, *Children of Coyote*, 204, 212–213.

Chapter 3: Under the Husband's Government

1. Abigail Abbot Bailey, *Religion and Domestic Violence in Early New England: The Memoirs of Abigail Abbot Bailey*, ed. Ann Taves (Bloomington: Indiana University Press, 1989), 87–88; Hendrik Hartog, *Man and Wife in America: A History* (Cambridge, MA: Harvard University Press, 2000), chapter 2. By 1799, twelve states and the Northwest Territory recognized a legal right to divorce; Norma Basch, *Framing American Divorce: From the Revolutionary Generation to the Victorians* (Berkeley: University of California Press, 1999), 23; Nancy F. Cott, "Divorce and the Changing Status of Women in Eighteenth-Century Massachusetts," *William and Mary Quarterly* 33, no. 4 (1976): 594.
2. Ellen K. Rothman, *Hands and Hearts: A History of Courtship in America* (New York: Basic Books, 1984), 31; Benjamin Wadsworth, *The Well-Ordered Family*, 2nd ed. (Boston, 1719), 35–37.
3. Richard Godbeer, *Sexual Revolution in Early America* (Baltimore: Johns Hopkins University Press, 2002), 56–60; Anne Bradstreet, "To My Dear and Loving Husband," in *Several Poems* (Boston, 1678), reprinted in *The Works of Anne Bradstreet in Prose and Verse*, ed. John Harvard Ellis (Charlestown, 1867).
4. Thomas A. Foster, *Sex and the Eighteenth-Century Man: Massachusetts and the History of Sexuality in America* (Boston: Beacon Press, 2006), chapter 7.
5. Godbeer, *Sexual Revolution in Early America*, 235–236, 244.
6. Louis B. Wright and Marion Tinling, eds., *The Secret Diary of William Byrd of Westover, 1709–1712* (Richmond: Dietz Press, 1941), 345; Godbeer, *Sexual Revolution in Early America*, chapter 6; William Byrd, *The Westover Manuscripts: Containing the History of the Dividing Line Betwixt Virginia and North Carolina; A Journey to the Land of Eden, A. D. 1733; and A Progress to the Mines. Written from 1728 to 1736, and Now First Published* (Petersburg: Printed by Edmund and Julian C. Ruffin, 1841), 89.
7. Susan Juster, *Disorderly Women: Sexual Politics and Evangelicalism in Revolutionary New England* (Ithaca: Cornell University Press, 1994); Kathleen M. Brown, *Good Wives, Nasty Wenches, and Anxious Patriarchs: Gender, Race, and Power in Colonial Virginia* (Chapel Hill: University of North Carolina Press, 1996), chapter 8; Foster, *Sex and the Eighteenth-Century Man*, 69–75; Kelly A. Ryan, *Regulating Passion: Sexuality and Patriarchal Rule in Massachusetts, 1700–1830* (New York: Oxford University Press, 2014), chapter 2.
8. Rothman, *Hands and Hearts*, chapter 1.
9. Godbeer, *Sexual Revolution in Early America*, 246–255.
10. Cornelia Hughes Dayton, *Women Before the Bar: Gender, Law, and Society in Connecticut, 1639–1789* (Chapel Hill: University of North Carolina Press, 1995), chapter 5; Sharon Block, *Rape and Sexual Power in Early America* (Chapel Hill: University of North Carolina Press, 2006), chapter 4.
11. Rothman, *Hands and Hearts*, 46–48.
12. Daniel Scott Smith and Michael Hindus, "Premarital Pregnancy in America, 1640–1971: An Overview and Interpretation," *Journal of Interdisciplinary History* 4 (1975): 537–570; Godbeer, *Sexual Revolution in Early America*, 134, 228–229; Brown, *Good Wives, Nasty Wenches*, chapter 6; Mark E. Kann, *Taming Passion for the Public Good: Policing Sex in the Early Republic* (New York: New York University Press, 2012), 10.

13. Kirsten Fischer, *Suspect Relations: Sex, Race, and Resistance in Colonial North Carolina* (Ithaca: Cornell University Press, 2002), 53; Charles Woodmason, "A Report on Religion in the South," in *The Carolina Backcountry on the Eve of the Revolution: The Journal and Other Writings of Charles Woodmason, Anglican Itinerant*, ed. Richard J. Hooker (Chapel Hill: University of North Carolina Press, 1969), 80–81; Godbeer, *Sexual Revolution in Early America*, 8, 119–122; Jon Butler, *Awash in a Sea of Faith: Christianizing the American People* (Cambridge, MA: Harvard University Press, 1992), 167.
14. Basch, *Framing American Divorce*, chapter 1; Mary Beth Sievens, *Stray Wives: Marital Conflict in Early National New England* (New York: New York University Press, 2005); Nancy F. Cott, *Public Vows: A History of Marriage and the Nation* (Cambridge, MA: Harvard University Press, 2000), 37–38.
15. Roxanne Harde, "'I Consoled My Heart': Conversion Rhetoric and Female Subjectivity in the Personal Narratives of Elizabeth Ashbridge and Abigail Bailey," *Legacy* 21, no. 2 (2004): 163; Helena M. Wall, *Fierce Communion: Family and Community in Early America* (Cambridge, MA: Harvard University Press, 1990), chapter 3; Amanda Porterfield, *Female Piety in Puritan New England: The Emergence of Religious Humanism* (New York: Oxford University Press, 1992), chapter 3.
16. Ann Taves, introduction, in Bailey, *Religion and Domestic Violence*, 28, 38.
17. Mary Beth Norton, *Liberty's Daughters: The Revolutionary Experience of American Women, 1750–1800* (Ithaca: Cornell University Press, 1980), 72–73; Herbert Klein, *A Population History of the United States*, 2nd ed. (Cambridge: Cambridge University Press, 2012), 57, 73–75; Susan E. Klepp, *Revolutionary Conceptions: Women, Fertility, and Family Limitation in America, 1760–1820* (Chapel Hill: University of North Carolina Press, 2009), 4, 73; U.S. Census Bureau, "Chapter Z: Colonial and Pre-Federal Statistics, Series Z 1–19, Estimated Population of American Colonies: 1610–1780," in *Bicentennial Edition: Historical Statistics of the United States, Colonial Times to 1970* (Washington, DC: U.S. Government Printing Office, 1975), 1168.
18. Page Smith, *Daughters of the Promised Land: Women in American History* (Boston: Little, Brown and Company, 1970), 232; Angus McLaren, *Reproductive Rituals: The Perception of Fertility in England from the Sixteenth Century to the Nineteenth Century* (London: Methuen, 1984), introduction.
19. Cornelia Hughes Dayton, "Taking the Trade: Abortion and Gender Relations in an Eighteenth-Century New England Village," *William and Mary Quarterly* 48, no. 1 (1991): 19–20; Gloria L. Main, "Rocking the Cradle: Downsizing the New England Family," *Journal of Interdisciplinary History* 37, no. 1 (2006): 48; Etienne van de Walle, "Flowers and Fruits: Two Thousand Years of Menstrual Regulation," *Journal of Interdisciplinary History* 28, no. 2 (1997): 183–203; Janet Farrell Brodie, *Contraception and Abortion in 19th-Century America* (Ithaca: Cornell University Press, 1994), 42; Andrea Tone, *Devices and Desires: A History of Contraception in America* (New York: Hill and Wang, 2001), 13; Klepp, *Revolutionary Conceptions*, 195, 212.
20. Klepp, *Revolutionary Conceptions*, 57–64, chapter 4.
21. Unless otherwise noted, the following descriptions of the Bailey household are drawn from Bailey, "Memoirs," in *Religion and Domestic Violence in Early New England*, 57–95.
22. Clare A. Lyons, *Sex Among the Rabble: An Intimate History of Gender and Power in the Age of Revolution, Philadelphia, 1730–1830* (Chapel Hill: Omohundro Institute of Early American History and Culture, University of North Carolina Press, 2006), 247–256.

23. Toby L. Ditz, "Shipwrecked; or, Masculinity Imperiled: Mercantile Representations of Failure and the Gendered Self in Eighteenth-Century Philadelphia," *Journal of American History* 81, no. 1 (1994): 51–56, 66; Fischer, *Suspect Relations*, 141–142; Foster, *Sex and the Eighteenth-Century Man*, chapters 3 and 4.
24. Block, *Rape and Sexual Power*, 148–149, 163–164, 171.
25. Lyons, *Sex Among the Rabble*, 154–175; Linda K. Kerber, *No Constitutional Right to Be Ladies: Women and the Obligations of Citizenship* (New York: Hill and Wang, 1998), chapter 1; Cott, *Public Vows*, 17–23; Jan Lewis, "The Republican Wife: Virtue and Seduction in the Early Republic," *William and Mary Quarterly* 44, no. 4 (1987): 689–721.
26. Godbeer, *Sexual Revolution in Early America*, chapter 8; Lyons, *Sex Among the Rabble*, 249–250; Brown, *Good Wives, Nasty Wenches*, 87–88, 359.
27. Taves, introduction, 27.
28. Bailey, *Religion and Domestic Violence*, 189n66; Sharon Halevi, "'A Variety of Domestic Misfortunes': Writing the Dysfunctional Self in Early America," *Early American Literature* 44, no. 1 (2009): 98–105.
29. Block, *Rape and Sexual Power*, chapter 6; G. J. Barker-Benfield, *The Culture of Sensibility: Sex and Society in Eighteenth-Century Britain* (Chicago: University of Chicago Press, 1992), 148–153.
30. Hartog, *Man and Wife in America*, 60–61; Eileen Razzari Elrod, *Piety and Dissent: Race, Gender, and Biblical Rhetoric in Early American Autobiography* (Amherst: University of Massachusetts Press, 2008), 95–97; Nancy F. Cott, "Eighteenth-Century Family and Social Life Revealed in Massachusetts Divorce Records," *Journal of Social History* 10, no. 1 (1976): 29–30; Steven Mintz, *Huck's Raft: A History of American Childhood* (Cambridge, MA: Belknap Press of Harvard University Press, 2004), chapter 3.
31. Bailey, *Religion and Domestic Violence*, 194n216.
32. Abigail's description of her captivity, flight, and reunion with her children appear in Bailey, "Memoirs," 145–178.
33. *Massachusetts, U.S., Town and Vital Records, 1620–1988*, 541v, Ancestry.com.
34. Abiel Abbot and Ephraim Abbot, *Genealogical Register of the Descendants of George Abbot of Andover* (Boston: James Munroe and Co., 1847), 29.
35. Klepp, *Revolutionary Conceptions*, 8, 47–48.
36. Kelly A. Ryan, *Everyday Crimes: Social Violence and Civil Rights in Early America* (New York: New York University Press, 2019).

Chapter 4: Slavery's Intimate Bonds

1. Ira Berlin, *Many Thousands Gone: The First Two Centuries of Slavery in North America* (Cambridge, MA: The Belknap Press of Harvard University Press, 1998), 370, table 1; J. David Hacker, "From '20. and Odd' to 10 Million: The Growth of the Slave Population in the United States," *Slavery and Abolition* 41, no. 4 (2020): 840–855; "Pop Culture: 1790," United States Census Bureau: History, https://www.census.gov/history/www/through_the_decades/fast_facts/1790_fast_facts.html; Stanley L. Engerman, Richard Sutch, and Gavin Wright, "Slavery," *Historical Statistics of the United States: Earliest Times to the Present*, ed. Susan B. Carter (New York: Cambridge University Press, 2006) 2:369–385.
2. Engerman, Sutch, and Wright, "Slavery," 370.

3. Hacker, "'From 20. and Odd," 14.
4. Wilma A. Dunaway, *Slavery in the American Mountain South* (Cambridge: Cambridge University Press, 2003), 196.
5. Drew Gilpin Faust, ed., *The Ideology of Slavery: Proslavery Thought in the Antebellum South, 1830–1860* (Baton Rouge: Louisiana State University Press, 1981), 78.
6. Daina Ramey Berry, *"Swing the Sickle for the Harvest Is Ripe": Gender and Slavery in Antebellum Georgia* (Urbana: University of Illinois Press, 2007), 55–56; Deborah G. White, *Ar'n't I a Woman?: Female Slaves in the Plantation South*, rev. ed. (New York: W. W. Norton, 1999), chapter 3; Brenda E. Stevenson, *Life in Black and White: Family and Community in the Slave South* (New York: Oxford University Press, 1996), chapter 8.
7. Tera W. Hunter, *Bound in Wedlock: Slave and Free Black Marriage in the Nineteenth Century* (Cambridge, MA: Harvard University Press, 2017), 31–33; Berry, *"Swing the Sickle,"* chapter 3; Stevenson, *Life in Black and White*, 231; Thelma Jennings, "'Us Colored Women Had to Go Through a Plenty': Sexual Exploitation of African-American Slave Women," *Journal of Women's History* 1, no. 3 (1990): 53–54.
8. Berry, *"Swing the Sickle,"* 53–59; Hunter, *Bound in Wedlock*, 29, 32–33.
9. Victoria E. Bynum, *Unruly Women: The Politics of Social and Sexual Control in the Old South* (Chapel Hill: University of North Carolina Press, 1992), 94–95; Hunter, *Bound in Wedlock*, 72–73; *The State v. Zadock Roland*, 28 N.C. 241 (N.C. 1846); Jessica Millward, *Finding Charity's Folk: Enslaved and Free Black Women in Maryland* (Athens: University of Georgia Press, 2015).
10. Anthony E. Kaye, *Joining Places: Slave Neighborhoods in the Old South* (Chapel Hill: University of North Carolina Press, 2007).
11. Edward E. Baptist, *The Half Has Never Been Told: Slavery and the Making of American Capitalism* (New York: Basic Books, 2014), 261–262; "My Master Was a Mean Man," in *The American Slave: A Composite Autobiography*, ed. George P. Rawick (Westport: Greenwood Publishing Company, 1972), 6:81–82. For another example, see Berry, *"Swing the Sickle,"* 56.
12. Bynum, *Unruly Women*, 9; Kirsten Fischer, *Suspect Relations: Sex, Race, and Resistance in Colonial North Carolina* (Ithaca: Cornell University Press, 2002), 149–151.
13. Kathleen M. Brown, *Good Wives, Nasty Wenches, and Anxious Patriarchs: Gender, Race, and Power in Colonial Virginia* (Chapel Hill: University of North Carolina Press, 1996), chapter 9; Martha Hodes, *White Women, Black Men: Illicit Sex in the Nineteenth-Century South* (New Haven: Yale University Press, 1997).
14. Bynum, *Unruly Women*, 11, 14, 19–25; Stephanie McCurry, *Masters of Small Worlds: Yeoman Households, Gender Relations, and the Political Culture of the Antebellum South Carolina Low Country* (New York: Oxford University Press, 1995); Martha Hodes, "The Sexualization of Reconstruction Politics: White Women and Black Men in the South after the Civil War," *Journal of the History of Sexuality* 3, no. 3 (1993): 402–417.
15. Nell Irvin Painter, "Soul Murder and Slavery: Toward a Fully-Loaded Cost Accounting," in *U.S. History as Women's History: New Feminist Essays*, eds. Alice Kessler-Harris, Linda K. Kerber, and Kathryn Kish Sklar (Chapel Hill: University of North Carolina Press, 1995), 125–146; Baptist, *The Half Has Never Been Told*; Daina Ramey Berry, *The Price for Their Pound of Flesh: The Value of the Enslaved, from Womb to Grave, in the Building of a Nation* (Boston: Beacon Press, 2017), 61–62, 78–80; Brenda E. Stevenson, "What's Love Got to Do with It? Concubinage and Enslaved Women and

Girls in the Antebellum South," *Journal of African American History* 98, no. 1 (2013): 99–125; Heather V. Vermeulen, "Thomas Thistlewood's Libidinal Linnaean Project: Slavery, Ecology, and Knowledge Production," *Small Axe* 22, no. 1 (2018): 18–38.

16. Joshua D. Rothman, *Notorious in the Neighborhood: Sex and Families Across the Color Line in Virginia, 1787–1861* (Chapel Hill: University of North Carolina Press, 2003), 17–18; Annette Gordon-Reed, *The Hemingses of Monticello: An American Family* (New York: W. W. Norton, 2008).
17. Stevenson, "What's Love Got to Do with It?," 100.
18. Stevenson, "What's Love Got to Do with It?," 99–100, 105–106, 112; Baptist, *The Half Has Never Been Told*, 242.
19. Stephanie E. Jones-Rogers, *They Were Her Property: White Women as Slave Owners in the American South* (New Haven: Yale University Press, 2019), 102–118; Thavolia Glymph, *Out of the House of Bondage: The Transformation of the Plantation Household* (Cambridge: Cambridge University Press, 2008).
20. Thomas A. Foster, *Rethinking Rufus: Sexual Violations of Enslaved Men* (Athens: University of Georgia Press, 2019), 102–111.
21. Stevenson, "What's Love Got to Do with It?," 116.
22. Stevenson, "What's Love Got to Do with It?," 115.
23. Foster, *Rethinking Rufus*, 12–15; Ronald G. Walters, "The Erotic South: Civilization and Sexuality in American Abolitionism," *American Quarterly* 25 (1973): 177–201; Leslie M. Harris, *In the Shadow of Slavery: African Americans in New York City, 1626–1863* (Chicago: University of Chicago Press, 2003), 193.
24. Manisha Sinha, *The Slave's Cause: A History of Abolition* (New Haven: Yale University Press, 2016), 456–459.
25. April R. Haynes, *Riotous Flesh: Women, Physiology, and the Solitary Vice in Nineteenth-Century America* (Chicago: University of Chicago Press, 2015), 58; Harris, *Shadow of Slavery*, 190–199.
26. Berry, *"Swing the Sickle,"* 77–83; Jennings, "Us Colored Women," 49–51; Marie Jenkins Schwartz, *Birthing a Slave: Motherhood and Medicine in the Antebellum South* (Cambridge, MA: Harvard University Press, 2006), 67; "Rose Williams," in *When I Was a Slave: Memoirs from the Slave Narrative Collection*, ed. Norman R. Yetman (Mineola, NY: Dover Publications, Inc., 2002), 147.
27. Emily Jeannine Clark, "'Their Negro Nanny Was with Child by a White Man': Gossip, Sex, and Slavery in an Eighteenth-Century New England Town," *William and Mary Quarterly* 79, no. 4 (2022): 559–560; Berry, *Pound of Flesh*, 10–15, 19–21; Wendy Warren, "'Thrown upon the World': Valuing Infants in the Eighteenth-Century North American Slave Market," *Slavery & Abolition* 39, no. 4 (2018): 623–641.
28. David Doddington, "Manhood, Sex, and Power in Antebellum Slave Communities," in *Sexuality and Slavery: Reclaiming Intimate Histories in the Americas*, eds. Daina Ramey Berry and Leslie M. Harris (Athens: University of Georgia Press, 2018), 150; Hunter, *Bound in Wedlock*, 38, 51; Heather Andrea Williams, *Help Me to Find My People: The African American Search for Family Lost in Slavery* (Chapel Hill: University of North Carolina Press, 2012), chapter 2.
29. Deirdre Cooper Owens, *Medical Bondage: Race, Gender, and the Origins of American Gynecology* (Athens: University of Georgia Press, 2017), 84–85; Jennings, "Us Colored Women," 47; Foster, *Rethinking Rufus*, 1–2, chapter 3; Jacqueline Jones, *Labor of Love*,

Labor of Sorrow: Black Women, Work and the Family, from Slavery to the Present (New York: Basic Books, 2010), 33; Doddington, "Manhood, Sex, and Power," 153–154; Sharon Block, *Rape and Sexual Power in Early America* (Chapel Hill: University of North Carolina Press, 2006), 85; "Rose Williams," 146–149.

30. Schwartz, *Birthing a Slave*, 10–13, 19–20, 67, 74–75; William N. Morgan, "A Case of Rupture of the Uterus, with Artificial Anus at the Point of Rupture," *Western Journal of Medicine and Surgery* 2, no. 6 (1844), 498–501.
31. Cooper Owens, *Medical Bondage*, 50–51; Schwartz, *Birthing a Slave*, 50, 146–153; Stevenson, *Life in Black and White*, 290–291; Sharla M. Fett, "Consciousness and Calling: African American Midwives at Work in the Antebellum South," *New Studies in the History of American Slavery*, eds. Edward E. Baptist and Stephanie M. H. Camp (Athens: University of Georgia Press, 2006), 65–86.
32. Schwartz, *Birthing a Slave*, 93–104.
33. Cooper Owens, *Medical Bondage*, 1–2, 26, 36–39, and chapters 1–3 generally; Schwartz, *Birthing a Slave*, 164–165.
34. Jennings, "Us Colored Women," 54–58; Schwartz, *Birthing a Slave*, 127–131; Jones, *Labor of Love*, 18; Narrative of Nehemiah Caulkins of Waterford, Connecticut, in [Theodore D. Weld], *American Slavery As It Is: Testimony of a Thousand Witnesses* (New York: American Anti-Slavery Society, 1839), 12, excerpted in Gerda Lerner, ed., *Black Women in White America: A Documentary History* (New York: Vintage Books, 1992), 47.
35. Schwartz, *Birthing a Slave*, 191; Jones, *Labor of Love*, 18, 33–34; Richard Follett, "Heat, Sex, and Sugar: Pregnancy and Childbearing in the Slave Quarters," *Journal of Family History* 28, no. 4 (2003): 510–539; Dorothy E. Roberts, *Killing the Black Body: Race, Reproduction, and the Meaning of Liberty* (New York: Pantheon Books, 1997), 36.
36. Jennings, "Us Colored Women," 57; Jones, *Labor of Love*, 33; Liese M. Perrin, "Resisting Reproduction: Reconsidering Slave Contraception in the Old South," *Journal of American Studies* 35, no. 2 (2001): 255–274.
37. Foster, *Rethinking Rufus*, 87–91; Hunter, *Bound in Wedlock*, 233–244; Nancy F. Cott, *Public Vows: A History of Marriage and the Nation* (Cambridge, MA: Harvard University Press, 2000), 83–88.
38. Berry, *"Swing the Sickle,"* 89; Hunter, *Bound in Wedlock*, 209–210; Williams, *Help Me to Find My People*, chapter 2.

Chapter 5: A Woman of Pleasure

1. Elizabeth Schlappa, "Onania's Letters and the Female Masturbator: Women, Gender, and the 'Abominable Crime' of Self-Pollution," *Journal of the History of Sexuality* 32, no. 3 (2023): 313–339; Andrea Haslanger, "What Happens When Pornography Ends in Marriage: The Uniformity of Pleasure in 'Fanny Hill,'" *ELH* 78, no. 1 (2011): 163–188; Hal Gladfelder, *Fanny Hill in Bombay: The Making and Unmaking of John Cleland* (Baltimore: Johns Hopkins University Press, 2012).
2. John Cleland, *Memoirs of Fanny Hill, a woman of pleasure / written by herself ; with plate, engraved by a member of the Royal Academy; two volumes in one. Vol I[-II]* (London [i.e., United States?]: G. Felton's Press, in the Strand. Copy right secured to the Royal fam-

ily, according to law, 1832). Original held by the American Antiquarian Society, which notes, "The imprint is false. Another edition, with imprint 'London: Printed for G. Felton, in the Strand. 1787,' is ascribed to the press of Munroe & Francis in Boston, and dated ca. 1810. The uncovered boards (of spruce or fir) used to bind this edition suggest that it too is an American production." Citing pages 8, 10–11, 13–14, 28–30, and 34–39.

3. Clorinda Donato, "Just an 'English Whore'?: Italian Translations of Fanny Hill and the Transcultural Novel," *Eighteenth-Century Life* 43, no. 2 (2019): 137–161; Marcus Allen McCorison, "Two Unrecorded American Printings of 'Fanny Hill,'" *Vermont History* 40, no. 1 (1972): 64–66; Clare A. Lyons, *Sex Among the Rabble: An Intimate History of Gender and Power in the Age of Revolution, Philadelphia, 1730–1830* (Chapel Hill: The Omohundro Institute of Early American History and Culture, by the University of North Carolina Press, 2006), 133n20; "A Brief History of Copyright in the United States," U.S. Copyright Office, copyright.gov/timeline/.
4. Ava Chamberlain, "Bad Books and Bad Boys: The Transformation of Gender in Eighteenth-Century Northampton, Massachusetts," *New England Quarterly* 75, no. 2 (2002): 179.
5. William J. Gilmore-Lehne, *Reading Becomes a Necessity of Life: Material and Cultural Life in Rural New England, 1780–1835* (Knoxville: University of Tennessee Press, 1989), 177.
6. Lyons, *Sex Among the Rabble*, 116–120, 171–180, 185.
7. Lyons, *Sex Among the Rabble*, 127–130, 132.
8. Helen Lefkowitz Horowitz, *Rereading Sex: Battles over Sexual Knowledge and Suppression in Nineteenth-Century America* (New York: Alfred A. Knopf, 2002); Patricia Cline Cohen, *The Murder of Helen Jewett: The Life and Death of a Prostitute in Nineteenth-Century New York* (New York: Alfred A. Knopf, 1999); Timothy J. Gilfoyle, *City of Eros: New York City, Prostitution, and the Commercialization of Sex, 1790–1920* (New York: W. W. Norton, 1992); Patricia Cline Cohen, Timothy J. Gilfoyle, and Helen Lefkowitz Horowitz, *The Flash Press: Sporting Male Weeklies in 1840s New York* (Chicago: University of Chicago Press, 2008), 138; Donna Dennis, *Licentious Gotham: Erotic Publishing and Its Prosecution in Nineteenth-Century New York* (Cambridge, MA: Harvard University Press, 2009).
9. *Fanny Hill*, 1832 edition at AAS, 41.
10. Sharon Block, *Rape and Sexual Power in Early America* (Chapel Hill: University of North Carolina Press, 2006), 23; Richard Godbeer, *Sexual Revolution in Early America* (Baltimore: Johns Hopkins University Press, 2002), 195–196; Lyons, *Sex Among the Rabble*, 251; *Fanny Hill*, 1832 edition at AAS, 46.
11. Rashauna Johnson, "Spectacles of Restraint: Race, Excess, and Heterosexuality in Early American Print Culture," in *Heterosexual Histories*, eds. Rebecca L. Davis and Michele Mitchell (New York: New York University Press, 2021), 180–185.
12. Edward E. Baptist, *The Half Has Never Been Told: Slavery and the Making of American Capitalism* (New York: Basic Books, 2014), 236–237, 243–259.
13. Barbara Meil Hobson, *Uneasy Virtue: The Politics of Prostitution and the American Reform Tradition* (New York: Basic Books, 1987), 66–76; Carroll Smith-Rosenberg, "Beauty, the Beast, and the Militant Woman: A Case Study in Sex Roles and Social Stress in Jacksonian America," *American Quarterly* 23, no. 4 (1971): 562–584.
14. Janet Farrell Brodie, *Contraception and Abortion in 19th-Century America* (Ithaca: Cor-

nell University Press, 1994), 119–125; Lori D. Ginzberg, "'The Hearts of Your Readers Will Shudder': Fanny Wright, Infidelity, and American Freethought," *American Quarterly* 46, no. 2 (1994): 195–226.

15. Horowitz, *Rereading Sex*, 45–60; Robert Dale Owen, *Moral physiology: or, A brief and plain treatise on the population question* (London: J. Watson, 1834?), 30, Kress Library of Business and Economics, Harvard University, Gale Primary Sources.
16. Horowitz, *Rereading Sex*, 73–85.
17. Rodney Hessinger, *Seduced, Abandoned, and Reborn: Visions of Youth in Middle-Class America, 1780–1850* (Philadelphia: University of Pennsylvania Press, 2005), chapter 5; G. L. Barker-Benfield, *Horrors of the Half-Known Life: Male Attitudes Toward Women and Sexuality in Nineteenth-Century America* (New York: Harper & Row, 1976), chapter 15; April R. Haynes, *Riotous Flesh: Women, Physiology, and the Solitary Vice in Nineteenth-Century America* (Chicago: University of Chicago Press, 2015).
18. Haynes, *Riotous Flesh*, chapter 1; Horowitz, *Rereading Sex*, 92–107; Kara M. French, *Against Sex: Identities of Sexual Restraint in Early America* (Chapel Hill: University of North Carolina Press, 2021), 116–122.
19. Haynes, *Riotous Flesh*, 7, 26–28, 52.
20. Horowitz, *Rereading Sex*, 107–112; Erica Armstrong Dunbar, *A Fragile Freedom: African American Women and Emancipation in the Antebellum City* (New Haven: Yale University Press, 2008), chapter 4; Haynes, *Riotous Flesh*, chapter 5.
21. Haynes, *Riotous Flesh*, 144–146.
22. *Fanny Hill*, 1832 edition at AAS, 50.
23. Horowitz, *Rereading Sex*, 19–23; Otho T. Beall, "Aristotle's Master Piece in America: A Landmark in the Folklore of Medicine," *William and Mary Quarterly* 20, no. 2 (1963): 207–222; Mary E. Fissell, "Hairy Women and Naked Truths: Gender and the Politics of Knowledge in 'Aristotle's Masterpiece,'" *William and Mary Quarterly* 60, no. 1 (2003): 43; Vern L. Bullough, "An Early American Sex Manual, or, Aristotle Who?" *Early American Literature* 7, no. 3 (1973): 236–240.
24. Kirsten Fischer, *Suspect Relations: Sex, Race, and Resistance in Colonial North Carolina* (Ithaca: Cornell University Press, 2002), 4; Thomas Laqueur, *Making Sex: Body and Gender from the Greeks to Freud* (Cambridge, MA: Harvard University Press, 1990). For a critique of Laqueur's argument, see Helen King, *The One-Sex Body on Trial: The Classical and Early Modern Evidence* (Farnham: Ashgate Publishing, 2013).
25. Roy Porter, "'The Secrets of Generation Display'd': Aristotle's Master-Piece in Eighteenth-Century England," *Eighteenth Century Life* 9 (1984–1985): 1–16; Fissell, "Hairy Women," 66; Block, *Rape and Sexual Power*, chapter 1.
26. Bullough, "Early American Sex Manual," 242.
27. *A Letter from Richard P. Robinson, as connected with the Murder of Ellen Jewett*, was sold wholesale at 29 Ann Street in NYC. See Horowitz, *Rereading Sex*, 244; Cohen, *Murder of Helen Jewett*, 396–397.
28. Katie M. Hemphill, *Bawdy City: Commercial Sex and Regulation in Baltimore, 1790–1915* (Cambridge: Cambridge University Press, 2020), 1–2; Joshua D. Rothman, *Notorious in the Neighborhood: Sex and Families Across the Color Line in Virginia, 1787–1861* (Chapel Hill: University of North Carolina Press, 2003), 107; Cohen, *Murder of Helen Jewett*; Lyons, *Sex Among the Rabble*, 192; Stephanie E. Jones-Rogers, *They Were Her*

Property: White Women as Slave Owners in the American South (New Haven: Yale University Press, 2019), 146–149.

29. Hemphill, *Bawdy City*, 23–45; Gilfoyle, *City of Eros*, 30–31, 124–125; Leslie M. Harris, *In the Shadow of Slavery: African Americans in New York City, 1626–1863* (Chicago: University of Chicago Press, 2003), 190–191.
30. Hemphill, *Bawdy City*, 45; Rothman, *Notorious*, 111–129.
31. *Fanny Hill*, AAS 1832 edition, 3.
32. Hal Gladfelder, "Obscenity, Censorship, and the Eighteenth-Century Novel: The Case of John Cleland," *Wordsworth Circle* 35, no. 3 (2004): 134; Dennis, *Licentious Gotham*, 15.
33. Dennis, *Licentious Gotham*, 34; David Weed, "Fitting Fanny: Cleland's 'Memoirs' and the Politics of Male Pleasure," *NOVEL: A Forum on Fiction* 31, no. 1 (1997): 7–20; Lynn Hunt, "Introduction," in *The Invention of Pornography: Obscenity and the Origins of Modernity, 1500–1800*, ed. Lynn Hunt (New York: Zone Books, 1993), 10; Thomas Alan Holmes, "Sexual Positions and Sexual Politics: John Cleland's Memoirs of a Woman of Pleasure," *South Atlantic Review* 74, no. 1 (2009): 124–139; Margaret F. Walker, "Bookin' West Tall Tales and 'Books of Every Sort and Size from Fanny Hill to the Bible' on the Journey West," *Overland Journal* 25, no. 3 (2007): 166.
34. Whitney Strub, *Perversion for Profit: The Politics of Pornography and the Rise of the New Right* (New York: Columbia University Press, 2011), 70–71; Marc Stein, *Sexual Injustice: Supreme Court Decisions from Griswold to Roe* (Chapel Hill: University of North Carolina Press, 2010), 35–44.

Chapter 6: Perfect Confidence and Love

1. Elizabeth Hampsten, *Read This Only to Yourself: The Private Writings of Midwestern Women, 1880–1910* (Bloomington: Indiana University Press, 1982), 161–162, 167, 169.
2. Hampsten, *Read This*, 168.
3. Jonathan Ned Katz, *Love Stories: Sex between Men Before Homosexuality* (Chicago: University of Chicago Press, 2001), 134–146.
4. Katz, *Love Stories*, 74.
5. Martha Vicinus, "'They Wonder to Which Sex I Belong': The Historical Roots of the Modern Lesbian Identity," *Feminist Studies* 18, no. 3 (1992): 478; William N. Eskridge, *Dishonorable Passions: Sodomy Laws in America, 1861–2003* (New York: Viking, 2008), 20; Katz, *Love Stories*, 60–63.
6. Marylynne Diggs, "Romantic Friends or a 'Different Race of Creatures'? The Representation of Lesbian Pathology in Nineteenth-Century America," *Feminist Studies* 21, no. 2 (1995): 323–324.
7. Lillian Faderman, *Surpassing the Love of Men: Romantic Friendship and Love Between Women from the Renaissance to the Present* (New York: William Morrow Company, 1981), 147–177.
8. Richard Godbeer, *The Overflowing of Friendship: Love Between Men and the Creation of the American Republic* (Baltimore: Johns Hopkins University Press, 2009), 57–58; Martin B. Duberman, "'Writhing Bedfellows': 1826 Two Young Men from Antebellum South Carolina's Ruling Elite Share 'Extravagant Delight,'" *Journal of Homosexuality* 6, nos. 1–2 (1981): 87–88; E. Anthony Rotundo, *American Manhood: Transformations*

in *Masculinity from the Revolution to the Modern Era* (New York: Basic Books, 1993), chapter 4.

9. Katz, *Love Stories*, 3; Eve Kosofsky Sedgwick, *Between Men: English Literature and Male Homosocial Desire* (New York: Columbia University Press, 1985).

10. Philip Clayton Van Buskirk, *An American Seafarer in the Age of Sail: The Erotic Diaries of Philip C. Van Buskirk, 1851–1870*, ed. Barry Richard Burg (New Haven: Yale University Press, 1994), 74–75, 79, 114; B. R. Burg, "Sodomy, Masturbation, and Courts-Martial in the Antebellum American Navy," *Journal of the History of Sexuality* 23, no. 1 (2014): 53–67; Katz, *Love Stories*, 78–80, 134–135.

11. Susan Lee Johnson, *Roaring Camp: The Social World of the California Gold Rush* (New York: W. W. Norton, 2000), 51, 71–78, chapter 2, 170–173, 294.

12. Rotundo, *American Manhood*, 80–81.

13. Harriet A. Jacobs, *Incidents in the Life of a Slave Girl: Written by Herself*, ed. Jean Fagan Yellin (Cambridge, MA: Harvard University Press, 2000), 192; Jim Downs, "With Only a Trace: Same-Sex Sexual Desire and Violence on Slave Plantations, 1607–1865," in *Connexions: Histories of Race and Sex in North America*, eds. Jennifer Brier, Jim Downs, and Jennifer L. Morgan (Urbana: University of Illinois Press, 2016), 19; Aliyyah I. Abdur-Rahman, "'The Strangest Freaks of Despotism': Queer Sexuality in Antebellum African American Slave Narratives," *African American Review* 40, no. 2 (2006): 233; Thomas A. Foster, *Rethinking Rufus: Sexual Violations of Enslaved Men* (Athens: University of Georgia Press, 2019), 85–87, 91–112; Martin B. Duberman, *About Time: Exploring the Gay Past*, rev. and expanded (New York: Meridian, 1991), 43–44; Katz, *Love Stories*, 317–320.

14. Katz, *Love Stories*, 45–61; Greta LaFleur, *The Natural History of Sexuality in Early America* (Baltimore: Johns Hopkins University Press, 2018).

15. Katz, *Love Stories*, 134–135; Downs, "With Only a Trace," 17.

16. Farah Jasmine Griffin, ed., *Beloved Sisters and Loving Friends: Letters from Rebecca Primus of Royal Oak, Maryland and Addie Brown of Hartford, Connecticut, 1854–1868* (New York: Alfred A. Knopf, 1999), 12, 18, 21; Karen V. Hansen, "'No Kisses Is Like Youres': An Erotic Friendship Between Two African-American Women during the Mid-Nineteenth Century," *Gender & History* 7, no. 2 (1995): 155–156.

17. Griffin, *Beloved Sisters*, 19–20.

18. Griffin, *Beloved Sisters*, 21–22.

19. Faderman, *Surpassing*, 152.

20. Griffin, *Beloved Sisters*, 35, 49.

21. Griffin, *Beloved Sisters*, 65.

22. Griffin, *Beloved Sisters*, 35, 47–48.

23. Rachel Hope Cleves, *Charity and Sylvia: A Same-Sex Marriage in Early America* (New York: Oxford University Press, 2014).

24. Rachel Hope Cleves, "'What, Another Female Husband?': The Prehistory of Same-Sex Marriage in America," *Journal of American History* 101, no. 4 (2015): 1064–1068; Jen Manion, *Female Husbands: A Trans History* (Cambridge: Cambridge University Press, 2020); Emily Skidmore, *True Sex: The Lives of Trans Men at the Turn of the Twentieth Century* (New York: New York University Press, 2017).

25. Cleves, "'What, Another Female Husband?'" 1071–1072; Manion, *Female Husbands*, chapter 5; Faderman, *Surpassing*, 190–230.
26. Diggs, "Romantic Friends," 321.
27. Griffin, *Beloved Sisters*, 44–45, 77, 87; Hansen, "'No Kisses,'" 156.
28. Griffin, *Beloved Sisters*, 225–226, 228; Nancy Sahli, "Smashing: Women's Relationships Before the Fall," *Chrysalis*, no. 8 (1979): 17–27.
29. Griffin, *Beloved Sisters*, 9, 235, 281–282.
30. Hampsten, *Read This*, 168–169, 173.
31. Hampsten, *Read This*, 153–154.
32. Hampsten, *Read This*, 167, 177, 179–186.

Chapter 7: Then Shall They Be Gods

1. Benjamin E. Park, *Kingdom of Nauvoo: The Rise and Fall of a Religious Empire on the American Frontier* (New York: Liveright Publishing Corporation, 2020), 21–32.
2. Hendrik Hartog, *Man and Wife in America: A History* (Cambridge, MA: Harvard University Press, 2000), chapter 9.
3. Park, *Kingdom*, 61–63, 65–66; Laurel Thatcher Ulrich, *A House Full of Females: Plural Marriage and Women's Rights in Early Mormonism, 1835–1870* (New York: Alfred A. Knopf, 2017), 14, 61, 66–67, 71–72. About 20 percent of the women who entered plural marriages in Nauvoo were legally married to another man, or had been until recently; Ulrich, 105.
4. Ulrich, *House Full of Females*, 72, 89, 91, 93–94.
5. Ulrich, *House Full of Females*, 73–74; Sarah Barringer Gordon, *The Mormon Question: Polygamy and Constitutional Conflict in Nineteenth-Century America* (Chapel Hill: University of North Carolina Press, 2002), 29–52.
6. Park, *Kingdom*, chapter 7.
7. Park, *Kingdom*, 235–238.
8. Park, *Kingdom*, 264–267; Anne F. Hyde, *Empires, Nations, and Families: A History of the North American West, 1800–1860* (Lincoln: University of Nebraska Press, 2011), 451–459.
9. Gordon, *Mormon Question*, 66–68; Nancy Isenberg, *Sex and Citizenship in Antebellum America* (Chapel Hill: University of North Carolina Press, 1998), 159–167; Ellen Carol Du Bois, ed., *The Elizabeth Cady Stanton-Susan B. Anthony Reader: Correspondence, Writings, Speeches*, rev. ed. (Boston: Northeastern University Press, 1992), 36–43; Nancy F. Cott, *Public Vows: A History of Marriage and the Nation* (Cambridge, MA: Harvard University Press, 2000); Michael Grossberg, *Governing the Hearth: Law and the Family in Nineteenth-Century America* (Chapel Hill: University of North Carolina Press, 1985).
10. Kathryn M. Daynes, *More Wives than One: Transformation of the Mormon Marriage System, 1840–1910* (Urbana: University of Illinois Press, 2001); Julie Dunfey, "'Living the Principle' of Plural Marriage: Mormon Women, Utopia, and Female Sexuality in the Nineteenth Century," *Feminist Studies* 10, no. 3 (1984): 523–536.
11. Ulrich, *House Full of Females*, 230–231.
12. Timothy Marr, *The Cultural Roots of American Islamicism* (Cambridge: Cambridge Uni-

versity Press, 2006); "The Mormon Nuisance," *Daily Atlas* (Boston), November 14, 1856, 2; Gordon, *Mormon Question*, 45; J. Spencer Fluhman, *"A Peculiar People": Anti-Mormonism and the Making of Religion in Nineteenth-Century America* (Chapel Hill: University of North Carolina Press, 2012), chapter 2.

13. Ulrich, *House Full of Females*, 241; Gordon, *Mormon Question*, 93.
14. Cott, *Public Vows*, 49; Hartog, *Man and Wife*, 14.
15. Joanne Ellen Passet, *Sex Radicals and the Quest for Women's Equality* (Urbana: University of Illinois Press, 2003).
16. Patricia Cline Cohen, "The 'Anti-Marriage Theory' of Thomas and Mary Gove Nichols," *Journal of the Early Republic* 34, no. 1 (2014): 1–20.
17. Satomi Minowa, "'Free Love' in Sectional Debates over Slavery in Mid-Nineteenth-Century America," *Japanese Journal of American Studies*, no. 31 (2020): 158; Helen Lefkowitz Horowitz, *Rereading Sex: Battles over Sexual Knowledge and Suppression in Nineteenth-Century America* (New York: Alfred A. Knopf, 2002), 266–69; Cohen, "'Anti-Marriage Theory'"; Ellen Carol DuBois and Linda Gordon, "Seeking Ecstasy on the Battlefield: Danger and Pleasure in Nineteenth-Century Feminist Sexual Thought," *Feminist Studies* 9, no. 1 (1983): 16.
18. Gordon, *Mormon Question*, 29–32; Passet, *Sex Radicals*, 178n1; Ulrich, *House Full of Females*, 214.
19. Gordon, *Mormon Question*, 53–57; Sarah M. S. Pearsall, *Polygamy: An Early American History* (New Haven: Yale University Press, 2019), 154–155; Minowa, "'Free Love,'" 169.
20. Helen Lefkowitz Horowitz, "Victoria Woodhull, Anthony Comstock, and Conflict over Sex in the United States in the 1870s," *Journal of American History* 87, no. 2 (2000): 412–416; Amanda Frisken, *Victoria Woodhull's Sexual Revolution: Political Theater and the Popular Press in Nineteenth-Century America* (Philadelphia: University of Pennsylvania Press, 2004), chapter 1.
21. Minowa, "Free Love," 158; Horowitz, *Rereading Sex*, 267–268; Kara M. French, *Against Sex: Identities of Sexual Restraint in Early America* (Chapel Hill: University of North Carolina Press, 2021).
22. Rodney Hessinger, *Smitten: Sex, Gender, and the Contest for Souls in the Second Great Awakening* (Ithaca: Cornell University Press, 2022), 126–129.
23. Peter von Ziegesar, "Reinventing Sex: The Oneida Community Challenged American Standards of Sex and Marriage," *Latham's Quarterly*, n.d.; Ellen Wayland-Smith, *Oneida: From Free Love Utopia to the Well-Set Table* (New York: Picador, 2016), 55–56, 67–71; Hessinger, *Smitten*, chapter 5.
24. John Humphrey Noyes, *Male Continence* (Oneida, NY: Office of Oneida Circular, 1872), 7, 8, 12, 14–15.
25. Noyes, *Male Continence*, 13; Ben Barker-Benfield, "The Spermatic Economy: A Nineteenth Century View of Sexuality," *Feminist Studies* 1, no. 1 (1972): 45–74.
26. Entries for Thursday, [March] 26, [1868] and Tuesday, [September] 22, [1868], both in Excerpts from the Journal of Tirzah Miller, September 3, 1867–July 25, 1877, Oneida Community Collection, Syracuse University, box 66, Women and Social Movements.
27. Wayland-Smith, *Oneida*, 126–132; Horowitz, *Rereading Sex*, 254–256; Noyes, *Marital Continence*, 15.
28. Wayland-Smith, *Oneida*, chapter 10.
29. Gordon, *Mormon Question*, 81–83.

30. Gordon, *Mormon Question*, 97–98, 104–107.
31. Gordon, *Mormon Question*, 119–145, 150–159, 181; Pablo Mitchell, *Coyote Nation: Sexuality, Race, and Conquest in Modernizing New Mexico, 1880–1920* (Chicago: University of Chicago Press, 2005), 16.
32. Jennifer Graber, *The Gods of Indian Country: Religion and the Struggle for the American West* (New York: Oxford University Press, 2018), 119–120; Gordon, *Mormon Question*, 127; Jane E. Simonsen, *Making Home Work: Domesticity and Native American Assimilation in the American West, 1860–1919* (Chapel Hill: University of North Carolina Press, 2006), 11, 38–41; Cathleen D. Cahill, *Federal Fathers and Mothers: A Social History of the United States Indian Service, 1869–1933* (Chapel Hill: University of North Carolina Press, 2011), 34–35.
33. Graber, *Gods of Indian Country*, 71–74; Jacki Thompson Rand, *Kiowa Humanity and the Invasion of the State* (Lincoln: University of Nebraska Press, 2008), 29–30, chapter 3; "Treaty with the Kiowa, Etc., 1837," Tribal Treaties Database, Oklahoma State University Libraries, treaties.okstate.edu/treaties/treaty-with-the-kiowa-etc-1837-0489.
34. Rose Stremlau, *Sustaining the Cherokee Family: Kinship and the Allotment of an Indigenous Nation* (Chapel Hill: University of North Carolina Press, 2011), 52–57, 76–81; Cahill, *Federal Fathers and Mothers*, 39–41.
35. Stremlau, *Sustaining*, 129; Cahill, *Federal Fathers and Mothers*, 40–41; Rand, *Kiowa Humanity*, 29–30.
36. Kiowa Indian ledger drawings [manuscript], ca. 1880–1890, Edward E. Ayer Collection, Newberry Library, *American Indian Histories and Cultures*, Adam Matthew Digital.

Chapter 8: A Typical Invert

1. "SING" [Freda Ward] to YBIR [cypher for LOVE, aka Alice Mitchell], July 11, 1891, reprinted in Appendix B, Lisa Duggan, *Sapphic Slashers: Sex, Violence, and American Modernity* (Durham: Duke University Press, 2000), 214; "Sane or Insane?" *Memphis Weekly Commercial*, July 27, 1892, 2.
2. Freda Ward to YBIR, July 26, 1891, in Duggan, *Sapphic Slashers*, 215; "Testimony of B. F. Turner," in F. L. Sim, *The Trial of Alice Mitchell for Killing Freda Ward: Forensic Psychiatry*, 19, reprint from *Memphis Medical Monthly* 12, no. 8 (1892): 377–428.
3. "SING" [Freda Ward] to YBIR, 214.
4. Alice Mitchell to Freda Ward, August 1, 1891, in Duggan, *Sapphic Slashers*, 217–218.
5. Mrs. W. H. Volkmar to Alice Mitchell, August 1, 1891, in Duggan, *Sapphic Slashers*, 219; *Memphis Weekly Commercial*, "Sane or Insane?" 1.
6. *Memphis Weekly Commercial*, "Sane or Insane?" 1.
7. Peter Boag, *Re-Dressing America's Frontier Past* (Berkeley: University of California Press, 2011); Emily Skidmore, *True Sex: The Lives of Trans Men at the Turn of the Twentieth Century* (New York: New York University Press, 2017); Will Roscoe, *The Zuni Man-Woman* (Albuquerque: University of New Mexico Press, 1991), 2, chapter 3.
8. Duggan, *Sapphic Slashers*, 142–148; Jen Manion, *Female Husbands: A Trans History* (Cambridge: Cambridge University Press, 2020), 245–247; "The Plea for Bail," *The Public Ledger*, February 11, 1892, 2; *Memphis Weekly Commercial*, "Sane or Insane?"

2; Hugh Ryan, *When Brooklyn Was Queer* (New York: St. Martin's Press, 2019), 50–66.

9. Claire Sears, *Arresting Dress: Cross-Dressing, Law, and Fascination in Nineteenth-Century San Francisco* (Durham: Duke University Press, 2015), 41–44, 87–93; Manion, *Female Husbands*, 199; Katrina C. Rose, "A History of Gender Variance in Pre-20th Century Anglo-American Law," *Texas Journal of Women and the Law* 14, no. 1 (2004): 77–119; I. Bennett Capers, "Cross Dressing and the Criminal," *Yale Journal of Law & the Humanities* 20, no. 1 (2008): 9–10.
10. Boag, *Re-Dressing*, 52–53, 70.
11. Gail Bederman, *Manliness and Civilization: A Cultural History of Gender and Race in the United States, 1880–1917* (Chicago: University of Chicago Press, 1995), esp. chapter 5.
12. Katy Coyle and Nadiene Van Dyke, "Sex, Smashing, and Storyville in Turn-of-the-Century New Orleans: Reexamining the Continuum of Lesbian Sexuality," in *Carryin' on in the Lesbian and Gay South*, ed. John Howard (New York: New York University Press, 1997), 62; Nancy Sahli, "Smashing: Women's Relationships Before the Fall," *Chrysalis*, no. 8 (1979): 17–27; Lillian Faderman, *Odd Girls and Twilight Lovers: A History of Lesbian Life in Twentieth-Century America* (New York: Columbia University Press, 1991), 11, 18–21.
13. John D'Emilio and Estelle B. Freedman, *Intimate Matters: A History of Sexuality in America*, 3rd ed. (Chicago: University of Chicago Press, 2012), 190–194; Wendy L. Rouse, "'A Very Crushable, Kissable Girl': Queer Love and the Invention of the Abnormal Girl Among College Women in the Gilded Age and Progressive Era," *Journal of the Gilded Age and Progressive Era* 21, no. 3 (2022): 201–220.
14. Sim, *Forensic Psychiatry*, 13; "The Murder in Memphis," *Nashville Banner*, January 27, 1892, 9.
15. Peggy Pascoe, *What Comes Naturally: Miscegenation Law and the Making of Race in America* (New York: Oxford University Press, 2009), 40–43, 56–63, 80–85.
16. Lisa J. Lindquist, "Images of Alice: Gender, Deviancy, and a Love Murder in Memphis," *Journal of the History of Sexuality* 6, no. 1 (1995): 52–55; "Negro Demons," *The Fort Worth Daily Gazette*, October 11, 1892, 1; Estelle Freedman, *Redefining Rape: Sexual Violence in the Era of Suffrage and Segregation* (Cambridge, MA: Harvard University Press, 2013), 97.
17. Paula Giddings, *Ida: A Sword Among Lions: Ida B. Wells and the Campaign Against Lynching* (New York: Amistad, 2008), chapter 6; Crystal Nicole Feimster, *Southern Horrors: Women and the Politics of Rape and Lynching* (Cambridge, MA: Harvard University Press, 2009), chapter 4; Mia Bay, *To Tell the Truth Freely: The Life of Ida B. Wells* (New York: Hill and Wang, 2009), chapter 3.
18. Ida B. Wells, *Southern Horrors: Lynch Law in All Its Phases* ([New York]: New York Age, 1892), 4, Black Thought and Culture; Giddings, *Ida*, 205–208; Bay, *To Tell the Truth*, 103–104.
19. Giddings, *Ida*, 213–217; Bay, *To Tell the Truth*, 106, 122–127.
20. Duggan, *Sapphic Slashers*, 150–153; "United in Death," *The Public Ledger*, January 27, 1892, 1.
21. *Nashville Banner*, "The Murder in Memphis," 9; Duggan, *Sapphic Slashers*, 47–58.

22. *Memphis Weekly Commercial,* "Sane or Insane?" 2; "Testimony of J. H. Callendar," in *Forensic Psychiatry,* 30–31.
23. "Testimony of J. H. Callendar," 33.
24. "Sent for the Doctor," February 5, 1892, quoted in Lindquist, "Images of Alice," 56–57; Roscoe, *Zuni Man-Woman,* 67–69.
25. Kim Emery, "Steers, Queers, and Manifest Destiny: Representing the Lesbian Subject in Turn-of-the-Century Texas," *Journal of the History of Sexuality* 5, no. 1 (1994): 29.
26. Manion, *Female Husbands,* chapter 7; Skidmore, *True Sex,* chapter 1; Boag, *Re-Dressing,* chapter 5; Duggan, *Sapphic Slashers,* 163–164; Jennifer Terry, *An American Obsession: Science, Medicine, and Homosexuality in Modern Society* (Chicago: University of Chicago Press, 1999), 30–35. See also Bederman, *Manliness and Civilization,* chapter 5.
27. James G. Kiernan, "Sexual Perversion, and the Whitechapel Murders," *Medical Standard* 4, no. 5 (1888): 129–130, 170–172; Margaret Gibson, "Clitoral Corruption: Body Metaphors and American Doctors' Constructions of Female Homosexuality, 1870–1900," in *Science and Homosexualities,* ed. Vernon A. Rosario (New York: Routledge, 1997), 115–119.
28. Hubert Kennedy, "Karl Heinrich Ulrichs: First Theorist of Homosexuality," in Rosario, *Science and Homosexualities,* 26; Terry, *American Obsession,* 43–45; T. Griswold Comstock, "Alice Mitchell of Memphis: A Case of Sexual Perversion or 'Urning' (A Paranoiac)," *Journal of Orificial Surgery* 1, no. 7 (1893): 474–479.
29. Harry Oosterhuis, *Stepchildren of Nature: Krafft-Ebing, Psychiatry, and the Making of Sexual Identity* (Chicago: University of Chicago Press, 2000), 40, 50, 172–173; Terry, *American Obsession,* 49.
30. Sim, *Forensic Psychiatry,* 3; *Memphis Weekly Commercial,* "Sane or Insane?" 1–2.
31. *Memphis Weekly Commercial,* "Sane or Insane?" 1–2; George Chauncey, "From Sexual Inversion to Homosexuality: Medicine and the Changing Conceptualization of Female Deviance," *Salmagundi,* no. 58/59 (1982–1983): 114–146; Claudia Breger, "Feminine Masculinities: Scientific and Literary Representations of Female Inversion at the Turn of the Twentieth Century," *Journal of the History of Sexuality* 14, no. 1 (2005): 76–106; Heike Bauer, "Theorizing Female Inversion: Sexology, Discipline, and Gender at the Fin de Siècle," *Journal of the History of Sexuality* 18, no. 1 (2009): 84–102; Lindquist, "Images of Alice," 35; "Many Letters are Read," *Nashville Banner,* July 20, 1892, 5.
32. Comstock, "Alice Mitchell of Memphis," 475, 479.
33. Lindquist, "Images of Alice," 60–61.
34. "Alice Mitchell Dead," *The Nashville American,* April 1, 1898, 4; Paul Coppock, "Memphis' Strangest Love Murder Had All-Girl Cast," *The Commercial Appeal,* September 7, 1930, sec. 4, p. 5.
35. Martha Vicinus, "'They Wonder to Which Sex I Belong': The Historical Roots of the Modern Lesbian Identity," *Feminist Studies* 18, no. 3 (1992): 480–485.
36. Skidmore, *True Sex;* Carroll Smith-Rosenberg, "The New Woman as Androgyne: Social Disorder and Gender Crisis, 1870–1936," in *Disorderly Conduct: Visions of Gender in Victorian America* (New York: Oxford University Press, 1985), 245–296; Esther Newton, "The Mythic Mannish Lesbian: Radclyffe Hall and the New Woman," *Signs: Journal of Women in Culture & Society* 9, no. 4 (1984): 557–575.
37. Havelock Ellis, *Studies in the Psychology of Sex,* vol. 2, *Sexual Inversion,* 2nd ed. (Phil-

adelphia: The Medical Bulletin Printing-house, 1908), 120; Paul A. Robinson, *The Modernization of Sex: Havelock Ellis, Alfred Kinsey, William Masters, and Virginia Johnson* (Ithaca: Cornell University Press, 1989), 2–11; Douglas C. McMurtrie, "A Crime of Lesbian Love," *American Journal of Urology, Venereal, and Sexual Diseases* 10, no. 9 (1914): 433–434.

38. Oosterhuis, *Stepchildren*, 60–62; Terry, *American Obsession*, 55–60; Robinson, *Modernization*, 5–6; Mari Jo Buhle, *Feminism and Its Discontents: A Century of Struggle with Psychoanalysis* (Cambridge, MA: Harvard University Press, 1998), introduction and chapter 1.
39. James G. Kiernan, "Bisexuality," *Urologic and Cutaneous Review* 18, no. 7 (1914): 375.
40. Smith-Rosenberg, "New Woman as Androgyne," 283; Christina Simmons, "Companionate Marriage and the Lesbian Threat," *Frontiers* 4, no. 3 (1979): 57; Wendy L. Rouse, *Public Faces, Secret Lives: A Queer History of the Women's Suffrage Movement* (New York: New York University Press, 2022); Rebecca L. Davis, "'Not Marriage at All, but Simple Harlotry': The Companionate Marriage Controversy," *Journal of American History* 94, no. 4 (2008): 1137–1163.

Chapter 9: Obscene and Immoral

1. Andrea Tone, *Devices and Desires: A History of Contraceptives in America* (New York: Hill and Wang, 2001), 4–5; Judith Ann Giesberg, *Sex and the Civil War: Soldiers, Pornography, and the Making of American Morality* (Chapel Hill: University of North Carolina Press, 2017), 12–16; Helen Lefkowitz Horowitz, *Rereading Sex: Battles over Sexual Knowledge and Suppression in Nineteenth-Century America* (New York: Alfred A. Knopf, 2002), 225–227.
2. Amy Beth Werbel, *Lust on Trial: Censorship and the Rise of American Obscenity in the Age of Anthony Comstock* (New York: Columbia University Press, 2018), 67–69; Tone, *Devices and Desires*, chapters 1 and 2; "An Act for the Suppression of Trade in, and Circulation of, Obscene Literature and Articles of Immoral Use," March 3, 1873, Forty-Second Congress, Sess. III, Ch. 258, 1873, 598–599, memory.loc.gov.
3. Hubert Howe Bancroft, *The Book of the Fair* (Chicago: The Bancroft Company, 1893), 62.
4. "Cairo Street Open: Gates in Midway Plaisance Admit Throngs of Visitors," *Chicago Daily Tribune*, May 28, 1893, 1; "Will Be Like Cairo," *Chicago Daily Tribune*, April 23, 1893, 25; Robert Knutson, *The White City: The World's Columbian Exposition of 1893* (Ann Arbor: University Microfilms, 1960), 224.
5. Werbel, *Lust on Trial*, 77–86; Tone, *Devices*, 53–62; Margot Canaday, Nancy F. Cott, and Robert O. Self, eds., *Intimate States: Gender, Sexuality, and Governance in Modern US History* (Chicago: University of Chicago Press, 2021), 8; Susan Lee Johnson, *Roaring Camp: The Social World of the California Gold Rush* (New York: W. W. Norton, 2000), 162.
6. Giesberg, *Sex and the Civil War*, 61, 65–66; Anthony Comstock, *Traps for the Young*, 2nd ed. (New York: Funk & Wagnalls, 1884), ix.
7. Werbel, *Lust on Trial*, 52–53; Donna Dennis, *Licentious Gotham: Erotic Publishing and*

Its Prosecution in Nineteenth-Century New York (Cambridge, MA: Harvard University Press, 2009), 238–242.

8. Giesberg, *Sex and the Civil War,* 88–89; Werbel, *Lust on Trial,* 58; Dennis, *Licentious Gotham,* 252.
9. Tone, *Devices,* 26–30.
10. Werbel, *Lust on Trial,* 99–101; Jeffrey Escoffier, Whitney Strub, and Jeffrey Patrick Colgan, "The Comstock Apparatus," in Canaday, Cott, and Self, *Intimate States,* 43–45, 48.
11. Escoffier, Strub, and Colgan, "Comstock Apparatus," 43, 54; Janet Farrell Brodie, *Contraception and Abortion in 19th-Century America* (Ithaca: Cornell University Press, 1994), 229–230; Nicholas L. Syrett, *The Trials of Madame Restell: Nineteenth-Century America's Most Infamous Female Physician and the Campaign to Make Abortion a Crime* (New York: The New Press, 2023).
12. *Wonderful Trial of Caroline Lohman, Alias Restell, Reported in Full for the National Police Gazette* (New York: Burgess, Stringer & Co., 1847), HEINOnline.
13. "The Luxury of Crime," *Pomeroy's Illustrated Democrat* (Chicago), June 15, 1878, 6; *Wonderful Trial,* 2.
14. Leslie J. Reagan, *When Abortion Was a Crime: Women, Medicine, and Law in the United States, 1867–1973* (Berkeley: University of California Press, 1997), 10–15; Horatio Robinson Storer, *Criminal Abortion: Its Nature, Its Evidence, and Its Law* (New York: Little, Brown, 1868); James C. Mohr, *Abortion in America: The Origins and Evolution of National Policy, 1800–1900* (New York: Oxford University Press, 1978).
15. "The Criminal Record," *Daily Inter Ocean,* February 12, 1878, 2; Syrett, *Trials of Madame Restell,* 265–278; Tone, *Devices,* 33–34.
16. D. M. Bennett, *Anthony Comstock: His Career of Cruelty and Crime* (New York: Liberal and Scientific Publishing House, 1878), 1070; Syrett, *Trials of Madame Restell,* 279.
17. Werbel, *Lust on Trial,* 59, 105–10, 174–190, 203; Dennis, *Licentious Gotham,* chapter 7.
18. Tone, *Devices,* 32–40; Amy Sohn, *The Man Who Hated Women: Sex, Censorship, and Civil Liberties in the Gilded Age* (New York: Farrar, Straus and Giroux, 2021), 135–145.
19. John D'Emilio and Estelle B. Freedman, *Intimate Matters: A History of Sexuality in America,* 3rd. ed. (Chicago: University of Chicago Press, 2012), 160–161; Sohn, *Man Who Hated Women,* 152–155.
20. D'Emilio and Freedman, *Intimate Matters,* 174.
21. David Jay Pivar, *Purity Crusade: Sexual Morality and Social Control, 1868–1900* (Westport, CT: Greenwood Press, 1973); Barbara Leslie Epstein, *The Politics of Domesticity: Women, Evangelism, and Temperance in Nineteenth-Century America* (Middletown: Wesleyan University Press, 1981); "The Illinois Federation of Colored Women's Clubs," *Broad Axe,* October 19, 1901.
22. Ruth Birgitta Anderson Bordin, *Woman and Temperance: The Quest for Power and Liberty, 1873–1900* (Philadelphia: Temple University Press, 1981), 110–111.
23. Alison M. Parker, *Purifying America: Women, Cultural Reform, and Pro-Censorship Activism, 1873–1933* (Urbana: University of Illinois Press, 1997), chapter 6.
24. Tone, *Devices,* 37–45, chapter 4.
25. Leigh Eric Schmidt, *Heaven's Bride: The Unprintable Life of Ida C. Craddock, American*

Mystic, Scholar, Sexologist, Martyr, and Madwoman (New York: Basic Books, 2010), 16, 18.

26. Schmidt, *Heaven's Bride*, 18; "Egyptian Dancers Arrested," *The Milwaukee Journal*, December 5, 1893, 5; "No More Midway Dancing: Three of the Egyptian Girls Fined $50 Each," *New York Times*, December 7, 1893, 3.
27. Schmidt, *Heaven's Bride*, chapter 2.
28. Schmidt, *Heaven's Bride*, chapter 2.
29. Jesse F. Battan, "'The Word Made Flesh': Language, Authority, and Sexual Desire in Late Nineteenth-Century America," *Journal of the History of Sexuality* 3, no. 2 (1992): 231, 235, quoting Angela Heywood, "Sex Service—Ethics of Trust," *The Word*, October 1889, 2.
30. Tone, *Devices*, 36–40; Battan, "'The Word Made Flesh,'" 241–242; Hal D. Sears, *The Sex Radicals: Free Love in High Victorian America* (Lawrence: Regents Press of Kansas, 1977), 181–182.
31. Craddock pamphlet quoted in Schmidt, *Heaven's Bride*, 28–29.
32. Drew Gilpin Faust, *This Republic of Suffering: Death and the American Civil War* (New York: Alfred A. Knopf, 2008); Schmidt, *Heaven's Bride*, 123–129.
33. Craddock quoted in Schmidt, *Heaven's Bride*, 19, 28–29; *The Danse du Ventre (Dance of the Abdomen) as Performed in the Cairo Street Theatre, Midway Plaisance, Chicago: Its Value as an Educator in Marital Duties* (Philadelphia: n.p., 1893).
34. Schmidt, *Heaven's Bride*, 12, 16–18.
35. Schmidt, *Heaven's Bride*, 190–192, 195–197.
36. Schmidt, *Heaven's Bride*, 1, 212.
37. Ida Craddock, "Regeneration and Rejuvenation of Men and Women, through the Right Use of the Sex Function," 2, n.d., Ida Craddock papers, Special Collections Research Center, Southern Illinois University Carbondale.
38. Craddock, "Regeneration and Rejuvenation," 3.
39. Quoted in Schmidt, *Heaven's Bride*, 214; R. Marie Griffith, *Moral Combat: How Sex Divided American Christians and Fractured American Politics* (New York: Basic Books, 2017).
40. Emma Goldman, "Sex the Great Element for Creative Work," quoted in Candace Falk, *Love, Anarchy, and Emma Goldman*, rev. ed. (New Brunswick: Rutgers University Press, 1990), 99; Clare Hemmings, *Considering Emma Goldman: Feminist Political Ambivalence and the Imaginative Archive* (Durham: Duke University Press, 2018), 11.
41. Christine Stansell, *American Moderns: Bohemian New York and the Creation of a New Century* (New York: Metropolitan Books, 2000), 251–258; Ellen Kay Trimberger, "Feminism, Men, and Modern Love: Greenwich Village, 1900–1925," in *Powers of Desire: The Politics of Sexuality*, eds. Ann Snitow, Christine Stansell, and Sharon Thompson (New York: Monthly Review Press, 1983), 131–152.
42. Christina Simmons, *Making Marriage Modern: Women's Sexuality from the Progressive Era to World War II* (New York: Oxford University Press, 2009), 58; Gertrude Marvin, "Anthony and the Devil," *The Masses* (February 1914), 16; Jean H. Baker, *Margaret Sanger: A Life of Passion* (New York: Hill and Wang, 2011); Leigh Ann Wheeler, *How Sex Became a Civil Liberty* (New York: Oxford University Press, 2013), chapter 1.
43. Margaret Sanger, *Margaret Sanger: An Autobiography* (1938; reprint, New York: Dover Publications 1971), 215–223; Ellen Chesler, *Woman of Valor: Margaret Sanger and the*

Birth Control Movement in America (New York: Simon & Schuster, 1992), 168; Tone, *Devices*, 118; Cathy Moran Hajo, *Birth Control on Main Street: Organizing Clinics in the United States* (Urbana: University of Illinois Press, 2010), 12.

44. Sanger, *Autobiography*, 214–223, 230; Chesler, *Woman of Valor*, 159–160; Hajo, *Birth Control on Main Street*, 159; Tone, *Devices*, 106–108.

45. Mary Ware Dennett, *The Sex Side of Life: An Explanation for Young People*, rev. ed. (Woodside, NY: The author, 1928), 13.

46. Wheeler, *How Sex Became a Civil Liberty*, 35, 40–43; Lauren MacIvor Thompson, "The Politics of Female Pain: Women's Citizenship, Twilight Sleep and the Early Birth Control Movement," *Medical Humanities* 45, no. 1 (2019): 67–74.

47. Dennett, *The Sex Side of Life*.

48. Elizabeth Evens, "Plainclothes Policewomen on the Trail: NYPD Undercover Investigations of Abortionists and Queer Women, 1913–1926," *Modern American History* 4, no. 1 (2021): 49–66.

49. Robert Allen, *Horrible Prettiness: Burlesque and American Culture* (Chapel Hill: University of North Carolina Press, 1991), 230; Morton Minsky and Milk Machlin, *Minsky's Burlesque* (New York: Arbor House, 1986), 75; Andrea Friedman, *Prurient Interests: Gender, Democracy, and Obscenity in New York, 1909–1945* (New York: Columbia University Press, 2000), 66–68.

50. Shirley J. Burton, "Obscene, Lewd, and Lascivious: Ida Craddock and the Criminally Obscene Women of Chicago, 1873–1913," *Michigan Historical Review* 19, no. 1 (1993): 16; Knutson, *White City*, 224–225.

51. For an example, "Sally Rand-Fan Dance (1942)," see https://archive.org/details/youtube-zYeUx4kOQwI, YouTube.

Chapter 10: Plays Too Stirring for a Boy Your Age

1. Thirteenth Census of the United States, 1910 (NARA microfilm publication T624, 1,178 rolls), Records of the Bureau of the Census, Record Group 29, National Archives, Washington, DC, Ancestry.com; Robert Clyde Allen, *Horrible Prettiness: Burlesque and American Culture* (Chapel Hill: University of North Carolina Press, 1991), 192–193, 225; Andrea Friedman, *Prurient Interests: Gender, Democracy, and Obscenity in New York City, 1909–1945* (New York: Columbia University Press, 2000), 65; Gilberta R. Jacobs, "Burlesque Comes to Detroit," *Michigan Jewish History* 44 (2004): 38; Advertisement for Dewey, *The Plain Dealer*, February 18, 1900; Advertisement for Empire Theater, *The Plain Dealer*, September 10, 1905.

2. "Manuel Levine," in *The Judicial Biographies of the Municipal Court of Cleveland, 1912–2017* (n.d.), 566, clevelandmunicipalcourt.org; "Levine, Manuel V.," *Encyclopedia of Cleveland History*, Case Western Reserve University, www.case.edu/ech/; "Manuel Levine's Work," *The Plain Dealer*, October 27, 1907; "Burlesque Not for Boys," *The Plain Dealer*, October 18, 1909.

3. Alison M. Parker, *Purifying America: Women, Cultural Reform, and Pro-Censorship Activism, 1873–1933* (Urbana: University of Illinois Press, 1997), chapter 4; Leigh Ann Wheeler, "Battling over Burlesque: Conflicts Between Maternalism, Paternalism, and Organized Labor, Minneapolis, Minnesota, 1920–1932," *Frontiers* 20, no. 2 (1999): 148–174; Friedman, *Prurient Interests*, chapter 2.

4. *The Plain Dealer*, "Burlesque Not for Boys"; Jeffrey P. Moran, *Teaching Sex: The Shaping of Adolescence in the 20th Century* (Cambridge, MA: Harvard University Press, 2000).
5. Nicholas L. Syrett, "Age Disparity, Marriage, and the Gendering of Heterosexuality," in *Heterosexual Histories*, eds. Rebecca L. Davis and Michele Mitchell (New York: New York University Press, 2021), 96–119; Nicholas L. Syrett, *American Child Bride: A History of Minors and Marriage in the United States* (Chapel Hill: University of North Carolina Press, 2016); Stephen Robertson, *Crimes Against Children: Sexual Violence and Legal Culture in New York City, 1880–1960* (Chapel Hill: University of North Carolina Press, 2005), chapter 3.
6. Moran, *Teaching Sex*, chapter 1.
7. Gail Bederman, *Manliness and Civilization: A Cultural History of Gender and Race in the United States, 1880–1917* (Chicago: University of Chicago Press, 1995), chapter 3, 198–199.
8. Rebecca M. Kluchin, *Fit to Be Tied: Sterilization and Reproductive Rights in America, 1950–1980* (New Brunswick: Rutgers University Press, 2009), 15; Molly Ladd-Taylor, *Fixing the Poor: Eugenic Sterilization and Child Welfare in the Twentieth Century* (Baltimore: Johns Hopkins University Press, 2017); Alexandra Minna Stern, *Eugenic Nation: Faults and Frontiers of Better Breeding in Modern America* (Berkeley: University of California Press, 2005); Nancy Ordover, *American Eugenics: Race, Queer Anatomy, and the Science of Nationalism* (Minneapolis: University of Minnesota Press, 2003), part I; Wendy Kline, *Building a Better Race: Gender, Sexuality, and Eugenics from the Turn of the Century to the Baby Boom* (Berkeley: University of California Press, 2001); Daniel J. Kevles, *In the Name of Eugenics: Genetics and the Uses of Human Heredity* (New York: Alfred A. Knopf, 1985); Rebecca L. Davis, *More Perfect Unions: The American Search for Marital Bliss* (Cambridge, MA: Harvard University Press, 2010), chapter 1.
9. Moran, *Teaching Sex*, chapter 1; Bederman, *Manliness*, chapter 3.
10. Beth Bailey, *From Front Porch to Back Seat: Courtship in Twentieth-Century America* (Baltimore: Johns Hopkins University Press, 1988); David Nasaw, *Going Out: The Rise and Fall of Public Amusements* (New York: Basic Books, 1993); Kathy Peiss, *Cheap Amusements: Working Women and Leisure in Turn-of-the-Century New York* (Philadelphia: Temple University Press, 1986); John F. Kasson, *Amusing the Million: Coney Island at the Turn of the Century* (New York: Hill and Wang, 1978); Catherine Cocks, "Rethinking Sexuality in the Progressive Era," *Journal of the Gilded Age and Progressive Era* 5, no. 2 (2006): 93–118; Nan Enstad, *Ladies of Labor, Girls of Adventure: Working Women, Popular Culture, and Labor Politics at the Turn of the Twentieth Century* (New York: Columbia University Press, 1999); Lauren Rabinovitz, *For the Love of Pleasure: Women, Movies, and Culture in Turn-of-the-Century Chicago* (New Brunswick: Rutgers University Press, 1998).
11. Elizabeth Alice Clement, *Love for Sale: Courting, Treating, and Prostitution in New York City, 1900–1945* (Chapel Hill: University of North Carolina Press, 2006); Christina Simmons, *Making Marriage Modern: Women's Sexuality from the Progressive Era to World War II* (New York: Oxford University Press, 2009).
12. Don Romesburg, "'Wouldn't a Boy Do?': Placing Early-Twentieth-Century Male Youth Sex Work into Histories of Sexuality," *Journal of the History of Sexuality* 18, no. 3 (2009): 367–392.

13. Sharon R. Ullman, *Sex Seen: The Emergence of Modern Sexuality in America* (Berkeley: University of California Press, 1997), chapter 2.
14. Kevin White, *The First Sexual Revolution: The Emergence of Male Heterosexuality in Modern America* (New York: New York University Press, 1993).
15. Kathy Peiss, *Hope in a Jar: The Making of America's Beauty Culture* (New York: Owl Books, 1998), 191; Julio Capó, *Welcome to Fairyland: Queer Miami Before 1940* (Chapel Hill: University of North Carolina Press, 2017), 198–199, 225–227; "Club Women See Mild Burlesque," *The Plain Dealer,* January 1, 1907; Wheeler, "Battling over Burlesque," 148, 151, 158; Morton Minsky and Milt Machlin, *Minsky's Burlesque* (New York: Arbor House, 1986), 32–33.
16. Mary E. Odem, *Delinquent Daughters: Protecting and Policing Adolescent Female Sexuality in the United States, 1885–1920* (Chapel Hill: University of North Carolina Press, 1995), 13; Robertson, *Crimes Against Children,* chapter 4.
17. Ullman, *Sex Seen,* 28–44; Estelle B. Freedman, *Redefining Rape: Sexual Violence in the Era of Suffrage and Segregation* (Cambridge, MA: Harvard University Press, 2013), chapter 7.
18. Pablo Mitchell, *Coyote Nation: Sexuality, Race, and Conquest in Modernizing New Mexico, 1880–1920* (Chicago: University of Chicago Press, 2005), 68–72; Odem, *Delinquent Daughters,* 51, 163.
19. Cheryl D. Hicks, *Talk with You Like a Woman: African American Women, Justice, and Reform in New York, 1890–1935* (Chapel Hill: University of North Carolina Press, 2010), chapter 6; Robertson, *Crimes Against Children,* chapter 5; Ruth Alexander, *The "Girl Problem": Female Sexual Delinquency in New York, 1900–1930* (Ithaca: Cornell University Press, 1995), 105–122.
20. Hicks, *Talk with You,* 183–186; Alexander, *The "Girl Problem,"* 34.
21. Hicks, *Talk with You,* chapter 6; Regina G. Kunzel, *Fallen Women, Problem Girls: Unmarried Mothers and the Professionalization of Social Work, 1890–1945* (New Haven: Yale University Press, 1993); Karin L. Zipf, *Bad Girls at Samarcand: Sexuality and Sterilization in a Southern Juvenile Reformatory* (Baton Rouge: Louisiana State University Press, 2016); Odem, *Delinquent Daughters,* 155–156.
22. Philip A. Bruce, *The Plantation Negro as Freeman* (New York: Putnam, 1889); Dorothy E. Roberts, *Killing the Black Body: Race, Reproduction, and the Meaning of Liberty* (New York: Pantheon Books, 1997), 11–12.
23. Paula Giddings, *Ida: A Sword Among Lions: Ida B. Wells and the Campaign Against Lynching* (New York: Amistad, 2008), 269, 294–295.
24. Ida B. Wells, "Class Legislation," in *The Reason Why the Colored American Is Not in the World's Columbian Exposition* (Chicago: Privately published, 1893), 17, *Black Thought and Culture*; "Railroads and Colored Passengers," *Huntsville Gazette,* February 10, 1883; Evelyn Brooks Higginbotham, *Righteous Discontent: The Women's Movement in the Black Baptist Church, 1880–1920* (Cambridge, MA: Harvard University Press, 1993), chapter 7; Kevin Kelly Gaines, *Uplifting the Race: Black Leadership, Politics, and Culture in the Twentieth Century* (Chapel Hill: University of North Carolina Press, 1996); Michele Mitchell, *Righteous Propagation: African Americans and the Politics of Racial Destiny after Reconstruction* (Chapel Hill: University of North Carolina Press, 2004); Pippa Holloway, *Sexuality, Politics, and Social Control in Virginia, 1920–1945* (Chapel Hill: University of North Carolina Press, 2006), 89; Roberts, *Killing,* 85–86;

Simmons, *Making Marriage Modern*, chapter 1; Darlene Clark Hine, "Rape and the Inner Lives of Black Women in the Middle West: Preliminary Thoughts on the Culture of Dissemblance," *Signs: Journal of Women in Culture & Society* 14, no. 4 (1989): 912–920.

25. Mitchell, *Righteous Propagation*, 76–78, 87–88, 103–104, and chapter 3; Alison M. Parker, *Unceasing Militant: The Life of Mary Church Terrell* (Chapel Hill: University of North Carolina Press, 2021), 132–135; Cookie Woolner, *The Famous Lady Lovers: Black Women and Queer Desire Before Stonewall* (Chapel Hill: University of North Carolina Press, 2023), 29.

26. Lucie Cheng Hirata, "Chinese Immigrant Women in Nineteenth-Century California," in *Women of America: A History*, eds. Carol Ruth Berkin and Mary Beth Norton (Boston: Houghton Mifflin Co., 1979), 223–241; Amy Haruko Sueyoshi, *Discriminating Sex: White Leisure and the Making of the American "Oriental"* (Urbana: University of Illinois Press, 2018), 147–148; Yuji Ichioka, "Ameyuki-San: Japanese Prostitutes in Nineteenth-Century America," *Amerasia Journal* 4, no. 1 (1977): 2.

27. Eithne Luibhéid, *Entry Denied: Controlling Sexuality at the Border* (Minneapolis: University of Minnesota Press, 2002), chapter 2; Erika Lee, *At America's Gates: Chinese Immigration During the Exclusion Era, 1882–1943* (Chapel Hill: University of North Carolina Press, 2003); George A. Peffer, *If They Don't Bring Their Women Here: Chinese Female Immigration Before Exclusion* (Urbana: University of Illinois Press, 1999).

28. Peggy Pascoe, *Relations of Rescue: The Search for Female Moral Authority in the American West, 1874–1939* (New York: Oxford University Press, 1990), 94–95; Erika Lee, *America for Americans: A History of Xenophobia in the United States* (New York: Basic Books, 2021), chapter 3; Beth Lew-Williams, *The Chinese Must Go: Violence, Exclusion, and the Making of the Alien in America* (Cambridge, MA: Harvard University Press, 2018), 44–45; Judy Tzu-Chun Wu, "'Deviant Heterosexuality' and Model-Minority Families: Asian American History and Racialized Heterosexuality," in Davis and Mitchell, *Heterosexual Histories*, 124–129; Victor Jew, "'Chinese Demons': The Violent Articulation of Chinese Otherness and Interracial Sexuality in the U.S. Midwest, 1885–1889," *Journal of Social History* 37, no. 2 (2003): 389–410.

29. Joanne J. Meyerowitz, *Women Adrift: Independent Wage Earners in Chicago, 1880–1930* (Chicago: University of Chicago Press, 1988), 120–122.

30. Clement, *Love for Sale*, 79–80; Kevin J. Mumford, *Interzones: Black/White Sex Districts in Chicago and New York in the Early Twentieth Century* (New York: Columbia University Press, 1997), chapter 6.

31. Between 1913 and 1918, the United States deported about four hundred people per year for involvement with the sex industry. Stephen Robertson, "Harlem Undercover: Vice Investigators, Race, and Prostitution, 1910–1930," *Journal of Urban History* 35, no. 4 (2009): 499–500; Eva Payne, "Deportation as Rescue: White Slaves, Women Reformers, and the U.S. Bureau of Immigration," *Journal of Women's History* 33, no. 4 (2021): 43–44, 57; Grace Peña Delgado, "Border Control and Sexual Policing: White Slavery and Prostitution Along the U.S.–Mexico Borderlands, 1903–1910," *Western Historical Quarterly* 43, no. 2 (2012): 157–178; Stern, *Eugenic Nation*, chapter 2; Allan M. Brandt, *No Magic Bullet: A Social History of Venereal Disease in the United States Since 1880*, 2nd ed. (New York: Oxford University Press, 1987), chapter 2.

32. Jessica R. Pliley, *Policing Sexuality: The Mann Act and the Making of the FBI* (Cambridge,

MA: Harvard University Press, 2014); David J. Langum, *Crossing over the Line: Legislating Morality and the Mann Act* (Chicago: University of Chicago Press, 1994), 9–11.

33. Pliley, *Policing Sexuality*, 101–103.
34. Brandt, *No Magic Bullet*, 80–82.
35. Brandt, *No Magic Bullet*, 10–11, 77, 116.
36. Pliley, *Policing Sexuality*, 118–129; Estelle B. Freedman, *Their Sisters' Keepers: Women's Prison Reform in America, 1830–1930* (Ann Arbor: University of Michigan Press, 1979), chapter 7.
37. Brandt, *No Magic Bullet*, 62–63, 69; Simmons, *Making Marriage Modern*, 26; Walter Clarke, "Social Hygiene and the War," *Social Hygiene* 4 (April 1918): 294–297.

Chapter 11: A Society of Queers

1. Nicholas L. Syrett, *An Open Secret: The Family Story of Robert and John Gregg Allerton* (Chicago: University of Chicago Press, 2021), 48–49.
2. Sharon R. Ullman, *Sex Seen: The Emergence of Modern Sexuality in America* (Berkeley: University of California Press, 1997), 63–64; Syrett, *Open Secret*, 41; Julio Capó, *Welcome to Fairyland: Queer Miami Before 1940* (Chapel Hill: University of North Carolina Press, 2017), 96–98, 101–104, 112–131, 120–123, 163–165; Amy Haruko Sueyoshi, *Queer Compulsions: Race, Nation, and Sexuality in the Affairs of Yone Noguchi* (Honolulu: University of Hawai'I Press, 2012); Amy Haruko Sueyoshi, *Discriminating Sex: White Leisure and the Making of the American "Oriental"* (Urbana: University of Illinois Press, 2018), chapter 5.
3. Sueyoshi, *Discriminating Sex*, 151.
4. "Confessions Disclose Vice Ring in S.F.," *San Francisco Chronicle*, February 28, 1918, 2; "Four S.F. Vice Hearings Today," *San Francisco Chronicle*, March 15, 1918, 10; "Vice Fugitive on Way to Honduras," *San Francisco Chronicle*, May 24, 1918, 2; "Baker Street Vice Case Thrown Out of Court," *San Francisco Chronicle*, January 11, 1919, 8; Sueyoshi, *Discriminating Sex*, 151–155.
5. "First of Twenty Vice Defendants Convicted," *San Francisco Chronicle*, June 11, 1918, 4; 82 Cal. App. 17 (Cal. Ct. App. 1927), 255 p. 212, casetext.com/case/people-v-parsons-45; "In re Application of Clarence Lockett for a Writ of Habeus Corpus," Supreme Court of California, January 19, 1919, 582–83, 179 Cal. 581 (Cal. 1919), casetext.com/case/in-re-lockett#p582.
6. Peter Boag, *Same-Sex Affairs: Constructing and Controlling Homosexuality in the Pacific Northwest* (Berkeley: University of California Press, 2003), 157–168; Nayan Shah, *Stranger Intimacy: Contesting Race, Sexuality, and the Law in the American West* (Berkeley: University of California Press, 2011).
7. George Chauncey, "Christian Brotherhood or Sexual Perversion? Homosexual Identities and the Construction of Sexual Boundaries in the World War One Era," *Journal of Social History* 19, no. 2 (1985): 192.
8. Chauncey, "Christian Brotherhood," 192; George Chauncey, *Gay New York: Gender, Urban Culture, and the Making of the Gay Male World, 1890–1940* (New York: Basic Books, 1994), 12–13, 86–89; Boag, *Same-Sex Affairs*, 25–30; Chad C. Heap, *Slumming: Sexual and Racial Encounters in American Nightlife, 1885–1940* (Chicago: University of Chicago Press, 2009), 10.

9. Boag *Same-Sex Affairs*, 28; Capó, *Welcome to Fairyland*, 164–165.
10. Boag, *Same-Sex Affairs*, 1–6, chapters 3 and 4.
11. Boag, *Same-Sex Affairs*, 50.
12. Shah, *Stranger Intimacy*, 76–79, 150; Brian Stack, "From Sodomists to Citizens: Same-Sex Sexuality and the Progressive Era Washington State Reformatory," *Journal of the History of Sexuality* 28, no. 2 (2019): 185.
13. Hugh Ryan, *When Brookly Was Queer* (New York: St. Martin's Press, 2019), 83–89.
14. Margot Canaday, *The Straight State: Sexuality and Citizenship in Twentieth-Century America* (Princeton: Princeton University Press, 2009), 29–37; Jennifer Terry, *An American Obsession: Science, Medicine, and Homosexuality in Modern Society* (Chicago: University of Chicago Press, 1999), 43–50, 78–79; Susan M. Schweik, *The Ugly Laws: Disability in Public* (New York: New York University Press, 2009), chapter 6.
15. John Donald Gustav-Wrathall, *Take the Young Stranger by the Hand: Same-Sex Relations and the YMCA* (Chicago: University of Chicago Press, 1998); Chauncey, "Christian Brotherhood," 198–199; Chauncey, *Gay New York*, 155–159; Kathryn Lofton, "Queering Fundamentalism: John Balcom Shaw and the Sexuality of a Protestant Orthodoxy," *Journal of the History of Sexuality* 17, no. 3 (2008): 439–468.
16. Chauncey, *Gay New York*, 101–111.
17. Nan Alamilla Boyd, *Wide-Open Town: A History of Queer San Francisco to 1965* (Berkeley: University of California Press, 2003), 261n7.
18. Heap, *Slumming*, 84–85.
19. Judy Tzu-Chun Wu, *Doctor Mom Chung of the Fair-Haired Bastards: The Life of a Wartime Celebrity* (Berkeley: University of California Press, 2005), 98–99, chapter 7.
20. Ullman, *Sex Seen*, 51–55; Daniel Hurewitz, *Bohemian Los Angeles and the Making of Modern Politics* (Berkeley: University of California Press, 2007), 118–122; Chauncey, *Gay New York*, chapter 11; Heap, *Slumming*, 82–96, chapter 6; Esther Newton, "The Mythic Mannish Lesbian: Radclyffe Hall and the New Woman," *Signs: Journal of Women in Culture & Society* 9, no. 4 (1984): 557–575.
21. Heap, *Slumming*, chapter 6.
22. Heap, *Slumming*, 83–96, 232–233; Kevin J. Mumford, *Interzones: Black/White Sex Districts in Chicago and New York in the Early Twentieth Century* (New York: Columbia University Press, 1997).
23. Joanne J. Meyerowitz, *Women Adrift: Independent Wage Earners in Chicago, 1880–1930* (Chicago: University of Chicago Press, 1988), chapter 5; Stephen Robertson, Shane White, Stephen Garton, and Graham White, "Disorderly Houses: Residences, Privacy, and the Surveillance of Sexuality in 1920s Harlem," *Journal of the History of Sexuality* 21, no. 3 (2012): 443–466.
24. All quotations and details of Mabel Hampton's life are from Joan Nestle, "The Bodies I Have Lived With: Keynote for 18th Lesbian Lives Conference, Brighton, England, 2011," *Journal of Lesbian Studies* 17, nos. 3–4 (2013): 215–239; "Excerpts from the Oral History of Mabel Hampton," *Signs: Journal of Women in Culture & Society* 18, no. 4 (1993): 925–935; Joan Nestle, "'I Lift My Face to the Hill': The Life of Mabel Hampton as Told by a White Woman," in *Queer Ideas: The David R. Kessler Lectures in Lesbian and Gay Studies* (New York: Feminist Press at the City University of New York, 2003), 23–48; "Mabel Hampton (1902–1989)," in *The Persistent Desire: A Femme-Butch*

Reader, ed. Joan Nestle (Boston: Alyson Publications, Inc., 1992), 43–44; and "Oral History Recordings," Lesbian Herstory Archives, http://herstories.prattinfoschool.nyc/omeka/exhibits/show/mabel-hampton-oral-history/oral-history-recordings.

25. Robert Clyde Allen, *Horrible Prettiness: Burlesque and American Culture* (Chapel Hill: University of North Carolina Press, 1991), 276–277; Heap, *Slumming*, 234–236; Chauncey, *Gay New York*, 130, 296–297, 311–313; J. D. Doyle, "Hamilton Lodge Ball," Queer Music Heritage, last updated 2015, https://queermusicheritage.com/nov2014hamilton.html; Tim Lawrence, "A History of Drag Balls, Houses, and the Culture of Voguing," in Chantal Regnault (photographer), *Voguing and the House Ballroom Scene of New York City 1989–92* (London: Soul Jazz Books, 2011), 3.
26. Cookie Woolner, *The Famous Lady Lovers: Black Women and Queer Desire Before Stonewall* (Chapel Hill: University of North Carolina Press, 2023), 123–125.
27. Robertson et al, "Disorderly Houses," 464; Cynthia M. Blair, *I've Got to Make My Livin': Black Women's Sex Work in Turn-of-the-Century Chicago* (Chicago: University of Chicago Press, 2010), 175–180, 205–215; Victoria W. Wolcott, *Remaking Respectability: African American Women in Interwar Detroit* (Chapel Hill: University of North Carolina Press, 2001), 106–109; Woolner, *Famous Lady Lovers*, 73–83; Stephen Robertson, "Harlem Undercover: Vice Investigators, Race, and Prostitution, 1910–1930," *Journal of Urban History* 35, no. 4 (2009): 499–500.
28. Heap, *Slumming*, 260–264; Woolner, *Famous Lady Lovers*, chapter 2; Hazel Carby, "'It Jus Be's Dat Way Sometime': The Sexual Politics of Women's Blues," in *Unequal Sisters*, eds. Ellen Carol DuBois and Vicki L. Ruiz (New York: Routledge, 1990), 238–249.
29. Woolner, *Famous Lady Lovers*, 139; Elizabeth Lapovsky Kennedy and Madeline D. Davis, *Boots of Leather, Slippers of Gold: The History of a Lesbian Community* (New York: Routledge, 1993), 7.
30. Cheryl D. Hicks, *Talk with You Like a Woman: African American Women, Justice, and Reform in New York, 1890–1935* (Chapel Hill: University of North Carolina Press, 2010), 210–211.
31. Woolner, *Lady Lovers*, 28; Blair, *Make My Livin'*, chapter 3; Meyerowitz, *Women Adrift*, 114.
32. Hicks, *Talk with You*, 224; Woolner, *Famous Lady Lovers*, 10; Estelle B. Freedman, "The Prison Lesbian: Race, Class, and the Construction of the Aggressive Female Homosexual, 1915–1965," *Feminist Studies* 22, no. 2 (1996): 397; Regina Kunzel, *Criminal Intimacy: Prison and the Uneven History of Modern American Sexuality* (Chicago: University of Chicago Press, 2008), 28–33.
33. Hicks, *Talk with You*, 240, 250; Woolner, *Famous Lady Lovers*, 89. Hampton told Nestle that a nosy neighbor had reported her to the parole officer.
34. Chauncey, *Gay New York*, 334–342; Anna Lvovsky, *Vice Patrol: Cops, Courts, and the Struggle over Urban Gay Life before Stonewall* (Chicago: University of Chicago Press, 2021), chapter 1; Heap, *Slumming*, 90–93; Capó, *Welcome to Fairyland*.
35. Boyd, *Wide-Open*, 44–56.
36. Woolner, *Famous Lady Lovers*, 6, 29–31; Chauncey, *Gay New York*, 254–257; Michele Mitchell, *Righteous Propagation: African Americans and the Politics of Racial Destiny After Reconstruction* (Chapel Hill: University of North Carolina Press, 2004), 220–222.
37. Woolner, *Famous Lady Lovers*, 138.

38. Mabel Hampton said this to Joan Nestle in 1981, when she was eighty; quoted in Nestle, "Bodies," 218.

Chapter 12: Scientific Methods

1. Sarah E. Igo, *The Averaged American: Surveys, Citizens, and the Making of a Mass Public* (Cambridge, MA: Harvard University Press, 2007), 218–219; Paul H. Gebhard and Alan B. Johnson, *The Kinsey Data: Marginal Tabulations of the 1938–1963 Interviews Conducted by the Institute for Sex Research* (Bloomington: Indiana University Press, 1979), 11–20, questions cited, in order, 223, 151, 126, 145, 239.
2. Alfred C. Kinsey, Wardell B. Pomeroy, and Clyde E. Martin, *Sexual Behavior in the Human Male* (Bloomington: Indiana University Press, 1948), 158; Donna J. Drucker, *The Classification of Sex: Alfred Kinsey and the Organization of Knowledge* (Pittsburgh: University of Pittsburgh Press, 2014), 107–114, chapter 5; Janice M. Irvine, *Disorders of Desire: Sex and Gender in Modern American Sexology* (Philadelphia: Temple University Press, 1990), 31.
3. Igo, *Averaged American*, 194–195, 215; Drucker, *Classification of Sex*, chapter 4, 120.
4. Drucker, *Classification of Sex*, chapter 3; Regina Markell Morantz, "The Scientist as Sex Crusader: Alfred C. Kinsey and American Culture," *American Quarterly* 29, no. 5 (1977): 567; Jonathan Gathorne-Hardy, *Sex the Measure of All Things: A Life of Alfred C. Kinsey* (Bloomington: Indiana University Press, 2000); James H. Jones, *Alfred C. Kinsey: A Public / Private Life* (New York: W. W. Norton, 1997).
5. Drucker, *Classification of Sex*, 67–69; LaKisha Michelle Simmons, "'To Lay Aside All Morals': Respectability, Sexuality and Black College Students in the United States in the 1930s," *Gender & History* 24, no. 2 (2012): 442.
6. Jeffrey P. Moran, *Teaching Sex: The Shaping of Adolescence in the 20th Century* (Cambridge, MA: Harvard University Press, 2000), 15, chapter 2; Kristy L. Slominski, *Teaching Moral Sex: A History of Religion and Sex Education in the United States* (New York: Oxford University Press, 2021), 37–47, 79–86; Christina Simmons, *Making Marriage Modern: Women's Sexuality from the Progressive Era to World War II* (New York: Oxford University Press, 2009), 26–27.
7. Marie Carmichael Stopes, *Married Love: A New Contribution to the Solution of Sex Difficulties* (New York: Eugenics Publishing Co., 1932), viii, chapter 10; Simmons, *Making Marriage Modern*, chapter 5; Jennifer Terry, *An American Obsession: Science, Medicine, and Homosexuality in Modern Society* (Chicago: University of Chicago Press, 1999), 124; Theodoor H. van de Velde, *Ideal Marriage: Its Physiology and Technique*, trans. Stella Browne (New York: Random House, 1930 [1926]), 6.
8. Oliver M. Butterfield, "To Live Happily Even After," *The Reader's Digest*, May 1936, 27, 30.
9. Simmons, *Making Marriage Modern*, 188–207; Peter Laipson, "'Kiss Without Shame, for She Desires It': Sexual Foreplay in American Marital Advice Literature, 1900–1925," *Journal of Social History* 29, no. 3 (1996): 507–525; Michael Gordon, "From an Unfortunate Necessity to a Cult of Mutual Orgasm, 1830–1940," in *Studies in the Sociology of Sex*, ed. James Heslin (New York: Appleton-Century-Crofts, 1971), 53–77; Annamarie Jagose, *Orgasmology* (Durham: Duke University Press, 2013), chapter 1; Jessamyn Neuhaus, "The Importance of Being Orgasmic: Sexuality, Gender, and Mar-

ital Sex Manuals in the United States, 1920–1963," *Journal of the History of Sexuality* 9, no. 4 (2000): 447–473.

10. Drucker, *Classification of Sex*, 83.
11. Vern L. Bullough, *Science in the Bedroom: A History of Sex Research* (New York: Basic Books, 1994), 118–119.
12. Terry, *American Obsession*, 128–129, 195–196; David Allyn, "Private Acts/Public Policy: Alfred Kinsey, the American Law Institute and the Privatization of American Sexual Morality," *Journal of American Studies* 30, no. 3 (1996): 408–409.
13. Drucker, *Classification of Sex*, 70, 90–92; Katharine Bement Davis, *Factors in the Sex Life of Twenty-Two Hundred Women* (New York: Harper & Brothers, 1929), ix, xi, xvii; Terry, *American Obsession*, 129–135; Bullough, *Science in the Bedroom*, 112–118. See also Anya Jabour, "Out of the Closet? Reconstructing the Personal Life of Pioneering Sex Researcher Katharine Bement Davis," *Journal of the History of the Behavioral Sciences* 58, no. 4 (2022): 459–466.
14. Joanne Meyerowitz, "Sex Research at the Borders of Gender: Transvestites, Transsexuals, and Alfred C. Kinsey," *Bulletin of the History of Medicine* 75, no. 1 (2001): 82–86.
15. Henry L. Minton, *Departing from Deviance: A History of Homosexual Rights and Emancipatory Science in America* (Chicago: University of Chicago Press, 2002).
16. Joanne Meyerowitz, "'How Common Culture Shapes the Separate Lives': Sexuality, Race, and Mid-Twentieth-Century Social Constructionist Thought," *Journal of American History* 96, no. 4 (2010): 1067–1069.
17. Drucker, *Classification of Sex*, chapter 5; Alfred C. Kinsey, Wardell B. Pomeroy, Clyde E. Martin, and Paul Gebhard, *Sexual Behavior in the Human Female* (Bloomington: Indiana University Press, 1953), 5–16.
18. Igo, *Averaged American*, 219. Kinsey's team gathered more life histories from transgender individuals after 1948, an effort aided by trans activist Louise Lawrence, who introduced him to other "transvestites" and shaped Kinsey's understanding of cross-dressing as a significant category of human sexual behavior; see Meyerowitz, "Sex Research at the Borders of Gender," 72–90; Irvine, *Disorders of Desire*, 23–25.
19. Drucker, *Classification of Sex*, 142; Gathorne-Hardy, *Measure of All Things*, chapter 14; Igo, *Averaged American*, 237.
20. Kinsey et al, *SBHM*, 623.
21. Gathorne-Hardy, *Measure of All Things*, 168–169, 247–248.
22. Terry, *American Obsession*, 300–301.
23. Allan Bérubé, *Coming Out Under Fire: The History of Gay Men and Women in World War II* (Chapel Hill: University of North Carolina Press, 1990), 12; James H. Capshew, *Psychologists on the March: Science, Practice, and Professional Identity in America, 1929–1969* (Cambridge: Cambridge University Press, 1999); Ellen Herman, *The Romance of American Psychology: Political Culture in the Age of Experts* (Berkeley: University of California Press, 1995), 88–109.
24. Kinsey et al., *SBHF*, 282, 286, 298–302, 416 (extramarital sex), 453 (homosexual contact). In addition to vaginal sexual intercourse, sources of premarital outlet reported by the women surveyed included heterosexual and homosexual "petting"—defined as sexual stimulation other than coitus (227)—masturbation, and nocturnal dreams.
25. Igo, *Averaged American*, 220; Terry, *American Obsession*, 302; Morantz, "Scientist as Sex Crusader," 584; Irvine, *Disorders of Desire*, 25.

26. Marilyn E. Hegarty, *Victory Girls, Khaki-Wackies and Patriotutes: The Regulation of Female Sexuality During World War II* (New York: New York University Press, 2008); Anne Gray Fischer, *The Streets Belong to Us: Sex, Race, and Police Power from Segregation to Gentrification* (Chapel Hill: University of North Carolina Press, 2022), chapter 2.
27. Robert Westbrook, *Why We Fought: Forging American Obligations in World War II* (Washington, DC: Smithsonian Books, 2004), chapter 3; Meghan K. Winchell, *Good Girls, Good Food, Good Fun: The Story of USO Hostesses During World War II* (Chapel Hill: University of North Carolina Press, 2008); Joanne Meyerowitz, "Women, Cheesecake, and Borderline Material: Responses to Girlie Pictures in the Mid-Twentieth-Century U.S.," *Journal of Women's History* 8, no. 3 (1996): 9–35.
28. Amanda H. Littauer, *Bad Girls: Young Women, Sex, and Rebellion before the Sixties* (Chapel Hill: University of North Carolina Press, 2015), 86–96. See also Miriam G. Reumann, *American Sexual Character: Sex, Gender, and National Identity in the Kinsey Reports* (Berkeley: University of California Press, 2005), chapter 3.
29. R. Marie Griffith, *Moral Combat: How Sex Divided American Christians and Fractured American Politics* (New York: Basic Books, 2017), chapter 4.
30. Griffith, *Moral Combat*, 141–147; Irvine, *Disorders of Desire*, 42–43; Igo, *Averaged American*, 203–205.
31. Igo, *Averaged American*, 206–207.
32. Irvine, *Disorders of Desire*, 33; Estelle B. Freedman, "'Uncontrolled Desires': The Response to the Sexual Psychopath, 1920–1960," *Journal of American History* 74, no. 1 (1987): 89–91, 97–98.
33. Margot Canaday, *The Straight State: Sexuality and Citizenship in Twentieth-Century America* (Princeton: Princeton University Press, 2009), 219; Geoffrey R. Stone, *Sex and the Constitution: Sex, Religion, and Law from America's Origins to the Twenty-First Century* (New York: Liveright, 2017), 248–249.
34. David J. Garrow, *Liberty and Sexuality: The Right to Privacy and the Making of* Roe v. Wade (Berkeley: University of California Press, 1998), 277; Sarah E. Igo, *The Known Citizen: A History of Privacy in Modern America* (Cambridge, MA: Harvard University Press, 2018), 147; Melissa Murray, "Sexual Liberty and Criminal Law Reform," in *Reproductive Rights and Justice Stories*, eds. Melissa Murray, Katherine Shaw, and Reva B. Siegal (St. Paul: West Academic Publishing, 2019), 26–27; Leigh Ann Wheeler, *How Sex Became a Civil Liberty* (New York: Oxford University Press, 2013), chapter 4.
35. See, for example, Judith A. Reisman, Edward W. Eichel, Muir J. Gordon, and J. H. Court, *Kinsey, Sex and Fraud: The Indoctrination of a People* (Lafayette, LA: Huntington House Publishers, 1990).
36. Martin Meeker, *Contacts Desired: Gay and Lesbian Communications and Community, 1940s–1970s* (Chicago: University of Chicago Press, 2006), chapter 1; Lillian Faderman, *The Gay Revolution: The Story of the Struggle* (New York: Simon & Schuster, 2015), 54–61.
37. John D'Emilio, *Sexual Politics, Sexual Communities: The Making of a Homosexual Minority in the United States, 1940–1970* (Chicago: University of Chicago Press, 1983), 102–103; Marcia M. Gallo, *Different Daughters: A History of the Daughters of Bilitis and the Rise of the Lesbian Rights Movement* (New York: Carroll & Graf Publishers, 2006); Minton, *Departing from Deviance*, 174–175.

Chapter 13: Revolutionary Love

1. Unless otherwise noted, all biographical information about Steve Kiyoshi Kuromiya in this chapter draws from the Tommi Avicolli Mecca interview with Kiyoshi Kuromiya (Parts 1 and 2), March 15, 1983, John J. Wilcox Jr. LGBT Archives Digital Collections, William Way LGBT Community Center, Philadelphia, PA, https://digital.wilcoxarchives.org/islandora/object/islandora%3A129; Marc Stein interview of Kiyoshi Kuromiya, June 17, 1997, transcribed by Lisa Williams and Marc Stein, OutHistory.org.
2. Emily K. Hobson, "Policing Gay L.A.: Mapping Racial Divides in the Homophile Era, 1950–1967," in *The Rising Tide of Color: Race, State Violence, and Radical Movements Across the Pacific*, ed. Moon-Ho Jung (Seattle: University of Washington Press, 2014), 188–212.
3. Japanese-American Internee Data File, 1942–1946, Records of the War Relocation Authority, Record Group 210, National Archives at College Park, College Park, MD, Ancestry.com; "William Hosokawa: Heart Mountain," in *And Justice for All: An Oral History of the Japanese American Detention Camps*, ed. John Tateishi (Seattle: University of Washington Press, 1999), 20; Susan L. Smith, "Caregiving in Camp: Japanese American Women and Community Health in World War II," in *Guilt by Association: Essays on Japanese Settlement, Internment, and Relocation in the Rocky Mountain West*, ed. Mike Mackey (Powell, WY: Western History Publications, 2001), 191; Louis Fiset, "The Heart Mountain Hospital Strike of June 24, 1943," in *Remembering Heart Mountain: Essays on Japanese American Internment in Wyoming*, ed. Mike Mackey (Powell, WY: Western History Publications, 1998), 102; Arthur A. Hansen, *Barbed Voices: Oral History, Resistance, and the World War II Japanese American Social Disaster* (Louisville, CO: University Press of Colorado, 2018), 198–199; Helen Varney and Joyce Beebe Thompson, *A History of Midwifery in the United States: The Midwife Said Fear Not* (New York: Springer Publishing Company, 2016), 64–65.
4. *Seventeenth Census of the United States* (Washington, DC, 1950), Roll 1590, Sheet Number 28, Enumeration District 19–1242, Record Group 29, National Archives, Ancestry.com; Wesley G. Pippert, "The Economic Losses of Japanese-Americans Interned During World War II," *UPI*, June 15, 1983.
5. Anna Lvovsky, *Vice Patrol: Cops, Courts, and the Struggle over Urban Gay Life before Stonewall* (Chicago: University of Chicago Press, 2021); John Howard, "The Library, the Park, and the Pervert: Public Space and Homosexual Encounter in Post-World War II Atlanta," *Radical History Review*, no. 62 (1995): 166–187; Hobson, "Policing Gay L.A.," 196.
6. E. Patrick Johnson, *Sweet Tea: Black Gay Men of the South* (Chapel Hill: University of North Carolina Press, 2008); Will Fellows, *Farm Boys: Lives of Gay Men from the Rural Midwest* (Madison: University of Wisconsin Press, 1996); John Howard, *Men Like That: A Southern Queer History* (Chicago: University of Chicago Press, 1999); John Howard, ed., *Carryin' On in the Lesbian and Gay South* (New York: New York University Press, 1997). Barron quoted in Marc Stein, *City of Sisterly and Brotherly Loves: Lesbian and Gay Philadelphia, 1945–1972* (Chicago: University of Chicago Press, 2000), 344–345.
7. Lillian Faderman and Stuart Timmons, *Gay L.A.: A History of Sexual Outlaws, Power Politics, and Lipstick Lesbians* (New York: Basic Books, 2006), 112–113; Hobson, "Policing Gay L.A.," 189–190.

8. James Burkhart Gilbert, *A Cycle of Outrage: America's Reaction to the Juvenile Delinquent in the 1950s* (New York: Oxford University Press, 1986), 21–41, 125–142.
9. Pasadena, California, city directories list Charles Posner, a physician, as the only adult man with that last name. See, for example, "Pasadena, California, City Directory, 1951," 576, and "Pasadena, California, City Directory, 1958," 569, Ancestry.com.
10. Jennifer Terry, *An American Obsession: Science, Medicine, and Homosexuality in Modern Society* (Chicago: University of Chicago Press, 1999), 103–110, 162–163, 294–295, 287–295, 312–313; Martin B. Duberman, *Cures: A Gay Man's Odyssey*, 10th anniv. ed. (Boulder, CO: Westview Press, 2002); Ronald Bayer, *Homosexuality and American Psychiatry: The Politics of Diagnosis* (Princeton: Princeton University Press, 1987), chapter 1; Stephanie H. Kenen, "Who Counts When You're Counting Homosexuals? Hormones and Homosexuality in Mid-Twentieth-Century America," in *Science and Homosexualities*, ed. Vernon A. Rosario (New York: Routledge, 1997), 197–218.
11. David K. Johnson, *The Lavender Scare: The Cold War Persecution of Gays and Lesbians in the Federal Government* (Chicago: University of Chicago Press, 2004); John D'Emilio, *Sexual Politics, Sexual Communities: The Making of a Homosexual Minority in the United States, 1940–1970*, 2nd ed. (Chicago: University of Chicago Press, 1998), chapter 3; Margot Canaday, *The Straight State: Sexuality and Citizenship in Twentieth-Century America* (Princeton: Princeton University Press, 2009), 215–220; Mae M. Ngai, *Impossible Subjects: Illegal Aliens and the Making of Modern America* (Princeton: Princeton University Press, 2004); Eithne Luibhéid, *Entry Denied: Controlling Sexuality at the Border* (Minneapolis: University of Minnesota Press, 2002); Marc Stein, *Sexual Injustice: Supreme Court Decisions from Griswold to Roe* (Chapel Hill: University of North Carolina Press, 2010).
12. Johnson, *Lavender Scare*, 166–170; Carol L. Tilley, "Seducing the Innocent: Fredric Wertham and the Falsifications That Helped Condemn Comics," *Information & Culture: A Journal of History* 47, no. 4 (2012): 383–413; Andrew Grunzke, "Graphic Seduction: Anti-Homosexual Censorship of Comics in the Postwar Era," *Journal of American Culture* 44, no. 4 (2021): 300–317; Canaday, *Straight State*, chapter 5; Margot Canaday, *Queer Career: Sexuality and Work in Modern America* (Princeton: Princeton University Press, 2023), 36–37; Whitney Strub, *Perversion for Profit: The Politics of Pornography and the Rise of the New Right* (New York: Columbia University Press, 2011), 15.
13. Stephanie Foote, "Deviant Classics: Pulps and the Making of Lesbian Print Culture," *Signs: Journal of Women in Culture & Society* 31, no. 1 (2005): 169–190; Vito Russo, *The Celluloid Closet: Homosexuality in the Movies* (New York: Harper & Row, 1981).
14. David K. Johnson, *Buying Gay: How Physique Entrepreneurs Sparked a Movement* (New York: Columbia University Press, 2019); Martin Meeker, *Contacts Desired: Gay and Lesbian Communications and Community, 1940s–1970s* (Chicago: University of Chicago Press, 2006).
15. Yvonne Keller, "'Was It Right to Love Her Brother's Wife So Passionately?': Lesbian Pulp Novels and U.S. Lesbian Identity, 1950–1965," *American Quarterly* 57, no. 2 (2005): 385–410; Meeker, *Contacts Desired*, chapter 3.
16. Faderman and Timmons, *Gay L.A.*, 115–120; Craig M. Loftin, *Masked Voices: Gay Men and Lesbians in Cold War America* (Albany: State University of New York Press, 2012).
17. Nan Alamilla Boyd, *Wide-Open Town: A History of Queer San Francisco to 1965* (Berkeley: University of California Press, 2003), 221–223, 227–231; Johnson, *Buying Gay*, 198.

18. Peter B. Levy, "The Civil Rights Movement in Cambridge, Maryland, During the 1960s," *Viet Nam Generation* 6, no. 3/4 (1995): 97; Raymond Wong, "Monrovian Tells 'Bama Brutality: Attempts to Burn Marchers, Billyclub Beatings Described," *The Independent* (Pasadena, CA), March 19, 1965, copy located in Federal Bureau of Investigation (FBI) file on Kuromiya, Box 44, Identifier A, Kiyoshi Kuromiya Papers, Ms-Coll-18, John J. Wilcox, Jr. LGBT Archives, William Way LGBT Community Center; Charles A. Krause, "Free U. Studies Warfare, Resistance," *The Daily Pennsylvanian*, October 17, 1968, 4; Memo from SA Charles A. Durham Jr., Philadelphia, March 28, 1969, Kuromiya FBI File.
19. Stein, *Sisterly and Brotherly Loves*, 219–224; D'Emilio, *Sexual Politics*, 161–162; Loftin, *Masked Voices*, chapter 10.
20. Kuromiya was approximately five feet, four inches tall. The FBI either knew or guessed that he weighed 154 pounds in 1969; see Memo from Durham, 44.
21. Stein, *Sisterly and Brotherly Loves*, 246.
22. Stein, *Sisterly and Brotherly Loves*, 227, 232–236, 246, 251; Marc Stein, "'Birthplace of the Nation': Imagining Lesbian and Gay Communities in Philadelphia, 1969–1980," in *Creating a Place for Ourselves: Lesbian, Gay, and Bisexual Community Histories*, ed. Genny Beemyn (New York: Routledge, 1997), 255–259.
23. Stein, *Sexual Injustice*; Canaday, *Straight State*, 241–247; Luibhéid, *Entry Denied*, 85–96; Siobhan Somerville, "Queer Loving," *GLQ: A Journal of Lesbian and Gay Studies* 11, no. 3 (2005): 347–356.
24. Stein, "Birthplace of the Nation," 258; D'Emilio, *Sexual Politics*, 170–171; Stein, *Sisterly and Brotherly Loves*, 219–220.
25. Stein, *Sisterly and Brotherly Loves*, 245; Marc Stein, "Dewey's Sit-In in Philadelphia, 1965," *OutHistory.org*, April 20, 2015; Susan Stryker, *Transgender History: The Roots of Today's Revolution*, 2nd ed. (New York: Seal Press, 2017), 96–100; Emily K. Hobson, *Lavender and Red: Liberation and Solidarity in the Gay and Lesbian Left* (Berkeley: University of California Press, 2016), 20–21.
26. Stein, *Sisterly and Brotherly Loves*, 290.
27. Lillian Faderman, *The Gay Revolution: The Story of the Struggle* (New York: Simon & Schuster, 2015), 173–185; Marc Stein, *The Stonewall Riots: A Documentary History* (New York: New York University Press, 2019); Martin B. Duberman, *Stonewall* (New York: Dutton, 1993); D'Emilio, *Sexual Politics*, 231–237; David Carter, *Stonewall: The Riots That Sparked the Gay Revolution* (New York: St. Martin's Press, 2004).
28. David Allyn, *Make Love, Not War: The Sexual Revolution, an Unfettered History* (Boston: Little Brown, 2000), 119–131; Betty Luther Hillman, "'The Most Profoundly Revolutionary Act a Homosexual Can Engage In': Drag and the Politics of Gender Representation in the San Francisco Gay Liberation Movement," *Journal of the History of Sexuality* 20, no. 1 (2011): 156–158.
29. Elizabeth A. Armstrong and Suzanna M. Crage, "Movements and Memory: The Making of the Stonewall Myth," *American Sociological Review* 71, no. 5 (2006): 724–751.
30. Stein, *Sisterly and Brotherly Loves*, 315; Hobson, *Lavender and Red*, 72–73.
31. Stein, *Sisterly and Brotherly Loves*, chapter 12; Hobson, *Lavender and Red*, 2–3.
32. Hobson, *Lavender and Red*, 9; Terence Kissack, "Freaking Fag Revolutionaries: New York's Gay Liberation Front, 1969–1971," *Radical History Review*, 62 (1995): 104–134; Kevin J. Mumford, *Not Straight, Not White: Black Gay Men from the March on*

Washington to the AIDS Crisis (Chapel Hill: North Carolina University Press, 2016), chapter 4; Ian Lekus, "Queer Harvests: Homosexuality, the U.S. New Left, and the Venceremos Brigades to Cuba," *Radical History Review* 89 (2004): 57–91.

33. Faderman, *Gay Revolution*, chapter 16; Ronald Bayer, *Homosexuality and American Psychiatry: The Politics of Diagnosis* (Princeton: Princeton University Press, 1987), chapter 4.
34. Marc Stein, "Students, Sodomy, and the State: LGBT Campus Struggles in the 1970s," *Law and Social Inquiry* 48, no. 2 (2023): 531–560; Marc Stein, *Rethinking the Gay and Lesbian Movement* (New York: Routledge, 2012), 114; Faderman, *Gay Revolution*, 265–266.
35. Justin David Suran, "Coming Out Against the War: Antimilitarism and the Politicization of Homosexuality in the Era of Vietnam," *American Quarterly* 53, no. 3 (2001): 457–461.
36. Stein, *Rethinking*, 79–114.
37. Gillian Frank, "'The Civil Rights of Parents': Race and Conservative Politics in Anita Bryant's Campaign Against Gay Rights in 1970s Florida," *Journal of the History of Sexuality* 22, no. 1 (2013): 126–160; Faderman, *Gay Revolution*, chapters 18 and 19; Anita Bryant, *The Anita Bryant Story: The Survival of Our Nation's Families and the Threat of Militant Homosexuality* (Old Tappan, NJ: Revell, 1977), 111, 117.
38. Finn Enke, *Finding the Movement: Sexuality, Contested Space, and Feminist Activism* (Durham: Duke University Press, 2007); Stephen Vider, *The Queerness of Home: Gender, Sexuality, and the Politics of Domesticity After World War II* (Chicago: University of Chicago Press, 2021), chapter 3; Brock Thompson, *The Un-Natural State: Arkansas and the Queer South* (Fayetteville: University of Arkansas Press, 2010), chapter 13; Miriam Frank, *Out in the Union: A Labor History of Queer America* (Philadelphia: Temple University Press, 2014); Jonathan Bell, "Making Sexual Citizens: LGBT Politics, Health Care, and the State in the 1970s," in *Beyond the Politics of the Closet: Gay Rights and the American State Since the 1970s*, ed. Jonathan Bell (Philadelphia: University of Pennsylvania Press, 2020), 58–80; Christina B. Hanhardt, *Safe Space: Gay Neighborhood History and the Politics of Violence* (Durham: Duke University Press, 2013); Timothy Stewart-Winter, *Queer Clout: Chicago and the Rise of Gay Politics* (Philadelphia: University of Pennsylvania Press, 2016).

Chapter 14: Public Masturbator Number One

1. Betty Dodson, *Sex by Design: The Betty Dodson Story* (New York: Betty A. Dodson Foundation, 2015), 112, 223.
2. Jennifer Scanlon, *Bad Girls Go Everywhere: The Life of Helen Gurley Brown* (New York: Oxford University Press, 2009), chapter 4.
3. *The Goop Lab*, season 1, episode 3, "Understanding Sex and Female Pleasure: The Pleasure Is Ours," featuring Gwyneth Paltrow, Elise Loehnen, and Betty Dodson, aired January 24, 2020, on Netflix.
4. J. P. Edwards, "Do Women Provoke Sex Attack?" *Cosmopolitan*, March 1960, 36–40; Amanda H. Littauer, *Bad Girls: Young Women, Sex, and Rebellion before the Sixties* (Chapel Hill: University of North Carolina Press, 2015), chapter 4.
5. Betty Dodson, *Liberating Masturbation: A Meditation on Self Love* (New York: Betty

Dodson, 1974), 15; Thomas W. Laqueur, *Solitary Sex: A Cultural History of Masturbation* (Princeton: Princeton University Press, 2004), chapter 5.

6. Betty Dodson, handwritten personal narrative, [1972], 2, Dell Williams Papers, box 3, folder 66, Division of Rare and Manuscript Collections, Cornell University Library.
7. Joanne Meyerowitz, ed., *Not June Cleaver: Women and Gender in Postwar America, 1945–1960* (Philadelphia: Temple University Press, 1994); Littauer, *Bad Girls*, chapter 1; Wini Breines, *Young, White, and Miserable: Growing Up Female in the Fifties* (Boston: Beacon Press, 1992); Anne Gray Fischer, *The Streets Belong to Us: Sex, Race, and Police Power from Segregation to Gentrification* (Chapel Hill: University of North Carolina Press, 2022), chapter 3.
8. Dodson, *Sex by Design*, 15–23; Elizabeth Fraterrigo, *Playboy and the Making of the Good Life in Modern America* (New York: Oxford University Press, 2009).
9. Carlin Ross, "My Last Interview with Betty Dodson," YouTube video, October 28, 2021, https://www.youtube.com/watch?v=6SQtf824sC0; Joan McCracken Interview, 3–4, OH 378–036, Archives and Special Collections, Mansfield Library, University of Montana-Missoula; Elaine Tyler May, *America and the Pill: A History of Promise, Peril, and Liberation* (New York: Basic Books, 2010); Dodson, *Sex by Design*, 18–20.
10. Melissa Murray, "Sexual Liberty and Criminal Law Reform: The Story of *Griswold v. Connecticut*," in *Reproductive Rights and Justice Stories*, eds. Melissa Murray, Katherine Shaw, and Reva B. Siegel (St. Paul, MN: Foundation Press, 2019), 11–31; Sarah E. Igo, *The Known Citizen: A History of Privacy in Modern America* (Cambridge, MA: Harvard University Press, 2018), 149–159.
11. Dodson, *Sex by Design*, chapter 3.
12. "Betty's Talk–NOW's Sexuality Conference in 1973," featuring Carlin Ross and Betty Dodson, video, January 18, 2012, https://www.youtube.com/watch?v=w6oAGPA8MSs.
13. Carolyn Herbst Lewis, "Suburban Swing: Heterosexual Marriage and Spouse Swapping in the 1950s and 1960s," in *Heterosexual Histories*, eds. Rebecca L. Davis and Michele Mitchell (New York: New York University Press, 2021), 251–273; David Allyn, *Make Love, Not War: The Sexual Revolution, an Unfettered History* (Boston: Little Brown, 2000), chapter 17; Dodson, *Sex by Design*, 129–133.
14. Dodson, *Liberating Masturbation*, 11–13, 15.
15. Janice M. Irvine, *Disorders of Desire: Sex and Gender in Modern American Sexology* (Philadelphia: Temple University Press, 1990), 37–38, 65, 140; Dodson, *Sex by Design*, 131.
16. Geoffrey Stone, *Sex and the Constitution: Sex, Religion, and Law from America's Origins to the Twenty-First Century* (New York: Liveright, 2017), chapters 8 and 12; Mary Phillips, "The Fine Art of Lovemaking: An Interview with Betty Dodson," *Evergreen Review* 15, no. 87 (1971), 36–43, 73; "About," Evergreen, https://evergreenreview.com/about/; Dodson, *Sex by Design*, 94–100, 106–111.
17. Whitney Strub, *Perversion for Profit: The Politics of Pornography and the Rise of the New Right* (New York: Columbia University Press, 2011), 33–42, 60–68, 172–174; Stone, *Sex and the Constitution*, 269–78; Martin Meeker, *Contacts Desired: Gay and Lesbian Communications and Community, 1940s–1970s* (Chicago: University of Chicago Press, 2006), 53–59.
18. Stone, *Sex and the Constitution*, 287–293.

19. Strub, *Perversion for Profit*, chapter 5; Christie Milliken, "Rate It X?: Hollywood Cinema and the End of the Production Code," in *Sex Scene: Media and the Sexual Revolution*, ed. Eric Schaefer (Durham: Duke University Press, 2014), 25–52; Linda Williams, *Hard Core: Power, Pleasure, and the "Frenzy of the Visible"* (Berkeley: University of California Press, 1989); Eric Schaefer, "Gauging a Revolution: 16mm Film and the Rise of the Pornographic Feature," *Cinema Journal* 41, no. 3 (2002): 5, 7–8.
20. Lucas Hilderbrand, "Historical Fantasies: 1970s Gay Male Pornography in the Archives," in *Porno Chic and the Sex Wars: American Sexual Representation in the 1970s*, eds. Carolyn Bronstein and Whitney Strub (Amherst: University of Massachusetts Press, 2016), 327–328; Allyn, *Make Love, Not War*, 234–235; Jeffrey Escoffier, "Beefcake to Hardcore: Gay Pornography and the Sexual Revolution," in Schafer, *Sex Scene*, 319–348.
21. Nancy Semin Lingo, "Making Sense of Linda Lovelace," in Bronstein and Strub, *Porno Chic and the Sex Wars*, 104–105; Joseph Lam Duong, "San Francisco and the Politics of Hard Core," in Schafer, *Sex Scene*, 297–318.
22. Whitney Strub and Carolyn Bronstein, "Introduction," in *Porno Chic and the Sex Wars*, 1–2; Roger Ebert, "Behind the Green Door," December 11, 1973, https://www.rogerebert.com/reviews/behind-the-green-door-1973; Mireille Miller-Young, *A Taste for Brown Sugar: Black Women in Pornography* (Durham: Duke University Press, 2014), 73–75; Jennifer C. Nash, "Desiring Desiree," in Strub and Bronstein, *Porno Chic and the Sex Wars*, 73–103.
23. Irvine, *Disorders*, 78; Mari Jo Buhle, *Feminism and Its Discontents: A Century of Struggle with Psychoanalysis* (Cambridge, MA: Harvard University Press, 1998), introduction, chapter 1, 295–300; Patricia Cotti, "Sexuality and Psychoanalytic Aggrandizement: Freud's 1908 Theory of Cultural History," *History of Psychiatry* 22, no. 1 (2011): 58–74; Jane Gerhard, *Desiring Revolution: Second-Wave Feminism and the Rewriting of Twentieth-Century American Sexual Thought* (New York: Columbia University Press, 2001), 83; Allyn, *Make Love, Not War*, 202–205; Betty Dodson, "Cunt Positive Women . . ." in *Wet Dreams*, ed. William Levy (Amsterdam: Joy Publications, 1973), 51.
24. Joan Buck, "Some of my Best Friends Made Love There," in Levy, *Wet Dreams*, 27; Dodson, "Cunt Positive Women . . ." 50–51; Elena Gorfinkel, "Wet Dreams: Erotic Film Festivals of the Early 1970s and the Utopian Sexual Public Sphere," in Schafer, *Sex Scene*, 126–150; Benjamin Shephard, "Play as World-Making: From the Cockettes to the Germs, Gay Liberation to DIY Community Building," in *The Hidden 1970s: Histories of Radicalism*, ed. Dan Berger (New Brunswick: Rutgers University Press, 2010), 177–194.
25. Dell Williams, untitled draft, [1983], 1–2, Dell Williams Papers, box 3 folder 64.
26. Williams, untitled draft, [1983], 3; Mimi Lobell, "Last Word," [unknown publication], [ca. 1974], 127–128, Dell Williams Papers, box 1, folder 2.
27. Sandra Morgen, *Into Our Own Hands: The Women's Health Movement in the United States, 1969–1990* (New Brunswick: Rutgers University Press, 2002), 7–8; Hannah Dudley-Shotwell, *Revolutionizing Women's Healthcare: The Feminist Self-Help Movement in America* (New Brunswick: Rutgers University Press, 2020), 4, chapter 1; Judith A. Houck, *Looking through the Speculum: Examining the Women's Health Movement* (Chicago: University of Chicago Press, 2024), chapter 1; Michelle Murphy, "Immodest Witnessing: The Epistemology of Vaginal Self-Examination in the U.S. Feminist Self-Help Movement," *Feminist Studies* 30, no. 1 (2004): 115–147.

28. "Bodysex Workshops," flier, n.d., Dell Williams Papers, box 1, folder 8; various issues of *Women's Press* (1975), *Sojourner* (1976), and *New Women's Times* (1976–1979), Independent Voices.
29. Dodson, *Liberating Masturbation*, 21; "About Betty Dodson (bio)," n.d., 2, Dell Williams Papers, box 1, folder 4.
30. Laurie Johnson, "Women's Sexuality Conference Ends in School Here," *New York Times*, June 11, 1973, 10; N.O.W. Women's Sexuality Conference, "Statement of Purpose," [1972], Dell Williams Papers, box 3, folder 63.
31. Lobell, "Last Word"; Dodson, *Sex by Design*, 170–176; Dodson, *Liberating Masturbation*, 25.
32. Dell Williams, draft for "News and Views from Eve's Garden," n.d., Dell Williams Papers, box 3, folder 64; Lynn Comella, *Vibrator Nation: How Feminist Sex-Toy Stores Changed the Business of Pleasure* (Durham: Duke University Press, 2017), chapters 1–2; Margot Canaday, *Queer Career: Sexuality and Work in Modern America* (Princeton: Princeton University Press, 2023), 165–182.
33. Allison Miller, "A Legendary Erotic Archive Has Been Out of Public View for Decades. We Found It," *Observer*, October 19, 2022, https://observer.com/2022/10/a-legendary-erotic-archive-has-been-out-of-public-view-for-decades-we-found-it/; Irvine, *Disorders*, 84–85, 90–92.
34. Irvine, *Disorders*, 165.
35. "Worth Noting," *The Spokeswoman* 5, no. 9, March 15, 1975, 9; Ti-Grace Atkinson, "Why I'm Against S/M Liberation," in *Against Sadomasochism: A Radical Feminist Analysis*, eds. Robin Ruth Linden, Darlene R. Pagano, Diana E. H. Russell, and Susan Leigh Star (East Palo Alto, CA: Frog in the Well, 1982), 91; Jill Johnson, *Lesbian Nation: The Feminist Solution* (New York: Simon & Schuster, 1973); Alice Echols, *Daring to be Bad: Radical Feminism in America, 1967–1975* (Minneapolis: University of Minnesota Press, 1989), 170–175, quoted at 174; Emily K. Hobson, *Lavender and Red: Liberation and Solidarity in the Gay and Lesbian Left* (Berkeley: University of California Press, 2016), chapter 2; Sue, Nelly, Dian, Carol, and Billie, *Country Lesbians: The Story of the WomanShare Collective* (Grants Pass, OR: WomanShare Books, 1976), 19–20.
36. Anne M. Valk, *Radical Sisters: Second-Wave Feminism and Black Liberation in Washington, D.C.* (Urbana: University of Illinois Press, 2010), 162.
37. Alex Warner, "Feminism Meets Fisting: Antipornography, Sadomasochism, and the Politics of Sex," in Bronstein and Strub, *Porno Chic*, 254.
38. Lisa Duggan, "Feminist Historians and Antipornography Campaigns: An Overview," in *Sex Wars: Sexual Dissent and Political Culture*, eds. Lisa Duggan and Nan D. Hunter, 10th anniv. ed. (New York: Routledge, 2006), 68–73; Robin Morgan, "Theory and Practice: Pornography and Rape," in *Take Back the Night: Women on Pornography*, ed. Laura Lederer (New York: William Morrow, 1980), 134–140; Lorna N. Bracewell, *Why We Lost the Sex Wars: Sexual Freedom in the #MeToo Era* (Minneapolis: University of Minnesota Press, 2021), chapter 3, quoted at 116.
39. Charlie Jeffries, *Teenage Dreams: Girlhood Sexualities in the U.S. Culture Wars* (New Brunswick: Rutgers University Press, 2022), 40–41; Fischer, *Streets Belong to Us*, chapter 6.
40. Dodson, *Sex by Design*, 269, 362–365; Betty Dodson, "Porn Wars," in *The Feminist Porn Book: The Politics of Producing Pleasure*, eds. Tristan Taormino, Celine Parreñas Shi-

mizu, Constance Penley, and Mirielle Miller-Young (New York: Feminist Press at the City University of New York, 2013), 27. See also Gayle Rubin, "The Leather Menace: Comments on Politics and S/M," in *Coming to Power: Writings and Graphics on Lesbian S/M*, Samois, 3rd ed. (Boston: Alyson Publications, Inc., 1987), 221.

41. Rubin, "Leather Menace," 197, 213, 217; Patrick Califia, "A Personal View of the History of the Lesbian S/M Community and Movement in San Francisco," in Samois, *Coming to Power*, 280; Amanda H. Littauer, "Queer Girls and Intergenerational Lesbian Sexuality in the 1970s," *Historical Reflections* 46, no. 1 (2020): 95–108.

42. Janie Kritzman and Carole Vance, "Minutes from the Scholar and Feminist Planning Committee, 10/21/81," October 21, 1981, 3–4, Folder No. 12970: "The Scholar and the Feminist IX: Towards a Politics of Sexuality Conference, September 17, 1981–June, 1982 and undated," Lesbian Herstory Archives, Archives of Sexuality and Gender (Gale); "The Barnard Conference," Notes and Letters, *Feminist Studies* 9, no. 1 (1983): 177–182, quoted at 180; Warner, "Feminism Meets Fisting," 249; Gerhard, *Desiring Revolution*, 187–195; Rachel Corbman, "The Scholars and the Feminists: The Barnard Sex Conference and the History of the Institutionalization of Feminism," *Feminist Formations* 27, no. 3 (2015): 49–80; Carolyn Bronstein, *Battling Pornography: The American Feminist Anti-Pornography Movement, 1976–1986* (Cambridge: Cambridge University Press, 2011), 297–307; Patrick Califia, "Life Among the Monosexuals," *Journal of Bisexuality* 5, nos. 2–3 (2005): 139–148; Lauren Berlant, *The Queen of America Goes to Washington City: Notes on Sex and Citizenship* (Durham: Duke University Press, 1997), chapter 2.

43. Comella, *Vibrator Nation*, 54–56; "Radical Desire: Making *On Our Backs* Magazine," Cornell University, Human Sexuality Collection, online exhibition, last modified 2022, https://rmc.library.cornell.edu/radicaldesire/index.php.

44. Peter Alilunas, "Bridging the Gap: Adult Video News and the 'Long 1970s,'" in Bronstein and Strub, *Porno Chic*, 305–306; Various fliers, ca. 1991, Folder No. 13110, "Sexuality Sex Toys and Catalogues, April 29, 1989–1994 and undated," Lesbian Herstory Archives, Archives of Sexuality and Gender (Gale).

45. Phyllis Schlafly, ed., *Pornography's Victims* (Westchester, IL: Crossway Books, 1987), 114; Lisa Duggan, "Censorship in the Name of Feminism," in Duggan and Hunter, *Sex Wars*, chapter 2.

46. Strub, *Perversion for Profit*, 129–135, 198–206; Bronstein, *Battling Pornography*, chapters 6–8; Kelsy Burke, *Pornography Wars: The Past, Present, and Future of America's Obscene Obsession* (New York: Bloomsbury Publishing, 2023), 171.

47. Carole Vance, "Photography, Pornography, and Sexual Politics," *Aperture: The Body in Question* 121 (1990): 52–65; Dan Royles, *To Make the Wounded Whole: The African American Struggle Against HIV/AIDS* (Chapel Hill: University of North Carolina Press, 2020), 84–90.

48. Laura Kipnis, *Bound and Gagged: Pornography and the Politics of Fantasy in America* (Durham: Duke University Press, 1999), 178; Jeffries, *Teenage Dreams*, 96; Irvine, *Disorders*, 167, 173–174; Dodson, *Sex by Design*, 259.

49. Jeffries, *Teenage Dreams*, 46; Elizabeth Groeneveld, *Lesbian Porn Magazines and the Sex Wars: Reimagining Sex, Power, and Identity* (New York: Routledge, 2023).

50. *Betty Dodson's Bodysex Workshop*, 2012. DVD.

51. *Goop Lab*, "Understanding Sex."

Chapter 15: Irresponsible Intercourse

1. Steve Shirley, "Right-to-Life Chapter to Picket Women's Clinic," *The Missoulian*, December 8, 1978, 13.
2. Suzanne Pennypacker Morris, "Pro-Abortionist Succumbs to Gross Hysteria," *The Missoulian*, May 19, 1978, 4.
3. Sally Mullen Interview (transcript), OH 378–010, 9–10, Archives and Special Collections, Mansfield Library, University of Montana-Missoula.
4. Gayle Shirley, "Controversy Doesn't Reduce Demand for Clinic," *The Missoulian*, January 7, 1979, 11; Karissa Haugeberg, *Women Against Abortion: Inside the Largest Moral Reform Movement of the Twentieth Century* (Urbana: University of Illinois Press, 2017), 24–27.
5. Mary Ziegler, *After Roe: The Lost History of the Abortion Debate* (Cambridge, MA: Harvard University Press, 2015), 38–51.
6. Neil J. Young, *We Gather Together: The Religious Right and the Problem of Interfaith Politics* (New York: Oxford University Press, 2016), 96; Rebecca L. Davis, *More Perfect Unions: The American Search for Marital Bliss* (Cambridge, MA: Harvard University Press, 2010), 204–212.
7. Brianna Theobald, *Reproduction on the Reservation: Pregnancy, Childbirth, and Colonialism in the Long-Twentieth Century* (Chapel Hill: University of North Carolina Press, 2019), 20–21.
8. Todd L. Savitt, "Abortion in the Old West: The Trials of Dr. Edwin S. Kellogg of Helena, Montana," *Montana: The Magazine of Western History* 57, no. 3 (2007): 6; Janet Farrell Brodie, *Contraception and Abortion in 19th-Century America* (Ithaca: Cornell University Press, 1994), chapter 8; Judith Walzer Leavitt, *Brought to Bed: Childbearing in America, 1750–1950* (New York: Oxford University Press, 1986).
9. Joan Uda, "Abortion: *Roe v. Wade* and the Montana Dilemma," *Montana Law Review* 35, no. 1 (1974): 103–118; James Armstrong Interview (transcript), 2–3, OH 164–004, Archives and Special Collections, Mansfield Library, University of Montana-Missoula; Leslie J. Reagan, *When Abortion Was a Crime: Women, Medicine, and Law in the United States, 1867–1973* (Berkeley: University of California Press, 1997), 175–181; Rickie Solinger, *Pregnancy and Power: A Short History of Reproductive Politics in America* (New York: New York University Press, 2005), 157–160.
10. Regina G. Kunzel, *Fallen Women, Problem Girls: Unmarried Mothers and the Professionalization of Social Work, 1890–1945* (New Haven: Yale University Press, 1993), 26–29; Carole E. Joffe, *Doctors of Conscience: The Struggle to Provide Abortion Before and After* Roe v. Wade (Boston: Beacon Press, 1995), chapter 4; Armstrong Interview, 6–7.
11. Johanna Schoen, *Abortion After Roe* (Chapel Hill: University of North Carolina Press, 2015), 26; Rickie Solinger, ed., *Abortion Wars: A Half Century of Struggle, 1950–2000* (Berkeley: University of California Press, 1998); David J. Garrow, *Liberty and Sexuality: The Right to Privacy and the Making of* Roe v. Wade (Berkeley: University of California Press 1998), 270; Martha Coonfield Ward, *Poor Women, Powerful Men: America's Great Experiment in Family Planning* (Boulder: Westview Press, 1986), 22–23; Loretta J. Ross, "African-American Women and Abortion," in Solinger, *Abortion Wars*, 174.
12. Garrow, *Liberty and Sexuality*, 323–325, 411, 466; Mullen Interview, 2; Joan McCracken Interview (transcript), 6–7, OH 378–036, Archives and Special Collections, Mansfield

Library, University of Montana-Missoula; Gillian Frank, *A Sacred Choice: Liberal Religion and the Struggle for Reproductive Rights Before Roe v. Wade* (Chapel Hill: University of North Carolina Press, forthcoming); Reagan, *When Abortion Was a Crime*, 222–244; Laura Kaplan, *The Story of Jane: The Legendary Underground Feminist Abortion Service* (Chicago: University of Chicago Press, 1995).

13. Schoen, *Abortion After Roe*, 30–31.

14. Mullen Interview, 2–3, 7; Shirley, "Controversy Doesn't Reduce Demand," 11; Sandra Morgen, *Into Our Own Hands: The Women's Health Movement in the United States, 1969–1990* (New Brunswick: Rutgers University Press, 2002), 70–71; Judith A. Houck, *Looking Through the Speculum: Examining the Women's Health Movement* (Chicago: University of Chicago Press, 2024), chapter 4.

15. Gayle Shirley, "Clinic Doesn't Have Corner on Abortion," *The Missoulian*, January 7, 1979, 11.

16. Garrow, *Liberty and Sexuality*, 311–313; Leslie Woodcock Tentler, *Catholics and Contraception: An American History* (Ithaca: Cornell University Press, 2004), chapters 3 and 6; Haugeberg, *Women Against Abortion*, 29–31; Daniel K. Williams, *Defenders of the Unborn: The Pro-Life Movement before* Roe v. Wade (New York: Oxford University Press, 2019), 88–95; Suzanne P. Morris, "News of Dead Baby," (LTE) *The Journal Herald* (Dayton, Ohio), February 21, 1974, 4; Jennifer L. Holland, *Tiny You: A Western History of the Anti-Abortion Movement* (Berkeley: University of California Press, 2020), 54.

17. Suzanne P. Morris, "All the Numbers," (LTE) *Dayton Daily News*, November 17, 1974, 42; Williams, *Defenders*, 154; Louise Summerhill, *The Story of Birthright: The Alternative to Abortion* (Kenosha, WI: Prow Books, 1973), 117; Haugeberg, *Women Against Abortion*, 17–18; Holland, *Tiny You*, chapter 4; Ad copy, *The Missoulian*, July 7, 1979, 19; Suzanne P. Morris, "Pro-Lifers Work for Better World," *The Missoulian*, February 21, 1977, 4.

18. Suzanne P. Morris, "Rally Ignored," (LTE) *The Journal Herald*, February 11, 1975, 5; "Life Unit Pickets at Abortion Clinic," *Dayton Daily News*, October 23, 1975, 6; Suzanne P. Morris, "The Facts of Life," (LTE) *The Journal Herald* (Dayton, Ohio), December 9, 1974, 4; Suzanne P. Morris, "Abortion Is Wrong," (LTE) *The Missoulian*, August 11, 1974, 4; Ziegler, *After Roe*, 45; Williams, *Defenders*, 192–193, 206.

19. Suzanne P. Morris, "Not the Issue," (LTE) *Dayton Daily News*, May 16, 1976, 38; Morris, "Abortion Is Wrong"; Williams, *Defenders*, 88, 206.

20. Williams, *Defenders*, 97, chapter 7; Holland, *Tiny You*, chapter 1; Gillian Frank, "The Colour of the Unborn: Anti-Abortion and Anti-Bussing Politics in Michigan, United States, 1967–1973," *Gender & History* 26, no. 2 (2014): 351–378.

21. Ross, "African American Women," 180; Simone M. Caron, "Birth Control Politics and the Black Community in the 1960s: Genocide or Power Politics?" *Journal of Social History* 31, no. 3 (1998): 543–569; Jennifer A. Nelson, *Women of Color and the Reproductive Justice Movement* (New York: New York University Press, 2003), chapter 4; Frank, "Colour of the Unborn," 354.

22. Young, *We Gather*, 212–215; Frank, "Colour of the Unborn," 368; Robert O. Self, *All in the Family: The Realignment of American Democracy Since the 1960s* (New York: Hill and Wang, 2012), chapter 11; Marjorie Julian Spruill, *Divided We Stand: The Battle over Women's Rights and Family Values That Polarized American Politics* (New York:

Bloomsbury Publishing, 2018), chapter 5; Lisa McGirr, *Suburban Warriors: The Origins of the New American Right* (Princeton: Princeton University Press, 2001), chapter 6; Williams, *Defenders*, 96, 148–149.

23. Juli Loesch, quoted in Haugeberg, *Women Against Abortion*, 62; Carol Mattar, "Right to Life Will Picket," *The Journal Herald* (Dayton, Ohio) November 22, 1975, 23.
24. Shirley, "Controversy," 11; Linda L. Hanson, (LTE) *The Missoulian*, August 3, 1977, 4.
25. "Abortion Measure Aired; House Vote 'Imminent,'" *The Missoulian*, January 31, 1979, 13; Sara Dubow, *Ourselves Unborn: A History of the Fetus in Modern America* (New York: Oxford University Press, 2011); Schoen, *Abortion After Roe*, 145; Williams, *Defenders*, 134–142; Lauren Berlant, *The Queen of America Goes to Washington City: Notes on Sex and Citizenship* (Durham: Duke University Press, 1997), chapter 3.
26. Ellen S. Moore, *The Transformation of American Sex Education: Mary Calderone and the Fight for Sexual Health* (New York: New York University Press, 2022), 236–253; Janice Irvine, *Talk About Sex: How Sex Ed Battles Helped Ignite the Right*, 20th anniv. ed. (Philadelphia: Temple University Press, 2023), chapter 1; Steven Epstein, *The Quest for Sexual Health: How an Elusive Ideal Has Transformed Science, Politics, and Everyday Life* (Chicago: University of Chicago Press, 2022), 48–50.
27. Miriam S. Dapra, (LTE) *The Missoulian*, January 23, 1980, 6; Alan Rosenberg, "'Sex Ed' Needs Community Help," *The Missoulian*, May 10, 1981, 9; Heather White, *Reforming Sodom: Protestants and the Rise of Gay Rights* (Chapel Hill: University of North Carolina Press, 2015), chapter 4.
28. Lillian Faderman, *Odd Girls and Twilight Lovers: A History of Lesbian Life in Twentieth-Century America* (New York: Columbia University Press, 1999), 212.
29. Phyllis Schlafly, *The Power of the Positive Woman* (New York: Jove Publications, Inc., 1977), "special rights," 113, "prolesbian legislation," 228; Tom Newmann, "Right-to-Life Leaders Speaks in Missoula," *The Missoulian*, November 7, 1977, 3; Irvine, *Talk About Sex*, chapter 3.
30. Billy Graham, "My Answer," *Clarion-Ledger* (Jackson, Mississippi), August 28, 1961, 8; Young, *We Gather*, 98–106, 112–118. See also Gillian Frank and Neil J. Young, "What Everyone Gets Wrong About Evangelicals and Abortion," *Washington Post*, May 16, 2022, https://wapo.st/3LPLmJj; Paul K. Jewett, "The Relation of the Soul to the Fetus," *Christianity Today*, November 8, 1969, 6; Neil J. Young, "Fascinating and Happy: Mormon Women, the LDS Church, and the Politics of Sexual Conservatism," in *Devotions and Desires: Histories of Sexuality and Religion in the Twentieth-Century United States*, eds. Gillian Frank, Bethany Moreton, and Heather White (Chapel Hill: University of North Carolina Press, 2018), 193–213.
31. Holland, *Tiny You*, chapter 1; Whitney Strub, *Perversion for Profit: The Politics of Pornography and the Rise of the New Right* (New York: Columbia University Press, 2011), chapter 6; Young, *We Gather*, 160–165; Clayton Howard, *The Closet and the Cul-de-Sac: The Politics of Sexual Privacy in Northern California* (Philadelphia: University of Pennsylvania Press, 2019), 136–140, 236–238; Kristin Luker, *Abortion and the Politics of Motherhood* (Berkeley: University of California Press, 1984); Williams, *Defenders*, 91, 141–142; *The Missoulian*, "Abortion Measure Aired," 13.
32. D. A. Grimes, J. D. Forrest, A. L. Kirkman, and B. Radford, "An Epidemic of Antiabortion Violence in the United States," *American Journal of Obstetrics and Gynecology* 165 (1991): 1263–1268. There were reports of "110 cases of arson, firebombing, or bomb-

ing . . . 222 clinic invasions, 220 acts of clinic vandalism, 216 bomb threats, 65 death threats, 46 assault and batteries, 20 burglaries, and 2 kidnappings."

33. "Where Are They Now?," *The Missoulian*, December 31, 1989, B-1; "Notice of Time and Place of Hearing and Petition for Change of Name, Cause No. 72693," *The Missoulian*, June 15, 1990, 20.
34. John Stromnes, "NOW Vigil to Protest Clinic Bombings," *The Missoulian*, January 18, 1985, 9; Haugeberg, *Women Against Abortion*, 80–81.
35. Willa Craig Interview (transcript), 9–13, OH 378–008, Archives and Special Collections, Mansfield Library, University of Montana-Missoula.
36. Haugeberg, *Women Against Abortion*, 105; Schoen, *Abortion After Roe*, 186–197; Holland, *Tiny You*, 174–178.
37. Sherry Devlin, "Abortion Argument Hits Home," *The Missoulian*, November 24, 1991, 1.
38. Haugeberg, *Women Against Abortion*, 111–112; Holland, *Tiny You*, 13–14.
39. Michael Downs, "Fire Fans Flames of Abortion Argument," *The Missoulian*, April 4, 1993, 12; Haugeberg, *Women Against Abortion*, 76, 117; Bob Anez, "Stalking Bill Stuck in House," *The Missoulian*, March 12, 1993, B1; Michael Downs, "Abortion Doctor's Slaying Prompts Local Warnings," *The Missoulian*, March 12, 1993, B1.
40. Michael Moore, "Arson Fire Guts Clinic," *The Missoulian*, March 30, 1993, 1, 6; John Stromnes, "Rally Speakers Condemn Attack," *The Missoulian*, March 30, 1993, 1, 6; Michael Moore, "After Missoula Fire: Clinics Beef Up Security," *The Missoulian*, April 1, 1993, A1, 12.
41. Randi Erickson, "Anti-Abortion Activists Blamed for Blue Mountain Firebombing," *Missoula Independent*, April 2, 1993, 5, 14; John Stromnes, "Blaze Won't Stop Abortions: Clinic Director Promises Women Won't Lose Their Right to Choose," *The Missoulian*, March 31, 1993, C-8; Bob Anez, "State Politicians Condemn Attack on Missoula Clinic," *The Missoulian*, March 31, 1993, C-6; Randi Erickson, "Blue Mountain Suffers Firebomb's Legacy: No Insurance, and Patients Left in Need," *Missoula Independent*, August 6, 1993, 7.
42. Stromnes, "Blaze," C-5, C-8; Erickson, "Blue Mountain Suffers," 5; "Doctor to Reopen Abortion Clinic in Bozeman," *Great Falls Tribune*, March 21, 2008, 1M, 3M; Joe Kolman, "Abortion Doctor Will Sell Clinic," *The Billings Gazette*, June 1, 1997, 1, 9A; Susan Wicklund and Alan S. Kesselheim, *This Common Secret: My Journey as an Abortion Doctor* (New York: Public Affairs, 2007); Moore, "After Missoula Fire," A1, 12; Richard Wachs, "A Choice Alternative," *Missoula Independent*, September 5, 2002, 16; Ginny Merriam, "Up from the Ashes," *The Missoulian*, February 18, 1997, C1.
43. Haugeberg, *Women Against Abortion*, 132.
44. "Abortion Doctor Rebuilds Office," *The Missoulian*, December 8, 1994, B11; Patricia Sullivan, "Anti-Abortion Arson," *The Missoulian*, October 12, 1994, 1, 10; Rich Harris, "Abortion Activist Pleads Guilty to Torching Clinics in Montana," *Great Falls Tribune*, February 11, 1998, 9.
45. Kathleen McLaughlin, "Alleged Abortion Clinic Arsonist Left Long Trail of Evidence," *The Missoulian*, October 12, 1997, 1, 11; Cheryl Wilke (LTE) and Andrea Screnar (LTE), *The Missoulian*, April 4, 1993, 5.
46. Rich Harris, "Abortion Activist Pleads Guilty," 9; Jessica Mayrer, "Can't Do It All Alone," *Missoula Independent*, May 15, 2014, A16.

47. Dana S. Gershon, "Stalking Statutes: A New Vehicle to Curb the New Violence of the Radical Anti-Abortion Movement," *Columbia Human Rights Law Review* 26 (1994): 215–246; Haugeberg, *Women Against Abortion*, 139.
48. Matthew Berns, "Trigger Laws," *Georgetown Law Journal* 97, no. 6 (2009): 1639–1688; Center for Reproductive Rights, "After Roe Fell: Abortion Laws by State," July 2023, https://reproductiverights.org/maps/abortion-laws-by-state/.
49. Suzanne Pennypacker, "Dog Gripes Typical of Discourse," (LTE) *The Missoulian*, June 29, 1994, 5; A. E. Hirst, "Dogs, Owners Need Disciplining," (LTE), *The Missoulian*, July 5, 1994, 5.

Chapter 16: Sexual Advances

1. This description draws from my personal notes from the event, which I attended. See also Brandon Baker, "Anita Hill, Kimberlé Crenshaw, and Dorothy Roberts on Inequality and Sexual Harassment," *Penn Today*, University of Pennsylvania, October 11, 2018, https://penntoday.upenn.edu/news/legal-scholars-anita-hill-kimberle-crenshaw-and-dorothy-roberts-discuss-womens-equality-and.
2. Julie Berebitsky, *Sex and the Office: A History of Gender, Power, and Desire* (New Haven: Yale University Press, 2012), 264–273; "Chronology," in *Race, Gender, and Power in America: The Legacy of the Hill-Thomas Hearings*, eds. Anita Faye Hill and Emma Coleman Jordan (New York: Oxford University Press, 1995), xix–xxix.
3. Molly Ball et al., "Supreme Reckoning," *Time*, October 1, 2018, 22–27; Haley Sweetland Edwards et al., "She Said," *Time*, October 15, 2018, 20–25.
4. Kimberlé Crenshaw, "Demarginalizing the Intersection of Race and Sex: A Black Feminist Critique of Antidiscrimination Doctrine, Feminist Theory and Antiracist Politics," *University of Chicago Legal Forum* (1989): 139–167; Dorothy E. Roberts, *Fatal Invention: How Science, Politics, and Big Business Re-Create Race in the Twenty-First Century* (New York: New Press, 2011); Dorothy E. Roberts, *Killing the Black Body: Race, Reproduction, and the Meaning of Liberty* (New York: Pantheon Books, 1997); Dorothy E. Roberts, *Shattered Bonds: The Color of Child Welfare* (New York: Basic Books, 2002).
5. "The Race Problem—An Autobiography," by "A Southern Colored Woman," *The Independent* 56, no. 2885 (March 17, 1904), 587, 589, excerpted in *Black Women in White America: A Documentary History*, ed. Gerda Lerner (New York: Vintage Books, 1992), 158–159; LaKisha Michelle Simmons, *Crescent City Girls: The Lives of Young Black Women in Segregated New Orleans* (Chapel Hill: University of North Carolina Press, 2015), 69–79 and chapter 2; Anne Gray Fischer, *The Streets Belong to Us: Sex, Race, and Police Power from Segregation to Gentrification* (Chapel Hill: University of North Carolina Press, 2022), 94–100.
6. Danielle L. McGuire, *At the Dark End of the Street: Black Women, Rape, and Resistance—a New History of the Civil Rights Movement from Rosa Parks to the Rise of Black Power* (New York: Alfred A. Knopf, 2010).
7. Serena Mayeri, "Race, Sexual Citizenship, and the Constitution of Nonmarital Motherhood," in *Heterosexual Histories*, eds. Rebecca L. Davis and Michele Mitchell (New York: New York University Press), 274–300; Andrew Pope, "Making Motherhood a Felony: African American Women's Welfare Rights Activism in New Orleans and the End of Suitable Home Laws, 1959–1962," *Journal of American History* 105, no.

2 (2018): 291–310; Lisa Levenstein, *A Movement Without Marches: African American Women and the Politics of Poverty in Postwar Philadelphia* (Chapel Hill: University of North Carolina Press, 2009), chapter 1.

8. Alison Lefkovitz, *Strange Bedfellows: Marriage in the Age of Women's Liberation* (Philadelphia: University of Pennsylvania Press, 2018), chapter 4, quote at 106; Pope, "Making Motherhood a Felony," 292.

9. Serena Mayeri, "Intersectionality and the Constitution of Family Status," 32 *Constitutional Commentary* 377 (2017); Mayeri, "Race, Sexual Citizenship," in Davis and Mitchell, *Heterosexual Histories*, 279.

10. Mayeri, "Race, Sexual Citizenship," 280, quoting Weber v. Aetna Casualty, 406 U.S. 164 (1972). See also Kevin J. Mumford, "Untangling Pathology: The Moynihan Report and Homosexual Damage, 1965–1975," *Journal of Policy History* 24, no. 1 (2012): 57–59.

11. Natalia Molina, *Fit to Be Citizens?: Public Health and Race in Los Angeles: 1879–1939* (Berkeley: University of California Press, 2006), chapters 3 and 4.

12. Rebecca M. Kluchin, *Fit to Be Tied: Sterilization and Reproductive Rights in America, 1950–1980* (New Brunswick: Rutgers University Press, 2009), 34; Donald T. Critchlow, *Intended Consequences: Birth Control, Abortion, and the Federal Government in Modern America* (New York: Oxford University Press, 2001), 55–56; Emily Klancher Merchant, *Building the Population Bomb* (New York: Oxford University Press, 2021), 166–174; Matthew James Connelly, *Fatal Misconception: The Struggle to Control World Population* (Cambridge, MA: Belknap Press of Harvard University Press, 2008), 258–259; Linda Gordon, *The Moral Property of Women: A History of Birth Control Politics in America*, revised ed. (Urbana: University of Illinois Press, 2002), 190–203; Carole McCann, *Birth Control Politics in the United States, 1916–1945* (Ithaca: Cornell University Press, 1994), chapter 4; Roberts, *Killing*, 89–98; Alexandra Minna Stern, *Eugenic Nation: Faults and Frontiers of Better Breeding in Modern America* (Berkeley: University of California Press, 2005), 99–110.

13. Kluchin, *Fit to Be Tied*, 95; Critchlow, *Intended Consequences*, 91–96; Jennifer Nelson, *Women of Color and the Reproductive Rights Movement* (New York: New York University Press, 2003), 70.

14. Critchlow, *Intended Consequences*, 144–146; Philip Reilly, *The Surgical Solution: A History of Involuntary Sterilization in the United States* (Baltimore: Johns Hopkins University Press, 1991); Nelson, *Women of Color*, 65–67; Kluchin, *Fit to Be Tied*, 98–101, 151, 173–177; Roberts, *Killing*, 93.

15. Elena R. Gutiérrez, *Fertile Matters: The Politics of Mexican-Origin Women's Reproduction* (Austin: University of Texas Press, 2008), chapter 3; Kluchin, *Fit to Be Tied*, 84–85; Maya Manian, "Coerced Sterilization of Mexican-American Women: The Story of Madrigal v. Quilligan," in *Reproductive Rights and Justice Stories*, eds. Melissa Murray, Katherine Shaw, and Reva B. Siegel (St. Paul: Foundation Press, 2019): 97–116. Most Mexican migrants were, in fact, men with families in Mexico; see Ana Raquel Minian, *Undocumented Lives: The Untold Story of Mexican Migration* (Cambridge, MA: Harvard University Press, 2018).

16. Loretta J. Ross, "African American Women and Abortion," in *Abortion Wars: A Half Century of Struggle, 1950–2000*, ed. Rickie Solinger (Berkeley: University of California Press, 1998), 186, quoting Ninia Baehr, *Abortion Without Apology: A Radical History for the 1990s* (Boston: South End Press, 1990), 56; "Principles of Unity," *CARASA*

News 4, no.1 (1980): 3, 1978, Karen Stamm collection of Committee for Abortion Rights and Against Sterilization Abuse (CARASA) records, Sophia Smith Collection of Women's History, SSC MS 00811, Smith College Special Collections, Northampton, Massachusetts; Gutiérrez, *Fertile Matters*, 94–108.

17. Judith A. Houck, *Looking Through the Speculum: Examining the Women's Health Movement* (Chicago: University of Chicago Press, 2024), chapter 7; Jael Miriam Silliman, Marlene Gerber Fried, Loretta Ross, and Elena R. Gutiérrez, eds., *Undivided Rights: Women of Color Organize for Reproductive Justice* (Cambridge, MA: South End Press, 2004); Marlene Gerber Fried, ed., *From Abortion to Reproductive Freedom: Transforming a Movement* (Boston: Sound End Press, 1990).

18. Loretta Ross and Rickie Solinger, *Reproductive Justice: An Introduction* (Oakland: University of California Press, 2017), 65–66; Dorothy Roberts, "Reproductive Justice, Not Just Rights," *Dissent* 62, no. 4 (2015): 81–82; Loretta Ross, "Understanding Reproductive Justice: Transforming the Pro-Choice Movement," *Off Our Backs* 36, no. 4 (2006): 14–19; SisterSong Women of Color Reproductive Justice Collective, http://sistersong.net; Berebitsky, *Sex and the Office*, chapter 7, quoting *Redbook* at 225; Sarah B. Rowley, "Sexpo '76: Gender, Media, and the 1976 Hays-Ray Congressional Sex Scandal," *Journal of the History of Sexuality* 32, no. 2 (May 2023): 144–173.

19. Berebitsky, *Sex and the Office*, 239–243; Andrea Friedman, "The Price of Shame: Second-Wave Feminism and the Lewinsky-Clinton Scandal," in Davis and Mitchell, *Heterosexual Histories*, 362–363; Carrie N. Baker, *The Women's Movement Against Sexual Harassment* (New York: Cambridge University Press, 2008).

20. "Statement of Professor Anita F. Hill to the Senate Judiciary Committee October 11, 1991," in *Court of Appeal: The Black Community Speaks Out on the Racial and Sexual Politics of Clarence Thomas vs. Anita Hill*, eds. Robert Chrisman and Robert L. Allen (New York: Ballantine Books, 1992), 16–17.

21. Berebitsky, *Sex and the Office*, 266–267; Lauren Berlant, *The Queen of America Goes to Washington City: Notes on Sex and Citizenship* (Durham: Duke University Press, 1997), 240–241.

22. "Second Statement from Judge Clarence Thomas October 11, 1991," in Chrisman and Allen, *Court of Appeal*, 22; Estelle B. Freedman, *Redefining Rape: Sexual Violence in the Era of Suffrage and Segregation* (Cambridge, MA: Harvard University Press, 2013), chapter 13.

23. James Strong, "The Black Sexist Chauvinist Pig," *New Pittsburgh Courier*, November 2, 1991, 4; Berebitsky, *Sex and the Office*, 272.

24. Orlando Patterson, "Race, Gender, and Liberal Fallacies," *New York Times*, October 20, 1991, E15; Kimberlé Crenshaw, "Whose Story Is It, Anyway? Feminist and Anti-Racist Appropriations of Anita Hill," in *Race-ing Justice, En-Gendering Power: Essays on Anita Hill, Clarence Thomas, and the Construction of Social Reality*, ed. Toni Morrison (New York: Pantheon Books, 1992), 412–428.

25. "African American Women in Defense of Ourselves," advertisement, *New York Times*, November 11, 1991.

26. Nellie Y. McKay, "Remembering Anita Hill and Clarence Thomas: What Really Happened When a Black Woman Spoke Out," in Morrison, *Race-ing Justice*, 276–277; Susan Deller Ross, "Sexual Harassment Law in the Aftermath of the Hill-Thomas Hearings," in Hill and Jordan, *Race, Gender, and Power*, 229–237.

27. "Year of the Woman: November 3, 1992," Historical Highlights, United States Senate, https://www.senate.gov/artandhistory/history/minute/year_of_the_woman.htm.
28. Evelynn Hammonds, "Black (W)holes and the Geometry of Black Female Sexuality," *Differences: A Journal of Feminist Cultural Studies* 6, nos. 2 & 3 (1994): 134; bell hooks, *Wounds of Passion: A Writing Life* (New York: Henry Holt, 1997); bell hooks, "Selling Hot Pussy," in *Black Looks: Race and Representation* (New York: Routledge, 2015), 75–76. See also Hortense J. Spillers, "Mama's Baby, Papa's Maybe: An American Grammar Book," *Diacritics* 17, no. 2 (1987): 65–81.
29. Lauren Gail Berlant, ed., *Our Monica, Ourselves: The Clinton Affair and the National Interest* (New York: New York University Press, 2001).
30. Friedman, "Price of Shame," 358–386; Timothy Noah, "Bill Clinton and the Meaning of 'Is,'" *Slate*, September 13, 1998, https://slate.com/news-and-politics/1998/09/bill-clinton-and-the-meaning-of-is.html; Monica Lewinsky, "The Price of Shame," TED Talk, March 20, 2015, https://www.ted.com/talks/monica_lewinsky_the_price_of_shame?language=en;
31. Friedman, "Price of Shame," 380–381.
32. Ronan Farrow, *Catch and Kill: Lies, Spies, and a Conspiracy to Protect Predators* (New York: Little, Brown and Company, 2019); Jodi Kantor and Megan Twohey, *She Said: Breaking the Sexual Harassment Story That Helped Ignite a Movement* (New York: Penguin Press, 2019).
33. "Donald Trump Makes Lewd Remarks About Women on Video," NBC News, https://www.youtube.com/watch?v=fYqKx1GuZGg; "Donald Trump on 2005 Tape: 'This Was Locker-Room Talk,'" NBC News, https://www.youtube.com/watch?v=IEOO0MjhVsU.
34. Jamie Ducharme, "'Indelible in the Hippocampus Is the Laughter': The Science Behind Christine Blasey Ford's Testimony," *Time*, September 27, 2018, https://time.com/5408567/christine-blasey-ford-science-of-memory/.
35. Theresa Iker, "'All Wives Are Not Created Equal': Women Organizing in the Late Twentieth-Century Men's Rights Movement," *Journal of Women's History* 35, no. 2 (2023): 51–72; Laura Kipnis, *Unwanted Advances: Sexual Paranoia Comes to Campus* (New York: Harper, 2017); Jane Gallop, "Laura Kipnis, Unwanted Advances: Sexual Paranoia Comes to Campus," *Critical Inquiry* 45, no. 2 (2019): 557–558; Jennifer Senior, "'Unwanted Advances' Tackles Sexual Politics in Academia," *The New York Times*, April 5, 2017, https://www.nytimes.com/2017/04/05/books/review-laura-kipnis-unwanted-advances.html?smid=url-share; Christine Smallwood, "Laura Kipnis's Battle Against Vulnerability," *The New Yorker*, April 2, 2017, https://www.newyorker.com/culture/persons-of-interest/laura-kipniss-battle-against-vulnerability; Laura Smith, "This Feminist Has a Lot of Opinions About Sex on Campus," *Mother Jones*, April 4, 2017, https://www.motherjones.com/media/2017/04/feminist-campus-sexual-assault/; Katherine Angel, *Tomorrow Sex Will be Good Again: Women and Desire in the Age of Consent* (London: Verso, 2021), chapter 1.
36. "History of Women in the U.S. Congress," Center for American Women and Politics, Rutgers University, https://cawp.rutgers.edu/facts/levels-office/congress/history-women-us-congress.
37. Jessica Bennett, "How History Changed Anita Hill," *New York Times*, June 17, 2019.

Chapter 17: Family's Value

1. Max Smith, "Thoughts & Ideas," *Blacklines*, January 2004, 12; "Update: Mortality Attributable to HIV Infection Among Persons Aged 25–44 Years—United States, 1991 and 1992," *MMWR Weekly* 42, no. 45 (November 19, 1993): 869–872, https://www.cdc.gov/mmwr/preview/mmwrhtml/00022174.htm; "Update: Mortality Attributable to HIV Infection Among Persons Aged 25–44 Years—United States, 1994," *MMWR Weekly* 45, no. 6 (February 16, 1996): 121–125, https://www.cdc.gov/mmwr/preview/mmwrhtml/00040227.htm. For 1980–1996 statistics, see "HIV/AIDS: Snapshots of an Epidemic," AmfAR, http://tinyurl.com/hm6w8vhk; Lisa C. Moore and Anthony R. G. Hardaway, "Southern Sanctified Sissy," in *Spirited: Affirming the Soul and Black Gay/Lesbian Identity*, eds. G. Winston James and Lisa C. Moore (Washington, DC: RedBone Press, 2006), 159–160.
2. Phil Tiemeyer, *Plane Queer: Labor, Sexuality, and AIDS in the History of Male Flight Attendants* (Berkeley: University of California Press, 2013), 161–165; Michael Callen, Richard Berkowitz, and Joseph Sonnabend, *How to Have Sex in an Epidemic: One Approach* (New York: Tower Press, 1983).
3. "Family Album," *Family and Friends*, November 2001, 50; Kath Weston, "Parenting in the Age of AIDS," in *Sisters, Sexperts, Queers: Beyond the Lesbian Nation*, ed. Arlene Stein (New York: Plume, 1993), 175.
4. Centers for Disease Control, "*Pneumocystis* Pneumonia—Los Angeles," *Morbidity and Mortality Weekly Report* 30, no. 21 (June 5, 1981); Lawrence K. Altman, "Rare Cancer Seen in 41 Homosexuals," *New York Times*, July 3, 1981, 20.
5. Jennifer Brier, *Infectious Ideas: U.S. Political Responses to the AIDS Crisis* (Chapel Hill: University of North Carolina Press, 2009), 21; Paula A. Treichler, "AIDS, Homophobia, and Biomedical Discourse: An Epidemic of Signification," *October* 43 (1987): 52–53, 60; Gilbert C. White, II, "Hemophilia: An Amazing 35-Year Journey from the Depth of HIV to the Threshold of Cure," *Transactions of the American Clinical and Climatological Association* 121 (2010): 61–75.
6. Ann Cvetkovich, *An Archive of Feelings: Trauma, Sexuality, and Lesbian Public Cultures* (Durham: Duke University Press, 2003), 169; Kath Weston, *Families We Choose: Lesbians, Gays, and Kinship* (New York: Columbia University Press, 1991), 125–126; Nan Alamilla Boyd, *Wide-Open Town: A History of Queer San Francisco to 1965* (Berkeley: University of California Press, 2003), chapters 4–5.
7. Katie Batza, *Before AIDS: Gay Health Politics in the 1970s* (Philadelphia: University of Pennsylvania Press, 2018), chapter 5; Brier, *Infectious Ideas*, 15–19.
8. Lillian Faderman, *The Gay Revolution: The Story of the Struggle* (New York: Simon & Schuster, 2015), 418–421.
9. Dan Royles, *To Make the Wounded Whole: The African American Struggle Against HIV/AIDS* (Chapel Hill: University of North Carolina Press, 2020), 55–56; Brier, *Infectious Ideas*, 12–13, 39–40.
10. For a sampling of newspaper articles about allegations of racism against LGBT bars, see The Allan Berube Papers, box 102, folder 53, Gay, Lesbian, Bisexual, and Transgender Historical Society, Archives of Sexuality and Gender (Gale). See also Keith Boykin, *One More River to Cross: Black and Gay in America* (New York: Anchor Books, 1996), chapter 6; Lucas Hilderbrand, *The Bars Are Ours: Histories and Cultures of Gay Bars*

in America, 1960 and After (Durham: Duke University Press, 2023), chapter 4; La Shonda Mims, *Drastic Dykes and Accidental Activists: Queer Women in the Urban South* (Chapel Hill: University of North Carolina Press, 2022), 47.

11. Royles, *To Make the Wounded Whole,* 21–23 and chapter 4; Gregory D. Smithers, *Reclaiming Two-Spirits* (Boston: Beacon Press, 2022), 173–177.
12. United States Congress, "S.Amdt.963 to H.R.3058 - 100th Congress (1987–1988)," October 14, 1987, https://www.congress.gov/amendment/100th-congress/senate-amendment/963/text.
13. Karma R. Chávez, *The Borders of AIDS: Race, Quarantine, and Resistance* (Seattle: University of Washington Press, 2021), chapters 2 and 3.
14. Seth Dowland, *Family Values and the Rise of the Christian Right* (Philadelphia: University of Pennsylvania Press, 2015); Cynthia Burack, *Sin, Sex, and Democracy: Anitgay Rhetoric and the Christian Right* (Albany: State University of New York Press, 2008); Susan B. Ridgely, *Practicing What the Doctor Preached: At Home with Focus on the Family* (New York: Oxford University Press, 2017); Mark R. Kowalewski, "Religious Constructions of the AIDS Crisis," *Sociological Analysis* 51, no. 1 (1990): 93.
15. Brier, *Infectious Ideas,* chapter 3, and 88–91. The commission was formally known as the "Presidential Commission on the Human Immunodeficiency Virus Epidemic"; Faderman, *Gay Revolution,* 428–429.
16. Sarah Schulman, *Let the Record Show: A Political History of ACT UP New York, 1987–1993* (New York: Farrar, Straus and Giroux, 2021); Anthony Petro, *After the Wrath of God: AIDS, Sexuality, and American Religion* (New York: Oxford University Press, 2015), chapter 4; Douglas Crimp, "Mourning and Militancy," *October* 51 (Winter 1989): 3–18; Cvetkovich, *Archive of Feelings,* chapter 5, quote at 169; Deborah B. Gould, *Moving Politics: Emotion and ACT UP's Fight Against AIDS* (Chicago: University of Chicago Press, 2009).
17. Royles, *Make the Wounded Whole,* chapter 6.
18. Priscilla Alexander, "Sex Workers Fight Against AIDS: An International Perspective," in *Women Resisting AIDS: Feminist Strategies of Empowerment,* eds. Beth E. Schneider and Nancy E. Stoller (Philadelphia: Temple University Press, 1995), 99–123; Emma Day, "The Fire Inside: Women Protesting AIDS in Prison since 1980," *Modern American History* 5, no. 1 (2022): 79–100; Caroline Wolf Harlow, "HIV in U.S. Prisons and Jails," U.S. Department of Justice, Office of Justice Programs, *Bureau of Justice Statistics: Special Report* (September 1993), 1–8; Brier, *Infectious Ideas,* chapter 5; Royles, *Make the Wounded Whole,* 202–205; Schulman, *Let the Record Show,* chapter 7; Tamar W. Carroll, *Mobilizing New York: AIDS, Antipoverty, and Feminist Activism* (Chapel Hill: University of North Carolina Press, 2015), chapter 5.
19. Royles, *Make the Wounded Whole,* 74–75; Cathy J. Cohen, *The Boundaries of Blackness: AIDS and the Breakdown of Black Politics* (Chicago: University of Chicago Press, 1999), chapter 3.
20. For a sample of Brothers United events, see "Bulletin," *Family and Friends,* November 2000, 12; "Brothers' United Will Host Safe Sex Workshop [sic]," *Triangle Journal News,* September 2000, 5; Anita Moyt, "Conrad Pegues: Local Memphian to Sign Books," *Family and Friends,* August 1999, 38; Anita Moyt, "Brothers United to Host Book-signing Event," *Family and Friends,* May 2000, 48; Anita Moyt, "Sanford Gaylord to Speak in Memphis," *Family and Friends,* November 2001, 15. On Black queer art and

literature, see Jafari S. Allen, *There's a Disco Ball Between Us: A Theory of Black Gay Life* (Durham: Duke University Press, 2021), chapters 1 and 2; Eric Darnell Pritchard, *Fashioning Lives: Black Queers and the Politics of Literacy* (Carbondale: Southern Illinois University Press, 2017), chapter 2; Darius Bost, *Evidence of Being: The Black Gay Cultural Renaissance and the Politics of Violence* (Chicago: University of Chicago Press, 2019); E. Patrick Johnson, *Black. Queer. Southern. Women: An Oral History* (Chapel Hill: University of North Carolina Press, 2018), chapter 7.

21. "BU Members Take Retreat," *Family and Friends*, January 2002, 17.
22. Marc Stein, *City of Sisterly and Brotherly Loves: Lesbian and Gay Philadelphia, 1945–1972* (Chicago: University of Chicago Press, 2000), 322; Stephen Vider, *The Queerness of Home: Gender, Sexuality, and the Politics of Domesticity after World War II* (Chicago: University of Chicago Press, 2021), chapter 3; Shulamith Firestone, *The Dialectic of Sex: The Case for Feminist Revolution* (New York: William Morrow and Company, Inc., 1970), 39, 61.
23. Weston, *Families We Choose*, chapter 5.
24. Vider, *Queerness of Home*, 210.
25. Moore and Hardaway, "Southern Sanctified Sissy," 157.
26. Moore and Hardaway, "Southern Sanctified Sissy," 158–159; Anthony R. G. Hardaway, interview with the author, March 22, 2023; James S. Tinney, "Why a Black Gay Church?" in *In the Life: A Black Gay Anthology*, ed. Joseph Beam (Boston: Alyson Publications, Inc., 1986), 73. See also Kevin J. Mumford, *Not Straight, Not White: Black Gay Men from the March on Washington to the AIDS Crisis* (Chapel Hill: University of North Carolina Press, 2016), chapter 7.
27. E. Patrick Johnson, *Sweet Tea: Black Gay Men of the South* (Chapel Hill; University of North Carolina Press, 2008), 255–257; John Howard, *Men Like That: A Southern Queer History* (Chicago: University of Chicago Press, 1999), 48–54. On the problematic concept of the "down low" as a mode of simultaneously naming Black male same-sex experience and rendering it invisible, see C. Riley Snorton, *Nobody Is Supposed to Know: Black Sexuality on the Down Low* (Minneapolis: University of Minnesota Press, 2014), introduction; Hardaway, interview with the author.
28. Moore and Hardaway, "Southern Sanctified Sissy," 159; Thomas F. Rzeznik, "The Church and the AIDS Crisis in New York City," *US Catholic Historian* 34, no. 1 (2016): 143–165.
29. Lynne Gerber, "We Who Must Die Demand a Miracle: Christmas 1989 at the Metropolitan Community Church of San Francisco," in *Devotions and Desires: Histories of Sexuality and Religion in the Twentieth-Century United States*, eds. Gill Frank, Bethany Moreton, and Heather White (Chapel Hill: University of North Carolina Press, 2018), 253–276; Gregg Drinkwater, "AIDS Was Our Earthquake: American Jewish Responses to the AIDS Crisis, 1985–92," *Jewish Social Studies* 26, no. 1 (2020): 133; Moshe Shokeid, *A Gay Synagogue in New York* (New York: Columbia University Press, 1995); Tinney, "Why a Black Gay Church?," in Beam, *In the Life*, 70–86; Johnson, *Sweet Tea*, 184.
30. Huntly Collins, "The Renaissance Man as Radical," *Philadelphia Inquirer*, June 9, 1994, F4.
31. Douglas Martin, "Kiyoshi Kuromiya, 57, Fighter for the Rights of AIDS Patients," *New York Times*, May 28, 2000, 34; Huntly Collins, "Support for Marijuana Use Grows in Medical Circles," *Philadelphia Inquirer*, March 21, 1999, E1; *Kuromiya v. United*

States, 37 F. Supp. 2d 717 (E.D. Pa.1999), https://law.justia.com/cases/federal/district-courts/FSupp2/37/717/2415755/.

32. These descriptions of Kiyoshi Kuromiya's final illness draw from the untitled notebook log kept by his friends, May 1–10, 2000, Kiyoshi Kuromiya Papers, John J. Wilcox, Jr. Archives, William Way LGBT Community Center, as well as the author's email exchange with Jeff Maskovsky. See also Mark Bowden, "Act Up Will Make You Pay Attention to AIDS—Or Die Trying," *Philadelphia Inquirer Magazine*, June 14, 1992, 23, 27; Jeff Maskovsky, "'Fighting for Our Lives': Poverty and AIDS Activism in Neoliberal Philadelphia," dissertation (Temple University, 2000; University of Michigan microfilm, 2005).
33. Alfredo Sosa (@Alfie79), "KIYOSHI," Vimeo, June 10, 2010, https://vimeo.com/12474786; Susan FitzGerald, "K. Kuromiya, tireless AIDS Activist, Dies," *Philadelphia Inquirer*, May 12, 2000, 1; Scott Tucker, "Heart Mountain's Kiyoshi Kuromiya," *Casper Star-Tribune*, June 4, 2000, 38.
34. The Haven Memphis (@thehavenmemphis901), "Have you signed up yet?!," Instagram reel, August 18, 2022, https://www.instagram.com/reel/ChaScJmAJft/.
35. Marlon M. Bailey, *Butch Queens Up in Pumps: Gender, Performance, and Ballroom Culture in Detroit* (Ann Arbor: University of Michigan Press, 2013); Ricky Tucker, *And the Category Is . . . Inside New York's Vogue, House, and Ballroom Community* (Boston: Beacon Press, 2022); "Female Impersonators," *Ebony*, March 1953, 64.
36. Tucker, *And the Category*, 63–64; Simon Frank, dir., *The Queen* (Evergreen Film, 1967); https://www.youtube.com/watch?v=RYCQEl8TPeM; Jennie Livingston, dir., *Paris Is Burning* (New York: Miramax, 1991).
37. Tim Lawrence, "A History of Drag Balls, Houses, and the Culture of Voguing," in Chantal Regnault (photographer), *Voguing and the House Ballroom Scene of New York City 1989–92* (London: Soul Jazz Books, 2011), 4–5; Bailey, *Butch Queens*, 5.
38. Lawrence, "History of Drag Balls," 5–6, 9, quoting Guy Trebay, "Legends of the Ball," *Village Voice*, January 11, 2000, https://www.villagevoice.com/2000/01/11/legends-of-the-ball/; Bailey, *Butch Queens*, 19, chapters 4 and 5; Joseph Plaster, *Kids on the Street: Queer Kinship and Religion in San Francisco's Tenderloin* (Durham: Duke University Press, 2023), chapters 1 and 5.
39. Moore and Hardaway, "Southern Sanctified Sissy," 161.

Chapter 18: Save the Children

1. "Drag Story Hour," https://www.dragstoryhour.org/.
2. "Drag Queen Story Hour Goes on Despite Neo-Nazi's Attempt to Burn Church Down," *The Guardian* (online), April 3, 2023; Lola Fadulu, "Ohio Man Who Threw Molotov Cocktails at a Church Gets 18 Years in Prison," *New York Times*, January 30, 2024, nytimes.com; Stacy Nick, "Drag Queen Story Hour Shows Denver Kids that Different Is Fabulous, Darling," KUNC, July 13, 2017, https://www.kunc.org/arts-life/2017-07-13/drag-queen-story-hour-shows-denver-kids-that-different-is-fabulous-darling.
3. Erik Bottcher (@ebottcher), "Today I witnessed," Instagram reel, December 17, 2022, https://www.instagram.com/p/CmSEZUKKy_7/.
4. Tasseli McKay, Christine H. Lindquist, and Shilpi Misra, "Understanding (and Acting

On) 20 Years of Research on Violence and LGBTQ+ Communities," *Trauma, Violence, and Abuse* 20, no. 5 (2017): 665–678.

5. Karen Graves, *And They Were Wonderful Teachers: Florida's Purge of Gay and Lesbian Teachers* (Urbana: University of Illinois Press, 2009).
6. Daniel Winunwe Rivers, *Radical Relations: Lesbian Mothers, Gay Fathers, and Their Children in the United States since World War II* (Chapel Hill: University of North Carolina Press, 2013); Marie-Amélie George, *Family Matters: Queer Households and the Half-Century Struggle for Legal Recognition* (New York: Cambridge University Press, forthcoming), introduction and chapter 2; Lauren Jae Gutterman, *Her Neighbor's Wife: A History of Lesbian Desire Within Marriage* (Philadelphia: University of Pennsylvania Press, 2020), chapter 7.
7. William N. Eskridge, Jr., *Gaylaw: Challenging the Apartheid of the Closet* (Cambridge, MA: Harvard University Press, 1999), 271–277.
8. Lisa Duggan, "Queering the State," in *Sex Wars: Sexual Dissent and Political Culture*, eds. Lisa Duggan and Nan D. Hunter, 10th anniv. ed. (New York: Routledge, 2006), 177–178; Rachel Guberman, "'No Discrimination and No Special Rights': Gay Rights, Family Values, and the Politics of Moderation in the 1992 Election," in *Beyond the Politics of the Closet: Gay Rights and the American State Since the 1970s*, ed. Jonathan Bell (Philadelphia: University of Pennsylvania Press, 2020), 165–186.
9. Paul M. Renfro, *Stranger Danger: Family Values, Childhood, and the American Carceral State* (New York: Oxford University Press, 2020).
10. Renfro, *Stranger Danger*, 10–11, chapter 1.
11. Judith A. Reisman and Edward W. Eichel, *Kinsey, Sex and Fraud: The Indoctrination of a People* (Lafayette, L.A.: Lochinvar Inc., 1990); Janice M. Irvine, *Talk About Sex: How Sex Ed Battles Helped Ignite the Right*, 20th anniv. ed. (Philadelphia: Temple University Press, 2023), chapter 8; Kristin Luker, *When Sex Goes to School: Warring Views on Sex—and Sex Education—Since the Sixties* (New York: W. W. Norton, 2006), chapter 8.
12. Courtney D. Tabor, "'This Is What a 13-Year Old Girl Looks Like': A Feminist Analysis of *To Catch a Predator*," *Crime, Media, Culture* 19, no. 2 (2023): 233–251.
13. Bret Vetter, "Protestors Clash with Supporters of Drag Queen Story Hour in Pittsford," *News 10 WHEC.com* (online), April 23, 2023; Susan Stryker, *Transgender History: The Roots of Today's Revolution*, 2nd ed. (New York: Seal Press, 2017), 202; Jaime M. Grant et al., *Injustice at Every Turn: A Report of the National Transgender Discrimination Survey* (Washington, DC: National Center for Transgender Equality and National Gay and Lesbian Task Force, 2011); Sandy E. James et al., *The Report of the 2015 U.S. Transgender Survey* (Washington, DC: National Center for Transgender Equity, 2015); "Early Insights Report," *2022 U.S. Trans Survey*, February 7, 2024, ustranssurvey.org; Amit Paley, "2022 National Survey on LGBTQ Youth Mental Health," *The Trevor Project*, published 2022, https://www.thetrevorproject.org/survey-2022/; "Research Brief: Age of Gender Identity Outness and Suicide Risk," *The Trevor Project*, March 29, 2023, https://www.thetrevorproject.org/research-briefs/age-of-gender-identity-outness-and-suicide-risk-mar-2023/.
14. "Gender-Affirming Care and Young People," HHS Office of Population Affairs, March 2022, https://opa.hhs.gov/sites/default/files/2022-03/gender-affirming-care-young-people-march-2022.pdf.
15. Erin Reed, "Erin's Anti-Trans Risk Map: Early Legislative Session Edition," *Erin in the*

Morning, January 16, 2024, https://www.erininthemorning.com/p/erins-anti-trans-risk-map-early-legislative; Erin Reed, "LGBTQ+ Legislative Tracking 2023," Google Sheet, (linked from legislative map); "Anti-Transgender Medical Care Bans," *Equality Federation*, n.d., https://www.equalityfederation.org/tracker/anti-transgender-medical-care-bans; Elana Redfield, Kerith J. Conron, Will Tentindo, and Erica Browning, "Prohibiting Gender-Affirming Medical Care for Youth," UCLA Williams Institute, March 2023, https://williamsinstitute.law.ucla.edu/publications/bans-trans-youth-health-care/.

16. Jojo Macaluso, "Where Gender-Affirming Care for Youth is Banned, Intersex Surgery May be Allowed," *NPR News*, April 11, 2023, npr.org; Jason Rafferty, "Ensuring Comprehensive Care and Support for Transgender and Gender-Diverse Children and Adolescents," *Pediatrics* 142, no. 4 (2018), https://publications.aap.org/pediatrics/article/142/4/e20182162/37381/Ensuring-Comprehensive-Care-and-Support-for?autologincheck=redirected.
17. Hanna Rosin, "Boys on the Side," *The Atlantic*, September 2012, www.theatlantic.com/magazine/archive2012/09/boys-on-the-side/309062/.
18. Rosin, "Boys on the Side"; Paula England, "Is a 'Warm Hookup' an Oxymoron?" *Contexts* 15, no. 4 (2016): 58–59; Paula England, Emily Fitzgibbons Shaffer, and Alison C. K. Fogarty, "Hooking Up and Forming Romantic Relationships on Today's College Campuses," in *The Gendered Society Reader*, eds. M. Kimmel and A. Aronson, 5th ed. (New York: Oxford University Press, 2012), 559–572; Katherine Rowland, *The Pleasure Gap: American Women and the Unfinished Sexual Revolution* (New York: Seal Press, 2020).
19. Kate Julian, "Why Are Young People Having So Little Sex?" *The Atlantic*, December 2018, https://www.theatlantic.com/magazine/archive/2018/12/the-sex-recession/573949/.
20. Asa Seresin, "On Heteropessimism: Heterosexuality is Nobody's Personal Problem," *The New Inquiry*, October 9, 2019, https://thenewinquiry.com/on-heteropessimism/.
21. adrienne maree brown, *Pleasure Activism: The Politics of Feeling Good* (Chico, CA: AK Press, 2019).
22. Christopher M. Gleason, *American Poly: A History* (New York: Oxford University Press, 2023); Nona Willis Aronowitz, *Bad Sex: Truth, Pleasure, and an Unfinished Revolution* (New York: Plume, 2022); Molly Roden Winter, *More: A Memoir of an Open Marriage* (New York: Doubleday, 2024); Rachel Krantz, *Open: An Uncensored Memoir of Love, Liberation, and Non-Monogamy* (New York: Harmony, 2022). See also "KAP: Kink Aware Professionals," n.d.; Harlan White, "Polyamory in Liberal Religion," 2009; and Loving More, "FAQ for Open Relationships and Polyamory," n.d., all in box: "Miscellaneous," Widener Sexuality Archives, Chester, PA.

Coda: The Ghost of Anthony Comstock

1. Decision: Case 2:22-cv-00223-Z, United States District Court for the Northern District of Texas, Amarillo Division, *Alliance for Hippocratic Medicine, et al., v. U.S. Food and Drug Administration, et. al.*
2. Pat Schroeder, "Comstock Act Still on the Books," Congressional floor speech, September 24, 1996, Iowa State University Archives of Women's Political Communication, awpc.cattcenter.iastate.edu/2017/03/21/Comstock-act-still-on-the-books-sept-24-1996/.

3. Kelsy Burke, *Pornography Wars: The Past, Present, and Future of America's Obscene Obsession* (New York: Bloomsbury Publishing, 2023), 75–87; Jeff Kosseff, *The Twenty-Six Words that Created the Internet* (Ithaca: Cornell University Press, 2019); Reid Kanaley, "No Matter the Outcome, AIDS Activists Vowed to Stay Online," *Philadelphia Inquirer*, June 27, 1997, A11; Pamela Mendels, "AIDS Activist's Dilemma Proved Decisive in Decency Act Case," *New York Times*, June 18, 1996.
4. ACLU, "Defending Reproductive Rights in Cyberspace," October 31, 1996, https://www.aclu.org/documents/defending-reproductive-rights-cyberspace; Whitney Strub, *Perversion for Profit: The Politics of Pornography and the Rise of the New Right* (New York: Columbia University Press, 2010), 273–276.
5. Alejandra Caraballo, "The Abortion Medication Ruling Threatens Free Speech Online," *Wired*, April 12, 2023, www.wired.com/story/abortion-pill-comstock-free-speech-internet/; House Journal, Eighty-Eighth Legislature, Proceedings, March 13, 2023, 614, https://journals.house.texas.gov/hjrnl/88r/pdf/88RDAY21FINAL.PDF; H.F. 510 (Iowa), "An Act relating to the Iowa human life protection act," February 28, 2023, 24–27, legis.iowa.gov/docs/publications/LGI/90/HF510.pdf; "Planned Parenthood to Resume Offering Abortions in Wisconsin Next Week After Court Ruling," *PBS News Hour*, September 14, 2023, https://www.pbs.org/newshour/.
6. Zach Schonfeld, "Supreme Court Rules in Favor of Christian Designer in Gay Wedding Website Case," *The Hill*, June 30, 2023, https://thehill.com/regulation/court-battles/4061169-supreme-court-rules-in-favor-of-christian-designer-in-gay-wedding-website-case/.

Image Credits

ii Nini Treadwell Inc.

3 Library of Congress, Geography and Maps Division.

23 John K. Hillers Photographs of Zuni, Hopi, and Rio Grande River Pueblos in New Mexico and Arizona, Newberry Library.

33 The Miriam and Ira D. Wallach Division of Art, Prints, and Photographs: Photography Collection, The New York Public Library.

37 "Cheney family" of Massachusetts, c. 1795, Gift of Edgar William and Bernice Chrysler Garbisch, National Gallery of Art, Washington, DC.

44 Reproduced from Gustave-Joseph Witkowski, *Histoire des accouchements chez tous les peuples* (Paris: G. Steinheil, 1887), National Library of Medicine, Images from the History of Medicine Collection.

55 *Joshua Johnson, Grace Allison McCurdy (Mrs. Hugh McCurdy) and Her Daughters, Mary Jane and Letitia Grace*, c. 1806, oil on canvas, Corcoran Collection, museum purchase through the gifts of William Wilson Corcoran, Elizabeth Donner Norment, Francis Biddle, Erich Cohn, Hardinge Scholle, and the William A. Clark Fund, National Gallery of Art, Washington, DC.

57 Slavery Images: A Visual Record of the African Slave Trade and Slave Life in the Early African Diaspora. Reproduced from *Narrative of the life and adventures of Henry Bibb, an American slave, written by himself* (New York: 1849).

68 Slave auction at Richmond, Virginia, 1856, LOT 4422-A-1, Library of Congress, Prints and Photographs Division.

73 Courtesy, American Antiquarian Society.

81 Photography © New-York Historical Society.

85 National Library of Medicine.

87 National Library of Medicine.

88 Courtesy, American Antiquarian Society.

89 Courtesy, American Antiquarian Society.

93 Prudence Crandall Museum.

111 Mrs. T. B. H. Stenhouse, *"Tell it All": The Story of a Life's Experience in Mormonism* (Hartford, Conn.: A.D. Worthington & Co, 1878), HathiTrust and The New York Public Library, Astor, Lenox, and Tilden Foundations.

122 Courtesy, Oneida Community Mansion House.

128 Kiowa Indian ledger drawings between 1880 and 1890, Edward E. Ayer Collection, Newberry Library.

130 The Miriam and Ira D. Wallach Division of Art, Prints and Photographs: Print Collection, The New York Public Library.

134 National Anthropological Archives, Smithsonian Institution, NAA INV 02440800.

149 L. M. Glackens, "St. Anthony Comstock, the Village Nuisance" (New York: Ottmann Lith. Co., 1906), Library of Congress, Prints and Photographs Division.

156 Photography © New-York Historical Society.

160 Ida Craddock Papers, Special Collections Research Center, Morris Library, Southern Illinois University Carbondale.

165 Bain News Service Photograph Collection, Library of Congress, Prints and Photographs Division, LC-DIG-ggbain-23669 (digital file from original negative).

168 Courier Company, Joseph Brooks, Alfred Thompson, and Imperial Burlesque Co., *The Arabian Nights Aladdin's Wonderful Lamp* (Buffalo, NY: Courier Lith. Co., 1888), Library of Congress, Prints and Photographs Division, Theatrical Poster Collection.

169 *New York World-Telegram & Sun* collection, Library of Congress, Prints and Photographs Division.

171 "Gilda Gray herself in person" (Portland, OR: Holly Press, 19—?), Library of Congress, Prints and Photographs Division, Theatrical Poster Collection.

177 Bernarr McFadden, *McFadden's System of Physical Training* (New York: Hulbert Bros. & Co., 1895), Library of Congress.

184 Thomas Nast, "A Picture for Employers. Why they can live on 40 cents a day, and they can't," *Puck*, August 21, 1878, Library of Congress, Prints and Photographs Division, LC-USZC2–1242 (color film copy slide).

188 San Francisco History Center, San Francisco Public Library.

201 Smithsonian National Museum of African American History and Culture.

206 Lesbian Herstory Archives, Mabel Hampton Collection.

209 "The project staff of the Institute for Sex Research," Image No. SIA2008-4843, Smithsonian Institution Archives, Accession 90-105, Science Service Records.

215 Bain News Service, ca. 1910, Library of Congress, Prints and Photographs Division, LC-DIG-ggbain-15043 (digital file from original negative).

219 From the Collections of the Kinsey Institute, Indiana University. All rights reserved.

221 U.S. Public Health Service, United States, 1940s, National Library of Medicine.

227 Photo by Kay Tobin © Manuscripts and Archives Division, The New York Public Library.

234 *Physique Pictorial*, Spring 1955, Manuscripts and Archives Division, Digital Collections, The New York Public Library.

241 Courtesy, Hal Tarr / Gay Liberation Front Philadelphia, ephemera files, Ms. Coll. 35, John J. Wilcox Jr. Archives, William Way LGBT Community Center.

243 Jo Hofmann, photographer, 1973, Ms. Coll. 12, John J. Wilcox Jr. Archives, William Way LGBT Community Center.

249 © Betty Dodson Foundation.

259 © Betty Dodson Foundation.
261 © Betty Dodson Foundation.
262 Bettye Lane Photo. Courtesy Schlesinger Library, Harvard Radcliffe Institute.
266 "Handkerchief Color Code for Lesbians," Samois, Women's Press, 1978, no registered copyright. Courtesy of Gayle Rubin.
267 Photography © New-York Historical Society.
272 © Meg Handler.
282 Library of Congress, Prints and Photographs Division, Yanker Poster Collection, LC-USZC4–2856 (color film copy transparency).
290 © Meg Handler.
292 R. Michael Jenkins, photographer. Courtesy of Library of Congress, Prints and Photographs Division, LC-DIG-ppmsca-65032 (digital file from original).
310 © Harvey Finkle
315 Bebashi Transition to Hope, Philadelphia, PA. Courtesy of John J. Wilcox Jr. Archives, William Way LGBT Community Center.
318 © Harvey Finkle
325 © Harvey Finkle
331 Gay Freedom Day—Man with Rainbow Suspenders (1 of 2), Crawford Wayne Barton Papers, collection no. 1993–11, Gay, Lesbian, Bisexual, Transgender Historical Society.

Index